EU Law and Private International Law

Nijhoff Studies in EU Law

VOLUME 1

Nijhoff Studies in European Union Law is a refereed scholarly monographs series dedicated to the critical analysis of the current state and development of European Union law in a broad sense. Apart from constitutional, institutional and substantive issues of EU law, the series also embraces state-of-the-art interdisciplinary, comparative law and EU policies research with a clear link to European integration. Titles in the *Nijhoff Studies in European Union Law* series will be of particular interest to academics, policy makers and practitioners dealing with EU law and policies, as well as national and international (non) governmental institutions and bodies.

The titles published in this series are listed at www.brill.nl/seul

EU Law and Private International Law

The Interrelationship in Contractual Obligations

By

Jan-Jaap Kuipers

MARTINUS NIJHOFF PUBLISHERS

LEIDEN • BOSTON
2012

This book is printed on acid-free paper.

Library of Congress Cataloging-in-Publication Data

Kuipers, Jan-Jaap.
EU law and private international law : the interrelationship in contractual obligations / by Jan-Jaap Kuipers.
p. cm. -- (Nijhoff studies in European Union law, 2210-9765 ; v. 1)
Includes bibliographical references and index.
ISBN 978-90-04-20673-1 (hardback : alk. paper) 1. Conflict of laws--Contracts--European Union countries. 2. Contracts--European Union countries. 3. European Parliament. Regulation (EC) No 593/2008 of the European Parliament and of the Council of 17 June 2008 on the law applicable to contractual obligations (Rome I) I. Title. II. Title: European Union law and private international law.
KJE983.C66K85 2011
346.2402--dc23

2011034632

ISSN 2210-9765
ISBN 978-90-04-20673-1

CONTENTS

ACKNOWLEDGEMENTS

The present book builds upon my Ph.D dissertation 'The interrelationship between EU law and private international law in contractual obligations: Private autonomy, overriding mandatory provisions and a European justice area' defended at the European University Institute on 17 January 2011. I'm heavily indebted to the members of my jury, Marie-Ange Moreau, Hans-Wolfgang Micklitz, Gerard-René de Groot and Jean-Michel Jacquet for their valuable comments. I'm particularly grateful to my supervisor, Marie-Ange Moreau, who patiently listened to my thoughts and provided invaluable support in helping to structure my ideas. A special word of thanks goes to Gerard-René de Groot who was always willing to provide me with his advice, not only relating to my research, but as well about the pursuit of my wider academic career.

My research has benefitted immensely from the discussions in the Working Group on Private International Law at the European University Institute. Many thanks go to Claire Staath, Sara Migliorini and Benedict Wray for the stimulating discussions in and outside the classrooms on the future orientation of Private International Law. A special word of thanks goes to Guilherme Vasconcelos Vilaça. The fruits of our exchanges of ideas on law and legal theory at the kitchen table of our apartment in Florence can be found throughout this book.

Last, but certainly not least, many thanks for the support of my family and friends in the Netherlands. During my years in Florence I have developed profound new friendships. Since the writing of a thesis can be at times a very lonely experience, the warmth and encouragement provided by family and friends has been indispensable.

The manuscript was submitted for publication on 15 March 2011. Any subsequent new developments have not been incorporated in the book.

Nijmegen, March 2011

CHAPTER 1

INTRODUCTION: EU PRIVATE INTERNATIONAL LAW

The aim of this contribution is to analyse the interaction between European Union law and the conflict of laws rules in the area of contractual obligations.[1] Conflict of laws norms designate the law applicable to a legal relationship. For example, a contract between a French seller and a German buyer could potentially be governed by German or French law. International trade would be hampered if French courts were to always apply French contract law and German courts were to apply always German contract law when confronted with an international case. The outcome of a legal proceeding would then depend entirely upon the forum before which it was brought. The legal uncertainty, the threat of a rush to court and the risk of forum-shopping is detrimental to international trade.

With the problems that might follow from divergences in national private law, one would expect the European Union to have a major interest in Private International Law (PIL). A lack of confidence in cross-border trade could hinder the smooth functioning of the internal market if both parties were established in the Union, but in different Member States. This first chapter will therefore explore the general influence of Union law upon PIL. It will be demonstrated that although the relationship between these two areas has had an uneasy start, the Union is becoming increasingly active in PIL. The gradual broadening of competences and subsequent adaptation of PIL measures is only one side of the coin. The case-law of the European Court of Justice affecting PIL has necessitated the modification of the conflict of laws process in areas of PIL that have not yet been touched by harmonisation.

---

[1] The effects of Union law upon PIL have been object of extensive study within the framework of the Hague Academy: Badiali, G., "Le droit international privé des Communautés européennes", *Recueil des Cours*, Vol. 191, 1985, pp. 9–182; Struycken, A., "Les conséquences de l'intégration européenne sur le développement du droit international privé," *Recueil des Cours*, Vol. 232, 1992, pp. 257–383 ; Fallon, M., "Les conflits de lois et de juridictions dans un espace économique intégré", *Receuil des Cours*, Vol. 253, 1995, pp. 9–281 ; Borrás, A., "Le droit international privé communautaire : réalités, problèmes et perspectives d'avenir", *Recueil des Cours*, Vol. 317, 2005, pp. 323–526.

The increasing influence of Union law has caused tensions in traditional conflict of laws thinking. Whereas Union law appears to have sometimes ignored the rich history that underlies PIL, some PIL lawyers have been rather keen in denying any influence of the Union on the conflict of laws norms at all. This first chapter will use the general analysis of the interface between Union law and PIL to identify the key features that will be explored in subsequent chapters.

1.1 *Private International Law at a Turning Point*

European Union law is far from being the sole pressure upon the traditional perception of conflict of laws mechanisms. Outside of the European Union, PIL is also a legal discipline currently undergoing transformation. Traditional paradigms do not always hold ground. The expansion of international trade and the emergence of the internet have led to a sharp increase in international transactions. It has in practice become very difficult for a state to insist upon the application of its (mandatory) norms, while traditional connecting factors based on territoriality seem unapt to deal with the specific features of the internet.[2] The habitual place of residence of the party rendering the most characteristic performance may, in online contracts, be completely arbitrary. How should the question where a service is geographically performed be answered when it is rendered exclusively online? Another example of pressure upon traditional PIL paradigms is that of international norms which directly intervene with national private law.[3] International human rights in particular generate rights and even impose obligations upon individuals, directly affecting the relationship between individuals and transferring direct causes of action against

[2] Basedow, J., "The Efffects of Globalization on Private International Law", in: J. Basedow and T. Kono (eds.), Legal Aspects of Globalization, Kluwer Law International, The Hague, 1999, pp. 1–10; Wai, R., "Transnational Liftoff and Juridicial Touchdown: The Regulatory Function of Private International Law in an Era of Globalization", *Columbia Journal of Transnational Law*, Vol. 40, 2002, pp. 209–274; Svantesson, B., *Private International Law and the Internet*, Kluwer Law International, Deventer, 2007.

[3] Kinsch, P., "Droits de l'Homme, Droits Fondamentaux et Droit International Privé", *Recueil des Cours*, Vol. 318, 2005, pp. 19–331. With regard to labour law: Moreau, M., H. Muir Watt and P. Rodière (eds.), *Justice et mondialisation en droit du travail : Du rôle du juge aux conflits alternatifs*, Dalloz, Paris, 2010.

other private actors.[4] PIL norms themselves could moreover be set aside in cases where they breach international law. An example would be a conflict of laws rule that would directly or indirectly discriminate on the basis of race or ethnic origin.[5] Therefore the perception that PIL is exclusively a branch of national law can no longer be maintained.

Traditionally, public law regulated the state, whereas private law was exclusively concerned with individuals. A state did not have a regulatory interest and private law was left to the citizens. However, this idea of private law as an unregulated area, free of state interests[6] has been proven to be a fallacy,[7] and the use of private law to satisfy public interests has put pressure on the public-private divide. Without a doubt, a certain confluence between public and private law is currently taking place.[8] Consequently, the distinction between public international law and private international law, where the former dealt with the right of a state to regulate conduct not exclusively of domestic concern and the latter determined the applicable law in a specific case, has been increasingly fading. Although more reluctant in contract than in torts, private law is increasingly being perceived as a regulatory tool.[9] Overriding mandatory provisions, whose observance in a horizontal dispute is crucial for the functioning of the state, are a primary manifestation of this. The growing interference of state interests raises the question

[4] Steele, J., "Damages in Tort and Under the Human Rights Act: Remedial or Functional Separation", *Cambridge Law Journal*, Vol. 67 No. 3, 2008, pp. 606–634. The topic is object of a Ph.D research by Claire Staath (European University Institute) forthcoming 2012.

[5] Mills, A., *The Confluence of Public and Private International Law: Justice, Pluralism and Subsidiarity in the International Constitutional Ordering of Private Law*, Cambridge University Press, Cambridge, 2009, pp. 264–288.

[6] Kegel, G., "The Crisis of Conflict of Laws", *Recueil des Cours*, Vol. 95, 1964, pp. 91–268.

[7] Bucher, A., "L'Ordre Public et le But Social des Lois en Droit International Privé", *Recueil des Cours*, Vol. 239, 1993, pp. 9–116; Jansen, N. and R. Michaels, "Private Law and the State Comparative Perceptions and Historical Observations", *RabelsZ*, Vol. 71, 2007, 345–397; Jansen, N., and R. Michaels, "Beyond the State – Rethinking Private Law", *American Journal of Comparative Law*, Vol. 56, 2008, pp. 527–540; Dagan, H., "The Limited Autonomy of Private Law" *American Journal of Comparative Law*, Vol. 56, 2008, pp. 809–834.

[8] Bagheri, M., International Contracts and National Economic Regulation, Kluwer Law International, The Hague, 2000; Jansen, N. and R. Michaels, "Private Law Beyond the State? Europeanization, Globalization and Privatization", *American Journal of Comparative Law*, Vol. 54, 2006, pp. 843–890; Lecuyer, S., *Appréciation critique du droit international privé conventionnel*, L.G.D.J., Paris, 2007; Mills, *supra* note 5.

[9] Collins, H., *Regulating Contracts*, Oxford University Press, Oxford, 1999, pp. 57–87.

whether the determination of the applicable law has not in essence become the allocation of the regulatory authority between states.

Although the changing nature of PIL is widely acknowledged, responses have differed. Some have proposed to widen the recognition of non-State law,[10] or view PIL as public international law,[11] while others have proposed to make public law also subject to the conflict of laws mechanism.[12] The aim of the present contribution is not, however, to challenge the basic assumptions of PIL nor to develop a normative view towards the most suitable role for PIL in the international arena. Instead, the analysis will mainly focus upon the role of PIL, and that of overriding mandatory provisions in particular, in a common European justice area. General issues of globalisation and the increasing inclusion of public interests in private law will only be addressed if to do so would lead to a better understanding of the main topic.

1.2 *The Structure of the Book*

This book will thus be limited to an analysis of the interaction between Union law and private international law in the area of contractual obligations. For that purpose, the first chapter will address main problems and outline the general context. A detailed analysis will only be provided in subsequent chapters. Before exploring more thoroughly the influence of Union law upon PIL, the second chapter will provide a bird's eye-view of the conflict of laws rules in the area of contractual obligations. The discussion of the system of the Rome I Regulation has a twofold objective. On the one hand, it will explain the fundamental principles of conflict of laws. That discussion will enable the good understanding of the subsequent chapters by lawyers who are not confronted with private international law on a daily basis. Secondly, the bird's eye view will demonstrate that Rome I follows a conflict of laws methodology in line with pre-existing national traditions without

---

[10] Michaels, R., "The Re-*State*-ment of Non-State Law: The State, Choice of Law and the Challenges from Global Legal Pluralism", *Wayne Law Review*, Vol. 51, 2005, pp. 1209–1259; Loquin E., "Les règles matérielles internationals", *Recueil des Cours*, Vol. 322, 2006, pp. 21–241.

[11] Mills, *supra* note 5.

[12] Muir Watt, H., "Choice of Law in Integrated and Interconnected Markets: A Matter of Political Economy": *Electronic Journal of Comparative Law*, Vol 7, No. 3, 2003, available at: http://www.ejcl.org/ejcl/73/art73-4.html, as of 15 March 2011.

adopting a specific orientation towards the objectives of the market. Since the conflict of laws norms in the Rome Convention lacked until recently a supreme arbiter, national courts have continued to interpret the Rome Convention in the light of pre-exisitng national traditions. The nationalistic interpretation of the Rome Convention will be demonstrated by using the example of overriding mandatory provisions. The conceptions of overriding mandatory provisions in France, Germany, the Netherlands and the United Kingdom are therefore discussed in chapter three.

The fourth chapter will analyse the interaction between Union law and Private International Law in harmonised areas. To what extent can the traditional PIL approach be applied to secondary Union law? It will be attempted to reconcile the unification of the conflict of laws norms on a Union level with the adoption of provisions indicating the international scope of application of secondary legislation. It will be argued that these latter provisions are only exceptionally conflict of laws norms in a traditional sense, but more often scope rules indicating the degree of mandatory nature of a rule in an international context. Consequently the international scope of application of secondary law in the area of contractual obligations will depend upon Rome I instead of being established autonomously.

The fifth chapter will analyse the role of Private International Law on the internal market. The harmonisation of substantive private law has already been on the agenda for years. Conflict of laws would loose their function on the internal market when all law would be uniform. However also the harmonisation of sectorial fields, if pursued systematically, could reduce the importance of Rome I. The competence of the Union to enact European Civil Code, Contract Code or optional instrument will therefore be explored. Subsequently it will be attempted to demonstrate in which areas it would be feasible to strive for closer convergence between the legal systems of the Member States and in which areas legal pluralism should continue to exist. In the latter areas, the potential obstacles to cross border trade that may follow from divergening national rules can be adequately remedied by a mix between mutual recognition and conflict of laws.

The final chapter will aim to further define the mix between mutual recognition and conflict of laws by analysig the interaction between Union law and Private International Law in non-harmonised areas. For the purpose of this chapter, it does not matter whether differences between national private laws occur due to a total absence of harmonisation or due to minimum harmonisation. The question will be answered whether the country of origin principle contains a hidden conflict of laws rule or, if that question should be answered in the negative, to what extent rules of contract law are able to constitute an obstacle to the functioning of the internal market. It will be argued that rules concerning administrative authorisations, prudential supervision and product quality ought to be treated differently than rules applicable between private parties. The application of the principle of mutual recognition towards this later category of rules is less appropriate.

1.3 *The Communautarisation of Private International Law*

PIL has always taken a particular position in the legal system of the Member States.[13] The idea that a court might not apply its own law, but instead that of a foreign, or give effect to rights acquired under a foreign law has captured academic minds for centuries. It is perhaps the reason why the determination under what conditions a foreign law could be applied was often left by the legislator to the judiciary. In the area of contracts, the Rome Convention (1980) constituted even for countries such as Belgium, France and the Netherlands the first codification of conflict of laws rules.[14]

---

[13] Boele-Woelki, K., "Unification and Harmonization of Private International Law in Europe", J. Basedow *et al* (eds.) *Private Law in the International Arena: Liber Amicorum Kurt Siehr*, T.M.C. Asser Press, The Hague, 2000, pp. 61–78; Basedow, J., "The Communitarisation of the Conflict of laws under the Treaty of Amsterdam", *Common Market Law Review*, Vol. 37, No. 3, 2000, pp. 687–708; Israël, J., "Europees Internationaal Privaatrecht", *Nederlands Internationaal Privaatrecht*", Vol. 18, 2001, pp. 135–149; Jessurun d'Oliveria, H., "The EU and a Metamorphosis of Private International Law", J. Fawcett (ed.), *Reform and Development of Private International Law: Essays in honours of Sir Peter North*, Oxford University Press, Oxford, 2002, pp. 111–136; Lagarde, P. "Développement futurs du droit international privé dans une Europe en voie d'unification: quelques conjectures", *RabelsZ*, Vol. 68, 2004, pp. 225–24; Dickinson, A., "European Private International Law: Embracing New Horizons or Mourning the Past", *Journal of Private International Law*, Vol. 1, No. 2, 2005, pp. 197–236; Vékás, L., "Der Weg zur Vergemeinschaftung des Internationalen Privat- und Verfahrensrechts – eine Skizze", J. Erauw *et al* (eds.), *Liber Memorialis Petar Šarčević, Universalism, Tradition and the Individual*, Sellier, München, 2006, pp. 171–187; Bogdan, M., *Concise Introduction to EU Private International Law*, Europa Law Publishing, Groningen, 2006, pp. 6–14; Meeusen, J., "Who is afraid of European Private International Law", G. Venturini and S. Bariatti (eds), *Liber Fausto Pocar: New Instruments of Private International Law*, Giuffrè, Milano, 2009, pp. 685–700.

[14] See par. 3.1.1 and 3.3.1.

PIL and Union law was not really love at first sight. At first instance, that may seem surprising because both PIL and Union law fulfil a similar function; they both try to resolve a conflict of laws. Mutual recognition combined with a country of origin approach does no more than to settle a claim of application of the laws of the host Member State and the home Member State in favour of the latter. PIL and Union law, however, do not have the same starting point. Union law evolves around the creation of an internal market in which it is perceived to be an obstacle to the proper functioning of the latter when a producer would be subject to the laws of both the host and the home Member State. PIL is not, or at least before the influence of Union law was not, concerned with the political aim of European integration. European PIL tries to serve international trade and transnational relationships by bringing back a legal relationship to its natural seat and finding the applicable law. Traditionally, the conflict of laws rules have been understood as being value free and rule blind.[15] Although PIL is unfamiliar with the political nature of Union law, its ambitions are wider, in the sense that its tries to serve international trade as a whole and not just the needs of intra-Union commerce. The international harmony of decisions, where the outcome of a dispute is similar regardless before which court the proceedings are brought, is a goal in itself. Consequently, the application of Union law and PIL are supported by different rationales. Union law is concerned with whether the imposition of a rule constitutes a restriction to the internal market whereas PIL in the Savignian tradition does not seek to neutralise the disadvantages that result from discrepancies between national laws but instead tries to locate the centre of the relationship, that being in contracts the law of the place that is most closely connected to the contract.[16]

The different rationale means that a notion used in general Union law is not necessarily transposable in PIL. For example the definition of services will have a different meaning in the context of art. 56 of the Treaty on the Functioning of the European Union (TFEU) than in

---

[15] On the incorporation of substantive considerations in PIL: Brilmayer, L., "The Role of Substantive and Choice of Law Policies in the Formation and Application of Choice of Law Rules", *Recueil des Cours*, Vol. 252, 1995, pp. 9–122; Vrellis, S., "Conflit ou Coordination de Valeurs en Droit International Privé : Al la recherche de justice", *Recueil des Cours*, Vol. 328, 2007, pp. 189–485.

[16] Fallon, M., "Libertés communautaires et règles de conflit de lois", A. Fuchs *et al* (eds.), Les conflits de lois et le système juridique communautaire, Dalloz, Paris, 2004, pp. 31–80 (34).

the context of art. 4 (1b) Rome I Regulation. Art. 56 TFEU aims to contribute to the realisation of the internal market by guaranteeing the free movement of services. In order to achieve its effect, a wide definition is necessary to cover the performance of any economic activity. However, art. 4 (1b) Rome I operates as one of the presumptions to determine with which jurisdiction the closest connection exists. The law applicable to a contract for the provisions of services is the law of the place where the party who has to provide the service is established. In order not to deprive the other presumptions establishing a close connection of their effect a more narrow definition of the notion 'services' is appropriate.[17]

The autonomous interpretation of PIL instruments does not apply only vis-à-vis other Union instruments. The conflict of laws rules are to be defined independently from the legal systems of the Member States. Despite similar wording, European conflict of laws concepts do not necessarily mean the same as pre-existing national concepts. The development of an autonomous concept facilitates a uniform interpretation and avoids, at least with regard to the internal market, several traditional PIL problems. Should, for example, the question whether a contract constitutes a contract for the sale of goods or the provision of services be answered according to the *lex fori* (law of the forum) or to the law that putatively governs the contract? PIL uses the doctrine of characterisation to solve that issue. Due to the autonomous construction it should not matter whether that question is governed by the *lex fori* or the putative applicable law since the question will be answered identical anyway.[18]

1.3.1 *Legal Basis*

In its early years the Union tried to create the internal market by removing obstacles to trade artificially created by Member States with the implementation of the fundamental freedoms.[19] The EEC Treaty was,

---

[17] C-533/07 *Falco Privatstiftung and Rabitsch* [2009] ECR I-3327; Case C-381/08 *Car Trim v Keysafety* [2010] ECR I-0000.

[18] Another PIL difficulty is directly solved in Rome I. Does the determination of the applicable law mean the applicability of that whole legal system including its rules of PIL or only the substantive private law? What happens if the conflict of laws rules of the applicable legal system refers back to the law of the forum? Rome I excludes renvoi, meaning that the conflict of laws norms refer only to the substantive law.

[19] Basedow, J., "The Gradual Emergence of European Private Law", T. Einhorn and K. Siehr (eds.), *Intercontinental Cooperation through Private International Law: Essays in Memory of Peter E Nygh*, TMC Asser Press, The Hague, 2004, pp. 1–18 (8).

save for its provisions on competition law, only addressed to Member States and not to private parties. In the landmark cases *Van Gend & Loos* and *Costa v E.N.E.L.* it became clear that individuals could directly invoke the provisions of the EEC Treaty and that Union law would, in a case of conflict with national law prevail. Individuals could thus directly rely on norms contained in the Treaty even if this would contravene national law. Union law gained increasing importance for PIL lawyers when it was accepted that it could not only confer rights upon individuals, but also impose obligations. In *Defrenne II*,[20] the European Court of Justice (ECJ) held that the non-discrimination principle embodied in art. 141 EC (157 TFEU) also applied to a contract between an employee and a private employer. In the nineties, the Court recognised the direct applicability of art. 39 EC (45 TFEU) in a purely private dispute.[21] The effective application of Union law would be undermined if Member States could, by transferring competences to a private body, prevent the application of the free movement of workers.[22] Art. 45 TFEU should therefore also be applied against private law bodies that could effectively regulate the employment market. The Court later accepted the same with regard to the freedom of establishment.[23] With regard to arts. 45 and 49 TFEU it follows that their application is not limited to quasi-public organisations or to associations exercising a regulatory task and having quasi-legislative powers.[24] It has also been widely accepted that not only primary law, but also regulations can be directly applied between two individuals.[25]

---

[20] Case 43/75 *Defrenne II* [1975] ECR 455.

[21] Case C-415/93 *Bosman* [1995] I-4921. See: Van den Bogaert, S., "Horizontality: The Courts Attacks?" C. Barnard (ed.), *The Law of Single European Market*, Hart Publishing, Oxford, 2002, pp. 123–152.

[22] Case 36/74 *Walrave and Koch* [1974] ECR 1405, paras. 17, 18, 23 and 24; Case 13/76 *Donà* [1976] ECR 1333, paras. 17 and 18; Joined Cases C- 51/96 and C-191/97 *Deliège* [2000] ECR I-2549, para. 47; Case C-176/96 *Lehtonen and Castors Braine* [2000] ECR I-2681, para. 35; Case C-309/99 *Wouters and Others* [2002] ECR I-1577, paras. 120; Case C-519/04 P *Meca-Medina and Majcen* v *Commission* [2006] ECR I-6991.

[23] Case C-438-05 *Viking* [2007] ECR I-10779. The prevailing opinion is that the Court attributed also in *Laval* direct horizontal effect to art. 49, see: Wyatt, D., "Horizontal Effect of Fundamental Freedoms and the Right to Equality after Viking and Mangold, and the Implications for Union Competence", Oxford Legal Studies Research Paper No. 20/2008; Reich, N., "The Public/Private Divide in European Law", H. Micklitz and F. Cafaggi, *European Private Law after the Common Frame of Reference*, Edward Elgar, Cheltenham, pp. 56–89 (63).

[24] *Viking*, Supra note 23, par. 64.

[25] Case 93/71 *Leonesio v Italian Ministry of Agriculture* [1972] ECR 293; Case 39/72 *Commission v Italy* [1973] ECR 101.

The gradually increasing importance of Union law in private relations led to an overlap with PIL, a situation for which both PIL and Union law have been struggling to find a satisfactory solution. With the creation of an internal market by taking away obstacles to trade artificially created by Member State at the centre, it might not come as a surprise that the original EEC Treaty did not really address PIL. It merely made one reference, stipulating that Member States will enter with each other into negotiations concerning the simplification of recognition and enforcement of judicial decisions (art. 220 EEC, which ceased to exist with the entry into force of the TFEU). The result was the Brussels Convention on Jurisdiction and the Enforcement of Judgments in Civil and Commercial Matters, hence not a Union instrument but a 'regular' international treaty. The Rome Convention was even more loosely connected to the Union legal order and lacked any explicit legal basis in the Treaty.[26]

Both the Brussels Convention and the Rome Convention were negotiated by PIL experts, rather than Union lawyers, and followed a modern version of traditional PIL patterns instead of any specific orientation towards the objectives of the Treaty.[27] The difference in approach is very well demonstrated by their respective attitude towards international conventions. Whereas art. 351 TFEU provided that the Treaty will not affect the obligations of Member States arising under other international conventions that entered into force before 1 January 1958, it requires the Member State or States concerned to take all appropriate steps to eliminate the existing incompatibilities. It follows from the ECJ decisions in *ERTA* and *Open Skies* that the Union enjoys the power to act externally in so far as ir is necessary for the fulfilment of its internal powers.[28] Member States lose their ability to enter into international

[26] Plender, R., *The European Contracts Convention: The Rome Convention on the Law Applicable to Contractual Obligations*, Sweet & Maxwell, London, 2001, 6. The question whether the Rome Convention is part of the EU legal order or not becomes relevant at the stage of interpretation. The Rome Convention may, provided that it is part of the EU legal order, also be used to guide the interpretation of other EU instruments.

[27] Jessurun d'Oliveria, *supra* note 13, 121.

[28] Case 22/70 *Commission v Council (ERTA)* [1971] ECR 263; case C-476/98, *Commission v. Germany (Open Skies)* [2002] ECR I-9855, see: Boele-Woelki, K., and R. Van Ooik, "The Communitarization of Private International Law", *Yearbook of Private International Law*, Vol. 4, 2002, pp. 1–36 (18-24); Eeckhout, P., *External Relations of the European Union: Legal and Constitutional Foundations*,: Oxford University Press, Oxford, 2004, pp. 58–100; Van Ooik, R., "The European Court of Justice and the Division of Competence in the European Union", D. Obradovic and N. Lavranos (eds.),

conventions once the Union has exercised its competences internally and the possibility exists that the convention envisaged may affect the scope of the common rules. The doctrine of implied powers was codified in the Lisbon Treaty.[29]

Art. 21 Rome Convention takes a completely different approach, the Convention 'shall not prejudice the application of international conventions to which a Contracting State is, or becomes, a party'. Hence, Member States did not lose the possibility to conclude new conventions. Art. 23 read in conjunction with art. 24 required a Contracting State to merely notify the intention to ratify an international convention (or even amend its internal choice of law rule) to the Secretary-General of the Council of the European Communities. If no other Contracting State requested consultations within six months, or after a period of two years after the notification no consensus had been reached, the Contracting State could ratify the convention concerned. The ratification of an international convention by a Member State in an area that has been harmonised by the Union would undermine the uniform application of Union law and would be unthinkable in the context of the Union.[30] However, from a PIL perspective, a flexible approach to international conventions is necessary in order to strive for its broader aim: the facilitation of trade on the international level and the international harmony of decisions.[31]

Interface between EU Law and National Law, European Law Publishers, Groningen, 2007, pp. 11–40; Neframi, E., *Les Accords Mixtes de la Communauté Européenne: Aspects Communautaires et Internationaux*, Bruylant, Brussels, 2007, pp. 52–76.

[29] Art. 216 (1) TFEU 'The Union may conclude an agreement with one or more third countries or international organisations where the Treaties so provide or where the conclusion of an agreement is necessary in order to achieve, within the framework of the Union's policies, one of the objectives referred to in the Treaties, or is provided for in a legally binding act of the Union or is likely to affect common rules or alter their scope.' Cremona, M., "Defining competence in EU external relations: lessons from the Treaty reform process", A. Dashwood and M. Maresceau (eds.), *Law and Practice of EU External Relations*, Cambridge University Press, Cambridge, 2008, pp. 34–69.

[30] The area covered by the Brussels I Regulation has now become an exclusive EC competence. Opinion 1/03 *Lugano Convetion* [2006] ECR I-1145. Brand, R., "The Lugano Case in the European Court of Justice: Evolving European Union Competence in Private International Law", *ILSA Journal of International & Comparative Law*, Vol. 11, 2005, pp. 297–303; Cremona, M., EU External Action in the JHA Domain: A Legal Perspective, EUI Working Papers Law, No. 24 (2008).

[31] Art. 25 Rome I still contains a clause giving prevalence to international conventions entered into before the adoption of Rome I. The provision on conventions concluded after the adoption of Rome I has been repealed, but has become less pressing in the light of the accession of the EU to the Hague Conference.

1.3.2 *Maastricht, Amsterdam and Nice*

Some conflict of laws lawyers predicted that in the light of the modification of the national PIL systems by the Brussels and Rome Conventions and the initiatives of the Hague Conference on Private International Law the influence of the Union on national PIL would be fairly limited and only gradual.[32] This prediction could not have been farther from the reality. The problem of competence was resolved in the Treaty of Maastricht (1991) which formalised the desire, as expressed by the Rome Convention, to continue the unification of PIL and it incorporated two articles on judicial cooperation in civil matters providing for the legal basis for the negotiation and adoption of PIL conventions in Title VI of the EU Treaty. The Treaty of Amsterdam (1997) moved Title VI to title IV in the EC Treaty and generated a Union law-making competence. The adoption of PIL measures was simplified by the Treaty of Nice (2000) by changing the voting requirements, save in family law matters, from unanimity to qualified majority. Despite its placement in the Title on Visa, Asylum and Immigration the competence of the Union was not limited to migration related PIL. The reason for the placement of the PIL competence in Title IV is rather co-incidental and may be due to the limited amount of time available for the Amsterdam negotiations[33] and the fact that immigration law is in some Member States, such as France, traditionally regarded as part of PIL.

The placement of the PIL competence in Title IV was, however, not without consequences. Ireland and the United Kingdom enjoy the possibility of an opt-out to the whole title and could decide ad hoc whether they desired to take part in the preparations of a specific measure. Denmark was not at all bound by measures adopted under Title IV,

---

Von Wagner, R., "Die Haager Konferenz für Internationales Privatrecht zehn Jahre nach der Vergemeinschaftung der Gesetzgebungskompetenz in der justiziellen Zusammenarbeit in Zivilsachen", *RabelsZ*, Vol. 73, 2009, pp. 215–240.

[32] North, P., "Is European Harmonisation of Private International Law a Myth or Reality", T. de Boer (ed.) *Forty Years on: the Evolution of Postwar Private International Law in Europe*, Kluwer, Deventer, 1990, pp. 29–48.

[33] Kohler, C., "Interrogations sur les sources de droit international privé européen après le traité d'Amsterdam", *Revue Critique de Droit International Privé*, Vol. 88, No. 1, 1999, pp. 3–30; Kessedjian, C., Le droit international privé et l'intégration juridique européene, T. Einhorn and K. Siehr (eds.), *Intercontinental Cooperation through Private International Law: Essays in Memory of Peter E Nygh*, TMC Asser Press, The Hague, 2004, pp. 187–196 (191).

but could conclude international conventions with the Union to reach the same substantial effects.[34] Moreover, art. 68 (1) EC limited the possibility for making a preliminary reference concerning measures adopted on Title IV to the ECJ to national courts against whose decisions was no remedy possible. That situation was far from satisfying, and was actually worse than under the interpretation protocol to the Rome Convention, under which appellate courts also had the power to refer a case for a preliminary ruling to the ECJ. Particularly in the light of the gradual communautarisation of PIL, the fact that a reference could only be made by a court against whose decision was no remedy possible became increasingly untenable. The limited possibility of appeal to the ECJ by national courts resulted in divergent and often contradictory interpretations and seriously undermined the goal of attaining more legal certainty in cross-border conflicts. From a commercial perspective as well as from the perspective of access to effective judicial remedies it could not be regarded as feasible that parties to a contract who disagree about interpretation of the conflict of laws rules first had to go all the way to the highest national court before the ECJ could address their claim.

The relationship between art. 65 and art. 95 EC was also debated. Art. 95 conferred power upon the Union to approximate national laws insofar necessary for the functioning of the internal market. Should art. 65 EC be understood as a *lex specialis* of art. 95 EC, or did art. 65 have an autonomous meaning?[35] Differences in conflict of laws rules and the existence of concurrent fora made the applicable law somewhat unpredictable. The resulting legal uncertainty could discourage traders from entering into international contracts. Therefore, in principle there appeared not to be a convincing argument why conflict of laws would fall outside the reach of art. 95. However art. 95 only allowed for the approximation of national laws, whereas art. 65 empowered the Union to take measures to progressively establish an area of freedom, security and justice. In contrast with art. 95, the Union was thus empowered

---

[34] Chalmers, D., *et al*, *European Union Law*, Cambridge University Press, Cambridge, 2006, 620–621. With regards to Brussels I: Agreement between the European Union and the Kingdom of Denmark on jurisdiction and the recognition and enforcement of judgments in civil and commercial matters OJ L 299.

[35] Israël, J., "Conflicts of Law and the EC after Amsterdam: A Change for the Worse?", *Maastricht Journal of European and Comparative Law*, Vol. 7, No. 1, 2000, pp. 81–99.

under art. 65 to issue both directives and regulations in this area. It is the regulation that has proven to be the preferred instrument of Union legislation. Whether art. 65 could be attributed an autonomous meaning or not, it was clearly drafted to cover a number of concrete aspects of cross-border private law. It should therefore be adopted as basis for legislative measures concerning PIL rather than more generally framed competences, such as on the internal market (art. 95) or transport (art. 71).[36]

1.3.3 *Union Instruments*

The controversies and the limited control of the ECJ have not stopped the Union from further engaging in PIL. The Tampere European summit (1999) adopted an action plan on the implementation of the provisions of the Treaty of Amsterdam in the area of freedom, security and justice. The mutual recognition of judicial decisions was considered a cornerstone of a common justice area. Following Tampere and Nice the Union has extensively used its acquired competences,[37] not only have the Brussels and Rome Conventions been transformed into regulations, but the Union has also entered new areas. Instruments have been adopted relating to insolvency proceedings (Regulation 1346/2000), the service in the Member States of judicial and extrajudicial documents in civil or commercial matters (Regulation 1348/2000), cooperation between the courts of the Member States in the taking of evidence in civil or commercial matters (Regulation 206/2001), to improve access to justice in cross-border disputes by establishing minimum common rules relating to legal aid for such disputes (Directive 2003/8), concerning jurisdiction and the recognition and enforcement of judgements in matrimonial matters and the matters of parental responsibility (Brussels II bis Regulation, 2201/2003), a European Enforcement Order for uncontested claims (Regulation 805/2004), a European Small Claims Procedure (Regulation 861/2007), the Law Applicable to Non-Contractual Obligations (Rome II Regulation, 864/2007), on the service in the Member States of judicial and extrajudicial documents in civil or commercial matters (Regulation 1393/2007), jurisdiction, applicable law, recognition and enforcement of decisions and cooperation in matters relating to maintenance

[36] Boele-Woelki/Van Ooik, *supra* note 28, 17.
[37] Brand, R., "The European Magnet and the U.S. Centrifuge: Ten Selected Private International Law Developments of 2008", University of Pittsburgh Working Paper No. 2009-01.

obligations (Regulation 4/2009). Initiatives in the area of succession and wills, matrimonial property regime and alternative dispute resolution have been undertaken.[38] It cannot be excluded that within the next two decades national PIL will have been completely replaced by PIL adopted at a Union level.[39]

1.3.4 *A New Legal Basis in the Lisbon Treaty*

The Treaty of Lisbon sets another step in the direction of replacement of PIL by Union law. It will continue the trend of communautarisation of PIL and solves some of the difficulties.[40] Art. 81 TFEU provides as follows:

1. The Union shall develop judicial cooperation in civil matters having cross-border implications, based on the principle of mutual recognition of judgments and of decisions in extrajudicial cases. Such cooperation may include the adoption of measures for the approximation of the laws and regulations of the Member States.
2. For the purposes of paragraph 1, the European Parliament and the Council, acting in accordance with the ordinary legislative procedure, shall adopt measures, particularly when necessary for the proper functioning of the internal market, aimed at ensuring:
   (a) the mutual recognition and enforcement between Member States of judgments and of decisions in extrajudicial cases;
   (b) the cross-border service of judicial and extrajudicial documents;
   (c) the compatibility of the rules applicable in the Member States concerning conflict of laws and of jurisdiction;
   (d) cooperation in the taking of evidence;
   (e) effective access to justice;
   (f) the elimination of obstacles to the proper functioning of civil proceedings, if necessary by promoting the compatibility of the rules on civil procedure applicable in the Member States;
   (g) the development of alternative methods of dispute settlement;
   (h) support for the training of the judiciary and judicial staff.

---

[38] Green Paper on alternative dispute resolution in civil and commercial law, COM(2002), 0196 final; Green Paper on maintenance obligations, COM(2004), 254 final Green Paper on Succession and Wills COM (2005) 65 final; Green Paper on the conflict of laws in matters concerning matrimonial property regimes, including the question of jurisdiction and mutual recognition, COM(2006), 400 final.

[39] Lagarde, *supra* note 13, 225–233.

[40] De Groot, G., and J. Kuipers, "The New Provisions on Private International Law in the Treaty of Lisbon", *Maastricht Journal of European and Comparative Law*, Vol. 15, No. 1, 2008, pp. 109-114; Mansel, H., K. Thorn and R. Wagner, "Europäisches Kollisionsrecht 2009 : Hoffnungen durch den Vertrag von Lissabon", *IPRax*, Vol. 30, No. 1, 2010, pp. 1–27; Barrière Brousse, I., "Le Traité de Lisbonne et le droit international privé", *Journal du Droit International*, Vol. 137, No. 1, 2010, pp. 3–34.

3. Notwithstanding paragraph 2, measures concerning family law with cross-border implications shall be established by the Council, acting in accordance with a special legislative procedure. The Council shall act unanimously after consulting the European Parliament. The Council, on a proposal from the Commission, may adopt a decision determining those aspects of family law with cross-border implications which may be the subject of acts adopted by the ordinary legislative procedure. The Council shall act unanimously after consulting the European Parliament. The proposal referred to in the second subparagraph shall be notified to the national Parliaments. If a national Parliament makes known its opposition within six months of the date of such notification, the decision shall not be adopted. In the absence of opposition, the Council may adopt the decision.

The Union shall be empowered to adopt measures *in particular* when necessary for the functioning of the internal market. The adoption of measures does therefore not strictly depend upon the internal market criterion. Art. 81 thus provides for a wider competence than envisaged by art. 114 TFEU (art. 95 EC). Although art. 81 TFEU maintains the requirement of unanimity voting in family matters, a special PIL passerelle clause has been introduced to enable the adoption of specific measures on the basis of qualified majority voting (QMV). The Lisbon Treaty, moreover, does away with the limited jurisdiction of the ECJ: the normal preliminary ruling procedure is also applicable to measures adopted on the basis of art. 81 TFEU. National courts may therefore refer a preliminary question to the ECJ, whether appeal against that courts final decision is possible or not. Finally, Denmark seized the opportunity to modify its position towards art. 81 TFEU. It may notify the other Member States that it will enjoy a more flexible position as provided for in the annex to the protocol.[41] Denmark would after notification acquire a position similar to that of Ireland and the United Kingdom.

1.3.5 *External Competences*

It was open to doubt whether art. 65 EC also conferred competence to harmonise the national conflict of laws rules that cover relationship with third countries.[42] To what extent is harmonisation of these rules

[41] Art. 8 (1) of Protocol 22 on the Position of Denmark as Annexed to the TFEU.

[42] Hess, B., "Les compétences externes de la Communauté européenne dans le cadre de l'article 65 CE", A. Fuchs *et al* (eds.), *Les conflits de lois et le système juridique communautaire*, Dalloz, Paris, 2004, pp. 81–100.

necessary for the functioning of the internal market? Despite the slight widening of competence, also art. 81 TFEU does not address the external power of the Union. However under the ERTA doctrine the Union acquires international competence if it has exercised its internal competence and acting on the international plane is necessary for the fulfilment of that purpose.[43] In *Owusu*, the Court in a very brief argument stated that the common rules of jurisdiction contained in the Brussels Convention were 'not intended to apply only to situations in which there is a real and sufficient link with the working of the internal market, by definition involving a number of Member States.' It sufficed to observe that 'the consolidation as such of the rules on conflict of jurisdiction and on the recognition and enforcement of judgments, effected by the Brussels Convention in respect of cases with an international element, is without doubt intended to eliminate obstacles to the functioning of the internal market which may derive from disparities between national legislations on the subject.'[44] The Brussels Convention thus also applied to the question whether an English court could decline jurisdiction over a tort allegedly committed in Jamaica on the grounds that the Jamaican court was in a much better position to adjudicate the case (*forum non conveniens*). That does however not answer the question whether the Union was competent to act in the international arena. In the *Lugano Opinion* the Court held that the area of jurisdiction and recognition and enforcement of judgments in civil matters had become an exclusive implicit external competence.[45] The Lugano Convention should therefore be signed by the Union exclusively and not by the Member States. The competence of the Member States would potentially affect the scope of the common rules. It could be doubted whether the harmonisation of PIL with regard to the relations with third countries was really necessary

---

[43] Eeckhout, *supra* note 28, 58–100; De Vareilles-Sommières, P., "La Compétence internationale de l'espace judicaire européen", T. Azzi *et al* (eds.), *Vers de nouveaux équilibres entre ordres juridiques, Liber amicorum Hélène Gaudemet-Tallon*, Dalloz, Paris, 2008, pp. 397–417.

[44] Case C-281/02 *Owusu* [2005] ECR I-1383, par. 34.

[45] Opinion 1/03 *Lugano Convetion* [2006] ECR I-1145, para. 143–146. Fallon, M., "L'applicabilité du règlement ‹Bruxelles I› aux situations externes après l'avis 1/03", TAzzi *et al* (eds.), *Vers de nouveaux équilibres entre ordres juridiques, Liber amicorum Hélène Gaudemet-Tallon*, Dalloz, Paris, 2008, pp. 241–264 ; Kuijper, P., "The Opinion on the Lugano Convention and Implied External Relations Powers", B. Martenczuk and S. van Thiel, *Justice, Liberty and Security: New Challenges for EU External Relations*, Brussels University Press, Brussels, 2008, pp. 187–210

for the functioning of the internal market. The widening of Union competence to *in particular* when necessary for the internal market therefore corresponds better with the reality of *Owusu* and the *Lugano Opinion*.

In the past decade the Union has become an important player in the negotiations of international conventions laying down PIL rules. The increasing activity of the European legislator in PIL resulted in April 2007 into the accession of the EC to the Hague Conference on Private International Law.[46] In early 2009 the Union signed its first convention, the Hague Convention on Choice of Court Agreements (2005).[47] The coherency of Union law is protected by a so-called 'disconnection clause', which provides that Member States shall apply the relevant international instrument externally, but amongst each other the Union rules.[48] However, the disconnection clause in PIL[49] is different from traditional disconnection clauses in so far as it does not seek to ensure the applicability of Union law every time that it is applicable but rather coordinates the application of the international agreement and the common rules in situations where both are applicable.[50] In that way, the disconnection contributes in striving towards uniform rules in PIL, which is the aim of the Hague Conference.

---

[46] http://www.hcch.net/index_en.php?act=states.details&sid=220, as of 15 March 2011. See also: Brand, R., "Union Competence for Matters of Judicial Cooperation at the Hague Conference on Private International Law: A View from the United States", *Journal of Law and Commerce*, Vol. 21, 2002, pp. 191–208; Traest, M., *De Europese Gemeenschap en de Haagse Conferentie voor het Internationaal Privaatrecht*, Maklu, Antwerpen, 2003; Schulz, A., "The Accession of the European Union to the Hague Conference on Private International Law", *International and Comparative Law Quarterly*, Vol. 56, 2006, pp. 939–950; Van Loon, H., and A. Schulz, "The European Union and the Hague Conference on Private International Law", B. Martenczuk and S. van Thiel, *Justice, Liberty and Security: New Challenges for EU External Relations*, Brussels University Press, Brussels, 2008, pp. 257–299.

[47] Von Wagner, R., Das Haager Übereinkommen vom 30. 6. 2005 über Gerichtsstandsvereinbarungen, *RabelsZ*, Vol. 73, No. 1, 2009, pp. 100–149.

[48] Art. 26 (6) Hague Convention on Choice of Court Agreements (2005).

[49] Borrás, A., "Les clauses de déconnexion et le droit international privé communautaire", H. Mansel *et al* (eds.), *Festschrift für Erik Jayme*, Sellier, München, 2004, pp. 57–72.

[50] See with regard to the interface between Brussels I and the Hague Convention on Choice of Court Agreements: Hartley, T., and M. Dogauchi, Explanatory Report Convention of 30 June 2005 on Choice of Court Agreements, para. 309 and 310. Available at: http://www.hcch.net/upload/expl37e.pdf, as of 15 March 2011.

1.3.6 *Regulation 662/2009*

With the entry into force of Rome I on July 24 2008, the area of conflict of laws rules regarding contractual obligations has been exhaustively harmonised by the Union legislator. If one would apply the Courts reasoning in the *Lugano Opinion*, concerning Brussels I, to Rome I one has to conclude that the Union has gained an exclusive external competence in the area of the law applicable to contractual obligations. In art. 25 (1), Rome I still gives prevalence to existing international conventions which lay down conflict of laws rules concerning contractual obligations. Rome I does not, however, mention the possibility for Member States to conclude new international conventions. The possibility, which existed under the Rome Convention of concluding an international convention that would take prevalence over the common rules, even at the opposition of other Member States, has been removed.

Member States thus appear to have lost their competence to enter into bi- or multilateral conventions with third countries on matters covered by Rome I. Council Regulation 662/2009 however establishes a procedure for the negotiation and conclusion of agreements between Member States and third countries on particular matters concerning the law applicable to contractual and non-contractual obligations.[51] The Regulation authorises Member States, subject to a special procedure, to modify or conclude a new international convention in areas where an exclusive Union competence exists. The Commission has to consent to both the opening of the negotiations and the signing of the agreement. The Commission will refuse to do so if the Member State concerned fails to demonstrate that it has a specific interest in concluding the agreement resulting from the economic, geographic, cultural, historical, social or political ties between the Member State and the third country concerned or when the envisaged agreement would render Union law ineffective and undermine the proper functioning of the system established by that law.[52]

---

[51] The Regulation is the product of the call for a proposal concerning the procedure and conditions under which Member States could enter into international conventions made by the 42nd recital of the preamble to Rome I.

[52] Art. 4 (2) Regulation 662/2009. The third criterion is 'the envisaged agreement would not undermine the object and purpose of the Union's external relations policy as decided by the Union.'

Rome I lays down a principle of universal application, which will mean that Rome I is also applicable to a contract with connections to the Member State and the third country concerned. Regulation 662/2009 seemed therefore to move away from the structure of Rome I. Under Rome I deviation from the normal conflict of laws rules is possible with regard to specific issues, but not with regard to specific countries. Authorisation should thus by definition be refused because a bilateral agreement with a third country will always undermine the functioning of the common rules. In any case, the impact of Regulation 662/2009 is marginal and does not intend to establish real conflict of laws rules, but is most likely limited to micro-treaties providing for specific cooperation between a Member State and a third country. In order to achieve the purpose of the micro-treaty, the treaty may provide for some rules on applicable law.[53] An example would be the joint exploitation of a bridge crossing a river that constitutes the natural border between a Member State and a third country. Regulation 662/2009 does therefore not challenge the exclusive nature of the Union's external competence in matters relating to the law applicable to contractual obligations.

The influence of the Union legislator on the PIL of the Member States is significant. More and more national regulations are being replaced by European ones. That is mirrored on the international level by increasing use of external competences. The growing activity of the European legislator in PIL is not surprising. The general consensus seems to be that, despite the repetitive calls of the European Parliament for the creation of a European Civil Code,[54] the Union has no competence to introduce a comprehensive codification.[55] Even the Commission has acknowledged that some areas of private law will not

[53] Kuipers, J., "The Exclusive External Competence of the Union under art. 81 TFEU: Lugano re-opened?", M. Cremona, J. Monar and S. Poli (eds.), *The External Dimension of the Area of Freedom Security and Justice* (forthcoming).

[54] OJ C 158 [1989], 400; OJ C 205, [1994], 518; OJ C 140 E, [2002], 538; OJ C 76 E, [2004], 95.

[55] Smits, J., *The Making of European Private Law: Toward a Ius Commune Europaeum as a Mixed Legel System*, Intersentia, Antwerpen, 2002; Legrand, P., "A Diabolical Idea", A. Hartkamp (ed.), *Towards a European Civil Code*, Kluwer Law International, Nijmegen, 3rd edition, 2004, pp. 245–272; Van Gerven, W., "The ECJ Case-Law as a Means of Unification of Private Law?", A. Hartkamp (ed.), *Towards a European Civil Code,* Ars Aequi Libri, Nijmegen, 2005, pp. 101–124 (102); Smits, J., "The Principles of European Contract Law and the Harmonisation of Private Law in Europe", Antoni Vacquer (ed.), *La Tercera Parte de Los Principios de Derecho Contractual Europeo*, Tirant, Valencia, 2005, pp. 567–590; Röttinger, M., "Towards a European Code Napoléon/ABGB/BGB? Recent EC Activities for a European Contract Law", *European*

be harmonised in the near future, or even never.[56] Such areas will essentially be governed by national private law. Private international law constitutes a good alternative to substantive harmonisation of private laws since it is able to enhance legal certainty while at the same time does not necessitate any change of substantive law and is therefore better able to respect legal diversity.[57]

1.4 *Conflict of Laws Rules in Sectoral Instruments*

Art. 81 TFEU is not the only legal basis on which the Union may enter the terrain of conflict of laws. Directives laying down rules applicable in the horizontal relation between private parties will also cover cross-border legal relationships. The whole purpose of the internal market is that a consumer may shop in different Member States or that an employee may move to a Member State where conditions are more advantageous to him. The international scope of application of those rules should therefore also be established. Two alternatives are available. The first is to establish the international scope of application of a directive on the basis of an autonomous construction of its object and purpose. The second is making the scope of application of secondary Union law dependent upon traditional conflict of laws norms.

The approach taken by the Union is not really clear. On the one hand, the codification of national PIL at the Union level according to

Law Journal, Vol. 12, 2006, pp. 807–827; Vogenauer, S. and S. Weatherill, "The EC's Competence to Pursue Harmonisation", S. Vogenauer and S. Weatherill (eds.), *The Harmonisation of European Contract Law; Implications for European Private Laws, Business and Legal Practice*, Hart Publishing, Portland, 2006, pp. 105–148; Weatherhill, S., "Constitutional Issues – How Much is Best Left Unsaid?", *The Harmonisation of European Contract Law,* 2006, pp. 89–104; Micklitz, H., "Review of Academic Approaches to the European Contract Law Codification Project", M. Andenas *et al* (eds.), *Liber Amicorum Guido Alpa: Private Law beyond the National Systems*, British Institute of International and Comparative Law, London, 2007, pp. 699–726.

[56] Commissioner Vitorino: 'Il existe certains domaines du droit civil en du droit pénal, tant en ce qui concerne le fond que la procédure, que ne seront pas harmonisés pendant très longtemps entre les membres de l'Union europééne, et peut-être même jamais', quoted in: Remien, O., "Private International Law, the European Union and its Emerging Area of Freedom, Security and Justice," *Common Market Law Review,* 2001, pp. 53–86 (63).

[57] Muir-Watt, H., "European Integration, legal diversity and the Conflict of Laws", *Edinburgh Law Review*, Vol. 9, 2005, pp. 6–31. A critical view is adopted by: Harris, J., "Understanding the English response to the Europeanisation of Private International Law", *Journal of Private International Law*, Vol. 4, No. 3, 2008, pp. 347–395. In more detail: see chapter 5.

the lines of the traditional conflict of laws mechanisms would suggest that the Union does not intend to change the operation of the traditional conflict of laws norms. On the other hand, provisions in secondary law addressing the international scope of application diverge in method and criteria used and are difficult to translate in traditional PIL mechanisms. The precise meaning of these provisions, that appear particular frequently in the area of consumer law, is open to debate. In the process of drafting Rome I, Member States could not agree to more than that an evaluation of the conflict of laws norms with regard to consumer contracts should be carried out by the Commission, with the object of study being the coherence of Union law on the application of the special protective connective factor for consumers in the light of the *acquis communautaire* in the area of consumer law.[58]

An autonomous approach would mean a paradigm change. The international scope of application of a rule would be established on the basis of the rule instead of the legitimate expectations of the parties or determining the spatially most appropriate law. One can wonder whether a unilateral approach will in the long run best serve the interests of the Union or whether the Union is making the same mistake as the early post-Glossators did when for the first time confronted with PIL question: to overlook the coordinative function of the conflict of laws rules[59] and to focus exclusively on the perceived needs of the own legal order.

However, a traditional conflict of laws approach also has its difficulties. Problematic is that upon a strict construction of the traditional conflict of laws norms a contract between a French and a German citizen is just as international as a contract between a French and a Russian citizen. The existence of a common market with its own set of rules was not translated in the conflict of laws process. Under the system of the Rome Convention the French and German citizen were awarded full party autonomy. They could therefore elect the application of the law of a third country and avoid the application of mandatory norms of Union law even though all connections pointed exclusively to the Union. Rome I does more justice to the specificities of the internal market. It draws a parallel to situations that are completely internal

---

[58] Art. 27 (1b) Rome I.

[59] Jacquet, J., "La Fonction Supranationale de la Règle de Conflit de Lois", *Recueil des Cours*, Vol. 292, 2001, pp. 155–248 ; Mayer, P., "Le Phénomène de la Coordination des Ordres Juridiques Étatiques en Droit Privé" *Recueil des Cours*, Vol. 327, 2007, 23–377.

to one Member State. Party autonomy is in such circumstances limited to non-mandatory rules. Art. 3 (4) Rome I provides that when all elements are located in one or more Member States a choice of law may not lead to the non-application of the mandatory rules of Union law.

1.5 *Influence of Primary Union Law upon the Conflict of Law Rules*

The increasing influence of Union law upon private law did not only generate the desire to codify PIL at a Union level, but had already of its own motion a major impact upon PIL. In a seminal article Roth analysed the influence of the internal market upon the PIL of the Member States.[60] He observed an interplay whereby PIL could both be used as instrument to advance the internal market, but that on the other hand Union law could impose limits on the conflict of laws norms.

> Primäres Gemeinschaftsrecht und mitgliedstaatliches IPR stehen in doppeleter Beziehung zueinander: Internationales Privatrecht läßt sichals ein Instrument begreifen, mit dem die Ziele eines Gemeinsamen Marketes gefördert werden können. Umgekehrt kann das primäre Gemeinschaftsrecht kollisionsrechtlichen Gestaltungen Schranken auferlegen, wenn sie mit den Freiheiten des EWG-Vertrages kollidieren.[61]

With regard to primary law it was discussed whether conflict of laws could form a barrier to intra-Union trade.[62] It was debated whether the fundamental freedoms implied a *favor offerentis*.[63] According to Basedow the law that is the most favourable to the Union trade of goods

[60] Roth, W., "Der Einfluß des Europäischen Gemeinschaftsrechts auf das Internationale Privatrecht", *RabelsZ*, Vol. 55, 1991, pp. 623–673.

[61] Roth, *supra* note 60, 637. 'Primary Union law and the PIL of Member States are in a double relation towards each other: Private International Law lets itself to be understood as an instrument, with which the goal of a common market could be advanced. On the other hand primary law could impose boundaries upon conflict of laws norms when they collide with the freedoms of the EC Treaty.'

[62] Radicati di Brozolo, L., "L'influence sur les conflits de lois des principes de droit communautaire en matière de liberté de circulation", *Revue Critique de Droit International Privé*, Vol. 82, No. 3, 1993, pp. 401–423.

[63] Basedow, J., "Der kollisionsrechteliche Gehalt der Produktfreiheiten im europäischen Binnenmarkt: favor offerentis", *RabelsZ*, Vol. 95, 1995, pp. 1–55; critical: Wilderspin, M., and X. Lewis, "Les relations entre le droit communautaire et les règles de conflits de lois des Etats membres", *Revue Critique de Droit International*

should be applied. Hence, the fundamental freedoms require application of the least restrictive law to a foreign trader (Günstigkeitsprinzip, favor offerentis), since it are the producers and traders that constitute the real engine of European integration. The principle of mutual recognition then becomes a conflict of laws rule also affecting the private law relations.

From the outset it must be observed that the idea of the application of the law that is most favourable to the Union trade in goods does often not conflict with the result obtained under Rome I. The presumptions determine in general terms that, in absence of a choice of law, the law of the place where the party that has to render the most characteristic performance is situated shall be applicable. The party rendering the characteristic performance will, statistically, often be a 'repeat player' and will be the most adversely affected by the application of varying legal regimes. Applying the law of the country of the party that renders the characteristic performance thus promotes efficiency by allowing the 'repeat player' to anticipate his behaviour on the basis of a single law without having to make a choice of law.[64] The connecting factor for contracts thus tries to promote international trade and that goal coincides with the Union goals if the two contracting partners are established within the Union, but in different Member States.

The existence of a *favor offerentis* however seems implausible. The Union does not engage in an abstract balancing of which law would be most beneficial to the manufacturer or provider of services. The fundamental freedoms imply the principle of mutual recognition, which requires Member States to take into account economic legislation already applied in the home Member State. It has been correctly noted[65] that the fundamental freedoms do not only protect the manufacturer or producer but equally the recipient.[66] They do not

---

Privé, 2002, pp. 1–37 ; Heuzé, V., "De la compétence de la loi du pays d'origine en matière contractuelle ou l'anti-droit Européen", B. Ancel, *Le droit international privé : esprit et méthodes ; Mélanges en l'honneur de Paul Lagarde*, Dalloz, Paris, 2005, pp. 393–415.

[64] Solomon, D., "The Private International Law of Contracts in Europe: Advances and Retreats", *Tulane Law Review*, Vol. 82, 2008, 1709–1740 (1715–1717). See also par. 2.6.2.

[65] Von Wilmowsky, P., "EG-Vertrag und kollisionsrechtliche Rechtswahlfreiheit", *RabelsZ*, Vol. 62, 1998, pp. 1–37; De Baere, G., "Houdt het Communautair herkomstlandbeginsel een verborgen conflictregel in?", *Revue Belge de Droit International*, Vol. 36, 2003, pp. 131–201 (180).

[66] Cases 286/82 and 26/83 *Luise and Carbone* [1984] ECR 377; Case 186/87 *Cowan* [1989] ECR 195.

therefore favour the manufacturer or service provider over the recipient.

Instead of implying a *favor offerentis*, one can instead detect an impulse given by the fundamental freedoms to party autonomy. The choice of law is not restricted to the laws of the host Member State or the Member State of origin. Parties to an international contract can avoid the rules of private law of both Member States, even in situations when they are in a domestic setting mandatory, since in theory even the law of Afghanistan could be chosen to govern the contract. The connecting factor shall only be applied when parties have failed to make a choice of law. Rules whose application can be avoided by the parties by a simple choice of law are not able to constitute a restriction to the internal market[67] and primary law does not implicitly favour any national private law.

1.5.1 *The Compatibility of Connecting Factors with the TFEU*

A short review of the case-law makes it clear that primary law has a direct impact upon the conflict of laws rule.[68] The application of a conflict of laws rule is incompatible with the TFEU insofar it constitutes an obstacle to trade or amounts to discrimination on the grounds of nationality that cannot be justified by an overriding public interest. Until now, the ECJ has never ruled a connecting factor to be contrary to the free movement provisions. In *Boukhalfa*,[69] the law applicable to employment contracts of all German staff members of the German embassy in Algeria was German, whereas the law applicable to the employment contract of all other staff members was determined on the basis of the *lex loci laboris*.[70] A Belgian staff member successfully complained against the application, of the less favourable, Algerian law. Art. 18 TFEU establishes within the scope of the Treaties a general principle of non-discrimination on the grounds of nationality, art. 45 (2) TFEU does specifically with regard to workers the same. The ECJ held that not the connecting factor as such, but the fact that

[67] Case C-339/89 *Ahlstom Atlantique* [1991] ECR 107, par. 29. See par 5.7.

[68] A different view: Kohler, C., "Travaux de Comité français de droit international privé (1993–94)", 75–76.

[69] Case C-214/94 *Boukhalfa* [1996] ECR I-2253.

[70] The lex loci laboris is the law of the place where the labour is habitually carried out.

different connecting factors were applied to EU nationals according to their nationality, was contrary to the EC Treaty.[71]

In *Johannes* the Court held that the nationality of the parties to the proceedings was solely to be taken into consideration as a connecting factor, pursuant to the rules of PIL, for the purposes of determining the substantive national law applicable to the effects of a divorce. A German couple residing in Belgium got divorced. The husband worked as Commission official and the wife brought an action seeking a share of his pension rights, which would be higher according to German law than according to Belgian law. The Commission official complained that if the law applicable to the allocation of pension rights were established on the basis of nationality, he would face a heavier burden than a Belgian official merely because of his German nationality. Since the facts of the case occurred before the entry into force of the Treaty of Amsterdam the Court held that the situation fell outside the scope of Union law and that Union law did therefore not 'preclude the laws of a Member State from taking the spouses' nationality into consideration as a connecting factor for the purposes of determining the substantive national law applicable to the effects of a divorce.'[72] In the light of *Grunkin-Paul* it is doubtful whether the Court would have taken a different decision even if the facts had fallen into the temporal scope of the Treaty of Amsterdam.[73]

In *Grunkin-Paul*[74] the ECJ carefully avoided ruling upon the compatibility with primary Union law of the use of nationality as connecting factor for establishing the law governing the determination of a surname. Despite the fact that the referring court explicitly asked the ECJ to assess the compatibility of the connecting factor with the EC Treaty, the ECJ limited its reply and held that the refusal of recognition of a surname was incompatible with European Citizenship. The AG, however, did assess the use of nationality as a connecting in this context:

[71] Wilderspin/Lewis *supra* note 63 (7).

[72] Case C-430/97 *Johannes v Johannes* [1999] ECR I-3475, par. 28.

[73] Puljak, M., *Le droit international privé à l'épreuve du principe communautaire de non-discrimination en raison de la nationalité*, Presses Universitaires d'Aix-Marseille, Aix en Marseille, 2003; Meeusen, J., "Instrumentalisation of Private International Law in the European Union: Towards a European Conflicts Revolution? " *European Journal of Migration and Law*, Vol. 9, 2007, pp. 287–305 (291–295).

[74] Case C-353/06 *Grunkin Paul* [2008] ECR I-7639.

> It is true that the rule in Paragraph 10 of the EGBGB (nationality as connecting factor, JJK) *distinguishes* between individuals according to their nationality, but such distinctions are inevitable where nationality serves as a link with a particular legal system. It does not, by contrast, *discriminate* on grounds of nationality. The purpose of the prohibition of such discrimination is not to efface the distinctions which necessarily flow from possession of the nationality of one Member State rather than another (which are clearly maintained by the second sentence of Article 17(1) EC) but to preclude *further* differences of treatment which are based on nationality and which operate *to the detriment* of a citizen of the Union.[75]

As *Grunkin Paul* demonstrates, Union law undoubtedly impacts upon the national PIL systems. Nationality as a connecting factor cannot be used in the traditional manner.[76] In *Hadadi* the Court was confronted, in respect of the Brussels II bis Regulation on jurisdiction and the recognition and enforcement of judgments in matrimonial matters and in matters of parental responsibility, with a situation where both spouses possessed French and Hungarian nationality.[77] The ECJ held that in reviewing the competence of the Hungarian court that pronounced a divorce, the French court could not overlook that the spouses possessed also the nationality of the other Member State. French courts were not allowed to apply the doctrine of effective nationality to establish with which nationality the most genuine link existed. Rather the French court had to recognise that also the Hungarian court could assume jurisdiction on the basis of nationality. The courts of either country whose nationality the spouses possess will thus be competent to hear the case.

In the case-law of the ECJ, conflict of laws norms are interpreted in a manner compatible with Union law, instead of requiring a specific conflict of laws methodology. As will be explored in further sections, further influences of primary law upon the application of the conflict of laws rule may be observed, in particular with regard to the free

[75] AG Sharpston, *Grunkin Paul*, par. 62. Critical about the AG's opinion: Meeusen, J., "Grunkin and Paul judgment" *Zeitschrift für Europäisches Privatrecht*, Vol. 18, No. 1, 2010, pp. 186–201 (193).

[76] Vonk, O., *Dual Nationality in the European Union*, EUI Thesis (2010), 10–130.

[77] Case C-168/08 *Hadadi* [2009] ECR I-6871. See: Van den Eeckhout, V., "Het beroep op het bezit van een nationaliteit in geval van dubbele nationaliteit", *Nederlands Tijdschrift voor Europees Recht*, Vol. 15, 2009, 307–316.

movement provisions. In *Arblade*,[78] the application of overriding mandatory provisions came under the scrutiny of the freedom to provide services and in *Centros* and *Überseering* the freedom of establishment of legal persons prevented Member States from applying their own PIL rules to a company duly set up under the laws of another Member State.[79] In some cases, the Court follows PIL methodology, while in other cases the PIL dimension is completely neglected.

1.6 *The Method of Interpretation*

Although the barrier between PIL and Union law has now been broken, the uneasy relationship between them has not yet been resolved. The ECJ has been accused of being unable to reach reasonable decisions in private law disputes.[80] Undeniably, the method of interpretation deployed by the Court does not always produce sensible results. The Court has, in a series of judgments with regard to the Brussels Convention, focussed on the mandatory observance of Union law and the principle of mutual trust of judicial systems between the Member States rather than on the reasonable expectations of the parties. Brussels I attempts to enhance legal certainty in the internal market by introducing clear and predictable rules on jurisdiction. Rules of special jurisdiction must be interpreted strictly and cannot be given an interpretation going beyond the cases expressly envisaged by Brussels I.[81] On first glance, that argument could also be applied with regard to Rome I. Legal certainty thus plays a larger role in Union PIL than previously in the Member States. First the Court held in *Gasser* that the *lis pendens* rule (art. 21) interpreted in the light of mutual trust required that the courts of a Member State, even in clear contravention of a choice of forum agreement, must stay proceedings when proceedings have already been commenced in another Member State, irrespective how long it takes for the courts of the latter Member State to declare the case inadmissible.[82] Private parties can thus even in bad faith lodge

[78] Case C-374/96 *Arblade* [1999] ECR I-8453.

[79] Case C-212/97 *Centros* [1999] ECR I-1459; Case C-208/00 *Überseering* [2002] ECR I-9919

[80] Hartley, T., "The Modern Approach to Private International Law: International Litigation and Transactions from a Common-Law Perspective: General Course on Private International Law", *Recueil des Cours*, Vol. 319, No. 9, 2006, pp. 9–324 (183).

[81] Case 150/77 *Bertrand* [1978] ECR 1431, par. 17; Case C-464/01 *Gruber* [2005] ECR I-439, par. 32; Case C-103/05 *Reisch Montage* [2006] ECR I-6827, par. 23

[82] Case C-116/02 *Gasser* [2003] ECR I-14693

proceedings before the court of another Member State which manifestly has no jurisdiction to delay proceedings. In PIL terminology the technique of lodging proceedings before a notoriously slow, but incompetent court in order to gain time is referred to as an 'Italian Torpedo'.[83] This literal interpretation opens the door for forum shopping and abuse.[84]

In *Freeport v Arnoldsson* the ECJ refused a national court the possibility to decline jurisdiction in a case where it was apparent that a defendant was merely being sued in order to be able to sue co-defendants in the same court.[85] The ECJ held it was not necessary to establish separately whether 'claims were not brought with the sole object of ousting the jurisdiction of the courts of the Member State where one of the defendants is domiciled'.[86] In both cases the ECJ reasoned that since the Brussels Convention did not provide for an exception, there could be none, and thereby ignored the role courts traditionally have played in the development of PIL.

Glaxosmithkline is another striking example.[87] An employee worked first for a French company in France and subsequently for an English company in the United Kingdom belonging to the same group of undertakings. The parties agreed that the English undertaking would safeguard all rights that the employee enjoyed under the contract with the French company. The employee launched proceedings in France against both employers jointly. On a literal interpretation that was not possible. An employer could only be sued in the courts where he was domiciled or where the employee habitually carried out his work. The English company was neither established in France nor did the employee perform the labour contract with the English company in France. The general rules of Brussels I, including the possibility of joining linked claims as laid down in art. 6 (1), are not applicable to labour contracts. The ECJ reiterated again that in order to safeguard the

---

[83] Franzosi, M., "Worldwide Patent Litigation and the Italian Torpedo", *European Intellectual Property Law Review*, Vol. 19, No. 7, 1997, pp. 382–385; Betti, I., "The Italian torpedo is dead: long live the Italian torpedo, *Journal of Intellectual Property Law & Practice*, Vol. 3, No. 1, 2008, 6–7.

[84] This problem is aggravated by the fact that the ECJ does not allow common law anti-suit injunctions to restrain proceedings in other Member States who are competent on the basis of the Brussels instruments. Case C-159/02 *Turner v Grovit* [2005] ECR I-3565 and case C-185/07 *West Tankers* [2009] ECR I-663.

[85] Case C-98/06 *Freeport v Arnoldsson* [2007] ECR I-8319.

[86] *Supra* note 85, par. 54.

[87] Case C-462/06 *Glaxosmithkline* [2008] ECR I-3965.

predictability of the rules the derogations to the rule that a person may be sued in a court other than where is domiciled should be interpreted strictly. It set aside the plea for a teleological interpretation as proposed by several intervening governments and ruled instead that 'the transformation by the Community courts of the rules of special jurisdiction, aimed at facilitating sound administration of justice, into rules of unilateral jurisdiction protecting the party deemed to be weaker would go beyond the balance of interests which the Community legislature has established in the law as it currently stands.'[88] That reasoning holds little ground. Sound administration of justice, and in particular procedural economy and aversion of risk of conflicting decisions would be promoted if the employee would be allowed to bring a related action against both employees in a single court. The 13th recital to Brussels I provides that the weaker party should be protected by rules of jurisdiction more favourable to his interests than the general rules provide for. If the general rules in fact afford a greater protection to the employee than the rules designed to protect him, a strong argument could be made to depart from the literal wording. Legal predictability has become an overriding value *per se*.

Where the perspective of traditional PIL on jurisdiction matters is the safeguard of the rights of litigants, the ECJ is more concerned with the maintaining the coherence and uniform application of the Brussels regime.[89] Not only does the Court not seem willing to take the PIL rationale underlying the Brussels instruments into account, the resulting consequences of the formalistic reading, such as the Italian Torpedo, seem hardly able to promote the confidence of traders in the common market.

1.6.1 *The Method of Interpretation Relating to Rome I*

Although the ECJ only had the possibility to develop a large body of case-law in the context of the Brussels Convention, it seems that the Court emphasises legal certainty over flexibility. The legal certainty should avoid divergent interpretations of national courts and promote the forseeability of parties engaged in cross border contracts. In essence, the Court is adopting the same interpretation techniques with regard to PIL as it had done in the pre-Maastricht era to provisions of public

[88] *Glaxosmithkline*, *supra* note, par. 32.
[89] Harris, *supra* note 57, 372.

law. It is however doubtful whether it is feasible to expand the interpretation paradigms of public law or competition law, that are by definition mandatory, to areas of law that seek to balance the interests of private parties. When the objective of the rule is to strike a fair balance between private parties and the rule would produce unfeasible results in specific circumstances, much may be said in favour of allowing flexibility rather than stressing the mandatory nature of the rule. The burden of a legislative error is not born by the state or the legislator itself but by a private party. Interpretations as in *Gasser* and *Glaxosmithkline* do not only produce unfeasible results but are also self-defeating, in that they frustrate the objective of strengthening the confidence in the internal market. It can only be hoped that the Court does not adopt a similar approach towards the Rome Convention and Rome Regulations and that it modifies its stand on the Brussels instruments. The decisions of the Court have led to a large amount of critique, especially from common law lawyers.[90] It is should not be excluded that the ECJ decisions will be in one way or the other modified by the European legislator. At least the *Gasser* issue has been taken up in the Commission's Proposal to revise Brussels I.[91]

In its first decision on the Rome Convention, the Court opted for a less rigid approach. It was confronted with a contract where no choice of law had been made. The applicable law thus had to be established according to the presumptions of art. 4 Rome Convention. In answering the question under which circumstances national courts could make use of the escape clause and to override the presumptions in favour of a law that has a closer connection, the Court reiterated that art. 4 (5) was meant to counterbalance the rigidity of the presumptions by leaving courts a certain margin of flexibility. Instead of following the case-law prevalent in some Member States[92] that the presumption

[90] Hartley, T., "The European Union and the Systematic Dismantling of the Common Law of Conflict of Laws", *International Comparative Law Quarterly*, Vol. 54, 2005, pp. 813–828.

[91] Proposal for a Regulatoin of the European Parliament and of the Council on jurisdiction and the recognition and enforcement of judgments in civil and commercial matters (Recast) COM(2010) 748 final. The proposed art. 32 (2) would give priority to the chosen court to decide on its jurisdiction, regardless of whether it is first or second seised.

[92] Such as the Netherlands, see: Kuipers, J., "The Rome I Regulation: Ending the contradictory interpretation by national courts of art. 4 (5) Rome Convention?" *Prague Yearbook of Comparative Law*, Vol. 1, 2009, pp. 153–181.

could only be overridden when the place where the party who is to effect the performance which is characteristic of the contract is established has no genuine connecting value, the Court held that the exception was to be applied 'where it is clear from the circumstances as a whole that the contract is more closely connected with a country other than that determined on the basis of one of the criteria set out in Article 4(2) to (4) of the Convention'.[93] Although the ECJ leaves much to the imagination of national courts it is remarkable, in the light of the case-law under Brussels I, that the narrowest interpretation of the exception has been struck out.

1.7 *European Public Policy*

The final feature of EU conflict of laws is the development of a European public policy. In its case-law the Court is gradually identifying a set of values and principles belonging to the European public policy.[94] This would coexist alongside national public policy provisions, but be uniform as regards Union values are concerned. As regards applicable law, *Ingmar* is until so far the only case dealing with a Union public policy.[95] The ECJ held that the provisions protecting the agent after termination of an agency contract as laid down in the Agency Directive

[93] Case C-133/08 *Intercontainer Interfrigo (ICF) SC v Balkenende Oosthuizen BV and MIC Operations BV* [2009] ECR I-9687, par. 64.

[94] Liebscher, C., "Arbitral & Judicial Decision: European public policy after Eco Swiss", *American Review of International Arbitration*, Vol. 10. 1999, pp. 81–94; Muir-Watt, H., "Evidence of an Emergent European Legal Culture : Public Policy Requirements of Procedural Fairness under the Brussels and Lugano Conventions", *Texas International Law Journal*, Vol. 36, 2001, pp. 539–554 ; Poillot Peruzzetto, S.,"Ordre Public et loi de police dans l'ordre communautaire", *Travaux du Comité Français de Droit International Privé 2002–2004*, pp. 65–106 (88); Martiny, D., "Die Zukunft des europäischen ordre public im Internationalen Privat-Zivelverfahrensrecht", M. Coester, D. Martiny and K. Prinz von Sachsen Gessaphe (eds.), *Privatrecht in Europe, Festschrift für Hans Jürgen Sonnenberger*, Verlag C.H. Beck, München, 2004, pp. 523–548 ; Basedow, J., "Recherches sur la formation de l'ordre public européen dans la jurisprudence", B. Ancel, *Le droit international privé : esprit et méthodes ; Mélanges en l'honneur de Paul Lagarde*, Dalloz, Paris, 2005, pp. 291–319; Struycken, A., "L'ordre public de la Communauté Européenne", T. Azzi *et al* (eds.), *Vers de nouveaux équilibres entre ordres juridiques, Liber amicorum Hélène Gaudemet-Tallon*, Dalloz, Paris, 2008, pp. 617–632 (623). More careful : Meidanis, H., "Public Policy and *ordre public* in the private international law of the EC/EU: Traditional positions of the Member States and modern trends", *European Law Review*, Vol. 30, 2005, pp. 95–110.

[95] Case C-381/98 *Ingmar* [2000], ECR I-9305.

were mandatory up to the extent that they were applicable regardless of the applicable law.[96] A Union public policy is without a doubt in the making. Due to the division of competences, economic and monetary provisions will constitute the core of that European public policy.[97] The Court has been invited on several occasions to rule on the question whether the failure to observe a mandatory provision of Union law constitutes sufficient reason to refuse to recognise or enforce an arbitral decision. The Court held first in *Eco Swiss* that art. 101 TFEU should be categorised as a matter of public policy, whose non-observation could lead to the setting aside of an arbitral award.[98] The Court directly placed art. 101 in the category of public policy within the meaning of the New York Convention on Arbitration (1958). However, it appears that as regards consumer law the Court takes a more restrictive reading.[99] Rather than categorising the rules on consumer protection directly as provisions of public policy, the Court held the provisions to have equal standing with national public policy rules. The paragraph leaves it open for Member States to define the Union provisions as public policy, but not as provisions of international public policy. The more conservative approach is in line with earlier case-law, as the Court had already held earlier in *Renault v Maxicar* that not every (alleged) error in the application of Union law required, or even allowed, a court in a Member State to resort to the public policy exception in order to refuse a judgment handed down in another Member State.[100]

Despite the focus on economic law, it could be expected that after the entry into force of the Lisbon Treaty and its Charter on Fundamental Rights, fundamental rights may also start to become part of the Union public order.[101] Fundamental rights have been used to give shape to

---

[96] The provisions will only be part of the European public order, and overriding mandatory, insofar they implement the Union minimum standard. Steinmann, T., P. Kenel and I. Billotte, *Le contract d'agence commercial en Europe*, Schulthess, Zürich, 2005.

[97] Karydis, G. "Ordre public dans l'ordre juridique communautaire", *Revue Trimestrielle de Droit Européen*, Vol. 38, 2002, pp. 1–26 (12).

[98] Case C-126/97 *Eco Swiss* [1999] ECR I-3055.

[99] Case C-168/05 *Mostaza Claro* [2006] ECR I-10421; Case C-40/08 *Asturcom* [2009] ECR I-9579. The Court did not classify the Unfair Contract Terms Directive as public policy, but rather ruled it should standing equal to public policy in the Member States (*Asturcom*, par. 52).

[100] Case C-38/98 *Renault v Maxicar* [2000] ECR I-973.

[101] Picheval, C., *L'ordre public européen droit communautaire et droit européen des droit de l'homme*, CERIC, Aix-Marseille, 2001.

PIL doctrines, rather than constituting an autonomous source of obligations.[102] The Court has in *Krombach*[103] and *Gambazzi*[104] established that Union law does not prevent courts on the basis of national public policy to refuse to recognise a judgment rendered in another Member State on the grounds of the non-observance of a fundamental right, such as the right to a fair trial. Although solely addressed to the European institutions, the Charter may have the effect that instead of establishing the limits of national public policy, the Court will develop an autonomous construction of fundamental rights in the European public order.[105]

Although it can certainly no longer be maintained that Union law and PIL operate in isolation, there is still much to be improved. The insertion of a Union competence on PIL and the gradual replacement of national PIL with European codifications give the Union a direct opportunity to guide the developments in PIL. PIL can therefore no longer deny the impact of Union law. This does however not mean that it has no role left to play within the internal market. Uniform conflict of laws rules can ensure the harmony of decisions on a Union level without the need to harmonise the substantive law. Resort to the conflict of laws rules is therefore the exercise of subsidiarity par excellence. It should also be noted that Union law may have something to learn from PIL. The rich history of the subject has shown that it is unfeasible to solely approach international situations from the perspective of one's own laws. Regard should not only be had towards the desire to apply the laws of the forum, but also the interest of foreign legislation to be applied, as well as the reasonable expectations of private parties and the needs of international trade. Whether the Union will modify its stand and in the future adhere more to the multilateral PIL approaches dominant in the Member States and, be willing to apply a PIL rationale to PIL instruments is only a question that the future can answer.

---

102 Fawcett, J., "The Impact of Art. 6 (1) of the ECHR on Private International Law", *International and Comparative Law Quarterly*, Vol. 56, 2007, pp. 1–48 ; Kuipers, J., "The Right to a Fair Trial and the Free Movement of Civil Judgments", *Croatian Yearbook of European Law & Policy*, vol. 6, 2010, pp. 23–52.

103 Case C-7/98 *Krombach* [2000] ECR I-1935.

104 Case C-394/07 *Gambazzi* [2009] ECR I-2563.

105 Art. 6 (1) TFEU attributes to the Charter of Fundamental Rights the same legal value as the Treaties. The Charter is however addressed to European institutions and not the Member States.

CHAPTER 2

ROME I REGULATION: PARTY AUTONOMY AS ITS CORNERSTONE

The aim of this book is to attempt to redefine the relationship between Union law and PIL in the area of contracts. The Rome I Regulation is used to delimit the area of research rather than object of study as such. It will therefore not be attempted to analyse the instrument, but rather, where appropriate, explore specific provisions. Nevertheless, in order to conceptualise its relationship with Union law it is necessary to understand its underlying rationale.

Conflict of laws is at times a very complex topic with its own terminology. This chapter therefore tries to provide an introduction into the conflict of laws mechanism with regard to contractual obligations. First the legal status of the Rome Convention and Rome I will be discussed. It will be demonstrated why, despite the 1980 Convention, conflict of laws rules have depended much upon pre-existing national conceptions. Subsequently the principal rule in Rome I and the reasons for its existence will be analysed. In contracts, party autonomy as choice of law rule does not appear to be challenged any longer. The discussion tends to focus upon its limitations. Overriding mandatory provisions will be discussed as one of the limitations upon private autonomy. Overriding mandatory provisions deserve special attention because it is with regard to contracts the only mechanism to determine the applicable law that has not been unified at the Union level. Although Union law imposes certain limits, it is still left to a Member State to define which provisions it considers to be overriding mandatory within its jurisdiction. Finally, other limitations upon private autonomy will be discussed as well as their interaction with overriding mandatory provisions.

2.1 *A Birds-Eye View on the Development of Private International Law*

Private International Law only serves a purpose when there is more than one legal entity, differences exist between the laws of those entities and there is a certain amount of contact (e.g. trade) between them.[1] That is the reason why PIL did not emerge in the Greek and Roman period. The differences between the legal systems of the Greek and Roman cities were not sufficient to generate the need for PIL. English PIL only developed in the 18th century when the isolation of the British island was broken and international trade emerged. PIL commonly starts with the post-glossators, in particular Bartolus of Sassaferrato (1314–1357), who inferred a conflict of laws rule from the Corpus Iuris Civilis.[2] To answer the question whether a law could be applied to a citizen residing outside the relevant territory and whether a law could be applied to foreigners residing in the relevant territory, he divided laws as to groups (contracts, torts, goods etc.) and nature (permissive v prohibitive rules and rules that were advantageous or disadvantageous to the individual concerned). For example, a prohibitive rule could be applied extra-territorially when it was advantageous for the individual concerned, but not when it was disadvantageous.

The statute theory, and thus the determination of the sphere of application of a rule by ascertaining its object, was used throughout the medieval period.[3] Statutes were grouped into real, personal or mixed statutes. Whereas the application of the first group was strictly territorial, personal statutes would apply to all residents of the relevant territory. The statute theory was further refined by the French scholars Charles Dumoulin (1500–1566) and D'Argentré (1519–1590). The latter elaborated the distinction so as to encompass every legal relation:

---

[1] The general development of PIL is described in: Gutzwiller, M., *Der Einfluss Savignys auf die Entwicklung des International privatrechts*, Fribourg, 1923; Yntema, H., "The Historic Basis of Private International Law", *American Journal of Comparative Law*, Vol. 2, 1953, pp. 297–317; Kalenský, P., *Trends of Private International Law*, Brill Archive, London, 1971; Juenger, F., *Choice of Law and Multistate Justice*, Martinus Nijhoff, Dordrecht, 1993, 99. 6–42; North P., and J. Fawcett, *Cheshire and North Private International Law*,: Butterworths, London, Eleventh edition, 1987, pp. 14–39; Strikwerda, L., Inleiding tot het Nederlandse Internationaal Privaatrecht, Kluwer, Deventer, 2005, pp. 15–25; Ancel, B., Histoire du droit international privé, electronically available at: http://www.u-paris2.fr/44834992/0/fiche___document/&RH =COURS_TD, as of 15 March 2011.

[2] Woolf, C., *Bartolus of Sassoferrato. His position in the History of Political Medieval Thought*, Cambridge University Press Cambridge, 1913; Ryan, M., "Bartolus of Sassaferrato and free cities", *Transactions of the Royal Historical Society*, No. 10, 2000, pp. 65–89; Lepsius, S., "Bartolus de Sassoferrato", Compendium Auctorum Latinorum Medii Aevi, Edizioni del Galluzzo, Florence, 2005.

[3] Meijers, E., "L'Histoire des principes fondamentaux du droit international privé à partir du moyen âge spécialement dans l'Europe occidentale", *Recueil des Cours*, Vol. 3, 1934, pp. 543–686.

real statutes had as their principal object the regulation of an immovable and could only be applied on a territorial basis; personal statutes applied to individuals resident on the territory of the enacting Sovereign but followed that person also outside the territory; and mixed statutes formed the residual category and concerned, for example, acts and would then apply to all acts done in that territory, but not beyond. There is some evidence to suggest that Dumoulin[4] was the first proponent of party autonomy, but in any case party autonomy was not supported by D'Argentré.[5] He emphasised instead the principle of territoriality, as part of his efforts to secure the feudal privileges of the local French nobility against the desire for unification of the central government.

The statute theory was further developed in the 17th century by Dutch writers. If the powers of a Sovereign do not extend beyond its borders, should this principle then also not apply to personal statutes? Christiaan Rodenburg (1618–1668), Paulus Voet (1619–1667), Ulrik Huber (1636–1694) and Johannes Voet (1647–1714) answered this question in the affirmative.[6] They rejected, however, the absolute territorial application of statutes. Sovereigns were not obliged to give effect to each other's laws, but could do so voluntarily, on the basis of *comitas*.[7] According to Huber comity and the general pressure of international commerce required that acts duly performed in one jurisdiction should be sustained in other jurisdictions. This idea became very influential in common law jurisdictions, in the form of the vested rights doctrine.[8]

---

[4] Gamillscheg, F., *Der Einfluss Dumoulins auf die Entwicklung des Kollisionsrecht*, 1955, 112.

[5] Meili, F., "Argentraeus und Molinaeus und ihre Bedeutung im internationale Privat- und Strafrecht", *Zeitschrift für internationales Recht*, Vol. 5 (1895), pp. 363–544.

[6] Yntema, H., "The Comity Doctrine", E. von Caemmerer, A. Nikisch and K. Zweigert, (eds.), *Vom Deutschen zum Europäischen Recht, Festschrift für Hans Dölle*, Mohr Siebeck, Tübingen, bd. II, 1963, pp. 65–72; Veen, T. *Recht en nut: Studien over en naar aanleiding van Ulrik Huber (1636–1694)*, Tjeenk Willink, Zwolle, 1976; Lipstein, K., *Principles of the Conflict of Laws, National and International*, Brill Archive, London, 1981, 13–19; Sauveplanne, J., "De Leidse Invloed op het Internationaal Privaatrecht", *Rechtsgeleerde opstellen vervaardigd door leden van het Leids Juridisch Dispuut Juri Sacrum ter gelegenheid van het 100-jarig bestaan van het Dispuut*, Kluwer, Deventer, 1982, pp. 119–125.

[7] The comitas doctrine started with Paulus Voet. Rodenburg followed the distinction of d'Argentré and sought the legitimacy of PIL in *necessitas*.

[8] Strikwerda, L., "Fries recht in Amerika. Over Ulrik Huber, Jospeh Story en internationale contracten", *Groninger Opmerkingen en Medelingen IV*, 1987, pp. 55; North/Fawcett *supra* note 1, 21.

Friedrich Carl von Savigny (1779–1861) was unsatisfied with the statutist approach because of the historic impossibility in reaching consensus about the division of statutes in the three categories.[9] He considered the approach to be both incomplete and ambiguous. Von Savigny developed a theory based on the absolute division between public and private law, whereby the conflict rules are exclusively used to determine the applicable private law. He then turned the question around. The scope of application of private laws should not be deduced from the rule at stake, but rather from the legal relationship. The law of the jurisdiction where the legal situation had its 'Heimat' (home) or natural seat should be applied. The object, content and purpose of the rule thus became irrelevant. In the opinion of Von Savigny, PIL was as a matter of principle not interested in the outcome of the application of the substantive rule it held applicable. Rather it was only concerned with the establishment of the spatially most appropriate law. PIL thus became rule blind, value free, or neutral. The unilateral determination of the sphere of application of a rule was replaced by a multilateral one. Von Savigny specifically denounced the *comitas* doctrine and based the possible application of foreign laws instead on the 'völkerrechtliche Gemeinschaft der miteinder verkehrende Nationen'. The völkerrechtliche Gemeinschaft of civilised nations did not only, in his opinion, provide the justification for the application of foreign law, but equally required that every legal dispute had to be decided in the same way regardless where the proceeding was brought, in other words: an international harmony of decisions.

The Savignian conception of PIL with its rigid and neutral conflict of laws rules dominated the European conflict of laws arena well into the 20th century, but has proved over time to be inadequate. The universalism that underlies the Savignian system has been called into question.[10]

[9] Deelen, J., *De blinddoek van von Savigny*, Scheltema & Holkema, Amsterdam, 1966; Kollewijn, R., "Quelques considérations à propos de la doctrine de Savigny", *Nederlands Tijdschrift voor Internationaal Recht*, Vol. 15, 1968, pp. 237–258; Real, W., *Karl Friedrich von Savigny 1814–1875:Briefen, Akten, Aufzeichnungen eines Diplomaten der Reichsgrundungszeit*, Harald Boldt Verlag, Boppard am Rhein, 1981; Rückert, J., Idealismus, Jurisprudenz und Politik bei Friedrich Carl von Savigny, Gremer, Ebelsbach, 1984; Kegel, G., "Story and von Savigny", *American Journal of Comparative Law*, Vol. 37, No. 1, 1989, pp. 39–66.

[10] Ehrenzweig, A., *A Treatise on the Conflict of Laws*, West Publishing Co., St. Paul, 1962, pp. 322.

In Europe, without changing the essence of the multilateral conflict of laws rule several techniques were deployed to refine its application. So, in contracts, the principle of the closest connection was able to provide for flexibility while alternative connections sought to advance specific substantive interests. Examples include connecting factors favouring the validity of a contract or marriage, or the possibility of a divorce. Other connecting factors sought to protect the interest of one party, such as connecting factors that allowed the victim of an accident to choose between certain related legal systems or connecting factors protecting the weaker party, such as consumers and employees.[11]

2.1.1 *Rome Convention and Rome I Regulation*

The codification of the conflict of laws rules at the Union level does not call into the question the multilateral nature of the conflict of laws process. The common rules follow the traditions that already existed in the Member States. The Union was also never in a position to radically change the conflict of laws rules. The Union did originally not have any explicit power allowing for the harmonisation of the conflict of laws rules. The EEC Treaty only provided that Member States would enter with each into negotiations concerning the simplification of recognition and enforcement of judicial decisions, something which resulted in the Brussels Convention. The provision did however not address conflict of laws rules.[12] It was considered, however, to be at odds with the internal market for courts to use their national conflict of laws rules to establish the applicable law. The problem of competences was solved in the 3rd preamble of the Rome Convention, which provided that the Member States were '[anxious] to continue in the field of private international law the work of unification of law which has already been done within the Union, in particular in the field of jurisdiction and enforcement of judgments'. The Rome Convention, however, is not limited to internal market situations; it has a universal scope of application. Its connecting factors may lead to the application of any law, regardless whether it is the law of a Member State or not.

---

[11] Bonomi, A., "Mandatory Rules in Private International Law: The quest for uniformity of decisions in a global environment", *Yearbook of Private International Law*, Vol. 1, 1999, pp. 215–247 (217).

[12] Art. 220 EEC Treaty, which later became 293 EC Treaty, but did not return in the TFEU.

The lack of competence in the EC Treaty made the status of the Rome Convention unclear. Although the Convention was not a Union instrument, it was generally regarded to be in some way part of the *acquis communautaire*. Yet, due its status as international convention the ECJ did not enjoy the power of interpretation. The problem was solved by attributing this competence to the ECJ in a separate protocol that only entered into force on 1 August 2004.[13] However, it was only after the adaptation of Rome I and the entry into force of the Lisbon Treaty in 2009 that all national courts acquired the possibility to make a preliminary reference to the ECJ.

The transformation of the Rome Convention into a Union instrument was already identified as a priority in the Vienna Action Plan (1998) on how best to implement the provisions of the Treaty of Amsterdam on the creation of an area of freedom, security and justice.[14] It took the Commission five years to prepare a Green Paper inviting stakeholders to express their views on the revision of the Rome Convention.[15] The Commission finally presented in 2005 a proposal for a Rome I Regulation.[16] The proposal did not fully satisfy the parliament.[17] Although the United Kingdom decided not to opt-in to the process of preparation of Rome I, and therefore did not possess any voting rights, it did participate in the negotiations and remained quite influential.[18] The European Parliament agreed to the Common Position adopted in the Justice and Home Affairs Council in April 2008 and the Rome I Regulation was formally adopted in June 2008.[19] It applies to contracts concluded as from 17 December 2009.[20]

Because the Regulation is adopted on the basis of Title IV of the EC Treaty it is not applicable to Denmark. Denmark could either enter into

[13] First Protocol of 19 December 1988 on the interpretation of the 1980 Convention by the Court of Justice OJ C 027 (1998), 47–51.

[14] OJ 1999 C 19 /1.

[15] Green Paper of 14 January 2003 on the conversion of the Rome Convention of 1980 on the law applicable to contractual obligations into a Union instrument and its modernisation, COM (2002) 654 final.

[16] Proposal for a Regulation on the Law applicable to contractual obligations, COM (2005) 650 final.

[17] European Parliament Report on COM(2005) 650, A6-0450/2007

[18] UK Ministry of Justice, Rome I – should the UK opt in?, Consultation Paper CP05/08,

[19] Regulation EC NO. 593/2008 on the Law Applicable to Contractual Obligations (Rome I) OJ 2008 L 177/6.

[20] Art. 29 Rome I and Corrigendum Rome I, 13497/1/09 REV 1 JUR 369.

a parallel agreement with the EU, as it did with respect to the Brussels I Regulation,[21] or if such an agreement should be refused by the EU adopt the substantive rules as a national measure. Ireland opted-in to the process of negotiating the instrument and is therefore bound by Rome I.[22] After a public consultation, the United Kingdom also decided to opt into the final instrument.[23] Rome I will therefore also be applicable in the UK.

2.1.2 *The Content of the Common Rules*

In the process of transforming the Convention into a Regulation, the relation of the instrument with jurisdiction and recognition and enforcement of judgments in civil matters (Brussels I), and the law applicable to non-contractual obligations (Rome II), was deemed to be of particular importance (*Gleichlauf*).[24] It was therefore attempted to connect applicable law issues as much as possible with jurisdiction and to coordinate the issues addressed by the conflict of laws norms relating to contractual obligations and to non-contractual obligations.[25] The Union legislator also seized the opportunity to repair some of the weaknesses in the Convention. Some articles were therefore substantially modified, while others were copied without much modification.[26]

---

[21] Agreement between the European Community and the Kingdom of Denmark on jurisdiction and the recognition and enforcement of judgments in civil and commercial matters, OJ 2005 299R/62; see: Nielsen, P., "Brussels I and Denmark", *IPRax*, Vol. 27, No. 6, 2007, pp. 506–509. Agreement between the European Community and the Kingdom of Denmark on jurisdiction and the recognition and enforcement of judgments in civil and commercial matters

[22] Recital 44 Rome I.

[23] Commission Decision of 22 December 2008 on the request from the United Kingdom to accept the Rome I Regulation, OJ 2009 L 10/22.

[24] Lein, E., "The New Rome I / Rome II / Brussels I Synergy", *Yearbook of Private International Law*, Vol. 10, 2008, pp. 177–198.

[25] Rammeloo, S., "*Via Romana*. Van EVO naar Rome I – Nieuw Europees IPR inzake het recht dat van toepassing is op verbintenissen uit overeenkomst", *Nederlands Internationaal Privaatrecht*, Vol. 3, 2006, pp. 239–253.

[26] As already stated it is not my intention to review the substance of the Rome I Regulation in general. Differences between the two instruments are discussed by: Wilderspin, M., "The Rome I Regulation: Communitarisation and modernisation of the Rome Convention", *ERA Forum*, Vol. 9, 2008, pp. 259–274; Lando, O., and P. Nielsen, "The Rome I Regulation", *Common Market Law Review*, Vol. 45, 2008, pp. 1687–1725; Van der Plas, C., "Verbintenissen uit overeenkomst: van EVO-Verdrag naar Rome I-Verordening", *Nederlands Tijdschrift voor Europees Recht*, Vol. 14, 2008, pp. 318–329.

An example of a significant modification is the law applicable in the absence of a choice of law. Art. 4 Rome Convention adopted the principle of the closest connection.[27] It was presumed that the closest connection existed with the country where the party who is to effect the performance which is characteristic of the contract is established. Special presumptions applied for a contract that constituted a right in an immovable property and a contract of a carriage. Courts could derogate from the presumptions if it appeared from the circumstances as a whole that the contract had closer connections with another country. These presumptions gave rise to a lot of legal uncertainty since they were interpreted by the courts in the Member States in varying ways. In particular, national courts differed as to under what circumstances one could depart from the presumptions and establish a different applicable law. On one side of the spectrum, the Dutch courts favoured a very strict reading in order to provide a maximum degree of legal certainty to the presumptions. Deviation from the presumption of characteristic performance was only possible when the place of establishment of the party that had to render the most characteristic performance had in the light of the particular circumstances of the case no genuine value in establishing the applicable law.[28] The English courts, on the other hand, favoured flexibility and already deviated from the presumptions when the place of establishment of the party that had to render the most characteristic performance did not coincide with the place where the contractual obligation had to be performed.[29] In its first ruling on the

---

[27] Magagni, M., *La Prestazione Caratteristica nella Convenzione di Roma del 19 Giugno 1980*, Giuffrè, Milano, 1989 ; Gunst, D., *Die charakteristische Leistung: Zur funktionellen Anknüpfung im Internationalen Vertragsrecht Deutschlands der Schweiz und der Europäischen Gemeinschaft*, Hartung Gorre, Konstanz, 1994; Ancel, M., *La prestation caractéristique du contrat*, Economica, Paris, 2002.

[28] Hoge Raad 25 September 1992 *Nederlands Internationaal Privaatrecht Recht* 1993, 105; Hoge Raad 17 October 2008 LJN: BE7201. Rammeloo, S., "Die Auslegung von Art.4 Abs. 2 und Abs. 5 EVÜ: Eine niederländische Perspektive", *Iprax*, Vol. 14, 1994, pp. 234–245; Struycken, T., "Een *letter of credit* en accessoire aanknoping", *Nederlands Internationaal Privaatrechtrecht*, Vol. 19, 2001, pp. 204–206.

[29] Queen's Bench Division (Commercial Court), *Bank of Baroda v Vysya Bank*, [1994] 2 Lloyd's Rep 87; Court of Appeal (Civil Division), *Marconi Communications International Ltd v PT Pan Indonesian Bank Ltd TBK*, [2007] 2 Lloyd's Rep 72; Queen's Bench Division (Commercial Court), *Definitely Maybe (Touring) Ltd v. Marek Lieberberg Konzertagentur* [2001] 2 Lloyd's Rep 455.

Rome Convention, the ECJ seemed to have set aside the narrow Dutch interpretation but failed to specify under precisely which circumstances deviation from the main presumption was possible.[30]

Art. 4 Rome I has been structurally revised.[31] The general principle of characteristic performance has been replaced by special presumptions. Art. 4 Rome I now reads:

1. To the extent that the law applicable to the contract has not been chosen in accordance with Article 3 and without prejudice to Articles 5 to 8, the law governing the contract shall be determined as follows:
   (a) a contract for the sale of goods shall be governed by the law of the country where the seller has his habitual residence;
   (b) a contract for the provision of services shall be governed by the law of the country where the service provider has his habitual residence;
   (c) a contract relating to a right in rem in immovable property or to a tenancy of immovable property shall be governed by the law of the country where the property is situated;
   (d) notwithstanding point (c), a tenancy of immovable property concluded for temporary private use for a period of no more than six consecutive months shall be governed by the law of the country where the landlord has his habitual residence, provided that the tenant is a natural person and has his habitual residence in the same country;
   (e) a franchise contract shall be governed by the law of the country where the franchisee has his habitual residence;
   (f) a distribution contract shall be governed by the law of the country where the distributor has his habitual residence;
   (g) a contract for the sale of goods by auction shall be governed by the law of the country where the auction takes place, if such a place can be determined;
   (h) a contract concluded within a multilateral system which brings together or facilitates the bringing together of multiple third-party buying and selling interests in financial instruments, as defined by Article 4(1), point (17) of Directive 2004/39/EC, in accordance with non-discretionary rules and governed by a single law, shall be governed by that law.

---

[30] Case C-133/08 *Intercontainer Interfrigo (ICF) SC v Balkenende Oosthuizen BV and MIC Operations BV* [2009] ECR I-9687.

[31] Magnus, U., "Article 4 Rome I Regulation: The Law Applicable in the Absence of a Choice", F. Ferrari and S. Leible, *Rome I Regulation: The Law Applicable to Contractual Obligations in Europe*, Sellier, Münich, 2009, pp. 27–50.

2. Where the contract is not covered by paragraph 1 or where the elements of the contract would be covered by more than one of points (a) to (h) of paragraph 1, the contract shall be governed by the law of the country where the party required to effect the characteristic performance of the contract has his habitual residence.
3. Where it is clear from all the circumstances of the case that the contract is manifestly more closely connected with a country other than that indicated in paragraphs 1 or 2, the law of that other country shall apply.
4. Where the law applicable cannot be determined pursuant to paragraphs 1 or 2, the contract shall be governed by the law of the country with which it is most closely connected.

The new provision does not solve all the controversies that existed under the Rome Convention.[32] However, although further guidance by the ECJ will be required, art. 4 Rome I offers less leeway for confusion. The necessity of resorting too often to the exception clause has been reduced since the general presumption is replaced by a number of specific presumptions. Resort to the exception clause should therefore be limited to situations where there exists a *manifest* closer connection.

2.1.3 *Party Autonomy*

The objective connecting factors will only apply when the parties have failed to make a choice of law. The freedom to choose the law applicable to a contract is nowadays well rooted in European PIL.[33] Although the meaning and extent have evolved over time, it gradually became the main rule in the Member States and was adopted in the Rome Convention. It reappears, without much significant change, in Rome I. The first origins of party autonomy can be traced back to the period after the decline of the Roman Empire.[34] The application of the various laws depended upon the ethnic origin of the parties.[35] The *professio*

---

[32] Kuipers, J., "The Rome I Regulation: Ending the contradictory interpretation by national courts of art. 4 (5) Rome Convention?" *Prague Yearbook of Comparative Law*, Vol. 1, 2009, pp. 153–181.

[33] The various national approaches are described in: Bermann, G., (ed.), *Party autonomy: constitutional and international law limits in comparative perspective, XVIth Quadrennial Congress of Comparative Law*, Juris Publishing, New York, 2005.

[34] A more detailed historical account is given by: Ranouil, V., *L'autonomie de la volonté. Naissance et evolution d'un concept*, PUF, Paris, 1980.

[35] Stein, P., *Roman Law in European History*, Cambridge University Press, Cambridge, 1999, pp. 12.

iuris was initially meant as a declaration to evidence the parties ethnicity, but evolved and was later deployed in a fictitious manner so that parties could manipulate the applicable law by declaring to belong to a certain ethnic group.[36] By condoning this practice, it could be argued that courts, at least implicitly, recognised a principle of party autonomy.[37]

There is some evidence to suggest that Dumoulin (1501–1566) explicitly recognised party autonomy.[38] It is however more likely that he meant to use the implied intention of the parties to apply the law of the place of performance rather than that of conclusion of the contract. In an example he justified on this basis the application of the law of domicile of the husband to a marriage contract rather than the place of marriage, which would often coincide with the domicile of the wife.[39] It is more likely that the first explicit confirmation of party autonomy originates in the work of Mancini (1817–1888). He recognised that party autonomy should only be subordinate to laws that touch upon public policy, sovereignty and rights in real estate.[40]

English courts already appear to have accepted much ealier, in 1796, that parties could choose the law applicable to their relationship.[41] It took Continental courts significantly longer to accept party autonomy.[42] Some German authors still perceive party autonomy to be a solution of convenience rather than a good conflict of laws rule in itself.[43] The codification of private autonomy in the Rome Convention,

---

[36] Meijers, E., "L'Histoire des principes fondamentaux du droit international privé à partir du moyen âge spécialement dans l'Europe occidentale", *Recueil des Cours,* Vol. 3, 1934, pp. 543–668 (558–559).

[37] Juenger, *supra* note 1, 10.

[38] Gamillscheg, *supra* note 4, 112; Juenger *supra* note 1, 16.

[39] Nygh, P., *Autonomy in International Contracts*, Clarendon Press, Oxford, 1999, 4.

[40] Jayme, E., *Pasquale Stanislao Mancini, Internationales Privatrecht zwischen Risorgimento und praktischer Jurisprudenz*, Gremer, Ebelsbach, 1980, 3.

[41] *Gienar v Meyer* (1796) 2 Hy Bl 603.

[42] See chapter 3.

[43] Kegel, G. and H. Schurig, *Internationales Privatrecht*, Verlag C.H. Beck, München, 8. Auflage, 2001, pp. 569. For discussion: Kühne, G., "Die Parteiautonomie zwischen kollisionsrechtlichter und materiellrechtlichter Gerechtigkeit", H. Krüger and H. Mansel, *Liber Amicorum Gerhard Kegel*, C.H. Beck Verlag, München, 2002, pp. 65–82; Leible, S., "Parteiautonomie im IPR – Allgemeines Anknüpfungsprinzip oder Verlegenheitslösung?", H. Mansel *et al* (eds.), *Festschrift für Erik Jayme*, Band I, Sellier, München, 2004, pp. 485–503.

however, did not go beyond the existing practices in most Member States.[44] Art. 3 (1) allows party to choose the law of any state as law governing their contract. An Italian seller and a Spanish buyer are free to choose Portuguese law to govern their contract, even if the contract has no factual connections with Portugal whatsoever. Parties can also decide to choose a law to govern only a part of the contract (dépeçage),[45] although whether a contract should in such circumstances be separable into different parts or not is debated.[46] In the latter opinion, the Italian seller and Spanish could, for example, agree to apply Portuguese law to the validity of the performance and to make the rest of the contract subject to Italian law. Parties are also free to modify the law governing their contract at any point.[47] That applies even when, for example, performance has already occurred. Although it might seem slightly surprising, the underlying rationale of the latter provision is not the possibility to change the applicable law but rather to provide parties the possibility to choose an applicable law when a legal dispute has arisen and no choice of law was made in the contract.

The choice of law must be expressed or demonstrated with reasonable certainty by the terms of the contract or the circumstances of the case. It is thus not necessary that the parties expressly stipulate the applicable law. An implicit choice of law will be assumed when a genuine will of the parties can with a reasonable degree of certainty be deduced from the contract and the surrounding circumstances.[48] It will thus depend much upon the factual circumstances.[49] Such a deduction will not be possible when connections with too many different jurisdictions exist.[50] On the other hand the fact that parties base their

---

[44] Williams, P., "The EEC Convention on the Law Applicable to Contractual Obligations", *International and Comparative Law Quarterly*, Vol. 35. 1986, pp. 1–31.

[45] Resp. Art. 3 (1) Rome Convention and Rome I Regulation.

[46] In favour of seperability: Kegel/Schurig, *supra* note 43, 570; Kropholler, J., *Internationales Privatrecht*, 4. Auflage, Mohr Siebeck, Tübingen, 2001, pp. 441; Stone, P., *European private international law*, Edward Edgar, Cheltenham, 2006, pp. 277. The requirement seemed to implicit in: Gerechtshof 's-Gravenhage 12 November 2003 LJN: AN7590. Against a requirement of separability: Siehr, K., *Internationales Privatrecht*, C.F. Müller Verlag, Heidelberg, 2001, pp. 125. Support could be drawn from OLG Franfurt am Main 13 February 1992 (cited in *Siehr*); Rechtbank Arnhem (District Court) 7 September 2000, *Nederlands Internationaal Privaatrecht* 2001, no. 19.

[47] Resp. Art. 3 (2) Rome Convention and Rome I Regulation.

[48] Magagni, *supra* note 27, 17–27; Juenger *supra* note 1, 213–220; Mankowski, P., "Stillschweigende Rechtswahl und wählbares Recht", S. Leible (ed.), *Das Grünbuch zum Internationalen Vertragsrecht*, Sellier, München, 2004, pp. 63–108.

[49] Other possible indicators are listed in: Nygh, *supra* note 39, 113–120.

[50] Bundesgerichtshof 26 June 2004, VIII ZR 273/03.

submissions upon the arguments derived from one law only or an exclusive jurisdiction clause in a contract[51] are strong indications for an implicit choice of law.

2.1.4 *Party Autonomy in Rome I*

The popularity of the Rome Convention with international traders can for a large part be credited to the wide recognition of party autonomy. The operation of art. 3 produced satisfying results for the contracting parties. It should therefore not come as a surprise that art. 3 was not a subject of controversy in the transformation of the Convention into a Regulation. The Commission proposed further bolstering the impact of the will the parties by incorporating a provision that would allow private parties to opt for principles and rules of the substantive law of contract recognised internationally or in the Union.[52] This would include for example the UNIDROIT principles or a future Union opt-in instrument, but exclude the *lex mercatoria* which was allegedly not precise enough. Although no such provision was adopted in the final document the 13th recital of the preamble to Rome I provides that the Regulation 'does not preclude parties from incorporating by reference into their contract a non-State body of law or an international convention.' The preamble thereby ensures that a possible optional European contract law instrument would not clash with PIL.[53]

Neither the Rome Convention, nor Rome I address the bootstrap problem.[54] The material validity of a choice of law clause, or the question whether a party consented to that clause will be governed by the law that is designated by it instead of, for example, the otherwise applicable law.[55] A party may only invoke the law of the place of habitual

[51] The 12th recital in the preamble to the Rome I Regulation identifies an exclusive choice of court clause as one of the factors to be taken into account in determining whether a choice of law has been clearly demonstrated. Art. 3 (1) Proposal for a Regulation on the Law applicable to contractual obligations, COM (2005) 650 final even raised in these circumstances a presumption.

[52] Art. 3 (2) of the Proposal. Such a choice was allegedly under art. 3 Rome Convention not possible: Court of Appeal, *Halpern v Halpern* [2007] EWCA Civ 291. Roth, W., "Zur Wälbarkeit nichtstaatlichen Rechts", H. Mansel *et al* (eds.), *Festschrift für Erik Jayme*, Band I, Sellier, München, 2004, pp. 757–772; Heiss, H., "Party Autonomy", F. Ferrari and S. Leible, *Rome I Regulation: The Law Applicable to Contractual Obligations in Europe*, Sellier, Münich, 2009, pp. 1–16.

[53] In more detail: par. 5.2.1

[54] Briggs, P., *Agreements on Jurisdiction and Choice of Law*, Oxford University Press, Oxford, 2008, pp. 396–399.

[55] Art. 10 (1) Rome I.

residence if he can demonstrate that it would be unreasonable to determine the effects of his conduct in accordance with the law designated in the choice of law clause. A contract is formally valid if it would be upheld by the law that the parties designated in their choice of law clause.[56]

Serious problems may arise if the parties are allowed to choose the law that governs the validity of their choice of law clause. In the US, art. 187 Second Restatement provides that the *lex fori* governs issues as misrepresentation, duress, undue influence or mistake while the law chosen governs all other issues such as formation and validity.[57] Abusive behaviour by private parties can only be sanctioned by the general safeguard clauses, such as the protection of the fundamental policy of the state with a materially greater interest whose law would be applicable in the absence of a choice of law.[58] A similar safeguard does not exist in Rome I, but by analogy the public policy may operate in cases of abusive behaviour by the parties. English courts, for example, will strike down a choice of law clause if the choice is not bona fide. Bona fide in this context means that the parties cannot choose to contract under one law in order to validate an agreement that manifestly has its closest connection with another law, under which law the contract would have been invalid.[59]

2.1.5 *The Success of Party Autonomy*

Party autonomy is thus maintained in Rome I as the corner-stone of the conflict of laws mechanism. Traditionally, the main reason advanced

---

[56] Art. 11 Rome I. A contract is also formally valid if it is valid according to the *lex loci contractus* if both parties are at the time of conclusion in that jurisdiction; or in case when the parties are in different countries according to the law of either place where they are present at the time of conclusion or according to either law of their habitual residence (art. 11 (1) and (2)).

[57] Symeonides, S., *American Private International Law*, Kluwer Law International, Deventer, 2008, pp. 208–209.

[58] Art. 187 (2) SR: 'The law of the state chosen by the parties to govern their contractual rights and duties will be applied, even if the particular issue is one which the parties could not have resolved by an explicit provision in their agreement directed to that issue, unless either (...) (b) application of the law of the chosen state would be contrary to a fundamental policy of a state which has a materially greater interest than the chosen state in the determination of the particular issue and which, under the rule of s 188, would be the state of the applicable law in the absence of an effective choice of law by the parties.'

[59] See par. 3.4.1.

against party autonomy was that parties should not be able to place themselves above the objectively applicable law.[60] Despite the emergence of the welfare state and increased regulatory intervention of the state private autonomy has been increasingly recognised. Four principal factors may be able to explain this apparent triumph of party autonomy.

The first factor is the principle of freedom of contract. It is accepted in national contract law that parties should, within the limits defined by the mandatory laws of a state, be free to determine the terms and content of their contractual obligations. If it is accepted that in national contract law parties can shape their relations, it would make sense to accept the same on the international level.[61]

Private autonomy cannot, however, be explained in PIL by referring only to the acceptance of private autonomy in a national context. It would only provide that parties would have the possibility to opt out of the default rules, something which they could already do anyway. The second factor recognises that private parties actually enjoy an even a greater autonomy on the international level. There is no state that can effectively control international contracts. Parties to an international contract have the possibility to adjudicate their case before several fora. Mandatory rules can thus be avoided by avoiding the relevant forum. In particular, recent technological developments have provided the individual with more factual possibilities to escape the state model, *de facto* enhancing private autonomy.[62] Even if freedom to choose the applicable law were denied, private parties could manipulate the connecting factors by cleverly choosing the place of conclusion of the contract, place of performance or currency of the contract.[63] Because states

[60] The influential French scholar Henri Batiffol therefore said that a choice of law could not be attributed more force than a mere contractual stipulation. See: Jacquet, J., *Le Contrat International*, Dalloz, Paris, 1992, pp. 37. In The Netherlands the argument was advanced by: Bervoets, Th., "Een rechtstheoretisch onderzoek naar het beginsel van rechtskeuze", *Partij-invloed in het international privaatrecht; Vier opstellen ter gelegenheid van het 25-jarig bestaan van het Centrum voor Buitenlands Recht en Internationaal Privaatrecht aan de Universiteit van Amsterdam,* Deventer, Kluwer, 1974, pp. 31–45.

[61] Leible, *supra* note 61, 485–503.

[62] Pamboukis, C., "La renaissance-métamorphose de la méthode de reconnaissance", *Revue Critique de Droit International Privé*, Vol. 97, No. 3, 2008, pp. 513–560 (519).

[63] Nygh *supra* note 39, 2.

cannot *de facto* control international contracts, they should recognise it *de iure*.

The third factor is that a legislator is the full and exclusive sovereign of his territory. He can push through his convictions because he is the sole competent creator of laws.[64] On the international level, the legislator loses his position as exclusive sovereign. Private parties are confronted with a number of competent sovereigns. The collision of his laws with those of a foreign sovereign makes that a sovereign cannot push through his convictions as he could do if a situation were exclusive to his territory. Restraint is appropriate. It means that private parties should be afforded a larger degree of autonomy on the international plane than in a national context. Although this restraint may be a limitation on authority, it is not necessarily a limitation on sovereignty. Rather it is a question of striking the right balance between the regulatory authority of the forum state against the equal authority of other states. The issue thus does not concern the limitation of sovereignty, but rather its proper exercise.[65]

The final factor is promotion of certainty and efficiency.[66] The determination of the applicable law on the basis of an objective operation of the conflict of laws rules is not always an easy and predictable discourse. The forseeability of the outcome of the operation of the conflict of laws norms is moreover hampered when several fora are available that may answer the question of applicable law differently. Parties may therefore decide not to take any risks and provide the maximum degree of legal certainty by indicating the applicable law themselves. The enhanced legal certainty which this generates will make international trade more attractive. Closely related to this argument is the argument that a choice of law clause will make sure that every court decides upon the applicable law in the same manner and that a choice of law thus promotes the international harmony of decisions.[67] The outcome of a case will be similar regardless where the proceedings are brought.

---

[64] Michaels, R., and H. Kamann, "Grundlagen eines allgemeinen gemeinschaftlichten Richtlinienkollisionsrechts – "Amerikanisierung" des Gemeinschafts-IPR?", *Europäisches Wirtschafts- & Steuerrecht*, Vol. 12, No. 6, 2001, pp. 301–311 (305).

[65] Brand, R., "Balancing Sovereignty and Party Autonomy in Private International Law", Erauw J., *et al* (eds.), *Liber Memorialis Petar Šarčević, Universalism, Tradition and the Individual*, Sellier, München, 2006, pp. 35–52 (40).

[66] Kassis, A., *Le nouveau droit européen des contrats internationaux*, LGDJ, Paris, 1993, pp. 194.

[67] Pommier, J., *Principe d'autonomie et loi du contrat en droit international privé conventionnel*, Economica, Paris, 1980, pp. 30–36.

Moreover, an English and an Iranian trader who wish to conclude a contract but distrust each other's laws might want to make their contract subject to a neutral law. Swiss law could therefore be chosen on legitimate grounds although the contract has no factual connections with Switzerland whatsoever. A producer which uses national distribution networks for the marketing of its products in various countries might wish to proceed on equal terms with all of its national distributors and therefore deviate from the general rule that distribution contracts are governed by the law of the country where the distributor has his habitual residence. All are good reasons to deviate from the objective applicable law.

From a law and economics perspective it is argued that party autonomy is the most efficient solution to the conflict of laws problem.[68] It does not really matter what the reasons for the choice of law are, as long as the parties agree on the applicable law and the choice of law does not lead to a reduction in welfare of third parties, efficiency is promoted.

> (..) individuals are assumed to be rational maximizers of their own welfare and have idiosyncratic knowledge about their preferences unavailable to anybody else. Therefore, they do not enter a choice-of-law agreement unless they believe that it will make them better off.[69]

Private autonomy also has its downsides. If the producer were to lodge proceedings for breach of contract against one the national distributors he would have initiate his actions in the courts of the home Member State of the distributor (D). Assume that the producer (P) has chosen the law of his own Member State to govern the contract. The courts of Member State D would now be obliged to apply the law of Member State P, instead of the law they are familiar with. The courts of Member State D have to invest in order to get acquainted with the laws of Member State P. Depending upon the system of court fees in the Member States, the courts may be unable to recover the extra costs.[70]

---

[68] Muir Watt, H., "Choice of Law in Integrated and Interconnected Markets: A Matter of Political Economy", *Electronic Journal of Comparative Law*, Vol 7, No. 3, 2003. Available at: http://www.ejcl.org/ejcl/73/art73-4.html, as of 15 March 2011; O'Hara, E. and L. Ribstein, "From Politics to Efficiency in Choice of Law", George Mason Law and Economics Working Paper No. 00-04, 1999; Rühl, G., "Party Autonomy in the Private International Law of Contracts: Transatlantic Convergence and Economic Efficiency", CLPE Research Paper 4/2007, Vol. 03 No. 1, 2007, pp. 32–34.

[69] Rühl, *supra* note 68, 33.

[70] Rühl, G., "Die Kosten der Rechtswahlfreiheit: Zur Anwendung ausländischen Rechts durch Deutsche Gerichte", *Rabelsz*, Vol. 71, 2007, pp. 559–596.

However, this argument is only of limited effect against party autonomy since courts would have to bear similar costs when foreign law is applied on the basis of the objective connecting factors. There seems to be a wide consensus in law and economics that society is better off as a whole with party autonomy.

There is of course a risk that private parties abuse their private autonomy or that private autonomy is abused to the detriment of the party with less bargaining power who sees a choice of law imposed upon him.[71] Accepting private autonomy thus necessarily brings with it the need to introduce some limitations and safeguards.[72] Examples of the former include overriding mandatory provisions or the prohibition on contracting out of mandatory provisions when all relevant factors are located within the same jurisdiction; examples of the latter include provisions that protect consumer and employees against the deprivation of minimum standards due to a choice of law.

Where growing interference of the state in the private law arena made it doubtful whether party autonomy would not reach its peak, the opposite has proven to be true.[73] The principle of party autonomy in international contracts is no longer open to doubt. The discussion does not focus upon the feasibility of party autonomy *per se*, but rather on its limits.[74] Those limits will be discussed below.[75]

The recognition and further strengthening of party autonomy in Rome I must be seen in the wider Union framework. Party autonomy

[71] Johns, F., "Performing Party Autonomy", *Law and Contemporary Problems*, Vol. 71, No. 3, 2008, pp. 243–271.

[72] Jacquet, J., *Principe d'autonomie et contrats internationaux*, Economica, Paris, 1983.

[73] Nygh, *supra* note 39, 13.

[74] Woodward, J., "Contractual Choice of Law: Legislative Choice in an Era of Party Autonomy", *Southern Methodist University Law Review*, Vol. 54. No. 2, 2001, pp. 697–786; Rühl, *supra* note 68; Martiny, D., "Europäisches Internationales Vertragsrecht in Erwartung der Rom-I Verordnung", *Zeitschrift für Europäisches Privatrecht*, Vol.16, 2008, pp. 79–108 (87).

[75] Outside the area of contracts the principle of party autonomy has equally gained increasing ground. Art. 6 of the Hague Convention on the Law Applicable to Trusts (1985) provides that a trust shall be governed by the law chosen by the settler; art. 7 of the Hague Convention on the Law Applicable to International Sale of Goods (1986) has as primary conflict of laws rule that the applicable law is chosen by the parties; art. 5 (1) of the Hague Convention on the Law Applicable to Succession to the Estates of Deceased Persons (1989) provides for a choice of law if the deceased was a national or had his habitual residence in the state involved; finally a restricted choice of law is also allowed in art. 4 of the Hague Convention on the Law Applicable to Certain Rights in Respect of Securities held with an Intermediary (2006).

is also gaining increasing ground in European PIL codifications in areas where it used to be excluded. The issue of choice of law came up in the context of the Proposal on Succession and Wills.[76] Also, art. 14 of the Rome II Regulation on the Law Applicable to non-Contractual Obligations recognises party autonomy, albeit with regard to a party not pursuing a commercial activity, a choice of law may only be made after the event giving rise to the liability occurred.[77] Enhancing legal certainty and promoting legal simplicity was the main reason for the introduction of a choice of law, although restricted to the laws of jurisdictions that have a close connection to the marriage, in the Rome III Regulation on Jurisdiction and Applicable Law in Matrimonial Matters.[78] The adoption of party autonomy is remarkable if one considers that the possibility to choose the applicable law in matrimonial matters was before the proposal only recognised in four Member States.[79] The role of party autonomy in the Union may therefore end up becoming more important than as has been traditionally understood in the Member States.[80]

---

[76] Green Paper Succession and Wills COM 2005 65 (final); Proposal for a Regulation on jurisdiction, applicable law, recognition and enforcement of decisions and authentic instruments in matters of succession and the creation of a European Certificate of Succession, COM (2009) 154 final; Harris, J., "The Proposed EU Regulation on Succession and Wills: Prospects and Challenges", *Trust Law International*, Vol. 22, 2008, pp. 181–235; Nick, C., Ausweitung der Parteiautonomie und objektive Anknüpfung im Erbkollisionsrecht, *European Journal of Legal Studies*, Vol. 2, No. 1, 2008, pp. 286–324.

[77] De Boer, Th., "Party Autonomy and its Limitations in the Rome II Regulation", *Yearbook of Private International Law*, Vol. 9, 2007, pp. 19–29; Kadner Graziano, T., "Das auf außervertragliche Schuldverhältnisse anzuwendende Recht nach Inkrafttreten der Rom II-Verordnung", *RabelsZ*, Vol. 73, 2009, pp. 1–77 (5–7); Bertoli, P., "Party Autonomy and Choice-Of-Law Methods in the "Rome II" Regulation on the Law Applicable to Non-Contractual Obligations", *Il Diritto dell'Unione europea*, Vol. 14, 2009, pp. 229–264.

[78] Please note that Regulation 1259/2010 was adopted within the framework of enhanced cooperation and will only bind fourteen Member States.

[79] The countries were Belgium, Germany, the Netherlands and Spain. House of Lords, European Union Committee, 52nd Report of Session 2005–06 Rome III—choice of law in divorce: Report with Evidence, Paper 272.

[80] For example party autonomy is now introduced in the area of surname law in Switzerland: Schnyder, A., "Parteiautonomie im Internationalen Namensrecht", J. Basedow *et al* (eds.) *Private Law in the International Arena: Liber Amicorum Kurt Siehr*, T.M.C. Asser Press, The Hague (2000), pp. 667–672. The ECJ seems to have allowed for a similar party autonomy in case C-148/02 *Garcia Avello* ECR [2003], I-11613; Case C-353/06 *Grunkin Paul* [2008] ECR I-7639. The last cases have led one author to observe a constitutionalisation of private autonomy. Marzal Yetano, T., "The Constitutionalisation of Party Autonomy in European Family Law", *Journal of Private International Law*, Vol. 6, No. 1, 2010, pp. 155–193.

The cornerstone of Rome I is the freedom of parties to designate the applicable law by a choice of law. Rome I does not modify the Rome Convention on this point substantially. Choice of law in contracts has been successful because it could be seen as exponent of private autonomy on the international plane; states cannot exercise a *de facto* control over international contracts anyway, a sovereign must exercise more restraint when a situation has contacts outside its territory, and choice of law promotes legal certainty and economic efficiency. Choice of law has also gained increasing recognition on the international plane. The European PIL codifications have more widely embraced choice of law than Member States have traditionally done. The possibility to choose the applicable law will therefore be the cornerstone in the interface between the conflict of laws rules in contractual obligations and Union law.

2.2 *The Function and Operation of Overriding Mandatory Provisions*

Whereas recognising the possibility of choosing the applicable law has boosted party autonomy, the development of overriding mandatory provisions reaches the opposite result. Increasing interference of the state in private law has led to a set of rules that are private in nature but are embedded with a regulatory function. The emergence of that regulatory function in private law has challenged the distinction between public international law and private international law where the former dealt with the right of a state to regulate conduct not exclusively of domestic concern and the latter determined the applicable law in a specific case. The regulatory effect of these provisions would be nullified if their application were dependant upon the applicable law. Those provisions could then be avoided by cleverly manipulating the connecting factors or by simply electing a different law. The provisions therefore override the otherwise applicable law and thus also the law chosen by the parties.

From a Union perspective overriding mandatory provisions are problematic. Whereas it will be argued in subsequent chapters that the possibility of choosing the law applicable to a legal relationship prevents a rule being caught by the free movement provisions, overriding mandatory provisions do not allow for a choice of law. However, in the light of the specific function of overriding mandatory provisions one can question whether they should be subject to the same traditional scrutiny of the fundamental freedoms over national laws.

This section tries to give a better insight in the aim and function of overriding mandatory provisions in Rome I and its relation towards party autonomy. Overriding mandatory provisions represent a particular category in PIL. The function and operation of overriding mandatory provisions will be even more difficult to understand when one is not familiar with conflict of laws. Also in Rome I, overriding mandatory provisions have a particular function since they constitute the only mechanism for establishing the applicable law whose content has not been harmonised. Moreover, the meaning given to overriding mandatory provisions differs from Member State to Member State. The role of overriding mandatory provisions in the European legal system will be the first object of study. It will be demonstrated that the value free conflict of laws norms used in the Savignian tradition have been unapt for dealing with the gradual realisation of public interests via private law. In addition, growing international trade and the gradual acceptance that parties should be able to designate the law applicable to a contract themselves has put increasing pressure on the Savignian conflict of laws rule.

The concept of overriding mandatory provisions inherently requires a certain extent of vagueness in order to safeguard the flexibility necessary to fulfil its role as exception to the normal conflict of law process. Vagueness does not, however, mean that overriding mandatory provisions are open-ended or arbitrary. By distinguishing overriding mandatory provisions from mandatory provisions, *ordre public* and unilateral conflict of laws rules it will be attempted to more precisely define overriding mandatory provisions. The codification in Rome instruments that the normal conflict of laws norms did not prejudice the application of overriding mandatory provisions of the forum was widely seen as nothing more than self-evident. The position of overriding mandatory provisions not belonging to the forum has been much more controversial. However, by demonstrating that a restrictive interpretation of overriding mandatory provisions of the forum prevails and the, although not universally favoured, acceptance of the possibility to apply foreign overriding mandatory provisions it will be demonstrated that overriding mandatory provisions are not necessarily a protectionist, unilateral exercise but can be aimed at the genuine protection of legitimate national interests.

After understanding the meaning, purpose and rationale of overriding mandatory provisions its interaction with other conflict of laws mechanisms will be assessed. The Rome Convention laid down connecting factors for protection of consumers and employees. The protection for consumers and employees is maintained in Rome I and moreover special conflict of laws rules are introduced for contracts of carriage and insurance contracts. It will be argued that the role of overriding mandatory provisions is severely limited when a situation already falls within the scope of one of the protective connecting factors. There is no reason to give the consumer or employee a double standard of protection, but it cannot be excluded that a State has a strong interest in seeing its law applied. Finally, overriding mandatory provisions may have a residual function to avoid too harsh consequences when the consumer or employee falls outside the scope of application of the protective connecting factor.

2.2.1 *The Origins of Overriding Mandatory Provisions*

Overriding mandatory provisions (or: lois de police, règles d'application immédiate, Eingriffsnormen, voorrangsregels) are a relatively new concept in Private International Law. Once the law that governs (part of) the contract is established, rules outside the applicable law are normally to be disregarded. Even Von Savigny[81] already acknowledged the existence of some rules that were of a strictly positive and imperative nature and that carried vital policies for the state which could never be displaced by a foreign law.[82] Von Savigny was however of the opinion that due to the growing liberalisation of human relations, and decreasing unilateralism, these rules were bound to disappear.[83] History has proven him wrong. Initially such strictly positive and imperative rules could often not be directly applied, but under some circumstances effect could be given to their factual consequences. For example, English law recognised in 1920 that the proper law of the contract could be displaced insofar as performance was unlawful according to the law of the place where the obligation had to be performed (*lex loci*

[81] Von Savigny, F., *System des heutige Römische Recht*, VIII System, § 349. See also: Micheals, R., "Globalizing Savigny? The State in Savigny's Private International Law and the Challenge of Europeanization and Globalization", Duke Law School Working Paper Series 15, 2005.

[82] Martinek, M., "The Seven Pillars of Wisdom in Private International Law: The German and the Swiss Experience with the Codification of Conflicts Law Rules", *Chinese Yearbook of Private International Law and Comparative Law*, 2001, pp. 15–54. Von Savigny, *supra* note 81.

[83] Von Savigny, *supra* note 81, 276; Wojewoda, M., "Mandatory Rules in Private International Law", *Maastricht Journal of European and Comparative Law*, vol. 7, No. 2, 2000, pp. 183–213 (185).

solutionis)[84] and a few years later the House of Lords held that English public policy prevented upholding a contract that required the breach of the laws of a friendly state.[85] A certain category of foreign rules were thus via English law not deprived of their effect.

The application of strictly imperative laws carrying vital foreign interests depended therefore primarily upon national substantive law. German authors criticised just before the Second World War the operation of the conflict of laws mechanism towards the foreign 'semi-public law';[86] foreign semi-public law that was part of the *lex causae* was often refused application on the basis of the *ordre public* exception. These authors tried to make the application of such rules not to dependent upon the *lex causae* but upon the rule itself.[87] The direct cause of that theory was that during the 1920s German industry had issued large amount of bonds, most notably in the United States. After the introduction of exchange control in Germany in 1931 these bonds were no longer serviced and the US bondholders successfully brought claims in the US applying US law. The German doctrine developed the theory of *Sonderstatut*, aimed at the applicability of the German exchange control rules regardless the applicability of US law.[88] The theory failed in US courts and did originally not find much support in the German doctrine.

The next step towards overriding mandatory provisions was also taken in the context of exchange control. Art. VII section 2(b) of the International Monetary Fund Agreement (1944) provides that:

> Exchange contracts which involve the currency of any member and which are contrary to the exchange control regulations of that member maintained or imposed consistently with this Agreement shall be unenforceable in the territories of any member. (…)

---

[84] *Ralli v Naviera* [1920] 2 K.B. 287.

[85] *Foster v Driscoll* [1929] 1 K.B. 470

[86] The notion is as such not used by Wengler and Zweigert but borrowed from Strikwerda, L., *Semipubliekrecht in het conflictenrecht : verkenningen op een kruispunt van methoden*, Tjeen Willink, Alphen a/d Rijn, 1978. It signifies rules that are at the crossroad of public and private law.

[87] Wengler, W., "Die anknüpfung des zwingenden Schuldrechts im IPR", *ZVergRWiss*, 1941, pp. 168–212; Zweigert, K., Nichterfüllung auf Grund ausländische Leistungsverbote", *RabelsZ*, Vol. 14 (1942), pp. 283.

[88] Mann, F., "Contracts: Effects of Mandatory Rules", K. Lipstein (ed.), *Harmonisation of Private International Law by the E.E.C.*, Chameleon Press Limited, London, 1978, pp. 31–32.

The Bretton Woods agreement would be seriously undermined if exchange controls regulating the use of a currency could be circumvented by the application of a different law. Members of Bretton Woods therefore had to take into account each others' exchange controls. Although the provision does not specify how the exchange contract is deemed to be unenforceable, it is clear that the unenforceability does not depend upon the applicable law. The greatest pressure on the classical system of Von Savigny came not, however, from exchange controls but from the emerging welfare state. The welfare state led to the creation of rules with social aims (consumer protection, minimum labour standards) that were neither truly private, nor truly public but rather of a semi-public nature. The rules were enacted in areas where private autonomy was not believed to be able to reach fair results. Private autonomy and contractual obligations were overruled by state measures. The Savignian system, being based on a strict separation between public and private law, could not really cope with the new category of rules and the question arose what position they should take in PIL.[89]

The idea that a special category of rules could find application although they were not part of the *lex causae* or even the *lex fori* reappeared in the academic debate in the sixties.[90] Courts steadily accepted that the application of a foreign law could not displace the fundamental rules of the forum. The *ordre public* exception was equipped with a positive function; it could not only function as shield against rules that shocked the internal legal order, but also act as sword by requiring the application of forum rules that embodied fundamental policies.

The possibility that courts could give effect, under certain circumstances, to foreign overriding mandatory provisions was confirmed in the Netherlands by the Hoge Raad (Supreme Court) in 1966 in the famous *Alnati* case.[91] The Hoge Raad held that in principle a choice of law made by the parties should be upheld, but that a foreign State may

---

[89] Strikwerda, L., *Semipubliekrecht in het conflictenrecht. Verkenningen op een kruispunt van methoden*, Tjeenk Willink, Alphen a/d Rijn, 1978.

[90] Francescakis, Ph., "Quelque précisions sur les 'lois d'application immédiate' et leur rapports avec les règles de conflits de lois", *Répertoire Dalloz de droit international privé, V° Conflit de lois,* 1966, n° 137 ; De Boer, Th., "Forty years on : the evolution of postwar private international law in Europe", *Symposium in celebration of the 40th anniversary of the Centre of Foreign Law and Private International Law*, Kluwer, Deventer, 1990.

[91] Hoge Raad 13 May 1966, NJ 1967, 3

have such an interest in the observance of its mandatory rules outside its territory that these rules have to be respected by a Dutch court, even though the parties have favoured the application of Dutch law. Contracting parties can thus not exclude these rules.

Although *Alnati* is usually cited for its express consideration of Belgian overriding mandatory provisions, it is even more interesting for a different reason. In *Alnati* the acceptance of (foreign) overriding mandatory provisions coincided with the firm acceptance of a choice of law. The former were seen as a limitation to the latter. Especially in the field of contract law, where parties enjoy the benefit of a large autonomy, it would often not be desirable if parties could prevent the application of semi-public rules by a mere choice of law. The scope of this problem in *Alnati* becomes clear if one realises that parties could also have chosen a legal system that was not all related to the legal relationship involved.[92] This problem was not specific to the Netherlands. It is not surprising that the Savignian system initially had difficulties in dealing with the effects of party autonomy. Moreover, international trade had yet to achieve adulthood. Due to its relatively small scale, evasive behaviour by parties could not have major implications for state policies. As contracts tended to internationalise more and more, the consequences of a liberal attitude towards a choice of law on society as a whole became more and more fierce.

2.2.2 *The Rome Convention*

The distinction between mandatory rules and overriding mandatory provisions and the subsequent possibility of applying the latter category of rules to a contractual relationship regardless the governing law was consequently inserted in art. 13 of the Benelux Treaty concerning a Uniform Law on Private International Law (1969).[93] The article drew inspiration from the *Alnati* decision: subparagraph 1 provided for the possibility of applying the overriding mandatory provisions of the forum, while subparagraph 2 provided that a choice of law could not prejudice the application of overriding mandatory provisions of the

[92] De Winter, L., "Dwingend recht bij internationale overeenkomsten", *NTIR*, 1964, pp. 329–365, C. Dubbink, (red.), *Naar een sociaal IPR, Een keus uit het werk van L. de Winter*, Kluwer: Deventer (1979), pp. 182–217

[93] This Treaty however never came into force: Strikwerda, L., *Inleiding tot het Nederlandse Internationaal Privaatrecht*, Groningen, Wolters-Noordhoff, 1988, pp. 116

manifestly objective applicable law.[94] The possibility to apply overriding mandatory provisions of the forum gradually gained acceptance in international conventions.[95]

With respect to the EU art. 7(1) of the Rome Convention allowed Member States to apply the overriding mandatory provisions of another country, and art. 7(2) provided that Member States were entitled to apply, regardless the applicable law, their own overriding mandatory provisions. Although the introduction of an express article on overriding mandatory provisions might have been for some Contracting States a novelty, equally the removal of the requirement that the law the chosen by the parties should have a qualified link with the contract constituted for some signatories a change with the past. The principle of party autonomy went hand in hand with its limitations. With the deletion of one of the safeguards against abuse of private autonomy,[96] the remaining two (*ordre public*, mandatory rules) gained greater importance. Since, the *ordre public* exception is in itself incapable of the promotion of forum interests, that role has now to be solely fulfilled by protective connecting factors and overriding mandatory provisions. A similar development can also be observed in the field of non-contractual obligations.[97] The acceptation of party autonomy in the Rome II Regulation on the Law Applicable to Non-Contractual Obligations was followed by the introduction of overriding mandatory provisions.

Although art. 13 of the Benelux Treaty was expressly named as source of inspiration for art. 7 Rome Convention,[98] the latter provision

[94] Deelen, J., "Internationale Contracten", *Mededelingen van de Nederlandse Vereniging voor Internationaal Recht*, no. 63, 1971, pp. 69–80.

[95] Examples include art. 16 of the Hague Convention on the Law Applicable to Agency (1978), art. 16 of the Hague Convention on Trusts (1985), art. 17 of the Hague Convention on the International Sale of Goods (1986), art. 20 of the Hague Convention on the International Protection of Adults (2000); art. 31 (1) United Nations Convention on the Assignment of Receivables in International Trade (2001) and a limited possibility is laid down in art. 11 of the Convention on the Law Applicable to Securities held with an Intermediary (2006).[95] Outside of Europe, attention should be drawn to art. 11 of the Inter-American Convention on the Law Applicable to International Contracts (1994).[95] Art. 11 moreover gives a discretion to the forum to apply foreign overriding mandatory provisions.

[96] Zhang, M., "Party Autonomy: An International Perspective of Contractual Choice of Law", *Emory International Law Review*, Vol. 20, 2006, pp. 511–562.

[97] EC Regulation 864/2007 on the Law Applicable to non-Contractual Obligations, OJ L 199/40 (2007).

[98] Giulano-Lagarde report, electronically available at http://www.rome-convention.org/instruments/i_rep_lagarde_en.htm. Art. 13 Benelux is quoted as evidence to support that art. 7 RC 'merely embodies principles which already exist in the laws of the

went significantly further since it did not limit the application of foreign overriding mandatory provisions to situations involving a choice of law but instead only required a sufficiently close link. The forum could thus also apply its overriding mandatory provisions when the law was established on the basis of the objective operation of the conflict of laws norms. Whereas traditionally the primary function of overriding mandatory provisions was aimed at the protection of state interests in private law, a second generation of overriding mandatory provisions emerged. These provisions primarily protected an individual interest, such as the one of a weaker party, rather than state interests in a narrow sense.[99] Subjecting private autonomy on the international plane to state intervention, overriding mandatory provisions can perform a regulatory function in international cases.

2.2.3 *Acceptance of Overriding Mandatory Provisions*

Overriding mandatory provisions have appeared in the most recent national codifications. Art. 18 of the Swiss PIL statute[100] allows for the application of Swiss overriding mandatory provisions, while art. 19 contains a similar option for foreign overriding mandatory provisions. Art. 17 of the Italian PIL statute[101] and art. 20 of the Belgian PIL code[102] also allow for the application of overriding mandatory provisions of the forum and recognise the possibility of applying foreign overriding mandatory provisions. The concept of overriding mandatory provisions has not been limited to Europe. Art. 10 of the Venezuelan Private International Law Act (1998) provides for the possibility to apply Venezuelan overriding mandatory provisions, but the act remains silent, despite the Inter-American Convention on the Law Applicable to International Contracts, about the position of foreign overriding mandatory provisions.[103] Québec, on the other hand has introduced,

Member States of the Community'. Whether such a principle, especially with regard to foreign overriding mandatory provisions indeed existed is however doubtful.

[99] In more detail, see par. 2.6.1.3 and 3.5.2.

[100] Loi fédérale sur le droit international privé du 18 décembre 1987, *Recueil systématique du droit fédéral* (1987) 291.

[101] Act No. 218 of 31 May 1995, *Gazzetta Ufficiale, Supplemento Ordinario* (1995) No. 128.

[102] Loi portant le Code de droit international privé du 16 juilliet 2004, *Moniteur Belge* published on 27 July 2004.

[103] Private International Law Act (1998), Gaceta Oficial de la República de Venezuela, No. 36.511 ; Parra-Aranguren, G., "The Venezuelan Act on Private International Law of 1998", *Yearbook of Private International Law*, Vol. 1, 1999, pp. 103–117.

the possibility of applying foreign overriding mandatory provisions. Whereas art. 3076 Code Civil du Québec (CCQ) provides that the section on private international shall not prejudice the application of domestic rules, art. 3079 allows Québec courts to apply, in the light of the consequences of (non) application, foreign overriding mandatory provisions of a legal system that has a close connection to the case.

Overriding mandatory provisions operate in reverse as compared how PIL was envisaged by Von Savigny. The field of application of the provision is determined on the basis its object and purpose rather than the determination of the spatially most appropriate law. The reasons for this are twofold: firstly the acceptance that states may have an interest in seeing their laws applied necessitates a PIL instrument that stresses the fundamental nature of the rule rather than the perspective of the individuals; and secondly the more liberal acceptance of a choice of law combined with the proportional increase in international trade necessitates an instrument preventing the abuse of private autonomy. Overriding mandatory provisions have therefore been referred to as a functionalist trend in PIL.[104]

Overriding mandatory provisions are thus originally an academic creation and were subsequently taken over by courts before appearing in national codifications and international conventions.[105] The emergence of overriding mandatory provisions is closely connected with the emergence of the welfare state that led to the creation of rules that were neither truly public nor truly private in nature. States thereby gained a regulatory interest in private law. On the other hand, the acceptance of party autonomy and the deletion of a link with the legal system chosen as requirement for a valid choice of law created a risk that parties would try to circumvent the regulatory laws. Overriding mandatory provisions were able to formalise the semi-public rules in PIL and provide adequate safeguards against the evasion of fundamental state policies. The national interest involved explains why states have more willingly accepted the application of their own overriding mandatory provisions and been more reluctant towards those originating from abroad.

---

[104] Guedj, T., "The Theory of the Lois de Police, A Functional Trend In Continental Private International Law – A Comparative Analysis With Modern American Theories", *American Journal of Comparative Law*, Vol. 39, 1991, pp. 661–697.

[105] Struycken, A., "La Contribution de l'Académie au développement de la science et de la pratique du droit international privé", *Recueil des Cours*, Vol. 271, 1998, pp. 15–56 (44–55).

2.3 *What are Overriding Mandatory Provisions?*

The preceding paragraphs have touched upon overriding mandatory provisions, without trying to define what they are. The French language version of Rome I refers to 'lois de police', the German to 'Eingriffsnormen' and the Dutch to 'bepalingen van bijzonder dwingend recht'. Alongside *lois de police* French courts and legal authors refer to *lois d'application immédiate, lois d'ordre public, lois d'application impérative*[106] and *lois d'application territorial,*[107] whereas in the Netherlands the term 'voorrangsregels' is common.[108]

The French language version already provides for a better understanding of overriding mandatory provisions. '*Police*' finds it etymological origin in the Greek word 'politeia', which means 'organisation of the State'. *Lois de police* are thus rules for the organisation of the State. The etymological origin was perhaps a source of inspiration for Francescakis to define *lois de police* as: '*lois dont l'observation est nécessaire pour la sauvegarde de l'organisation politique, sociale ou économique d'un pays*'.[109] It might however be more useful to first describe what overriding mandatory provisions are not.

2.3.1 *Mandatory vs Overriding Mandatory Provisions*

Mandatory rules are national rules that cannot be deviated from by contract and have usually as goal the protection of the interests of one

[106] Van Hoek, A., *Internationale mobiliteit van werknemers: Een onderzoek naar de interactie tussen arbeidsrecht, EG-recht en IPR aan de hand van de detacheringsrichtlijn*, SDU Uitgevers: Den Haag, 2000, pp. 125–131.

[107] Vignal, T., *Droit international privé*, Dalloz, Paris, 2005, pp. 45.

[108] The other language versions confirm that different terms have been used to described the concept : The Danish (overordnede præceptive bestemmelser) and the Greek (υπερισχύουσες διατάξεις αναγκαστικού δικαίου) language versions follow the English term of 'overriding mandatory provisions' whereas the Spanish (leyes de policía) is more in line with the French language version, the Swedish language version (internationellt tvingande regler) translates to 'international mandatory rules' and the Italian (norme di applicazione necessaria) and Portuguese (normas de aplicação imediata) refer to rules of immediate application (*lois d'application immediate*). It is not yet sure whether any significance should be attributed to the differences in the language version.

[109] Francescakis, Ph., "Quelque précisions sur les 'lois d'application immédiate' et leur rapports avec les règles de conflits de lois", *Répertoire Dalloz de droit international privé, V° Conflit de lois,* 1966, n° 137.

of the (weaker) parties or to protect third parties from suffering harm.[110] They are the opposite of default rules, which are applied in the event that parties failed to reach an agreement about a specific legal issue. Mandatory rules are applied regardless the will of the parties. On the international plane, they are protected by art. 3 (3) Rome I and the Rome Convention: mandatory provisions are, not withstanding a choice of law, applicable when all elements are connected with one country only. When parties to an international contract desire to evade a mandatory rule they are unable to do so within that legal system, but they can evade application by evading the entire legal system all together.[111] It is therefore impossible to evade the application of Austrian mandatory law protecting a subcontractor in a contract between an Austrian subcontractor and a Slovenian main contractor when the contract is governed by Austrian law. The Austrian mandatory subcontracting legislation will however normally not apply when the applicable law is Slovenian.

The general rule does not apply to consumer and individual employment contracts.[112] A choice of law cannot deprive the consumer of the mandatory protection afforded to him by the law of the place of his habitual residence and a choice of law cannot deprive the employee of the mandatory protection of the law of the place where he habitually carries out his activities in performance of the employment contract (resp. Art. 6 (2) Rome I and art. 8 (2) Rome I). A choice of Slovenian law in a consumer or employment will therefore normally not deprive the consumer or employee of Austrian mandatory standards.

Mandatory rules are part of the domestic substantive legal system and a mandatory rule only becomes relevant for PIL when it can be classified as an overriding mandatory provision. Overriding mandatory provisions are not limited in application to the legal system in which they originate. Because of the interest they seek to protect, they also claim application outside the frontiers of their own legal system. Their claimed scope of application supersedes the objective connecting factor or a choice of law. Overriding mandatory provisions can therefore be seen as a special type of mandatory rules. As opposed to

---

[110] Fawcett, J., "Evasion of Law and Mandatory Rules in Private International Law", *Cambridge Law Journal*, Vol. 44, 1990, pp. 44–62 (53).

[111] Winchop, M., and Keyes, M., "Statutes Domains in Private International Law: An Economic Theory of the Limits of Mandatory Rules", (1998). Available at SSRN: http://ssrn.com/abstract=121599 as of 15 March 2011.

[112] Bonomi, *supra* note 11, 224.

contracts-mandatory they are internationally or conflicts-mandatory.[113]

2.3.2 *Ordre Public vs Overriding Mandatory Provisions*

Overriding mandatory provisions originated in France and Germany as positive operations of the *ordre public* exception. The negative function of the *ordre public* refuses to give application to a foreign law when that would result in a manifest violation of its public order. A French judge will not, for example, give effect to a rule that prohibits the wife from initiating a divorce. In *Bouchereau* the ECJ made clear that the public policy of a Member State must address a real and severe danger and not just a violation of a national rule and secondly, that the public policy must be aimed at the protection of a fundamental interest.[114] Having resort to public policy will only be possible when application of the foreign law would result in a manifest breach of a rule of law regarded as fundamental in the legal order of the forum.[115] This means that comparable to the application of overriding mandatory provisions, the use of *ordre public* exception has to remain limited to special circumstances.[116] The refusal to apply a foreign rule because the results would be contrary to the public policy of the forum does not in itself necessitate the application of the *lex fori*. The vacuum that the non-application of the foreign law creates is however usually filled with the *lex fori*. Overriding mandatory provisions on the other hand operate on the basis of their own claimed scope of application. The result of the application of the foreign law is less relevant, what is decisive is the interest of the state involved to see its own law applied. The broader public policy concerns may in such a case not refuse a certain result, but rather require a certain result. It has therefore been said the *ordre public* exception is meant for safeguarding the values of the forum, while overriding mandatory provisions protect the policies of the State involved.[117]

---

[113] Wojewoda, *supra* note 83, 191.

[114] Case 30/77 *Bouchereau* [1977] ECR 1999.

[115] In analogy with the meaning of public policy in Brussels I: Case C-7/98 *Krombach* [2000] ECR I-1935, par. 90; C-38/98 *Renault v Maxicar* [2000] ECR 2973; Case C-394/07 *Gambazzi* [2009] ECR I-2563.

[116] Plender, R., and Wilderspin, M., "The European Private International Law of Obligations", Sweet & Maxwell, London, Third Edition, 2009, pp. 362.

[117] Remy, B., *Exception d'ordre public et mécanisme des lois de police en droit international privé*, Dalloz, Paris, 2008, pp. 176–208.

Rome I separates the *ordre public* exception (art. 21) from overriding mandatory provisions (art. 9). The distinction between overriding mandatory provisions and *ordre public* is only relevant at the stage of determining the applicable law. On the stage of recognition of foreign judgments the overriding mandatory provisions are absorbed again in the *ordre public* exception. The failure of a foreign judge to take into account overriding mandatory provisions of the *lex fori* may be manifestly incompatible with the public order and justify a refusal to give effect to such a judgment.[118]

Although connected at the stage of determining the applicable law there are two main distinctions between the *ordre public* exception and overriding mandatory provisions. Whereas *ordre public* only operates to refuse the acceptance of a certain result of a conflict rule and therefore in a way corrects the conflict of laws mechanism, overriding mandatory provisions are aimed at establishing the applicable law and thereby operate within the conflict of law mechanism. It must be noted that contrary to this dogmatic distinction some authors argue that the *ordre public* exception is not only used to correct the substantial result, but also to correct connecting factors.[119] In any case, because overriding mandatory provisions contribute to establishing the applicable law, they operate before the *ordre public* exception. It is possible that the application of a (foreign) overriding mandatory provision is manifestly incompatible with the *ordre public* of the forum. The application of a foreign overriding mandatory provision can therefore still be refused on the basis of art. 21 Rome I.

Secondly, where courts in certain circumstances may give effect to foreign overriding mandatory provisions originating in the *lex loci solutionis*, and conversely see their own overriding mandatory requirements applied abroad, it is impossible to take the *ordre public* exception of other countries into account. Although the *ordre public*

---

[118] But this is not necessarily the case : Radicati di Brozolo, L., "Mondialisation, juridiction, arbitrage : vers des règles d'application semi-nécessaires ?", *Revue Critique de Droit International Privé*, 2003, pp. 1–36 (18). Radicati di Brozolo argues that because of the requirements of legal certainty, national judges should not refuse to recognise a decision merely because it does not apply the overriding mandatory provisions of the forum. Because the application of overriding mandatory provisions depends upon when they are invoked in the forum (original proceedings or at the stage of recognition and enforcement) overriding mandatory provisions than become instead of lois d'application impérative, lois d'application semi-nécessaire.

[119] Ancel, B., and Y. Lequette, *Grand arrêts de la jurisprudence française de droit international privé*, 4e édition, 2001, pp. 516.

exception is historically strongly linked to the concept of overriding mandatory provisions, *ordre public* is meant to keep foreign law out, not to bring it in.

2.3.3 *Overriding Mandatory Provisions vs Unilateral Conflict of Laws Rules*

Unilateral conflict of laws rules indicate the scope of application of a national rule, but say nothing about the application of foreign law.[120] For example, a national code could provide that the section on remedies available to creditors in case of default of payment apply to every contract to be performed on the national territory. The rule would give no indication as to what law applies when the contract has to be performed abroad. Multilateral conflict of law rules are often phrased as the opposite of unilateral conflict of laws rules.[121] The multilateral conflict of laws rule applies to both foreign and domestic law. A multilateral conflict of laws rule would be phrased in such a way: 'The remedies available to the creditor in case of default of payment are determined by the law of the place where the contract has to be performed'. Unilateral conflict of laws rules have been gradually replaced or transformed by courts into multilateral conflict rules. Unilateral conflict of laws rules nowadays relate mostly to specific, narrowly defined regulations. As *lex specialis* they take precedence over bilateral conflict of laws rules.

Overriding mandatory provisions delimit, in the same way as unilateral conflict of laws rules, their own sphere of application. Since they apply regardless the applicable law, they also take precedence over the multilateral conflict of laws rules. However, unilateral conflict of law rules and overriding mandatory provisions do not fulfil the same function.[122] Unilateral conflict of laws rules aim to resolve a conflict of laws, overriding mandatory provisions to advance a certain state interest. The protection of the interest of the overriding mandatory provision cannot depend on the normal conflict of law mechanism but requires

---

[120] Kegel, G., and H. Schurig, *Internationales Privatrecht*, Verlag C.H. Beck, München:, 9. Auflage, 2004, pp. 301–303.

[121] Strikwerda, L., *Inleiding tot het Nederlandse Internationaal Privaatrecht*, Kluwer, Deventer, 2005, pp. 28–29.

[122] Guedj *supra* note 104, 677–679; Sonnenberger, H., "Eingriffsrecht – Das trojanische Pferd im IPR oder notwendige Ergänzung?", *IPRax*, vol. 23, 2003, pp. 104–116 (108).

direct application. Overriding mandatory provisions are sometimes equipped with a 'scope rule', a provision unilaterally delimiting the claimed scope of application of the overriding mandatory provision concerned but do not pursue any coordinative objectives.

Before the entry into force of the Rome Convention some Member States, such as Germany, predominantly used unilateral conflict of laws rules.[123] If it is accepted that in contracts the objective connecting factors only come into play when parties have failed to make a choice of law, the choice of law would also override the unilateral conflict of laws rule. It would be impossible to evade the application of an overriding mandatory provision by means of a choice of law. In contracts that distinction has lost relevance since Rome I exclusively employs multilateral conflict of laws rules. Member States have lost their ability to maintain conflict of laws rules relating to contractual obligations. In contract law, national rules that indicate a certain scope of application will therefore most often be scope rules.[124]

2.3.4 *Definition of Overriding Mandatory Provisions*

One of the major flaws of the Rome Convention was that it did not provide for an autonomous definition of overriding mandatory provisions. That deficiency has now been repaired, art. 9 (1) Rome I provides:

---

[123] Kropholler, J., *Internationales Privatrecht*, Mohr Siebeck, Tübingen, 5. Auflage, 2004, pp. 105.

[124] A German example: Par. 449 (1) Handelsgesetzbuch: Ist der Absender ein Verbraucher, so kann nicht zu dessen Nachteil von § 413 Abs. 2, den §§ 414, 418 Abs. 6, § 422 Abs. 3, den §§ 425 bis 438 und 447 abgewichen werden, es sei denn, der Frachtvertrag hat die Beförderung von Briefen oder briefähnlichen Sendungen zum Gegenstand. § 418 Abs. 6 und§ 447 können nicht zu Lasten gutgläubiger Dritter abbedungen werden. Par. 449 (3) HGB: Unterliegt der Frachtvertrag ausländischem Recht, so sind die Absätze 1 und 2 gleichwohl anzuwenden, wem nach dem Vertrag der Ort der Übernahme und der Ort der Ablieferung des Gutes im Inland liegen.

Dutch example: Art. 6:247 BW: 1) Op overeenkomsten tussen partijen die handelen in de uitoefening van een beroep of bedrijf en die beide in Nederland gevestigd zijn, is deze afdeling van toepassing, ongeacht het recht dat de overeenkomst beheerst. 2) Op overeenkomsten tussen partijen die handelen in de uitoefening van een beroep of bedrijf en die niet beide in Nederland gevestigd zijn, is deze afdeling niet van toepassing, ongeacht het recht dat de overeenkomst beheerst. 3) Een partij is in de zin van de leden 1 en 2 in Nederland gevestigd, indien haar hoofdvestiging, of, zo de prestatie volgens de overeenkomst door een andere vestiging dan de hoofdvestiging moet worden verricht, deze andere vestiging zich in Nederland bevindt. 4) Op overeenkomsten tussen een gebruiker en een wederpartij, natuurlijk persoon, die niet handelt in de uitoefening van een beroep of bedrijf, is, indien de wederpartij haar gewone verblijfplaats in Nederland heeft, deze afdeling van toepassing, ongeacht het recht dat de overeenkomst beheerst.

> Overriding mandatory provisions are provisions the respect for which is regarded as crucial by a country for safeguarding its public interests, such as its political, social or economic organisation, to such an extent that they are applicable to any situation falling within their scope, irrespective of the law otherwise applicable to the contract under this Regulation.

The definition indicates the difference with 'mandatory provisions'. As in the Rome Convention, the English language version draft did not distinguish between the overriding mandatory provisions in art. 8 Draft Proposal (they were simply referred to as mandatory provisions) from the mandatory rules protected by arts. 3 (4), 3 (5) and 6. The double meaning of mandatory rules in the Rome I proposal was criticised in the literature since it could give rise to confusion.[125] The Dutch, French and German version of the Rome I proposal did provide for such a difference. Art. 3 (4) referred respectively to 'dwingende bepalingen', 'disposition impératives' and 'zwingende Bestimmungen' while art. 8 referred to 'bepalingen van bijzonder dwingend recht', 'lois de police' and 'Eingriffsnormen'. The linguistic deficiency in the English language version has been rectified in the final document.

Another improvement of the definition of overriding mandatory provisions as compared to the definition in the draft version is the insertion of the words 'such as' after public interests. Art. 9 (1) thus makes it clear that the public interest listed in that provision (social, political and economical organisation) are not exhaustive. The definition now better connects to the case-law of the ECJ regarding the nature of the arts. 30, 46 and 55 EC. Although the grounds of public interests are exhaustively limited in these articles, the ECJ has, under the rule of reason, allowed other public interests to justify barriers to trade as long as the rule is applied in a non-discriminatory manner.

The definition provided for by art. 9 (1) is inspired by the judgement of the European Court of Justice (ECJ) in *Arblade,*[126] which in its turn is inspired by the definition of Francescakis.[127] *Arblade* as source for inspiration was not obvious. The referring court in *Arblade* asked whether the EC Treaty could '*render inoperative the first paragraph of Article 3 of the Civil Code relating to Belgian public-order legislation?*'.[128]

[125] Max Planck Institute for Foreign Private and Private International Law, "Comments on the European Commission's Proposal for a Regulation of the European Parliament and the Council on the law applicable to contractual obligations (Rome I)", RabelsZ, Vol. 71, 2007, pp. 225–344.

[126] Joined cases C-369/96 and C-376/96 *Arblade and Others* [1999], ECR I-8453, para. 30.

[127] Francescakis, Ph., "Conflit de lois (principes généraux)", *Répertoire Dalloz Droit International,* Vol. 1, 1968, pp. 470–497. Critical : Bonomi, *supra* note 11, pp. 231–4.

[128] *Arblade, supra* note 126, para. 24.

The ECJ held that the classification of a provision as one of public order did not place that provision outside the scope of Union law. The application of Union law should not depend upon the classification of a national rule by a national legislator. To be able to provide for a useful answer to the referring court the ECJ had however first to establish what the referring court meant with Belgian public-order legislation.[129] The ECJ thus clarified what it understood as Belgian public-order legislation, but did not intend to lay down a Union definition of overriding mandatory provisions. The development of overriding mandatory provisions in Belgium is inspired by the French doctrine,[130] but open it is to debate whether Rome I really adopts the French tradition.

German courts have held that in order for art. 7 (2) Rome Convention to bite, a provision must not merely protect an individual interest but also promote a public aim. The public interest must not be accessory to the protection of the individual interest, but an aim in itself. French courts have not imposed the requirement of public interest and have been willing to apply overriding mandatory provisions that purely protected the interests of the weaker party. The insertion of the requirement of 'public interest' in the definition of art. 9 (1) did not appear in either *Arblade* nor in the definition of Francescakis. At first sight, it appears therefore that the German view has prevailed. It can however not be excluded that a country classifies provisions of consumer or labour protection law as overriding mandatory provision because a Member State considers such rules as fundamental principles of its social and economic order.[131] The ECJ will therefore in the future have to decide on this issue.[132]

2.3.5 *Crucial for Safeguarding the Political, Social or Economic Organisation of the State*

Even when the ECJ has clarified the issue of public interest, the definition leaves a number of practical problems intact. How can one establish whether a provision is crucial for safeguarding the political, social

[129] Plender/Wilderspin, *supra* note 116, pp. 336.

[130] Meeusen, J., *Nationalisme en Internationalisme in het Internationaal Privaatrecht: Analyse van het Belgische Conflictenrecht*, Intersentia, Antwerpen, 1997.

[131] Max Planck Institute, *supra* note 125.

[132] Kuipers, J. and S. Migliorini, Qu'est-ce que sont les lois de police ? Une controverse franco-allemande, in: *European Review of Private Law*, vol. 18, No. 2, 2011, pp. 187–207. The obligation will be argued in more detail in par. 3.5.2.

or economical organisation of a state? Francescakis was of the opinion that the overriding nature of a mandatory provision could only be established *ex post*.[133] The appreciation of the interests involved necessarily means that a competent judge has to establish *ad hoc* whether a particular rule must be classified as an overriding mandatory provision.[134] There would however be some fields or specific objectives that would be naturally covered. If overriding mandatory provisions would be natural in some fields, independent of time and location, it would imply some form of European consensus.[135] Such a European consensus has not emerged following the implementation of the Rome Convention. Member States have found the imposition of overriding mandatory provisions 'natural' in not always the same areas.

The *ad hoc* establishment of a rule as an overriding mandatory provision was already the focus of the criticism of the definition of Francescakis. Every law aims to protect in some way or the other specific economic or social norms. That would bring down the difference between overriding mandatory provisions and mandatory provisions to a mere difference in degree, making it difficult to draw the distinction.[136] The criticism holds ground in that it is not always easy to establish whether a norm is mandatory or overriding mandatory. It boils down to the question of interpretation of the word 'crucial', which leaves a wide margin of appreciation to the judiciary. Drawing the line might prove to be difficult, but that applies to every rule that leaves a certain margin of discretion to the courts. By analogy, the concept of good faith requires a case by case interpretation by courts, but its inherent flexibility allows the concept of good faith to play an important role in the French, German and Dutch legal systems.

The Union or national legislator may ease the burden of the court by establishing the scope of application of a rule of semi-public origin. Such a PIL rule that delimitates the precise scope of a semi-public rule is in the Netherlands referred to as a 'scope rule'.[137] One has however to

---

[133] Francescakis, *supra* note 127, pp. 470–497.

[134] Rammeloo, S., "*Via Romana*. Van EVO naar Rome I – Nieuw Europees IPR inzake het recht dat van toepassing is op verbintenissen uit overeenkomst", *Nederlands Internationaal Privaatrecht*, Vol. 24, 2006, pp. 249.

[135] Bucher, A., "L'ordre public et but social des lois en droit international privé", *Recueil des Cours*, Vol. 239, 1993, pp. 9–116 (25).

[136] Loussouarn, Y., "Cours général de droit international privé", *Recueil des Cours*, Vol. 139, 1973, pp. 271–385.

[137] Strikwerda, *supra* note 121, pp. 74–75.

realise that not all semi-public regulation will contain a scope-rule and that national scope-rules do not bind national judges in other Member States. Consequently, foreign courts will then be required to assess independently whether the semi-public rule requires application and one can say that in a multilateral setting the overriding mandatory provision has to be legitimised.[138] The scope rule will nevertheless be useful for the foreign court to establish the intent of the legislator.

2.3.6 *Union Law*

Besides the difficulty of interpreting 'crucial', art. 9 (1) refers to rules that are crucial for the safeguard of the political, social or economical organisation of a *country*. What is the position of rules that are essential for the safeguarding of the political, social or economical organisation of the European Union?[139] Art. 3 (4) provides that the choice of law for a non-Member State is without prejudice to the application of mandatory rules of Union law, but Rome I does not provide for Union provisions that are applicable regardless the applicable law. It has been advocated that such rules already take precedence over the conflict laws by virtue of art. 23,[140] or that Union rules are part of the Member States legal order and therefore covered by the notion 'country'.[141]

The question of classifying provisions originating in Union law as overriding mandatory provisions is relevant in particular because Union law is regulatory law. Grundmann has even maintained that the Union exclusively regulates areas of mandatory law, while the Member States will ultimately only concern default law.[142] Whether this might become true or not, the Union policies do not only underlie substantive values, but already the enactment of Union law as such underlies a public interest since measures are meant to enhance the smooth functioning of the internal market. The rules originating in Union law therefore underlie a much stronger regulatory function than the private laws of the Member States.

---

[138] Wojewoda, *supra* note 83, pp. 190.

[139] Case 381/98 *Ingmar* [2000], ECR I-9305.

[140] Max Planck Institute, *supra* note 125. For a detailed discussion: see chapter 4.

[141] Dickinson, A., "The law applicable to contracts – uncertainty on the horizon?" *Butterworths Journal of International Banking and Financial Law*, 2006, pp. 171–173.

[142] Grundmann, S., "Internal Market Conflict of Laws…", A. Fuchs *et al* (eds.), *Les conflits de lois et le système juridique communautaire*, Dalloz, Paris, 2004, pp. 5–29.

The political, social or economical interest of individual Member States is not necessarily that of the Union as a whole. If one were to perceive the Union rules as being aimed at safeguarding the Union objective as covered in the definition of 'country' one would create rules that potentially protect conflicting interests in one country. These objections did apparently not persuade the German Bundesgerichtshof. The Bundesgerichtshof accepted in 2005 that overriding mandatory provisions derived from Union law may in principle be protected by the predecessor of art. 9 (2), art. 7 (2) Rome Convention.[143] As will be demonstrated later it is indeed preferable to cover overriding mandatory provisions of Union origin with the definition of country rather than to let Union overriding mandatory provisions systematically prevail over Rome I.[144]

In the first chapter attention was already drawn to the fact that a European public policy is developing alongside national public policy. The division of competences will mean that economic and monetary provisions will constitute the core of that European public policy. *Ingmar*, where the ECJ held that the provisions relating to the protection of the agent after termination of the agency agreement were applicable regardless the applicable law, is so far the sole example of the application of a Union overriding mandatory provision,[145] although the Timeshare Directive seems to be classified as a set of overriding mandatory provisions whenever the immovable is situated within the Union (art. 9 Timeshare Directive). Provisions of competition law would also be likely a likely candidate for the characterisation as overriding mandatory provision.[146]

The adoption of the Charter of Fundamental Rights could be an impetus for the development for a core of fundamental rights to apply regardless the applicable law.[147] It is not in the scope of the present research to provide a detailed analysis of the role of fundamental rights

143 Bundesgerichtshof December 13 2005, NJW 2006, 762. In the case, the claim was based on German implementation exceeding the directive. The BGH therefore held it was not necessary to address the issue further.

144 See chapter 4.

145 *Ingmar*, *supra* note 139.

146 Case C-126/97 *Eco Swiss* [1999] ECR I-3055.

147 Picheval, C., *L'ordre public européen droit communautaire et droit européen des droits de l'homme*, CERIC, Aix-Marseille, 2001.

in overriding mandatory provisions.[148] On first glance, the influence of fundamental rights in contract law is rather modest.[149] Courts in jurisdictions that deploy a fundamental rights reasoning do not, in similar cases, reach a substantially different outcome than courts who do not resort to fundamental rights methodology.[150] The gradual expansion of fundamental rights came at the expense of the hierarchal position of the doctrine. At best, a fundamental rights argument opens up a proportionality test, requiring a proper justification of the infringement of the fundamental right. That would not lead to a significantly different result than the application of open notions such as 'good faith' or 'fair dealings' traditionally employed in contract law.[151] Fundamental rights may however play an important role in particular kind of contracts, for example labour contracts. Before a general principle of Union law can apply the case must fall in the scope of Union law.[152] That may occur when a particular area has been harmonised by Union law.[153] An example would be the non-discrimination principle. If an employment contract governed by the law of a third country were to discriminate on the basis of race or ethnic origin, the contractual stipulation would have to

---

[148] It has been submitted that the technique of overriding mandatory provisions is insufficient to protect the fundamental rights contained in the ECHR. A particular difficulty is that the ECHR does not provide for precise rules. An autonomous approach should therefore be preferred. Marchadier, F., *Les objectifs généraux du droit international privé à l'épreuve de la convention européenne des droits de l'homme*, Bruylant, Bruxelles, 2007, pp. 601–609. Evidence for such an approach can be retrieved in French doctrine and case-law: Hammje, P., "L'ordre public de rattachement", *Travaux du Comité de Droit International Privé 2006–2008*, pp. 153–186.

[149] Recently authors have however started to apply human rights to general areas of private law. See: Cherednychenko, O., *Fundamental Rights, Contract Law and the Protection of the Weaker Party, A Comparative Analysis of the Constitutionalisation of Contract Law, with Emphasis on Risky Financial Transaction*, Sellier, München, 2007; Benöhr, I., *Consumer Law between Market Integration and Human Rights Protection*, EUI Thesis (2009). It should indeed be recognised that for example the anti-discrimination clause in the Charter exceeds the traditional field of labour law and may also impact upon the freedom to choose a contractual partner. Critically see: Basedow, J., "Freedom of Contract in the European Union", *European Review of Private Law*, vol. 16, 2008, pp. 901–923. One can wonder whether the formal incorporation of human rights language changes the outcome of a case. Mak, C., *Fundamental Rights in European Contract Law: A Comparison of the Impact of Fundamental Rights on Contractual Relationships in Germany, the Netherlands, Italy and England*, Wolters Kluwer, Alphen a/d Rijn, 2008, pp. 179.

[150] Examples are provided by: Mak, *supra* note 149, 179.

[151] Smits, J., "Private Law and Fundamental Rights: a skeptical view", Maastricht Working Papers Faculty of Law, no. 8, 2006.

[152] Case C-427/06 *Bartsch* [2008] ECR I-7245.

[153] Case C-555/07 *Kücükdeveci* [2010] ECR I-0000.

be set aside by a Union court on the basis of art. 14 (b) of the Race and Ethnic Origin Directive. Fundamental rights protect a value; they act as a shield, and will prevent the application of a rule or contractual stipulation that breaches the fundamental right concerned. The gap that is created is filled by the *lex fori.* Fundamental rights, and hence the Charter of Fundamental Rights, will therefore play a stronger role in the public policy exception than in the classification of a rule as an overriding mandatory provision.

An exception, where fundamental rights may play a stronger role in the characterisation of a provision as overriding mandatory provision, is data protection. That is because the protection granted in a jurisdiction risks being nullified if a similar protection is not afforded to the same individual outside the jurisdiction concerned. The Data Protection Directive aims to promote the smooth functioning of the internal market by striking a balance between the free circulation of personal data and protection of the right to private life. The ECJ accepted in *Österreichischer Rundfunk*[154] and *Lindqvist*[155] that a direct link between the internal market and the processing of data was not required. Both cases concerned situations that were exclusive to one Member State only. The acceptation that for the application of the Data Protection Directive the internal market does not necessarily have to be directly affected opens the door for the application of the directive to situations involving exclusively one Member State and a third country. Also in those circumstances the impact upon the common market is not obvious. The right to data protection has been classified, as part of the right to private life, as a fundamental right.[156] It is protected by art. 8 of the Charter of Fundamental Rights. When in a civil proceeding the question comes up whether a data subject has consented to the processing of his personal data, that question has to be answered on the basis of the contractual obligations between the parties. Insofar as the Data Protection Directive affects the mutual rights and obligations of private parties its protection should be extended to data subjects residing in the European Union. In particular in the online context, the right to private life could be jeopardised if data acquired under a foreign law with a laxer standard of consent could freely circulate the web.

[154] Case C-465/00 *Österreichischer Rundfunk* [2003] ECR I-4989
[155] Case C-101/01 *Lindqvist* [2003] ECR I-129711
[156] Case C-553/07 *Rijkeboer* [2009] ECR I-3889, par. 47.

The question whether consent has been acquired therefore has to be answered on the basis of the Directive, and in particular art. 7 (a), regardless the law that governs the horizontal relation between the data subject and data controller. It should however be borne in mind that the fundamental right standard protected by the Directive is merely a minimum. The ECJ has left, within the framework of the Directive, Member States a significant margin for balancing the protection of the right to a private life against other personal or fundamental rights.[157] Whereas there may be a Union minimum standard, data subjects will probably derive more protection from the data legislation as implemented in their respective national legal order.

2.3.7 *Conditions for Application*

Once a provision has been classified as overriding mandatory the question arises whether the provisions should be applied in the specific factual circumstances. Two situations have to be distinguished.[158] The first is where the governing law is the *lex fori* and the overriding mandatory provision also originates in this law. Are overriding mandatory provisions automatically applicable when part of the governing law, when the applicable law is that of the forum, even when the situation does not fall into its scope? The second is when the overriding mandatory provision prevails over a foreign *lex causae*.

The first question has been abundantly discussed in literature and solved differently in the Member States.[159] In brief, Germany and the Netherlands adhere to the special connection theory. Overriding mandatory provisions have to justify their own application regardless the *lex causae*. The fact the *lex causae* German or Dutch is in itself not sufficient to trigger the application of German or Dutch overriding mandatory provisions. The dogmatic solutions in France and the UK are less clear. In the latter Member State the prevailing opinion is that English public policy will in general not be applied unless there is an impact on the forum. In France, there is in general no hostility against applying overriding mandatory provisions. The fact that France does

[157] Case C-275/06 *Promusicae* [2008] ECR I-271, par. 63 and case C-73/07 *Satakunnan Markkinapörssi and Satamedia* [2008] ECR I-7075.

[158] The third possibility: the application of overriding mandatory provisions that are neither part of the *lex causae* nor the *lex fori* will be discussed in the next subsection.

[159] Rammeloo, S., Das Neue EG-Vertragskollisionrecht, Carl Heymanns Verlag KG, Köln, 1992, pp. 351–359 with further references.

not have an interest in seeing its law applied does not mean the law should not be applied. When the overriding mandatory provision adequately regulates the situation without being linked to a certain economical or social goal it can be applied.

The second question has received significantly less scholarly attention. Contrary to the first question it is clear that the factual circumstances should fall into the scope of the overriding mandatory provision. When the facts fall into scope, the notion '*règles d'application immédiate*' suggests that the overriding mandatory provision takes immediate precedence over the foreign *lex causae*. Also in art. 9 (2) Rome I seems to allow the automatic imposition of the overriding mandatory provisions of the forum. However, it is established case-law that the classification of a national provision as overriding mandatory, and the subsequent application under art. 9 (2), does not place the measure outside the scope of Union law.[160] It follows moreover from *Centros*[161] and *Inspire Art*[162] that the automatic imposition of an overriding mandatory provision without an analysis of the specific circumstances of the case will not be able to justify a restriction of one of the fundamental freedoms.[163] In cases with a Union element it is beyond doubt that the forum should analyse on a case by case basis the consequences of application or non-application of an overriding mandatory provision on the basis of the nature and purpose of the rule concerned. In international situations the notion of '*règles d'application immédiate*' adequately describes the process. Overriding mandatory provisions impose themselves upon the *lex causae* as soon as the factual situation falls within the scope of the protected interest.

Overriding mandatory provisions operate as an exception to the conflict of laws process. The fact that overriding mandatory provisions are defined narrowly should therefore not come as a surprise. Overriding mandatory provisions can only be imposed when it is crucial for the safeguard of an essential national policy. Legislators can aid the courts in the difficult task of establishing what an overriding mandatory provision is by equipping them with a scope rule. The strain that overriding mandatory provisions put on private parties is only justified

---

[160] Joined cases C-369/96 and C-376/96 *Arblade and Others* [1999], ECR I-8453, para. 31.

[161] Case C-212/97 *Centros* [1999] ECR I-1459

[162] Case C-167/01 *Inspire Art* [2003] ECR I-10155

[163] In more detail : chapter 6.

when the interest that is deemed worthy of protection is actually at stake. It should be welcomed that the Union legislator has attempted to define the notion of overriding mandatory provisions. The adaption of the definition of Francescakis will however probably not mean that the Court will follow the French legal tradition since the Rome I definition differs at one significant point. The insertion of the words 'public interest' makes the definition on first sight closely mirror the German tradition. The classification of provisions as overriding mandatory being an *ad hoc* exercise, the persistence of the various national approaches can be expected.

2.4 *Foreign Overriding Mandatory Provisions*

Although the provision in the Rome Convention stipulating that the instrument did not restrict the application of overriding mandatory provisions of the forum was perceived to be self-evident, the application foreign overriding mandatory provisions was quite the contrary. Traditionally, courts are reluctant to aid a foreign power in the enforcement of its public laws. Application of purely private foreign law on the basis of the conflict of laws norms was not regarded as a service rendered to the foreign state, but rather promoting the forums interest in the efficient and smooth regulation of transnational private law relationships.[164] Moreover, where one could accept that national overriding mandatory provisions override national conflict of laws rules, the acceptance that foreign rules might override national conflict of laws rules might be more difficult to make. The application of the overriding mandatory provisions of another jurisdiction has therefore been a controversial issue. A distinction could be drawn between foreign overriding mandatory provisions that belong to the *lex causae* and overriding mandatory provisions that are not *lex causae*, but neither belong to the *lex fori*.[165] In the first situation, there might be a stronger incentive to apply the overriding mandatory provisions of the *lex causae* since they

[164] Bogdan, M., "Foreign Public Law and Article 7 (1) of the Rome Convention: Some Reflections from Sweden", T. Azzi *et al* (eds.), *Vers de nouveaux équilibres entre ordres juridiques, Liber amicorum Hélène Gaudemet-Tallon*, Dalloz, Paris, 2008, pp. 671–682 (674).

[165] Kuckein, M., *Die 'Berüksichtigung' von Eingriffsnormen im deutschen und englischen internationalen Vertragsrecht*, Mohr Siebeck, Tübingen, 2008, pp. 12–13.

are already part of the governing law. There might be good reasons for a German court to apply an Austrian exchange regulation if the governing law is Austrian.[166] The German court will decide the case in the same way as the Austrian court, which would contribute to the international harmony of decisions.

The Rome instruments do not formally draw a distinction between overriding mandatory provisions originating in the *lex causae* and overriding mandatory provisions that do not.[167] The arguments often deployed against foreign overriding mandatory provisions have less force when the overriding mandatory provision originates in the *lex causae*. Party autonomy is not restricted and no legal uncertainty is created since the overriding mandatory provision was already part of the applicable law. The refusal to give effect to foreign overriding mandatory provisions that originate in the *lex causae* is therefore rather a decision based on legal principle, being that there is no point in wasting tax-payers' money on actively promoting the public interests of foreign states, rather than on legal reasons.

2.4.1 *The Scope of the Applicable Law*

Doubts have been raised about the applicability of first category foreign overriding mandatory provisions under the Rome Convention.[168] Rome I did not bring any clarification, but reproduced a provision defining the scope of the applicable law.[169] Art. 12 (1) provides:

> The law applicable to a contract by virtue of this Regulation shall govern in particular:
>
> (a) interpretation;
> (b) performance;

---

[166] Oberlandesgericht Schleswig-Holstein IPRspr. 1954/55, 463. Of course, the introduction of the euro has brought in this respect simplification.

[167] It is interesting to compare German and French authors on the issue. For example Radtke submits that the application of 1st and 2nd category foreign OMP underlie the same principle whereas Mayer/Heuzé submit that 'Du moment que le tribunal français a accepté de se reconnaître compétent, il ne peut refuser d'appliquer la loi de police étrangère sous le prétexte que, ce faisant, il servirait les intérêts de l'État étranger.' Radtke, R., "Schuldstatut und Eingriffsrecht", *Zeitschrift für Vergleichende Rechtswissenschaft*, Vol. 84, 1985, pp. 326–357; Mayer, P. and V. Heuzé, Droit International Privé, 9e édition, Paris, Montchrestien, 2007, pp. 93.

[168] Kropholler, *supra* note 123, pp. 501.

[169] Minor differences between art. 10 Rome Convention and art. 12 Rome I are discussed in Plender/Wilderspin *supra* note 116, pp. 395.

(c) within the limits of the powers conferred on the court by its procedural law, the consequences of a total or partial breach of obligations, including the assessment of damages in so far as it is governed by rules of law;
(d) the various ways of extinguishing obligations, and prescription and limitation of actions;
(e) the consequences of nullity of the contract.

Suppose that a Dutch employee works for a German employer for a period of two years every six months in a different country and that in the employment contract a choice of law in favour of Dutch law has been made. During employment in Germany the employer is forced to reorganise and has to dismiss the employee. If the employee were to argue that the employer unlawfully terminated the employment contract by not asking for prior authorisation of the appropriate Dutch authorities, art. 19 Brussels I would lead to the exclusive jurisdiction of German courts. The prior authorisation of dismissal is considered necessary for the regulation of the Dutch labour market and is from a Dutch perspective regarded as an overriding mandatory provision.[170] The regulation of the labour market has a strong public interest flavour. Since the various way of extinguishing obligations are part of the *lex causae*, a German court would have to apply the Dutch overriding mandatory provision since it affects the lawfulness of the termination.[171] The German court could only refuse to apply the Dutch provision on the ground that the provision itself does not require application in the specific circumstances or that application of the provision would be contrary to Union law.

The objection that a forum should not assist a foreign power in the enforcement of its claims still stands. The argument could be made that Private International Law in principle only refers to private law and leaves the applicability of (semi) public law untouched.[172] It must however be pointed out that there is no consensus on the Continent as to what is public and what is private and that the distinction has only limited effect in the United Kingdom. With respect to Brussels I, the

---

[170] Polak, M., *Arbeidsverhoudingen in het Nederlands internationaal privaatrecht*, Kluwer, Deventer, 1988, pp. 116.

[171] The German court would then be confronted with the difficult task whether art. 6 BBA requires in these specific circumstances application. See: par. 3.3.2

[172] Radtke, *supra* note 167, 332.

ECJ has been willing to give an autonomous interpretation to the notion of 'civil and commercial matters' and excluded rules of public international from its scope.[173] In a European context, the applicability of a foreign rule can therefore not depend upon the classification of the forum of that provision as private or public by the forum. The question whether a foreign overriding mandatory provision that is part of the *lex causae* should be applied is therefore a question of the scope of the governing law. That is an autonomous definition that will have to be developed by the ECJ. Rome I does not, for the purposes of the determining the scope of the applicable law, seem to draw a distinction on the basis of the overriding nature of a provision. It is therefore not open for the courts of a Member State to refuse the application of a rule that is part of the governing law on the grounds that the rule aims at the realisation of a public interest. The following section will therefore describe the application of the foreign overriding mandatory provisions that are neither part of the *lex fori* nor the *lex causae*.

2.4.2 *The Rome Convention*

The possibility of applying foreign overriding mandatory provisions was, as already mentioned earlier, accepted by the Dutch Hoge Raad in *Alnati* (1966). It held that a foreign State may have such an interest in the observance of its mandatory rules outside its territory that these rules have to be respected by a Dutch court. Contracting parties can thus not exclude these rules, not even by a choice of law.[174] The rationale was incorporated in the Rome Convention,[175] where art. 7 (1) provided that:

> When applying under this Convention the law of a country, effect may be given to the mandatory rules of the law of another country with which the situation has a close connection, if and in so far as, under the law of the latter country, those rules must be applied whatever the law applicable to the contract. In considering whether to give effect to these mandatory rules, regard shall be had to their nature and purpose and to the consequences of their application or non-application.

---

173 Case C-292/05 *Lechouritou* [2007] ECR 1519.

174 Hoge Raad 13 May 1966, NJ 1967, 3

175 Schultsz, J., "Dutch Antecedents and Parallels to Article 7 of the EEC Contracts Convention of 1980", *RabelsZ*, Vol. 47, 1983, pp. 267–283.

The codification of the *Alnati* decision in the Rome Convention was not without controversy. It constituted for many states a radical break with the past.[176] The development did not please all Contracting Parties equally. The arguments raised against the provision were manifold. The application of foreign overriding mandatory provisions would require an analysis of the foreign policies and introduce an element of the governmental interest analysis in Europe,[177] as well as splitting up the applicable law. A similar argument could however be made against the application of overriding mandatory provisions of the forum; in the absence of a scope rule, the degree of mandatory nature of a rule has to be established in the light of the object and purpose of the national relevant legislation.

The principal refusal to give effect to foreign (semi) public law can also not of itself carry sufficient weight to prevent the formal possibility to apply foreign overriding mandatory provisions. Even those Contracting Parties which did not foresee the formal possibility of applying foreign public law have found, through the use of alternative concepts or substantive law, ways to circumvent the most rigid consequences of the refusal.[178]

Another objection is that the application of foreign overriding mandatory provisions would unduly restrain party autonomy. Again, also overriding mandatory provisions of the forum restrain the contracting parties from choosing the applicable law. Party autonomy goes hand in hand with its limitations. Party autonomy only exists by the grace of states and is incapable of prejudicing the application of norms designed to protect the integrity of the judicial system and public policy. Party autonomy can therefore only be acceptable if appropriate check and balances are put into place. What can be deducted at best from this argument is that derogation from the principle of party autonomy must be both justifiable and proportionate to the objectives pursued.[179]

[176] Lando, O., "The EEC Convention on the Law Applicable to Contractual Obligations", *Common Market Law Review*, Vol. 24, 1987, pp. 172–180.

[177] Morse, C., "The EEC Convention on the Law applicable to Contractual Obligations", *Yearbook of European Law*, Vol. 2, 1982, pp. 107–171 (146).

[178] *supra* note 125, 317.

[179] Dickinson, A., "Third-Country Mandatory Rules in the Law Applicable to Contractual Obligations, so long, farewell, auf wiedersehem, adieu?" *Journal of Private International Law*, Vol. 3, No. 1, 2007, pp. 53–88 (59–61)

The most convincing argument against foreign overriding mandatory provisions is based on legal uncertainty. Indeed in the process of drafting art. 7 (1) Rome Convention, the Contracting Parties suggested that the introduction of such a clause would create a large amount of legal uncertainty.[180] It is admitted that the potential amount of legal uncertainty requires thorough drafting in order to avoid unfair surprises to parties. The fact that a large amount of discretion is left to courts does not, however, say anything about the feasibility of the possibility of applying foreign overriding mandatory provisions. In many continental legal systems the concept of good faith is able to fulfil an important role precisely because it leaves a large amount of flexibility to the courts. The fact that art. 7 (1) Rome Convention might lead to the application of overriding mandatory provisions of several legal orders does not alter that conclusion. The situation should have a sufficient close connection with the legal system in which the overriding mandatory provisions originate. In *Alnati* a sufficient close connection with Belgium did not exist although the order for the carriage of potatoes was placed by a Belgian agent and the port of departure was Antwerp. Hence, a provision such as art. 7 (1) does not refer to every potential legal system in the world but instead requires that some qualified link should exist. The fact that the precise conditions of that qualified link have yet to be crystallised in further case-law does not defeat the necessity of the provision as such.

The introduction of art. 7 (1) was deemed to be useful because it would codify the pre-existing practices to give in one way or the other effect to the public interests of foreign states.[181] Giving effect to foreign law is wider than the application of foreign law.[182] The first covers the giving effect to foreign semi-public law via open notions in national law such as good morals or public policy, whereas the latter is restricted to the actual application of the norm. The application of overriding mandatory provisions of third countries was, *inter alia*, defended on comity grounds. In the light of increasing social and economical

[180] Plender, R., "The European Contracts Convention : The Rome Convention on the Choice of Law for Contracts", Sweet & Maxwell, London, 1991, pp. 153.

[181] Mosconi, F., "Exceptions to the Operation of Choice of Law Rules", *Recueil des Cours*, Vol. 217, 1989, pp. 13–214 (153); Bonomi, A., "Note – Article 7(1) of the European Contracts Convention: Codifying the Practice of Applying Foreign Mandatory Rules", *Harvard Law Review*, Vol. 114, 2001, pp. 2462–2477.

[182] Remy, B., *Exception d'ordre public et mécanisme des lois de police en droit international privé*, Dalloz, Paris, 2008, pp. 352–356.

interdependence of states it was suggested that states should mutually respect each other's sociological and economical interests. It was hoped that, by giving under circumstances way to the application of foreign semi-public law, foreign states would do the same with regard to the semi public law of the forum.[183] Supposedly, the possibility of applying foreign overriding mandatory provisions would contribute to the prevention of forum shopping. With regard to Brussels I it has been pointed out that courts in different countries may possess concurrent jurisdiction. The court first seized would be competent to hear the case. Forum shopping would be encouraged if the application of overriding mandatory provisions would completely depend upon which court adjudicates the case.[184] Because a court could try a case in exactly the same way as a foreign court would, the international harmony of decisions would be promoted. Critics argue that forum shopping could also be adequately buttressed by adapting the rules on jurisdiction and that in any case the possible advantages are outweighed by the increased legal uncertainty.[185]

In the light of this controversy, Contracting Parties were, under art. 22 (1a), allowed to make a reservation and decide not to apply art. 7 (1). Germany, Ireland, Latvia, Luxembourg, Portugal, Slovenia and the United Kingdom made use of this possibility.[186] In the jurisdictions that did not make a reservation against art. 7 (1) courts have not been overwhelmingly enthusiastic in the application of foreign overriding mandatory provisions. It is hard to come up with examples where foreign overriding mandatory provisions have been applied by a court. This applies even in the Dutch *Alnati* case: the Hoge Raad did ultimately not apply the Belgian overriding mandatory provision because it found that Belgium did not have a sufficiently strong connection with the contract.

---

183 Kramer, L., "Return to Renvoi", *New York University Law Review*, Vol. 66, No. 4, 1991, pp. 979–1044 (1016); Chong, A., "The Public Policy and Mandatory Rules of Third Countries in International Contracts" *Journal of Private International Law*, Vol. 2, No. 1, 2006, pp. 27–70.

184 Bonomi, *supra* note 11, pp. 215–247.

185 Dickinson, *supra* note 179, pp. 86; Bogdan, *supra* note 164, pp. 680.

186 EU Council Agreements Office database at http://www.consilium.europa.eu/cms3_applications/Applications/accords/search.asp?lang=EN&cmsid=297, as of 15 March 2011.

In order for a court to give effect to foreign overriding mandatory provisions, art. 7 (1) Rome Convention requires that the foreign jurisdiction must classify the provision as overriding mandatory, that jurisdiction should have a close connection with the situation, and giving effect to the provision must be necessary in the light of its nature and purpose and consequences of their application or non-application. The classification of the overriding nature of the provision does therefore not depend upon the competent court, but upon the jurisdiction in which it originates.[187] What is to be regarded as crucial for the safeguard of the social or economical order of a state is in principle left to be determined by the state concerned itself.

Whereas the law in absence of a choice of law is determined on the principle of the closest connection, art. 7 (1) refers to 'close connection'. Although it is unclear what constitutes a close connection it is not unthinkable that a close connection could exist with several jurisdictions. This chance is increased because art. 7 (1) refers to 'situation' and not to a more narrow construction, e.g. 'contract'. It cannot be excluded that two jurisdictions with a close connection would require the application of each others' conflicting overriding mandatory provisions. The court seized would then be confronted with the difficult task of establishing which foreign overriding provision to give preference to. The national court may be inspired by the final criterion of art. 7 (1): the consequences of (non) application. It requires the weighing of interests.[188] Party autonomy would be unduly restricted if an overriding mandatory provision were to apply even though the goal it sought to promote is not affected in case of application or non-application.

2.4.3 *Article 9 (3) Rome I: A Solution to a Political Problem*

In the light of the failure of the Rome Convention to come up with a wording or solution that was that was acceptable to all Contracting

[187] A forum can only apply foreign overriding mandatory provisions if the foreign jurisdiction classifies those provisions as overriding mandatory, it does not prevent the national court from establishing whether the claimed scope is excessive. Pres. Rechtbank 's Gravenhage 17 September 1982 *Rechtspraak van de Week* (1982), 167.

[188] Bonomi *supra* note 11, pp. 235–239. Bonomi distinguishes between three interests, those of: 1) of the parties 2) the forum state 3) and the foreign state.

Parties it was not surprising that the controversy re-emerged in the transformation of the Convention into a Union instrument. The Commission proposed in art. 8 (3) to slightly redraft the wording of art. 7 (1) Rome Convention without changing it in substance.[189] The transformation of the Convention into a Regulation would forego the possibility for Member States to make a reservation. The United Kingdom realised it could not opt out of a specific provision and decided to use its special position under Title IV of the EC Treaty not to opt-in to the legislative process. The UK feared that London might lose its place as important centre of international arbitration due to a perceived increase in legal uncertainty and the threat for foreign litigants to be confronted with foreign public policy.[190] Art. 8 (3) was identified as one the key objections against Rome I. The desire to keep the United Kingdom onboard and facilitate the opt-in to the finalised document politicised the issue of foreign overriding mandatory provisions.

The European Parliament proposed to delete art. 8 (3) alltogether. The EP first referred to the reservations entered into by Germany, Ireland, Latvia, Luxembourg, Portugal, Slovenia and the United Kingdom. It repeated an argument that had often been raised by the United Kingdom: '*It is also considered that its discretionary nature, the uncertainty of the criteria which it employs and its potential breadth could detract from legal certainty and encourage speculative attempts to evade contractual obligations, thereby increasing uncertainty and risk for economic operators and entailing higher costs.*'[191]

---

[189] Art. 8 (3) of the proposal provided: 'Effect may be given to the mandatory rules of the law of another country with which the situation has a close connection. In considering whether to give effect to these mandatory rules, courts shall have regard to their nature and purpose in accordance with the definition in paragraph 1 and to the consequences of their application or non-application for the objective pursued by the relevant mandatory rules and for the parties.'

[190] Letter from Baroness Ashton of Upholland, Parliamentary Under Secretary of State, to Lord Grenfell, Chairman of the HL Select Committee on European Union, 16 May 2006; Note from General Secretariat of the Council to the Committee on Civil Law Matters (Rome I), 14708/06 JUSTCIV 240 CODEC 1219, 120: UK government 'We have serious concerns about the legal uncertainty inherent in this provision and the adverse economic consequences of that uncertainty, particularly in relation to complex financial transactions.' See as well: Financial Markets Law Committee, European Commission Final Proposal For a Regulation on the Law Applicable to Contractual Obligations (Rome I), April 2006, 8.

[191] Amendment 26, European Parliament Draft Report on COM(2005) 650, PE374.427.

The arguments raised by the EP show the political nature of the discussion. The same argument can be used against overriding mandatory provisions of the forum. Of course, the parallel between application of domestic overriding mandatory provisions and foreign overriding mandatory provisions can only be maintained up to a certain degree, but the legal certainty argument is being deployed selectively. Striking was the contrast with UK opposition to establish, in absence of a choice law, presumptions to indicate the jurisdiction with the closest connection. The presumptions reduce the difficulty of establishing the closest connection and significantly enhance legal certainty. The UK however feared it might lead to too much legal rigidity and favoured leaving a larger margin of discretion to the courts.[192] The UK's position is rather ambivalent but can be simply explained: the UK argued for the solutions that were already in place in its national legal orders.[193] Since the application of foreign overriding mandatory provisions has proven to be rare in practice and art. 8 (3) of the proposal would have created nothing more than a discretion for courts to take foreign overriding mandatory provisions into account, it may not be excluded that the strong opposition was pursued in order to gain a better bargaining position in other controversial topics such as cession, insurance or contracts of carriage.

In particular in a European justice area, which is characterised by a high degree of economic integration and mutual trust between the Member States, it would be unfeasible to completely ignore the overriding mandatory provisions of other Member States outside the *lex causae*.[194] The final version of Rome I contained a compromise, art. 9 (3) provides:

---

[192] UK Ministry of Justice, Rome I – should the UK opt in?, Consultation Paper CP05/08, 20–23.

[193] Harris, J., "Mandatory Rules and Public Policy under the Rome I Regulation", F. Ferrari and S. Leible, *Rome I Regulation: The Law Applicable to Contractual Obligations in Europe*, Sellier, Münich, 2009, pp. 269–342.

[194] The most recent PIL codifications outside the EU allow for a possibility to apply foreign overriding mandatory provisions. Reference can be made towards art. 3079 Code Civil du Québec, and art. 19 of the Swiss Private International Law Act (1987). See: Von Overbeck, A., "The Fate of Two Remarkable Provisions on the Swiss Statute on Private International Law", *Yearbook of Private International Law*, Vol. 1, 1999, pp. 119–133. On the other hand, art. 10 of the Venezuelan Private International Law Act (1998) does exclusively address overriding mandatory provisions of the forum. This is remarkable since art. 11 of the Inter-American Convention on the Law Applicable to International Contracts (1994) allows courts to give effect to overriding mandatory provisions.

> Effect may be given to the overriding mandatory provisions of the law of the country where the obligations arising out of the contract have to be or have been performed, in so far as those overriding mandatory provisions render the performance of the contract unlawful. In considering whether to give effect to those provisions, regard shall be had to their nature and purpose and to the consequences of their application or non-application.

The possibility of applying foreign overriding mandatory requirements is narrower than under the art. 7(1) of the Rome Convention and art. 8 (3) of the proposal. Effect shall be given to foreign overriding mandatory provisions of the *lex loci solutionis.* Art. 9 (3) approaches the solution under English law, which considers it to be an implied term to a contract that the contract is lawful according to the law of the place where it has to be performed. Rome I is however more restrictive than the common law doctrine. Under common law, English public policy would prevent upholding a contract that obliges the violation of the laws of a friendly State. Effect would be given to the overriding mandatory provisions of a friendly state if the parties to the contract wilfully breached the laws of that state. The typical example would be a contract to smuggle liquor to a friendly state that has prohibited the consumption of alcohol. The export of liquor does as such not contravene English public policy, but English courts would not want to offend a foreign sovereign. In a linguistic interpretation of art. 9 (3) there does not seem to be scope for the application of an overriding mandatory provision of a friendly state, unless performance of the contract happens to be required in that friendly state. The reason for exclusion of the doctrine can perhaps be sought on the continental emphasis on the separation of powers. Continental courts would not use concern for foreign relations or any other political ground as the basis for judicial reasoning.[195]

The UK also opposed the possibility of applying foreign overriding mandatory provisions in the Rome II Regulation. Art. 13 of the proposal provided the possibility for the forum to give effect to both its own overriding mandatory provisions as well as foreign overriding mandatory provisions. In art. 16 of the final version of the Rome II Regulation only the first possibility was maintained. The reason for the deletion of the latter possibility must again mainly be sought in the

---

[195] Bonomi *supra* note 11, 238.

position of the United Kingdom.[196] Although it is certainly correct that private autonomy has a stronger role in Rome I and Rome II and that art. 17 Rome II provides for the possibility to pay regard to the safety standards of the *lex loci delecti*, the difference in approach between the instruments cannot be fully explained from a legal perspective. Overriding mandatory provisions are broader than safety standards, and the application[197] of the overriding mandatory provisions of the forum is not adjusted to fit the different role of party autonomy. The advantage of the possibility of applying foreign overriding mandatory provisions is that a choice of court will also not enable evasion of the application of overriding mandatory provisions. If there exists no possibility for applying foreign overriding mandatory provisions, parties to a tort may, just like parties to a contract, resort to clever forum selection. The political nature of the compromises has lead to an inconsistent approach in the Rome instruments. The complete absence of foreign overriding mandatory provisions in Rome II and the limitation to overriding mandatory rules from the *lex loci solutionis* in Rome cannot be explained on the basis of the regulations. From a perspective of better law-making, as well as from a perspective of legal certainty, this has to be regretted. It is left up to lawyers to create some order in the chaos.

2.4.4 *Discretion or General Obligation to Apply Overriding Mandatory Provisions of Other Member States*

It has been argued that although the Rome instruments confer upon courts the possibility of applying foreign overriding mandatory provisions; Union law imposes a general duty to give effect to the overriding mandatory provisions of other Member States. Lang observes that the

---

[196] House of Lords, European Law Committee, 8th Report of Session 2003–2004, HL Paper 66, Report with evidence: The Rome II Regulation, in particular points 146 and 200. See also: Memorandum by R. Fentiman to European Law Committee, http://www.parliament.the-stationery-office.com/pa/ld200304/ldselect/ldeucom/66/66we10.htm, as of March 15, 2011.

[197] The Dutch State Committee on PIL mentioned health and safety standards in the Wet conflictenrecht cnrechtmatige daad (law on the law applicable to non-contractual obligations) specifically as an example of overriding mandatory provisions. Staatscommissie voor het Internationaal Privaatrecht, Rapport Algemene Bepalingen Wet Internationaal Privaatrecht (2002), par. 56. Art. 17 Rome II would exclude a rule of foreign competition law since it cannot be considered to be a health or safety standard. That may give rise to a problem under art. 6 (3b) Rome II.

principle of loyal cooperation (art. 4 TEU) requires Member States to take no action *'that could unnecessary or unjustifiably cause harm to another Member State'*. The prosperity of Member States is seen as a Union objective.[198] One could read into this analysis an obligation to apply an overriding mandatory provision of another Member State when the non-application would cause unnecessary or unjustifiable harm to the other Member State.

Another line is advanced by Israël.[199] He argues that public interests can be a justification to a restriction of one of the free movement provisions. In his opinion, the Member State is taking care of a Union objective that is not yet regulated by Union law. That is demonstrated by the fact that Member States may sometimes be under a duty to intervene. Member States are bound to assist each other in the implementation of Union law. Whenever an overriding mandatory provision is adopted on the basis of duty to regulate under Union law, other Member States should, as a matter of sincere cooperation, assist.[200] That obligation might work with regard to circumstances when there is duty of positive action, but has no general application. Union law allows Member States to apply a certain rule. Allowing Member States to apply a rule is however something different from requiring a Member State to apply its legislation. The decision to protect the public interest is within the discretion of the Member State involved; a Member State would not be in breach of its obligations under Union law if it failed to enact a measure for the protection of its cultural heritage. Union law cannot impose a duty upon Member States to regulate on areas not yet covered by harmonisation.

A third line of reasoning emphasises the special status of overriding mandatory provisions of other Member States. The free movement provisions are an effective guarantee against an excessive scope of application. European integration has reached such a degree that there exists a common consensus on social and economical policy. The legitimacy of those foreign overriding mandatory provisions paves the way

---

[198] Lang, T., "Community Constitutional Law: Article 5 EEC Treaty", *Common Market Law Review*, Vol. 27, 1990, pp. 645–682 (677).

[199] Israël, J., *European Cross-Border Insolvency Regulation*, Intersentia, Antwerpen, 2005, pp. 129–138; Israël, J., and K. Saarloos, "Europees Internationaal Privaat- en procesrecht", A. Hartkamp, C. Sieburg, L. Keus (eds.) *Serie Onderneming en Recht deel 42-II*, Deventer, Kluwer, 2007, pp. 629–698.

[200] That duty has now codified in art. 4 (3) TEU: 'Pursuant to the principle of sincere cooperation, the Union and the Member States shall, in full mutual respect, assist each other in carrying out tasks which flow from the Treaties'.

for an analogy with the governmental interest analysis in the US that supposedly, by taking the policies of the legislative policies as a basis for deciding the applicable law, presupposes a duty to give effect to the overriding mandatory provisions of other US states. The social and economical like-mindedness, combined with the legitimacy of the foreign overriding mandatory provisions, would justify a duty to apply the overriding mandatory provisions of other Member States. Even if social and economical like-mindedness could be authority for an obligation to apply the overriding mandatory provisions of the like-minded, it can be doubted whether European integration has reached such a degree of convergence.[201]

The second and third line of reasoning has some parallel with art. Art. VII section 2(b) IMF Agreement. When an exchange control is imposed in conformity with the IMF Agreement, contracts in contravention of that exchange control are unenforceable in other Contracting States. Similarly, contracts in violation of an overriding mandatory provision imposed in conformity with the TFEU would be unenforceable in other Member States. Exchange contracts are however a specific category of contracts and it does not appear the same reasoning could be expanded to contracts in general.

A fourth line of reasoning argues that Member States have, in the TFEU, committed themselves to the creation of an internal market. If the application of an overriding mandatory provision would completely depend upon the forum chosen, it would lead to the risk of divergent decisions between the Member States. The purported creation of an internal market can only be furthered by enhancing the international harmony of decisions. Due to the coexistence of multiple national legal systems, Member States are, as a matter of loyal cooperation, bound to reduce as far as possible the risk of resulting conflicts and frictions.[202]

There is definitely something to be said for the argument that overriding mandatory provisions from Member States are to be treated differently from overriding mandatory provisions from third countries since mutual trust in the conflict of laws system of other Member States is one of the pillars of Union PIL. This trust is most apparent in art.

---

[201] Fetsch, J., *Eingriffsnormen und EG-Vertrag*, Mohr Siebeck, Tübingen, 2002, pp. 237–239.

[202] Von Wilmowsky, P., "EG-Vertrag und kollisionsrechtliche Rechtswahlfreiheit", *RabelsZ*, Vol. 62, 1998, pp. 1–37, (25). Bonomi *supra* note 189, pp. 241.

33–58 Brussels I, where Member States only have limited possibilities to refuse the recognition or enforcement of a judicial order given in another Member State.[203] A general duty to apply the overriding mandatory provisions of other Member States would, in my opinion, be too far-reaching and would in any case not find any support in Union law.[204] It would go against the rationale of Rome I that allows courts in Member States to apply their own overriding mandatory provisions, why should the discretion be converted into an obligation when foreign overriding mandatory provisions are at stake?

The application of foreign overriding mandatory provisions has thus proven to be far more controversial than the application of overriding mandatory provisions of the forum. Art. 7 (1) Rome Convention was one of the most controversial provisions of that instrument. Although it seems to be impossible in a common European Justice Area to completely ignore the core public policy provisions of other Member States, the significant financial interests at stake in international arbitration have been able to politicise the discussion. As a result, the compromise reached in art. 9 (3) Rome I does not win any awards for legal coherency. It is both narrower than the Rome Convention and the pre-existing common law doctrine. Moreover the compromise is not consistent with the approach the approach taken by the Union legislator in other recent PIL codifications. It should therefore be hoped that the ECJ will not stick to a too formalistic interpretation of art. 9 (3), emphasising the mandatory nature of the Regulation, but rather that it will develop a more legally sound solution. It is however submitted that the interpretation which holds that, despite the codification in the Regulation of the possibility of applying foreign overriding mandatory provisions, there may be a general duty under Union law to apply foreign overriding mandatory provisions when it concerns those of other Member States is too far-reaching and has no basis in Union law.

---

[203] See for example: Case C-798 *Krombach v. Bamberski* [2000] ECR I-1395; Case C-394/07 *Gambazzi* [2009] ECR I-2563. See: Kramer, X., "Enforcement Under the Brussels Convention: Procedural Public Policy and the Influence of Article 6 ECHR", *International Lis*, 2003, pp. 16–20.

[204] Similar: Roth, W., "Der Einfluß des Europäischen Gemeinschaftsrechts auf das Internationale Privatrecht", *RabelsZ*, Vol. 55, 1991, pp. 623–673; Sonnenberger, H., "Eingriffsrecht – Das trojanische Pferd im IPR oder notwendige Ergänzung?", *IPRax*, 2003, pp. 114. Kuckein, *supra* note 165, pp. 62–63.

2.5 *Party Autonomy, Protective Connecting Factors and Overriding Mandatory Provisions*

Overriding mandatory provisions are thus a narrowly defined exception to the normal conflict of laws mechanism, in order to safeguard core state policies and correct private autonomy. However, they are certainly not the only limitation upon private autonomy in Rome I. What is the relationship between overriding mandatory provisions and other limitations upon private autonomy? It has already been observed that whereas traditionally the primary function of overriding mandatory provisions was aimed at the protection of state interests in private law, a second generation of overriding mandatory provisions emerged, which primarily protected the weaker party. Especially in cases of choice of law, weaker parties are in a vulnerable position since consumers and employees usually do not have the ability to oversee the consequences of a choice of law or a choice of law is imposed upon them.

The Rome Convention introduced connecting factors with regard to consumers (art. 5) and employees (art. 6) that tried to compensate the weaker party for any potential negative consequences of a choice of law. A choice of law could not deprive the consumer from the protection offered to him by the mandatory rules of the place where he had his habitual residence and a choice of law could not deprive the employee from the mandatory protection of the law of the place where he habitually carried out his work. Has Rome I thus two cumulative mechanisms to protect the same weaker party? Or, to what extent is the role of second generation overriding mandatory provisions limited by these 'protective' connecting factors?

2.5.1 *Distinguishing Between First and Second Generation Overriding Mandatory Provisions*

From the outset it must be observed that the distinction whether a provision is primarily aimed at the protection of a weaker party or also serves a state interest is difficult to make and may in some cases even appear arbitrary. Every rule aimed at the protection of a weaker party can be phrased in such a way that it also protects a higher good and *vice versa*. Does for example the Dutch provision that requires an employer to ask authorisation prior to dismissal from a governmental body primarily protect the employee against unfair dismissal or does the provision aim to regulate the labour market as a whole?[205] Reasonable arguments can be made for either position and the final answer is unclear. There is no single criterion that allows one to effectively distinguish between provisions that protect an individual interest and those provisions that protect the interest of a state. The question boils down to a matter of degree.[206]

The distinction between first and second generation overriding mandatory provisions becomes relevant in the light of the discussion whether second generation overriding mandatory provisions are at all covered by art. 9 Rome I. German authors in particular have argued that overriding mandatory provisions in principle only protect the interests of a state. The German doctrine does not require a rigid distinction between first and second generation overriding mandatory provisions, but for the application of art. 7 Rome Convention instead required that a provision should not protect purely private interests, but also a public interest. The protection of the public interest must be an aim as such and not merely ancilliary to the protection of the private interest. Aware of the numerous controversies, the Commission asked stakeholders in the Green Paper for the conversion of the Rome Convention into a Regulation whether it was necessary to clarify the meaning of 'mandatory provisions' in art. 3, 5, 6 and 7 of the Rome Convention.[207] In their reactions, stakeholders mostly commented upon the distinction between mandatory and internationally mandatory norms, and one stakeholder advanced that the proposal of the Commission did in fact not contribute at all in solving the problems concerning the relationship between art. 5 and 6 on the one hand, and art. 7 on the other hand.[208]

---

[205] The Hoge Raad has clarified that the authorisation is not required when the effects of a dismissal are not felt on the Dutch labour market, even though the law governing the employment contract is Dutch. The provision is therefore primarily concerned with the well-being of the Dutch labour market rather than the protection of the individual employee. Hoge Raad 5 June 1953, *Nederlandse Jurisprudentie* (1953), 613 (Melchers); Hoge Raad 23 oktober 1987, *Nederlandse Jurisprudentie* (1988), 842 (Sorensen).

[206] Bucher, *supra* note 135.

[207] Commission Green Paper Rome I Regulation COM (2002) 654 final, question 13. See: Bonomi, A., "Conversion of the Rome Convention on Contracts into an EC Instrument: Some Remarks on the Green Paper of the EC Commission", *Yearbook of Private International Law*, Vol. 5, 2003, pp. 53–98.

[208] Van Hoek, A., reaction to Green Paper, available at: http://ec.europa.eu/justice_home/news/consulting_public/rome_i/news_summary_rome1_en.htm, as of 15 March 2011.

The 37th recital to Rome I provides that considerations of public interest may justify, in exceptional cases, the application of overriding mandatory provisions. As already described, art. 9 (1) Rome I gives no limitative definition of public interests; it merely states that it includes a state's political, social or economical organisation. Despite the criterion of 'public interest' it cannot be concluded that art. 9 (1) only allows for the application of first generation overriding mandatory provisions. Public interest is not a synonym for state interest. It cannot be excluded that certain provisions of consumer or labour protection law will be classified as being overriding mandatory because a Member State considers such rules as fundamental principles of its political, social or economical organisation, and hence belong to its public interest.[209] Concerning the relationship between the protective connecting factors and art. 9, the 37th recital states: '*The concept of 'overriding mandatory provisions' should be distinguished from the expression 'provisions which cannot be derogated from by agreement' and should be construed more restrictively.*' It however fails to indicate how one should distinguish between the two concepts.

It is regrettable that the transformation of the Rome Convention into Rome I has not been seized as an opportunity to clarify the scope of overriding mandatory provisions. The Giuliano-Lagarde report identified consumer protection as such as one of the categories of rules that fall within the scope of art. 7 (2) Rome Convention.[210] German authors have however argued that second generation overriding mandatory provisions fall outside the scope of art. 7 Rome Convention.[211] The relationship between art. 29/30 EGBGB, the German provisions implementing arts. 5 and 6 Rome Convention, and art. 34 EGBGB is mutually exclusive; a provision can serve either the individual interests of the weaker party or public interests. Although the argument certainly holds water that the mandatory provisions which are applied on the basis of special connecting factors for consumer and labour contracts

---

[209] Max Planck Institute, *supra* note 125.

[210] Giulano-Lagarde report, electronically available at http://www.rome-convention.org/instruments/i_rep_lagarde_en.htm, as of 15 March 2011.

[211] Von Bar, C., and P. Mankowski, *Internationales Privatrecht, Band I: Allgemeine Lehren*, Beck'sche Verlagsbuchhandlung, München 2. Auflage, 2003, pp. 267. Kropholler, *supra* note 123, pp. 493–496. Discussion and references: Junker, A., "Empfiehlt es sich, Art. 7 EVÜ zu revidieren oder aufgrund der bisherigen Erfahrungen zu präzisieren?", *IPRax*, Vol. 20, 2000, pp. 65–73.

are limited to protective mandatory provisions,[212] the Rome instruments do not assume to exhaustively list all weaker parties. For example, art. 7 of the Rome I proposal introduced also a special connecting factor for agents, but was ultimately deleted from the final text.[213] If one were to adopt the German position it would mean that agents would not enjoy any protection at all. The same would apply to consumers that fall outside the scope of art. 5, such as the active consumer.[214]

Another academic view is that the provision that affords the highest standard of protection to the weaker party should prevail. Second generation overriding mandatory provisions should be applied when they increase the level of protection afforded by the law of the place of habitual residence of the consumer.[215] The principle of most favourable treatment however necessitates an analysis of what is the better law in the specific circumstances and will undoubtedly increase legal uncertainty. PIL is not well-equipped for an analysis of what from a substantive point of view, the 'better' law is.[216] It should moreover be questioned whether a system which compensates the weaker party for its vulnerable position in PIL should be used to enhance consumer and labour protection. Why should a Spanish consumer enjoy more protection when he enters into a contract with a Swedish undertaking on the Spanish market than his Spanish neighbour who enters into the same contract with a Spanish undertaking?

In the academic debate a middle positions is taken by giving arts. 5 and 6 Rome Convention relative priority over art. 7. Second generation mandatory provisions are then generally not applied, while mandatory consumer and labour protection rules are generally not seen as overriding mandatory.[217] English authors seem to favour the reverse. Art. 7 operates as an exception to the normal rules of the Convention:

> This suggests that Article 7 (2) should be regarded as a general exception to *all* the choice of law rules contained in the Convention, in the same

---

[212] The Giulano-Lagarde report states that art. 5 'should be interpreted in the light of its purpose which is to protect the weaker party'.

[213] Proposal for a Regulation on the Law applicable to contractual obligations, COM (2005) 650 final.

[214] This conclusion was indeed drawn by the Bundesgerichtshof, see: Bundesgerichtshof 19 March 1997 VIII ZR 316/96, 135.

[215] Kaye, P., *The New International Law of Contract of the European Community*, Aldershot, Brookfield, 1993, 263.

[216] Kegel/Schurig, *supra* note 120, pp. 131.

[217] Mankowski, P., "Keine Sonderanknüpfung deutschen Verbraucherschutzrechts über Art. 34 EGBGB", *Deutsche Zeitschrift fuer Wirtschaftsrecht*, 1996, pp. 273–280.

> way that public policy, which is more clearly worded in this respect, provides such an exception. This means that the special rules for particular issues, such as formal validity, and for special contracts will also be overridden.[218]

The Bundesgerichtshof held in 2005 that in order to trigger the application of art. 34 EGBGB, the provision implementing art. 7 (2) Rome Convention into the German legal order, a rule must promote at least a state interest. The Bundesgerichtshof subsequently refused to classify a provision of the *Verbraucherkreditgesetzes* (consumer credit law) as overriding mandatory because it was primarily aimed at the protection of the consumer and the German public interest was only subsidiary.[219]

The decision of the Bundesgerichtshof conflicts with the approach of the Cour de Cassation. In 1999 the latter already held that certain provisions of the *loi sur le crédit a la consummation* should be classified as overriding mandatory.[220] The Cour de Cassation was not concerned with the fact that the loi was primarily aimed at the protection of the consumer. Indeed, the Cour de Cassation did not limit the protection afforded by overriding mandatory provisions to consumers or employees, or even natural persons. In 2007 it classified two articles of the law on subcontracting that provided a claim to the subcontractor in case of insolvency of the main contractor against the *maître de l'ouvrage*.[221] The aim of the loi was the protection of the subcontractor, who was considered, as a Small or Medium sized Enterprise (SME), to be in a weaker position vis-à-vis the main contractor and the *maître de l'ouvrage*.

2.5.2 *The Position of the ECJ*

The ECJ has until now not had the opportunity to rule whether art. 7 Rome Convention covers second generation overriding mandatory

[218] North, P., and J. Fawcett, *Cheshire and North's Private International Law*, Butterworths, London, Thirteenth Edition, 1999, pp. 583.

[219] Bundesgerichtshof 13 December 2005 XI ZR 82/05.

[220] Cour de Cassation 19 October 1999, *Revue Critique de Droit International Privé*, 2000, pp. 29–34 (note P. Lagarde). The case is slightly more complex since the facts fell outside the temporal scope of the Rome Convention. The CdC therefore applied *lois de police* that existed in French case-law, a provision similar to art. 5 Rome Convention did however not exist.

[221] Cour de Cassation 30 November 2007, n° 260. The decision has been confirmed in: Cour de Cassation 25 February 2009, 07–20096.

provisions. The decision in *Ingmar* suggests, however, that the ECJ would answer such a question in the affirmative.[222] In *Ingmar*, the parties to an agency agreement had made a choice of law in favour of Californian law (the place of establishment of the principal) while the agent performed its activities in the United Kingdom. Arts. 17 and 18 of Directive 86/653 (Commercial Agents Directive) were aimed at guaranteeing the rights of the agent, who was considered to be the weaker party, after the termination of the agency agreement. The question arose whether these articles, notwithstanding the choice of law, should apply. Although the judgement itself only refers to mandatory provisions, the Court discussed the applicability of those rules regardless the *lex causae* and it must therefore be concluded that the Court actually referred to overriding mandatory provisions. The Court held that the articles in question were aimed at ensuring the freedom of establishment and the undistorted competition of the internal market, and were therefore essential for the functioning of the Union legal order. Despite the language of the Court it appears that the safeguard of the internal market was subsidiary to the protection of the agent since in the case at hand there appeared to be no real impact upon the internal market. Rather, the agent was protected against the deprivation of rights resulting from a choice of law.

The use of the internal market criterion may reveal the true reasoning of the ECJ, which in general strives for a uniform interpretation of Union instruments regardless whether the situation is wholly internal to the EU or has foreign elements. A wide scope of application of a directive to situations not wholly related to the internal market is perceived to enhance the uniform application of the directive to situations involving the internal market. The same interpretation technique can be discovered with regard to directives that address the functioning of the internal market but are interpreted to cover also situations that are completely internal to a Member State.[223] This concern with the uniform application of directives makes 'EU private law' differ on this point from national private law.

---

[222] Case 381/98 *Ingmar* [2000], ECR I-9305. The consequences for the German approach are described in: Reich, N., and H. Micklitz, *Europäisches Verbraucherrecht*, Nomos Verlagsgesellschaft, Baden-Baden, 4. Auflage, 2003, pp. 479–482.

[223] Case C-465/00 *Rechnungshof v Österreichischer Rundfunk and Others* [2002] ECR I-4989; Case C-101/01 *Lindqvist* [2003] ECR I-12971;

2.5.3 *Public or Private Interest in Article 9 (1) Rome I?*

In the process of drafting art. 9 Rome I, certain German authors proposed to clearly differentiate between first and second generation overriding mandatory provisions,[224] although the suggestion was not been incorporated in the final document. The final definition of overriding mandatory provisions in art. 9 (1) does not provide sufficient clarity. Moreover, there is no evidence to indicate that the European legislator intended in this respect to overturn *Ingmar*. It can therefore be presumed that second generation overriding mandatory provisions are not out of principle ineligible to be caught by art. 9 (1) Rome I.

The presumption that second generation overriding mandatory provisions are caught by art. 9 Rome I follows from the rationale of both Rome instruments. The Rome Convention, as most notably reflected in Germany, lifted the overriding mandatory provisions out of the *ordre public* exception in favour of an autonomous position. The abandonment of the perception that overriding mandatory provisions are positive operations of the *ordre public*, and towards overriding mandatory provisions, which have as their primary focus the limitation of the principle of choice of law, shifts the focus from pursuing a state policy to correcting private autonomy. Whereas one may doubt whether the protection of an individual is pursuing a state polity in a strict sense, there is no principal objection against the limitation of the choice of law in favour of weaker parties. It might be true that there is a fundamental difference between the first and second generation overriding mandatory provisions; the first tries to avoid that parties to a contract unjustifiably externalise costs whereas the second is aimed at preventing that the stronger party from unjustifiably transferring costs in a contract to its weaker opponent. In the second case the costs are contained within the contract and there is in theory still the choice for the weaker party not to conclude, and thus avoid the transfer of costs, the contract at all. The underlying principle, however, remains the same: both the first and second generation overriding mandatory provisions aim to prevent a choice of law that leads to an unjustifiable transferral of costs.[225]

---

[224] Mankowski, P., "Der Vorschlag für die Rom I-Verordnung", *IPRax*, Vol. 26, No. 2, 2006, pp. 101–113 (103).

[225] To what extent Rome I solves the controversy from the light of the pre-existing national practices, see par. 3.5.2.

Limitation of party autonomy may thus occur for two reasons. The first is in order to prevent that party autonomy be used by the stronger party to unjustifiably transfer costs to the weaker party. In that sense, the protection functions as a procedural guarantee for the genuine exercise of party autonomy. The second is to avoid the abuse of private autonomy to protect a greater good. There would be a genuine meeting of minds if parties to a waste processing contract were to agree to make their contract subject to a different law in order to avoid the prohibition of contracting with foreign waste producers. In such circumstances it would be unfeasible if the parties could by opting for a different private law, avoid the legislative policy concerned.[226]

If the limitation of the party autonomy is considered to be the core that underlies art. 9 Rome I, the question of priority of articles within the Rome I can be abandoned. Instead the focus should shift towards the question to what extent the protected interest is already realised by arts. 6 and 8.[227] The complexity of the matter merits a separate analysis.

2.5.4 *Consumers*

The Rome instruments favour the application of the law of the habitual residence of the party that delivers the goods or renders the service, in other words the party who has to render the most characteristic performance. The party rendering the characteristic performance will statistically be often a 'repeat player' and will be the most adversely affected by the applicability of varying legal regimes. Applying the law of the party that renders the characteristic performance thus promotes efficiency by allowing the 'repeat player' to anticipate his behaviour on the basis of a single law without having to make a choice of law. The application of this rule to business to consumer relations could, however, lead to unjust results since it would in Business to Consumer (B to C) cases structurally favour the economically stronger party.[228]

---

[226] Such a prohibition could justified on environmental grounds as well as public health reasons since 'waste is matter of a special kind whose accumulation, even before it becomes a health hazard, constitutes a danger to the environment, regard being had in particular to the limited capacity of each region or locality for waste reception, and secondly, such a prohibition cannot be regarded as discriminatory, in view of the principle that environmental damage should as a priority be rectified at source'. Case C-2/90 *Commission v Belgium* [1992] ECR I-4431.

[227] Fetsch, *supra* note 201, 41.

[228] Solomon, D., "The Private International Law of Contracts in Europe: Advances and Retreats", *Tulane Law Review*, Vol. 82, 2008, pp. 1709–1740 (1715–1717).

2.5.5 *Article 5 Rome Convention*

Article 5 (3) Rome Convention modified the presumption of the closest connection to a bias which favours the application of the law of the consumer. A choice of law in consumer contracts for the delivery of a good or the provision of a service is still possible, but may be subject to closer scrutiny. For example, the Cour de Cassation excluded the possibility of an implicit choice of law in consumer contracts.[229] In any case, in light of the stronger bargaining position of the professional, it was considered to be feasible to protect the consumer as opposed to a 'take it or leave it' choice of law clause in a contract. A protective mechanism should, it was thought, step in because it cannot be maintained that in such clauses a genuine meeting of minds has occurred.[230] The article provided that a choice of law made by the parties would not result in the deprivation of the protection afforded to the consumer by the mandatory rules of the law of the country in which the consumer has his habitual residence 'if (I) in that country the conclusion of the contract was preceded by a specific invitation addressed to him or by advertising, and he had taken in that country all the steps necessary on his part for the conclusion of the contract, or (II) the other party or his agent received the consumer's order in that country, or (III) the contract is for the sale of goods and the consumer travelled from that country to another country and there gave his order, provided that the consumer's journey was arranged by the seller for the purpose of inducing the consumer to buy.' A choice of law thus did not have the effect of evading the mandatory provisions of the law of the place where the consumer has his habitual residence. The choice of law however still had effect. The result was a complicated situation whereby the contract was governed by the law chosen by the parties while at the same time the mandatory provisions of the law of place of the habitual residence of the consumer had to be applied. Both were applied in parallel.

Art. 5 was subject to strong criticism and therefore altered in the Rome I proposal.[231] Art. 5 of the proposal declared the law of the place

---

229 Cour de Cassation 12 July 2005, 02-16915.

230 Mohamed Mahmoud, M., "Loi d'autonomie et méthodes de protection de la partie faible et droit international privé", *Recueil des Cours*, Vol. 315, 2005, pp. 141–264.

231 Mankowski, *supra* note 224, pp. 102; Rammeloo, *supra* note 134, pp. 239, 239–253; Schurr, F., "The relevance of the European consumer protection law for the development of the European Contract Law", *Victoria University of Wellington Law Review*, vol. 38, 2007, pp. 131–144; Wilderspin, *supra* note 26, pp. 268–270.

of habitual residence of the consumer applicable and gave no effect to a choice of law made by the parties. One could argue that all mandatory consumer laws had in fact become overriding mandatory provisions. It contained no limitation in respect of the subject matter of the consumer contract. The Commission argued that while both acceptance of the mandatory applicability of the law of the place of establishment of the undertaking and the law of the place of the habitual residence of the consumer could solve the legal complexities, only the latter option would be truly compatible with the high level of consumer protection that is required by the Treaty.[232] The proposed art. 5 was subject to fierce objections, mainly that it would create too great of a burden for smaller companies, and taking away the freedom to choose the applicable law would do more harm than good.[233]

2.5.6 *Article 6 Rome I*

The final version of Rome I opted for yet another solution.[234] Art. 6 no longer imposes any requirements with regard to the object of the contract. The special regime thus applies to all consumer contracts and not only to those which have as their object the sale of goods or the provision of services. Art. 6 provides that consumer contracts shall be governed by the law of the place where the consumer has his habitual residence, provided that the other party (I) 'pursues his commercial or professional activities in the country where the consumer has his habitual residence, or (II) by any means, directs such activities to that country or to several countries including that country'. Moreover, the contract must be concluded as a consequence of the targeting. A choice of law in favour of another law can still be made, but may not lead to the deprivation of protection afforded to the consumer by mandatory provisions of law of the place of the habitual residence of the consumer. The solution reached corresponds to art. 15 Brussels I, which contains special rules for jurisdiction in consumer contracts.[235]

---

232 Proposal for a Regulation on the Law applicable to contractual obligations, COM (2005) 650 final, 9.

233 Note from the Luxembourg Delegation on the Rome I Proposal, 2005/0261 (COD), 9670/07.

234 Ragno, F., "The Law Applicable to Consumer Contracts under the Rome I Regulation", F. Ferrari and S. Leible, *Rome I Regulation: The Law Applicable to Contractual Obligations in Europe*, Sellier, Münich, 2009, pp. 129–170.

235 Recital 24 to Rome I calls for a harmonious interpretation of art. 6 with art. 15 Brussels I, in the light of the joint declaration by the Council and the Commission on Article 15 of Regulation (EC) No 44/2001.

In particular as regards E-Commerce, the targeting criterion does not solve all problems. Instead of providing specific rules on e-commerce it was preferred to generalise the protective connecting factor so as to include e-contracts. It is not precisely clear when a website directs its activities to a certain market. Is the fact that a website is accessible from a Member State and the professional is willing to receive orders from that Member State sufficient? Factors such as language and currency used are not decisive.[236] The professional would suffer severe burdens if he were to operate on a global level and be subject to the different consumer laws of every jurisdiction. However since the professional can limit on his website the jurisdictions to whom he is willing to sell (ring-fencing),[237] he is in the best position to avoid the conflict of laws risk. For example, in the context of the online sale of music, companies have been able to distinguish between consumers from the different Member States on the basis of the billing address coupled to a credit card.[238] In *Pammer*, the ECJ found that the mere accessibility of a website was not sufficient to fulfil the targeting criterion.[239] The professional should have had the intention of contracting with foreign consumers, which may be evidenced by the mentioning of a telephone number with an international code, the use of a top-level domain name other than that of the Member State in which the trader is established, the mention of an international clientele composed of customers domiciled in various Member States or the language and currency used on the webiste.

Art. 6 thus simplifies, but maintains, the approach of art. 5 Rome Convention.[240] The criticised hybrid in consumer matters has been

---

[236] Gillies, L., "Choice-of-law Rules for Electronic Consumer Contracts: Replacement of the Rome Convention by the Rome I Regulation", *Journal of Private International Law*, Vol. 3, No. 1, 2007, pp. 89–112.

[237] Øren, J., "International Jurisdiction over Consumer Contracts in e-Europe", *International Comparative Law Quarterly*, Vol. 52, 2003, pp. 665–696; Smith, G., *Internet Law and Regulation*, Sweet & Maxwell, London, 2007, pp. 495–497.

[238] The music industry differentiated in prices between the Member States and refused to supply to some Member States on the grounds of insufficient protection against illegal copying. Farrand, B., "The Case that Never Was: An Analysis of the Apple iTunes Case Presented by the Commission and Potential Future Issues", *European Intellectual Property Law Review*, Vol. 31, 2009, pp. 508–513.

[239] Joined cases C-585/08 *Pammer v Reederei Karl Schlüter GmbH & Co KG* and C-144/09 *Hotel Alpenhof GesmbH v Olivier Heller* [2010] ECR I-0000. Both questions arose in the context of art. 15 (1c) Brussels I Regulation.

[240] Ragno, F., "The Law Applicable to Consumer Contracts under the Rome I Regulation", F. Ferrari and S. Leible, *Rome I Regulation: The Law Applicable to Contractual Obligations in Europe*, Münich: Sellier, 2009, pp. 129–170; Pizzolante, G., "I contratti con i consumatori e la nuova disciplina comunitaria in material di legge

maintained. Both the chosen law and the mandatory consumer law of the law of the place of habitual residence of the consumer are applied in parallel. Although the automatic application of the law of the habitual residence of the consumer might have been too intrusive for international trade, another solution was available. It would have been possible to give the professional the possibility to annul the choice of law and opt for the application of the entire law of the consumer. Although it was the professional who would have instigated the choice of law, what detriment would the consumer have suffered if the non-mandatory rules of his jurisdiction had also applied? Even if the consumer would have suffered detriment, what justifies the internationality bonus for consumers in a situation that is from their perspective an internal one? Art. 6 aims to protect the consumer against the negative consequences of a choice of law, but is not interested in raising the substantive level of consumer protection. Allowing the professional to annul the choice of law altogether would not therefore conflict with the rationale behind art. 6 (2). The consumer is protected against an imposed choice of law in an environment where he can assume that the law of his own jurisdiction will apply, but is not afforded any substantive protection.

Overriding mandatory provisions are thus at the same time wider and narrower than art. 6 Rome I. Narrower in the sense that overriding mandatory rules are always mandatory rules in the national sense, but mandatory rules are not necessarily mandatory on the international plane. Art. 6 thus refers to a wider set of norms. On the other hand, the scope of application of art. 9 is wider. Unlike the mandatory provisions, overriding mandatory provisions are not limited in the system in which they originate but may impose themselves upon the *lex causae*. Secondly, overriding mandatory provisions are not limited to situations involving a choice of law, but they can also be applied at the expense of the *lex causae* established on the basis of the objective connecting factors.

The status of consumer is in itself insufficient to trigger the application of art. 6 Rome I. The active consumer, the consumer who

applicablile obbiligazioni contrattuali", *Cuadernos de Derecho Transnacional*, Vol. 1, 2009, pp. 221–236.

approaches the professional out of his own initiative, is thus excluded.[241] Moreover, art. 6 (4) provides:

> Paragraphs 1 and 2 shall not apply to:
>
> (a) a contract for the supply of services where the services are to be supplied to the consumer exclusively in a country other than that in which he has his habitual residence;
> (b) a contract of carriage other than a contract relating to package travel within the meaning of Council Directive 90/ 314/EEC of 13 June 1990 on package travel, package holidays and package tours;
> (c) a contract relating to a right in rem in immovable property or a tenancy of immovable property other than a contract relating to the right to use immovable properties on a timeshare basis within the meaning of Directive 94/47/EC;
> (d) rights and obligations which constitute a financial instrument and rights and obligations constituting the terms and conditions governing the issuance or offer to the public and public take-over bids of transferable securities, and the subscription and redemption of units in collective investment undertakings in so far as these activities do not constitute provision of a financial service;
> (e) a contract concluded within the type of system falling within the scope of Article 4(1)(h).

The reason why the main rule of art. 6 Rome I does not apply to these contracts are various. When a service contract is performed outside the place of habitual residence of the consumer the connection with that place is not obvious and application of that law might lead to unfeasible results. Applying the law of the place of habitual residence of the consumer to the 'Big Bus Tour' in London, for example, would, even if a website accessible in various national languages specifically invites consumers to purchase their tickets in advance,[242] impose an unreasonable burden upon the company. The extension of the material scope of the provision made exceptions to specific type of contracts necessary.[243]

---

241 Stone, P., reaction to Green Paper, available at: http://ec.europa.eu/justice_home/news/consulting_public/rome_i/news_summary_rome1_en.htm, as of 15 March 2011.

242 Big Bus Tours London, http://www.bigbustours.com/eng/london/book_tickets.aspx, as of 15 March 2011.

243 Garcimartin Alfarez, F., "The Rome I Regulation: Exceptions to the Rule on Consumers Contracts and Financial Instruments", *Journal of Private International Law*, Vol. 5, No. 1, 2009, pp. 85–103.

With regard to the contracts referred to in sub (d) and (e) it was perceived that it was undesirable that different laws could be applied to each of the instruments issued, '*therefore changing their nature and preventing their fungible trading and offering*.'[244] The underlying rationale is that, with regard to insurance contracts and contracts of carriage, the appropriate level of protection should be set by specific provisions.[245] The reason for the exclusion of the main rule to these contracts lies thus rather in the peculiarities of the contract rather than in consumer protection.

2.5.7 *The Residual Function of Overriding Mandatory Provisions*

When the interest of the consumer has not been taken into account, art. 9 may play a residual role.[246] The national protection as a whole cannot be classified as an overriding mandatory provision, but the doctrine may guarantee the application of the core of consumer protection.[247] Such a residual function has been accepted in French courts. The Cour de Cassation, for example, applied art. L.311–37 Code de la Consommation conferring jurisdiction on a special court as an overriding mandatory provision to a contract governed by German law, while recognising that if all steps necessary for the conclusion of the contract had been taken in France art. 5 Rome Convention would have been applicable.[248] It is reasonable to limit in parallel with art. 6 Rome I the application of those second generation overriding mandatory provisions to situations involving a choice of law. When a Finnish consumer purchases a good in Sweden he can reasonably accept to be subject to Swedish consumer law and the consumer thus voluntarily gives up the protection afforded to him by Finnish law. The Swedish professional may however incorporate in his standard terms a choice of law for Romanian law, with presumably a lower level of consumer protection. The choice of law clause would, due to the lack of a transnational link, be void if the contract was concluded between the Swedish

[244] 28th recital to the Rome I Regulation.
[245] 32th recital to the Rome I Regulation.
[246] Junker *supra* note 211, pp. 68; Kuckein, *supra* note 165, pp. 46.
[247] Jacquet, J., Note sous CJCE 9 Novembre 2000, *Journal de droit international*, Vol. 128, 2001, pp. 517–523 (519).
[248] Cour de Cassation 23 May 2006, 03–15637.

professional and a Swedish consumer. Although the Finnish consumer gave up his Finnish protection, he did not reasonably expect to replace it with Romanian standards (rather Swedish). It would be unfair if the mobile consumer would be subject to a lower level of consumer protection than a non-mobile Finnish or Swedish consumer.[249] The choice of law in favour of Romanian law should therefore not deprive the Finnish consumer from the mandatory protection afforded to him by the *core* of Swedish consumer protection law.[250]

To support this conclusion the function of art. 6 as such must be recalled. Art. 6 seeks to undo the bias that is created by the characteristic performance test that in case of B to C relations structurally favours the economically stronger party. Art. 6 (2) seeks to safeguard the exchange of presumption by preventing that a mere choice of law could circumvent the mandatory provisions of the presumably applicable law. The gravity of consumer protection is therefore double: there is first the exchange of presumptions and second the protection against a choice of law. The list of presumption in art. 4 (1) are indicative. Equally, art. 6 has its limits: when in the case of a mobile consumer the contract is manifestly more connected with the law of the jurisdiction that the consumer enters, applying the law of the place of habitual residence of the consumer no longer holds any ground. If the consumer approaches the producer in the latter's home jurisdiction, the consumer voluntarily leaves his own jurisdiction. The presumption of applicable law does not have to be changed, and hence there is no need for a provision aimed at the enforcement of the mandatory laws of the otherwise applicable law in cases of a choice of law. The law of the stronger party will in such cases normally be the otherwise applicable law. Nevertheless, as the example with the Finnish consumer shows, it is necessary to maintain some minimum safeguards to avoid unfair results.

The differences in national solutions are noticeable. Due to the German interpretation that overriding mandatory provisions should primarily be aimed at the safeguard of state interests and not mainly

[249] The mobile consumer will still be worse off since art. 9 Rome I refers to internationally mandatory rules, whereas art. 6 refers to domestically mandatory rules.

[250] That would only apply to the Swedish consumer law not implementing a Union directive. As argued in par. 4.6.3, the appropriate solution would be to give a wide interpretation to the notion 'country'.

serve the protection of the weaker party, consumers that fall outside the scope of art. 6 are deprived of any residual protection. In this respect, the French solution seems preferable. Overriding mandatory provisions can ensure that a certain minimum of protection will be afforded to a consumer even though he falls outside the scope of art. 6.

When the facts fall into the scope of art. 6, the role of overriding mandatory provisions is severely restricted. The consumer sees already the law of the place of his habitual residence applied, or at least effect is given to the mandatory provisions of his law. The consumer enjoys exactly the same protection that would be afforded to him in a national situation. It is hard to justify why the mere existence of a transnational link should entitle a consumer to more protection than he would have enjoyed in purely domestic situation. The law chosen by the parties or the law of the place of establishment of the undertaking could provide for a higher level of protection to the consumer. The ECJ however held in *Alpine Investments* that enhancing the level of protection afforded to Belgian consumers is not an interest for the Dutch government.[251] When the weaker position of consumers has already been compensated by the protective connecting factor, there is in principle no role left for second generation overriding mandatory provisions. First generation mandatory provisions still have a role to play. Although the protection of Belgian consumers is not an interest for the Dutch government it does not mean that the Netherlands has no interest at stake at all. A rule prohibiting cold-calling aims, for example, at both the protection of consumers but also the safeguarding of the integrity of the Dutch financial market.[252]

2.5.8 *Employees*

The connecting factor protecting the employees is laid down in art. 6 Rome Convention and art. 8 Rome I. Both articles provide that a choice of law made by the parties in an individual employment contract will not result in the deprivation of the protection afforded to the employee by the law of the place where the employee habitually carries out his work in performance of the contract. The article therefore does not apply to collective agreements. If in an individual employment contract

[251] Case C-384/93 *Alpine Investments* [1995] ECR I-01141, par. 43.
[252] *Alpine Investments, supra* note 252, para. 43–44.

no choice of law has been made, the law of the place where the employee habitually carries out his performances shall be applicable. In the case where the employee habitually carries out his performances in several countries, the law of the place through which the employee was engaged was situated will be applicable.[253] The ECJ has interpreted the place of performance, within the context of art. 5 (1) Brussels Convention, to mean the place where the employee had established the effective centre of his working activities. For that purpose 'it is necessary to take into account the fact that the employee spends most of his working time in one of the Contracting States in which he has an office where he organizes his activities for his employer and to which he returns after each business trip abroad'.[254] The reasoning can be transposed to Rome I[255] since one of the principal reasons to award jurisdiction to this court is that from a point of view of employee protection the employee should be able to sue his employer where it is least expensive for him to commence proceedings and where the courts best suited to resolve disputes relating to the contract of employment are situated.[256] In principle that is the place where the employee spends most of his working time engaged in his employer's business.[257] The country where the employee spends most of his working time in his employers' business will normally also be the country that has the closest connection to the labour contract as well as having the largest regulatory interest.

Finally, the provision recognises that although an employee may habitually carry out work in a certain country, the employment contract may nonetheless have a closer connection with another country. In such a case, art. 6 (2) Rome Convention and art. 8 (4) Rome I provide that the law of that country applies.

---

[253] Clarification of how to establish the place through which the employee was engaged will be brought by: Case C-384/10 *Voogsgeerd* (pending case).

[254] Case C-125/92 *Mulox IBC* [1993] ECR I-4075, par. 26; Case C-383/95 *Rutten v Cross Medical* [1997] ECR I-0057, par. 25; Case C-37/00 *Weber* [2002] ECR I-2013, par. 58; Case C-437-00 *Pugliese* [2003] ECR I-3573, par. 19.

[255] Gerechtshof 's-Hertogenbosch, 20 September 2005, LJN: AU4725; Gerechtshof's Hertogenbosch, 10 April 2007, LJN: BB2826.

[256] Case C-29/10 *Heiko Koelzsch v État du Grand-Duché de Luxembourg* [2011] ECR I-0000.

[257] *Weber, supra* note 254, para. 49 and 50. The Cour de Cassation apparently answered the question in the affirmative and held that a French cyclist participating in international competitions on behalf of a Belgian team in various countries habitually carried out his work in France since he was training there. Cour de Cassation 3 December 2008, 06-45117. Note that in France, contrary to consumer law, an implied choice of law is possible: Cour de Cassation, 27 May 2009, 08-41908.

However, an employment contract is certainly not a uniform concept. What the *lex fori* could classify as an employment contract could be classified by the *lex loci solutionis* (the law of the place where the obligation has to be fulfilled) as a contract of agency. The role of art. 8 is in such cases not evident.[258] Should the ECJ develop an autonomous definition for the purpose of Rome I or should courts resort to the PIL mechanism of classification?[259] Since the aim of Rome I is the creation of uniform rules, the first option is preferable. Another difficulty is when an employee habitually works in one state and is subsequently transferred on the basis of the original employment contract to an establishment in another state. Does the law governing the employment contract change,[260] and should the place where the employee habitually carries out his work be determined at the time of the occurrence of the event leading to the disputed matter?[261]

Whereas there was substantial debate during the transformation of the Rome Convention into a Regulation about the connecting factor protecting consumers, the protective connecting factor for employees has been far less of a controversy.[262] In order to incorporate the case-law of the ECJ with regard to the Brussels Convention, art. 8 has been slightly modified from the place 'in which' to 'in which or, failing that, from which' the employee habitually carries out his work in performance of the contract in order to demonstrate that it also applies to, for example, personnel working on board of an aircraft, if there is a fixed base from which work is organised and where the personnel perform other obligations in relation to the employer.[263] Art. 8 Rome I does however not offer anything substantially new.

---

[258] Plender, R., *The European Contracts Convention: The Rome Convention on the Law Applicable to Contractual Obligations*, Sweet & Maxwell, London, Second Edition, 2001, pp. 163.

[259] Rammeloo, *supra* note 159, pp. 387–392.

[260] Morse, C., "Consumer Contracts, Employments Contracts and the Rome Convention", *International Comparative Law Quarterly*, Vol. 41, 1992, pp. 1–21. (17).

[261] Plender, *supra* note 258, 170.

[262] Hansen, L., "Applicable Employment Law after Rome I - The Draft Rome I Regulation and Its Importance for Employment Contracts", *European Business Law Review*, Vol. 19, 2008, pp. 767–774; Mankowski, P., "Employment Contracts under Article 8 of the Rome I Regulation", F. Ferrari and S. Leible, *Rome I Regulation: The Law Applicable to Contractual Obligations in Europe*, Sellier, Münich, 2009, pp. 171–216.

[263] Proposal for a Regulation on the Law applicable to contractual obligations, COM (2005) 650 final. Note that the Cour de Cassation did in a case involving a French flight attendant stationed in France held French law not applicable. That interpretation of art. 6 Rome Convention cannot be maintained under art. 8 Rome I. Cour de Cassation, 27 May 2009, 08-41908.

The original art. 6 Rome Convention implicitly presumes that mandatory rules must relate to employee protection.[264] With regard to the protective connecting factor for employees, the Giuliano-Lagarde report suggests that first generation overriding mandatory provisions are part of art. 6 Rome Convention. The report provides:

> The mandatory rules from which the parties may not derogate consist not only of the provisions relating to the contract of employment itself, but also provisions such as those concerning industrial safety and hygiene which are regarded in certain Member States as being provisions of public law

The implementation of art. 6 Rome Convention however leaves the health and hygiene regulations within the sphere of art. 7.[265] Even if one were to follow the Giuliano-Lagarde report it must be observed that contrary to second generation overriding mandatory provisions, the protective connecting factor for employees does not regulate first generation overriding mandatory provisions exhaustively. The paragraph in the Giuliano-Lagarde report merely fills in the notion 'mandatory' in the sense of art. 6 Rome Convention.[266] It must be realised that in order to warrant the application of overriding mandatory provisions, the legal system in which the overriding mandatory provisions originate should have a sufficiently close connection with the factual circumstances, but not necessarily the closest. Whereas there is in an individual employment contract only one weaker party, first generation overriding mandatory provisions may refer to several state policies. In other words, the fact that the first generation overriding mandatory provisions of the law of the place where the employee habitually carries out its performances are applied does not mean that another state does not have an interest in seeing its law applied. The problem then boils down to a conflict of overriding mandatory provisions.

Similar to art. 6 Rome I, art. 8 leaves gaps in employee protection. Most notably it does not provide for a specific regulation concerning posted workers. The conflict rule makes it possible to identify the

---

[264] Morse, *supra* note 260, 16.

[265] Mankowski, P., "Wichtige Klärungen im Internationalen Arbeitsrecht", *IPRax*, 1994, pp. 88–98. Czernich, D., and H. Heiss (eds.), EVÜ: Das Europäische Schuldvertragsübereinkommen, Wien: Verlag Orac, 1999, pp. 155.

[266] Kaye, P., *The New Private International Law of Contract of the European Community*, Dartmouth, Aldershot, 1993, pp. 224–225.

centre of gravity of the employment relationship, which in the case of the posting of workers is the Member State of origin. Although the employment contract is temporarily performed outside its territory the Member State of origin continues to have the closest relation with the employment contract. Art. 8 (2) tries to prevent the legal uncertainty that results from continuous adaption of places where the employee habitually carries out his work. Since the applicable law does not change, there is no procedural function for art. 8 to play. This does not, however, mean that the receiving state has no legitimate interest, such as the prevention of social dumping or to ensure the fair completion on the national labour market, in seeing its labour law applied. Similar to consumer contracts, the overriding mandatory provisions may fill the gap that is left by the protective connecting factor.

It follows from ECJ case-law that differences in labour law may be part of the comparative advantage of a foreign service provider.[267] Similarly as in consumer protection, art. 9 can therefore not be applied by full analogy to art. 8 in the sense that it could lead to the application of the mandatory rules that would be applied on the basis of art. 8, if the situation had fallen within its scope. Art. 9 can only refer to a much more narrow set of rules.

The exchange of presumptions for reasons of social protection such as with consumers is in principle not necessary with regard to employees. It is the employee who carries out in an employment contract the most characteristic performance. Application of the most characteristic performance test would therefore result in the application of the law of habitual residence of the employee. However, it is not this jurisdiction that has the largest regulatory interest in the private relationship but normally the country whose labour market is affected, that being the place where the employment contract has to be performed. It explains why the applicable law does not change when the employee temporarily fulfils his activities in another country, since the latter country's limited regulatory interest is outweighed by considerations of legal certainty and simplicity. It is impossible to determine *ex ante* whether the law of habitual residence of the employee or the *lex loci solutionis* offers a higher standard of protection. The modification of the connecting factor was, for the purpose of the protection of the

[267] Case C-341/05 *Laval* [2007] ECR I-11767; Case C-438/05 *Viking* [2007] ECR I-10779; Case C-346/06 *Dirk R&udacute;ffert* [2008] ECR I-1989.

employee, therefore also not strictly necessary. The modification and the choice of law protection must therefore be understood as a safeguard that parties cannot depart from due to the regulatory interest of a state. The interest of the state thus plays in art. 8 Rome I a much larger role than in art. 6 Rome I. To that extent it may be questioned whether art. 8 Rome I is truly a protective connecting factor or whether it aims to protect the regulatory interest of a state.

2.6 *Special Connecting Factors*

Rome I next introduced, for the protection of consumers and employees, a special connecting factor for contracts of carriage and insurance contracts. Those provisions limit the number of laws parties are allowed to choose. The requirement that a choice of law could only be made in favour of a related legal system existed in several European countries prior to the introduction of the Rome Convention, and is still commonly used in the US. In the context of contracts of carriage and insurance contracts it is believed that the weaker party is protected by requiring a qualified link of the contract with the legal system chosen.

2.6.1 *Contracts of Carriage*

After long deliberations it was decided not to exclude transport contracts from the scope of application of the Rome Convention.[268] It was however believed that it was inappropriate to submit contracts of carriage of goods to the presumption that the closest connection existed with the jurisdiction in which the transporter was established. In international transport, the place of establishment of the party that had to deliver the most characteristic performance often had no bearing with the contract whatsoever. A special presumption was therefore adopted stipulating that it was presumed that the law of the place of establishment of the carrier was applicable when the place of loading or the place of discharge or the principal place of business of the consignor

[268] Giuliano-Lagarde Report, 22. The reason for the possibility of excluding these contracts from the scope of the Rome Convention was that a large number of international conventions regulate contracts of carriage. Note that under art. 25 (1) Rome I international conventions laying down conflict of laws rules take precedence over the Regulation. Rome I therefore applies only to contracts of carriage not covered by an international convention the Member State concerned is party to.

was also situated in that country. Contracts for the carriage of passengers were excluded from the scope of art. 4 (4) but were also not covered by the special rules on consumer protection (art. 5 (4a)). A choice of law was possible in full, even when one of the parties to the contract was a natural person.

Art. 4 (4) Rome Convention only applied if the main purpose of the contract was the carriage of goods. The objective of the contractual relationship and all the obligations of the party who has to render the most characteristic performance have therefore to be ascertained. The connecting factor for the carriage of goods will not apply when the contract merely relates to making available the means of transport instead of the carriage of goods proper. This would exclude freight forwarding contracts since the primary function of the forwarding agent is to arrange the carriage for other people.[269]

The ECJ was in *ICF* confronted with a case where neither the place of loading, the place of discharge or the principal place of business coincided with the place of establishment of the carrier.[270] AG Bot convincingly argued that in those circumstances the court given the task of deciding the law applicable to the contract must refer to the general rule laid down in Article 4 (1) of the Rome Convention.[271] Application of one of the other presumption, such as that the closest connection exists with the country where the party that has to render the most characteristic performance is established would lead to the application of the law of the place where the carrier was established. Art. 4 (4) however implies that the place of establishment of the carrier is not a sufficiently strong connection to justify the application of that law. Resort to art. 4 (2) would nullify the requirement of art. 4 (4), that in order to justify the presumption that the law of the place of establishment of the carrier applies, the place of loading, the place of discharge or the principal place of business of the consignor has also to be situated in that country.

The presumption of art. 4 (4) was in the process of transformation of the Rome Convention into Rome I lifted out of the provision dealing with the applicable law in the absence of a choice of law altogether.

---

[269] Plender/Wilderspin, *supra* note 116, pp. 209.

[270] Case C-133/08 *Intercontainer Interfrigo (ICF) SC v Balkenende Oosthuizen BV and MIC Operations BV* [2009] ECR I-9687.

[271] AG Bot in *ICF*, para. 56–65.

Art. 5 (1) raises the same presumption,[272] but in addition provides that when the requirements of the presumption are not met, the law of the country where the place of delivery as agreed by the parties is situated will be applicable.[273]

Carriage contracts of passengers were thus excluded from the scope of both art. 4 (4) and art. 5 Rome Convention.[274] In order to mitigate the consequences courts could, in the case of an absence of choice, resort to the exception of a closer connection with the law of the consumer law (art. 4 (5) Rome Convention). For example the Amtsgericht Lübeck held that the provision applied and a closer link existed with Germany in a contract concluded on-line between a German national and an Irish airline for the transport of the former from a German to a Swedish airport.[275] Member States sought to realise a more consumer friendly solution. Art. 5 (2) Rome I addresses contracts for carriage of passengers. A presumption is raised in favour of the law of the country where the passenger has his habitual residence, provided that either the place of departure or the place of destination is situated in that country. If these requirements are not met, the law of the country where the carrier has his habitual residence applies.

Contracts for carriage of passengers are still excluded from the special protection for consumers (art. 6 (4b) Rome I). A choice of law is therefore possible in full, without any safeguard ensuring the application of the mandatory norms of the law of place where the natural person (consumer) is domiciled. However contrary to the Rome Convention, one should not resort to the general article on the possibility of choosing the applicable law. A choice of law is governed by art. 5 (2) itself, which limits a choice of law in carriage contracts of passengers to related legal systems. Parties can choose the law of the place where:

---

[272] The 22nd recital of the preamble of the Rome I Regulation specifically provides that, with regard to contracts for the carriage of goods, no change as to the substance of art. 4 (4) Rome Convention was intended.

[273] Nielsen, P., "The Law Applicable and Contracts of Carriage", F. Ferrari and S. Leible, *Rome I Regulation: The Law Applicable to Contractual Obligations in Europe*, Sellier, Münich, 2009, pp. 99–108.

[274] Art. 5 (4a) Rome Convention.

[275] AG Lübeck, 13 September 2007 - 28 C 331/07. The relevant considerations were that the website was accessible in the German language, one of the parties was German and the place of departure was located in Germany.

(a) the passenger has his habitual residence
(b) the carrier has his habitual residence
(c) the carrier has his place of central administration
(d) the place of departure is situated
(e) the place of destination is situated.

A choice of law for a legal system other than the ones mentioned will not be valid. Courts will then have to resort to the establishment of the applicable law on the basis of the objective connecting factors.[276] The underlying rationale is to allow with regard to contracts for the carriage of goods an unrestricted choice of law while imposing, with regard to contracts for the carriage of passengers, the requirement of a qualified link is that in the former type of contracts both parties will usually be experienced professionals, whereas the latter type of contracts often involves consumers. The restriction of choice of law to related legal systems acts as a safeguard against a deliberate choice for a legal regime with a very low level of consumer protection. Allowing commercial parties to choose their place of habitual residence or central administration on the other hand avoids carriers being confronted with a multiplicity of applicable laws.[277] It would be unfeasible if an Irish air carrier were to be confronted with the application of the (mandatory) law of the place of domicile of its passengers. Contracts for the carriage of passengers in the same flight would then be subject to different laws. In practice the present limitation will mean that carriers will opt for the law of its place of habitual residence or central administration. The protection can thus only be effective when the level of consumer protection does not play a role in selecting the place of habitual residence or central administration.

Art. 5 (2) Rome I does not distinguish between consumers and other natural persons. The requirement of a qualified link with the legal system declared applicable as well the presumption in favour of the law of the country where the passenger has his habitual residence, provided that either the place of departure or the place of destination is situated in that country therefore also applies to natural persons in exercise of a

[276] Plender/Wilderspin, *supra* note 116, pp. 216.
[277] UK Ministry of Justice, Rome I – should the UK opt in?, Consultation Paper CP05/08, 23–25.

trade or profession. The solution of art. 5 (2) has the obvious advantage of simplicity since it prevents a burden upon the carrier to establish whether a ticket is being purchased in the course of business or employment or strictly for personal reasons. However, in combination with 19 (1) Rome I, which provides that the habitual residence of a natural person acting in the course of his business activity shall be his principal place of business, art. 5 (2) could lead to strange outcomes. If a lawyer living in Belgium, but with his office in the Netherlands, purchased a ticket Amsterdam – London in order to attend a meeting in the City, in the absence of a choice of law Dutch law would govern that contract. If the lawyer left, however, from Brussels, the law of the place of establishment of the carrier would apply. If the lawyer were not acting within the course of his business he would for the purposes of Rome I have his habitual residence in Belgium. Consequently, if the lawyer were to go to visit old friends the reverse would happen. If he departed from Amsterdam, the law of the place of establishment of the carrier would apply whereas if he departed from Brussels, Belgian law would apply.[278]

The final provision of art. 5 Rome I is able to correct unforeseen consequences of the connecting factors provided for in subparagraph 1 and 2. Art. 5 (3) allows when it is clear from the circumstances of the case that the contract - in the absence of a choice of law - is manifestly more closely connected with a country for the application of the law of that country. Despite some lack of clarity, the new solution in art. 5 Rome I should be welcomed. A fair balance has been struck with regard to the carriage of persons between the protection of the weaker party and the interests of the carrier. Whereas the requirement that the chosen law should have a specified link with the contract prevents the abuse of private autonomy to impose a lenient law that provides no factual bearings with the contract whatsoever, the possibility for the carrier to choose the law of his habitual residence or central administration avoids the risk of having to deal with a multiplicity of national laws applicable to the same carriage.

---

[278] Example borrowed from: Claringbould, M., "Artikel 5 Rome I en vervoerovereenkomsten", *Nederlands Internationaal Privaatrecht*, Vol. 27, No. 4, 2009, pp. 426–436.

2.6.2 *Insurance Contracts*

A special connecting factor was also introduced with regard to insurance contracts. Rome I took over the conflict of laws rules of the Insurance Directives.[279] The incorporation of the conflict of laws rules contained in the directive into Rome I was the consequence of political impossibility in reaching a compromise and thus maintains the pre-existing patchwork.

Art. 1 (3) Rome Convention provided that it did not apply to contracts of insurance which cover risks situated in the territories of the Member States. The second Non-Life Insurance Directive (88/357/EEC) foresaw application of the law of the place where the risk is situated, as leading in general to the law of the place where the policy holder has his habitual residence. However insurance contracts covering buildings or motor vehicles were governed by the law of the place where the building was situated or where the motor vehicle was registered. Art. 1 (1g) Directive on Life Assurance (2002/83/EC) provided that a life insurance was governed by the habitual residence or establishment of the policyholder. The Directives had the aim of the strengthening of the internal market. They therefore only applied, including their conflict of laws rules, to insurers who were established in one of the Member States.

The second Non-Life Insurance Directive draws a distinction between large and other risks. A large risk is defined with regard to the nature of the risk, for instance a transport risk or on the basis of a set of objective criteria, such as the risk related to the operation of a medium sized undertaking on the basis of the net turnover, balance sheet total or average number of employees. Art. 7 (1f) allows parties to choose

---

[279] Heiss, H., "Insurance Contracts in Rome I: Another Recent Failure of the European Legislature", *Yearbook of Private International Law*, Vol. 10, 2008, pp. 261–283; Kramer, X., "The New European Conflict of Law Rules on Insurance Contracts in Rome I: A Complex Compromise", *The Icfai University Journal of Insurance Law*, Vol. 6, 2008, pp. 23–42; Merett, L., "Choice of Law in Insurance Contracts under the Rome I Regulation" *Journal of Private International Law*, Vol. 5, 2009, pp. 49–67; Merkin, R., "The Rome I Regulation and Reinsurance", *Journal of Private International Law*, Vol. 5, 2009, pp. 69–84; Gruber, U., "Insurance Contracts", F. Ferrari and S. Leible, *Rome I Regulation: The Law Applicable to Contractual Obligations in Europe*, Sellier, Münich, 2009, pp. 109–128; Heinze, C., "Insurance contracts under the Rome I Regulation", *Nederlands Internationaal Privaatrecht*, Vol. 27, 2009, pp. 445- 453; Perner, S., "Das Internationale Versicherungsvertragsrecht nach Rom I", *IPRax*, Vol. 29, 2009, pp. 218–222.

any law to govern their contract. The justification is that parties to an insurance contract covering a large risk will most often be both professionals, eliminating any necessity to protect a weaker party. Whereas for other risks the applicable law is that of the Member State where the risk is situated, the directive acknowledges the possibility of a wider choice of law in so far that is permitted by the otherwise applicable law.

The Life Assurance Directive provides that the law applicable is the law of the Member State of the habitual residence or establishment of the policyholder, that being the place of the commitment (art. 32 (1)). However again, where the law of that Member State allows, the parties may choose the law of another country. Risks situated outside the EU were governed by the normal rules of the Rome Convention. Also reinsurance contracts, whether the initial risk was situated in a Member State or not, fell within the scope of the Rome Convention. Choice of law was therefore subject to all the normal limitations.

The conflict of laws rules were therefore scattered over several instruments and left significant room for lacunae and inconsistencies with little reasonable justification.[280] It should therefore not be surprising that insurance law was identified as an area where discussion should take place in the process of the transformation of the Convention into a Regulation.[281] DG Internal Market did not favour an amendment of the conflict of laws rules without any previous study towards the operation of the conflict of laws norms in the Directives. A compromise was therefore reached incorporating all conflict of laws rules in Rome I, however without making any significant amendments.

One of the novelties is that art. 7 (1) does away with the distinction of whether the risk is situated in a Member State or not. A choice of law in accordance with art. 3 is possible: it means that most commercial

---

[280] Seatzu, F., *Insurance in Private International Law: A European Perspective*, Hart Publishing, Oxford, 2003; Cox, R., L. Merett and M. Smith, *Private International Law of Reinsurance and Insurance*, Informa, London 2006; De Korte, J., "De *ligging van het risico* in het conflictenrecht voor directe schadeverzekeringsovereenkomsten", *Aansprakelijkheid, Verzekering & Schade*, Vol. 5, No. 3, 2007, pp. 115–119.

[281] Joustra, C., "Het voorstel voor een Rome I Verordening: een nieuwe kans voor het ipr voor verzekeringsovereenkomsten?" *Nederlands Tijdschrift voor het Handelsrecht,* vol. 4, 2006, pp. 130–137; Financial Markets Law Committee, Insurance Contracts, Rome I, Issue 113, 2006; Max Planck Institute, *supra* note 125; Staudinger, A., "Internationales Versicherungsvertragsrecht – (k)ein Thema für Rom I?", F. Ferrari and S. Leible (eds.), *Ein neues Internationales Vertragsrecht für Europa, Jena: Jenaer Wissenschaftliche Verlagsgesellschaft*, 2007, pp. 226–243.

cases, which will usually concern large risks, the question of where the risk is situated has lost most of its relevance.[282] The same applies, due to their exclusion from the scope of art. 7, to insurances covering a non-large risk situated outside the territory of one of the Member State and reinsurance contracts. The applicability of the normal rules of the Rome Convention means that an insurance contract is also subject to the limitations upon private autonomy derived from mandatory rules and consumer protection. For a choice of law with regard to non-large risks situated within the territory of a Member State, however, a special regime applies. A choice of law is possible only with regard to related legal systems, being:

(a) the law of any Member State where the risk is situated at the time of conclusion of the contract;
(b) the law of the country where the policy holder has his habitual residence;
(c) in the case of life assurance, the law of the Member State of which the policy holder is a national;
(d) for insurance contracts covering risks limited to events occurring in one Member State other than the Member State where the risk is situated, the law of that Member State;
(e) where the policy holder of a contract falling under this paragraph pursues a commercial or industrial activity or a liberal profession and the insurance contract covers two or more risks which relate to those activities and are situated in different Member States, the law of any of the Member States concerned or the law of the country of habitual residence of the policy holder.

The strict limitations of the legal system private parties may elect is compensated by the second paragraph of art. 7 (3): a wider possibility of choice of law is recognised in so far as the Member State whose law is declared to be applicable allows for such a possibility. Apparently for the safeguard of adequate protection of policy holders it is necessary that the applicable law has a specified link with the contract. The opportunity for Member States to impose their law on insurance contracts covering commitments within their territories allows them to provide adequate safeguards for policy holders. That does not apply to large risks where both parties are usually commercial and therefore more likely to be acquainted with the consequences of a choice of law.

[282] Plender/Wilderspin, *supra* note 116, 263.

Although the incorporation of the choice of law rules for insurance contracts in Rome I already improves the transparency of the conflict of laws rules as such, there is a risk that lacunae may still occur. Due to the distinction between non-large risks situated in a Member State and not, Rome I is unnecessarily complex. To some extent, Rome I is a missed chance to improve the clarity of the conflict of laws rules in insurance contracts.[283] Constellation may be offered by the review clause in Rome I (27 (1a)), that obliges the Commission to present by 17 June 2013 'a study on the law applicable to insurance contracts and an assessment of the impact of the provisions to be introduced, if any'.

Besides protective connecting factors, another limitation upon private autonomy thus emerged. Special connecting factors do not as such impose a substantive floor of minimum protection. A legal system without consumer protection could theoretically be chosen, as long that legal system fulfils the qualified link with the contract. The special connecting factors for passenger carriage and insurance contracts allow a law to be chosen that is familiar to the professional. Special connecting factors thus pose a more limited interference with party autonomy (if assumed that the professional will usually opt for a law familiar to him) and international trade compared to protective connecting factors.

2.7 *Intermediate Conclusions*

Overriding mandatory provisions thus represent a particular category in PIL. They correct the private autonomy or objective connecting factors in order to safeguard the core of state policies and protection of the weaker party. The scope of applicability of the rule is deduced from the rule itself, rather than from the legal relationship. The correction is necessary because European conflict of laws is not concerned with the substantive policies that underlie a rule. The substantive outcome of the dispute does not matter: what is important is the resolution of competing claims for application. European conflict of laws differs on that point from for example US conflict of laws which takes the underlying legislative policies of the potentially applicable legal systems to decide

[283] Particularly strong: Heiss, *supra* note 279.

the applicable law. Europe instead places a heavier emphasis upon the individual and accordingly has a liberal acceptance of a choice of law. A safeguard against abuse of private autonomy and circumvention of essential national policies is therefore necessary. From that point of view, overriding mandatory provisions form the minimal interference with party autonomy.

The emphasis on private autonomy ensures that the exception does not become the rule. In other words, overriding mandatory provisions should be interpreted narrowly. The restriction of private autonomy should be proportionate and well-reasoned. Legislators can lighten the burden of the courts by clearly indicating the international field of application of an overriding mandatory provision. Overriding mandatory provisions differ from mandatory provisions. The involvement of several sovereigns requires mutual restraint. The fact that a situation is not domestic to one state makes it unreasonable for one state to require the application of all its mandatory rules. Interference with some fundamental policies should however not be tolerated. Resort to overriding mandatory provisions should be reserved to rules whose observance is crucial for the safeguard of a fundamental policy. If one adheres to such a strict approach, overriding mandatory provisions will not be a display of protectionist behaviour of Member States, but will aim at the genuine protection of legitimate aims. Particularly from this perspective, the very reluctant position that Member States take towards the application of foreign overriding mandatory provisions is less understandable. The principal refusal to assist foreign powers in the realisation of core governmental interests is particularly in a common European Justice Area hard to justify.

Overriding mandatory provisions are not the only mechanism used to correct the functioning of the conflict of laws mechanism. Special conflict of laws norms have been introduced for weaker parties. In the case of consumer contracts, the conflict of laws norm functions as a procedural guarantee to ensure the genuine exercise of private autonomy. In the case of employees, the protection of the weaker party is intertwined with the interest of a state in regulating the employment of persons habitually working on its territory. International trade would be unduly restricted if two cumulative functions for the protection of the weaker party would exist next to each other. Even from the perspective of the weaker party that is hard to justify. Why would a Spanish consumer that enters into a contract with a Swedish undertaking receive by operation of the conflict of laws mechanism a higher level of protection than his Spanish neighbour who happens to contract with a Spanish undertaking? Therefore, overriding mandatory provisions that protect the weaker party should not be applied if the weaker party already enjoys protection under a protective connecting factor. Those overriding mandatory provisions only play a residual role designed to counter the too harsh consequences of a choice of law through the operation of the conflict of laws rules.

Rome I failed to clarify the relationship between overriding mandatory provisions and protective connecting factors. A State may perceive the observation of consumer or labour as crucial for the safeguard of its political, social or economical order. The precise scope of art. 9 and its relation with the other provisions in Rome I therefore needs to be clarified by the ECJ. Due to a different limitation of private autonomy, the problem of first and second generation overriding mandatory provisions does not occur in the special connecting factor for contracts of carriage and insurance contracts. Those special connecting factors do not insist upon the application of mandatory rules, but rather require a predefined link of the contract with the law chosen. Cumulative protection of a weaker party in the conflict of laws process does therefore not occur.

CHAPTER 3

OVERRIDING MANDATORY PROVISIONS: THE NATIONAL PERSPECTIVE

The previous chapter discussed the general conflict of laws rules of Rome I. When assessing the interaction of private autonomy with overriding mandatory provisions and protective connecting factors it was often observed that Member States have taken differing approaches. Despite the principle of uniform application laid down in art. 18 Rome Convention,[1] Member States have continued to interpret provisions of the Rome Convention in the light of pre-existing national doctrine. This section will illustrate the national particularities of the Rome Convention by using the example of overriding mandatory provisions. Overriding mandatory provisions are chosen not only because national courts have rendered contradictory decisions on art. 7 Rome Convention, but also because the doctrine is in Rome I the only mechanism to determine the applicable law that is left to the Member States. In order to better understand the functioning of overriding mandatory provisions in the regime prior to Rome I, some general characteristics of the national conflict of laws mechanism will be discussed. The comparative overview will be limited to France, Germany, the Netherlands and the United Kingdom. The Member States chosen represent the three main legal traditions in Europe, while the Netherlands is considered since Dutch case-law has been influential in the process of drafting art. 7 Rome Convention. The section will conclude to what extent art. 9 Rome I leaves room for Member States to continue to apply their national conception of overriding mandatory provisions to Rome I.

3.1 *France*

The French language version of Rome I translates 'overriding mandatory provisions' as 'lois de police'. Besides *lois de police*, the notions *lois*

[1] Junker, A., "Die einheitliche europäische Auslegung nach dem EG-Schulvertragsübereinkommen", *RabelsZ*, Vol. 55, 1991, pp. 674–696.

d'application immediate, *lois d'ordre public* and *lois d'application imperative* can also be found in both case-law and legal writing.[2] Although the choice for the notion '*lois de police*' might have been understandable, it is certainly not without terminological problems. A closer look into the origin of overriding mandatory provisions in France, which is closely linked with the development of PIL in general, provides a better insight in the root of the problem.

PIL has in France never been comprehensively codified. Although some provisions on PIL existed in the Code civil and the Code de procedure civile, the main internal source of development of French PIL has been the case-law of the Cour de Cassation.[3] The starting point was however undoubtedly art. 3 (1) Code civil that reads:

> Les lois de police et de sûreté obligent tous ceux qui habitent le territoire.

It is impossible to discuss here all of the different interpretations that have been given to this article by the Cour de Cassation, and the description will be limited to the main themes.[4] A very influential approach is that based on the ideas of Henri Batiffol.[5] In the theory of Batiffol, the decisive criterion when establishing the applicable law is whether the legal situation relates to the status of a person, the good concerned or the source of the legal rights (*les actes et faits générateurs*

---

[2] With regard to French overriding mandatory provisions the notions are used interchangeably: Heuzé, V., *La réglementation française des contrats internationaux*, GLN Joly Éditions, Paris, 1990, pp. 192; Monéger, F., *Droit International Privé*, Litec, Paris, 2001, pp. 161; Vignal, T., *Droit International Privé*, Dalloz, Paris, 2005, pp. 243; Bureau, D., and H. Muir Watt, *Droit international privé*, Presses Universitaires de France, Paris, 2007, pp. 558. See as well: Van Hoek, A., *Internationale mobiliteit van werknemers: Een onderzoek naar de interactie tussen arbeidsrecht, EG-recht en IPR aan de hand van de detacheringsrichtlijn*, SDU Uitgevers, Den Haag, 2000, pp. 125–131; Bonomi, A., "Mandatory Rules in Private International Law: The quest for uniformity of decisions in a global environment", *Yearbook of Private International Law*, Vol. 1, 1999, pp. 215–247.

[3] Batifol, H., and P.Lagarde, *Traité de Droit International Privé*, Paris, Tome I, 8e édition, 1993, pp. 31–32.

[4] The case-law is extensively described in : Ancel, B., "Destinées de l'article 3 du Code civil", *Mélanges en l'honneur de Paul Lagarde ; Le droit international privé : esprit et méthodes*, Dalloz, Paris, 2005, pp. 1–18.

[5] Batiffol, H., *Traite élémentaire de droit international privé*, Librairie générale de droit et de jurisprudence, Paris, 1949, pp. 287. Especially in tort law, an 'Americanisation' of the conflict of laws rule took place, see: Moreau, M., *Structure du rattachement et conflits de lois en matière de responsabilité civile délictuelle*, Thèse Université de droit, d'économie et de sciences sociales de Paris, 1985.

de droits).[6] The latter category can further be subdivided in legal facts where the *lex loci delicti* is generally applied, the formation of legal acts which is governed by the *lex locus regit actum* and finally the substantive content of legal acts which is governed by the *loi d'autonomie*. The *loi d'autonomie* is the law that has been adopted by the parties. The adoption might either flow from an explicit choice or from the facts or circumstances of the case.[7] The Cour de cassation did not however, prior to the entry into force of the Rome Convention, base the validity of choice of law by parties to an international contract on the *loi d'autonomie* but on the principle of the binding force of contracts as laid down in art. 1134 CC.[8]

It is quite remarkable that a principle of party autonomy was developed by Battiffol from the *lois de police* in art. 3 (1) CC. The *loi d'autonomie* in the theory of Batifol should not, however, be confused with a choice of law in a traditional sense. According to Battiffol the choice made by the parties was only one of the factors that had to be taken into account by the forum when establishing the applicable law. The forum could, on the basis of objective criteria, decide to apply a law different from the one chosen by the parties involved. The system whereby a choice of law and objective criteria are assessed together by the forum in order to establish the applicable law is referred to as monism. Although Batiffol's conception of *loi d'autonomie* was already no longer prevailing in both doctrine and practice,[9] the entry into force of the Rome Convention marked its final death. Monism is not reconcilable with the principle of the freedom of choice of law in the Rome Convention, which only falls back on objective factors to establish the applicable law when parties have failed to make a choice of law. The approach whereby regard is first given to the will of the parties involved and where only in the event of absence of a will resort is taken to objective factors is referred to as dualism and widely accepted by contemporary French PIL.[10]

---

[6] The French conflict of laws system has not always been such multilateral. Prior to the ideas of Battifol, a unilateral approach based on the teachings of D'Argentré. The territorial application of French law was the main rule, save in cases where the *statut personnel* or the *statut réel* was the connecting factor. See: Ancel *supra* note 4.

[7] Cour de Cassation 10 December 1910 (American Trading Company).

[8] Ancel, *supra* note 4, 1–18.

[9] Ancel, *supra* note 4.

[10] Audit, B., *Droit International Privé*, Economica, Paris, 2e édition, 1997, pp. 655 ; Mayer, P., and V. Heuzé, *Droit International Privé*, Montchrestien, Paris, 9e édition, 2007.

3.1.1 *Classification*

The terminological confusion resulting from the development from territorial application to party autonomy becomes clear if one returns to the first category of the *générateurs de droits*, the legal facts. In the case of a tort, the territorial convictions that underlie the *lex loci delecti* are exclusive. There is no place for party autonomy in the connecting factor. The *lois de police* of art. 3 (1) CC becomes the applicable law and is classified as positive public order legislation. *Lois de police* than refer to legislation applied on the basis of territoriality. Such a wide conception, both in the sense of the substantive content of the applicable rules and connecting factor is incompatible with art. 9 (1) Rome I, which refers to rules that are regarded by a country as '*crucial for safeguarding its public interests, such as its political, social or economic organisation*'. The meaning of *lois de police* in art. 3 (1) is thus different from the meaning of *lois de police* in the Rome I and should be strictly separated from it.

The link between territoriality as connecting factor and the establishment of a close connection in the *lois de police* is however strongly present on the background and has even led modern scholars to classify *lois de police* as *lois d'application territoriale.*[11] Although habitual residence, the place of performance and the location of a good are strong indicators that a sufficient close connection exists, there are by no means exclusive. The most obvious example of other, non-territorial indicators would be nationality or choice of law. Moreover, overriding mandatory provisions might be applied extra-territorially. The classification of *lois de police as lois d'application territoriale* might give rise to confusion and must therefore be rejected.

With the strong connection between territoriality and overriding mandatory provisions in France, it is not surprising that the latter developed not as a correction to the autonomy granted to private parties but rather from the light of the classification of some rules as *clauses spéciales d'ordre public positif.*[12] The connection with *ordre public* suggests that *lois de police* may refer both to values and policies, giving the overriding mandatory provisions a rather broad notion. For example, most of the French labour law provisions are considered to be *lois de*

[11] Vignal, *supra* note 2, pp. 45.

[12] See : Rigaux, F., and M. Fallon, *Droit International Privé*, Larcier, Bruxelles, 3e édition, 2005, pp. 325.

police.[13] Is this really the protection of core state policies or rather the protection of social values? It can of course not be excluded that the social values are so fundamental that, when contained in a policy, they become rules for which the observance is crucial for the social organisation of the State.

As is demonstrated by the *Compagnie des Wagons-lits* case French courts do not shy away from classifying a provision as overriding mandatory. [14] An undertaking, Compagnie des Wagons-lits (Compagnie) established according to Belgian law with its statutory seat in Brussels, operated via various permanent establishments in France. The Ordonnance of 22 February 1945 concerning the workers participation committees required undertakings employing more than 50 persons to establish a workers participation committee. In addition art. 21 provided that a central committee had to be established if the undertaking operated via multiple establishments. The central committee was to convene at the location of the statutory seat of the undertaking. Compagnie did create workers participation committees at every individual establishment but failed to create a central committee. The Conseil d'État held that the Ordonnance, in order to guarantee the full application of all the rights contained in it, had to be applied to every legal or natural person exercising the capacity of employer in France. On a textual construction of the Ordonnance the central committee had to convene in Brussels. This was however not accepted by the Court. The central committee had to convene in France. It is striking to see that the content of the legislation is used to deduct the scope of application, but when the Ordonnance is found applicable, its literal construction is subsequently modified in order to reach the desired normative result.[15]

---

[13] Rodière, P., *La convention collective de travail en droit international*, Litec, Paris, 1987, pp. 65–66.

[14] Conseil d'État 29 juin 1973, *Journal de droit international privé* 1975, pp. 538 (note M. Simon-Depitre).

[15] One can similarly see the classification of art. 21 of the Ordonnance as an verriding mandatory provision as being rather wide if one realises that the workers were already represented in committees at every individual establishment. The European Works Council Directive (EC 94/45) however follows a similar rationale with regard to non-EU undertakings. Contrary to the French law, the EWCD however requires the setting up of a works council when the undertaking employs at least 1.000 workers within the EU and employs at least 150 workers in two or more Member States (Art. 2 (1a). In that sense the observance of the rule may be more essential since a central works council will be more essential for worker participation if the size of the undertaking increases.

The decision of the Conseil d'État shows the danger that overriding mandatory provisions might lead to lexforism. The original definition of lois de police in France however appears to be strict. 'Police' finds it etymological origin in the Greek word 'politeia', which means 'organisation of the State'.[16] According to Francescakis, one of the most influential French scholars on the topic, *lois de police* are: '*lois dont l'observation est nécessaire pour la sauvegarde de l'organisation politique, sociale ou économique d'un pays*'.[17]

In recent legal writing Bureau and Muir Watt proposed a definition that emphasises the special status of overriding mandatory provisions in the conflict of laws process rather than its special character among mandatory rules:

> Sont ainsi d'application immédiate les lois qui, assorties implicitement ou explicitement, de critères d'applicabilité spatiale propres, revendiquent un champ d'application sans tolérer l'intermédiation de la règle de conflit bilatérale[18]

The neutral conflict of laws rule is not adequately equipped to protect the interests that the overriding mandatory provision is aimed to protect. The overriding mandatory provision therefore takes matters into its own hand and corrects the connecting factor. Overriding mandatory provisions that demarcate their own field of application have to be followed by courts whereas the judiciary plays an important role with respect to rules that do not. Art. L. 333-3-1 of the Code de la consommation (CdC) contains a hint about its international field of application by providing that the section of the CdC covering overindebtedness also applies to: '*débiteurs de nationalité française en situation de surendettement domiciliés hors de France et qui ont contracté des dettes non professionnelles auprès de créanciers établis en France*'. In the latter type of situations it is left to the judge to deduct the scope of application from the underlying interest. However, also the definition of Bureau and Muir Watt does not, with regard to those implicit overriding mandatory provisions, solve the problem of classification.

---

[16] Allen, R., *The Penguin English Dictionary*, Penguin Books, London, 2nd edtion, 2003, pp. 1078.

[17] Francescakis, Ph., "Quelque précisions sur les 'lois d'application immédiate' et leur rapports avec les règles de conflits de lois", *Répertoire Dalloz de droit international privé, V° Conflit de lois*, 1966, n° 137.

[18] Bureau/Muir Watt, *supra* note 2, pp. 560.

The definition of Bureau and Muir Watt also covers the emergence of 'seconde génération' overriding mandatory provisions.[19] French PIL recognises, but does not distinguish between the two different categories of overriding mandatory provisions. Some authors place the second category outside the notion of *lois de police*. They argue that *lois de police* are only aimed at the essential interests of the state and not at the protection of an individual. While *lois de police* only refer to the first category, the term *lois d'application immédiate* is used as genus referring to both categories.[20] It is however a clear minority position. Regardless what dogmatic distinction one desires to follow, French private law rules in for example labour law that seek to protect the employee are frequently classified by courts as overriding mandatory provisions. France on this point differs from the Netherlands where the distinction is largely theoretical and courts rarely apply the second category of overriding mandatory provisions.[21]

The decision of the Cour de Cassation in *Agintis* provides for a recent illustration of the willingness to protect the weaker party.[22] A French undertaking, Basell, concluded with SAB (an undertaking established in Germany) a contract for the construction of an immovable for industrial use located in France. SAB subcontracted the construction of the lot 'tuyauterie' to the French undertaking Agintis. In the subcontracts a choice of law for German law was made. After completion of the works SAB was in a judgement of the International Court of Arbitration ordered to pay a sum of € 1.6 million of payments still due. SAB failed to comply and Agintis subsequently sought payment from Basell, as master of the works. Arts. 12 and 14 (1) of the *loi relative à la sous-traitance* allow a subcontractor to seek a direct redress against the master of the works in case of default of the main contractor.[23] Basell refused payment on the grounds that both the main contract and the

---

[19] Bureau/Muir Watt, *supra* note 2, pp. 561.

[20] Niboyet, M., and G. de Geouffre de La Pradelle, *Droit International Privé*, Librairie Générale de Droit et de Jurisprudence, Paris, 2007, pp. 119.

[21] Van Hoek, *supra* note 2, pp. 129. See for example on consumer law: Cour de Cassation 19 October 1999, *Revue Critique de Droit International Privé*, 2000, pp. 29–34 (note P. Lagarde) where some provisions of the loi sur le crédit a la consommation were declared overriding mandatory; Cour de Cassation, 23 May 2006, n° 258.

[22] Cour de Cassation 30 November 2007, 06-14006, but as well: Cour de Cassation 25 February 2009, 07-20096. See: Piroddi, P., "The French Plumber, Subcontracting and the Internal Market", *Yearbook of Private International Law*, Vol. 10, 2008, pp. 593–616.

[23] Loi n° 75-1334 du 31 décembre 1975 relative à la sous-traitance.

subcontract were governed by German law, which did not provide for a similar action. The Cour de Cassation held that the provisions protecting the subcontractor in the *loi relative à la sous-traitance* were mandatory provisions in both the sense of art. 3 (1) Code Civil and the art. 3 and 7 of the Rome Convention. Advocate General Guérin gave a broader insight in the courts decision; in his opinion he argued that the *loi relative à la sous-traitance* is aimed at ensuring equal competition for all subcontractors on the French market.[24] Smaller construction companies are protected against the bargaining power of larger undertakings and allowing foreign undertakings to evade the application of the *loi relative à la sous-traitance* would place small French construction companies in a competitive disadvantage *vis-a-vis* foreign competitors. The rule thus serves both the state interest of ensuring equal competition as well as the protection of the weaker party. AG Guérin therefore classified the relevant provisions as overriding mandatory provisions. The content of the rule therefore applies to all building projects situated in France. One must moreover realise that whereas overriding mandatory provisions of consumers and employees are aimed at the protection of a natural person, the *loi relative à la sous-traitance* protects legal persons. It is very doubtful whether the rationale underlying consumer and employee protection can be applied to B to B relations in the same way.[25] Small and medium sized enterprises (SME) have for that reason recently been excluded from the revision of the EC consumer acquis.[26]

The protective function of overriding mandatory provisions that may be broader than the protection of state interests in the strict sense probably justifies why a court does not have to investigate the applicability of overriding mandatory provisions of its own motion, but that the potential applicability of overriding mandatory provisions has to be raised by one of the parties.[27] It would be hard to justify that the applicability of provisions protecting the core of state interests should depend upon the plea of one of the parties to the dispute.

---

[24] Opinion AG Guérin in : *supra* note 22.

[25] In particular Agintis was an undertaking that was controlled by another group of undertakings and also operated as a general contractor.

[26] Proposal for a directive of the European Parliament and of the Council on consumer rights, COM (2008), 614.

[27] Cour de Cassation, 16 May 2007, 05–43949.

3.1.2 *Self Limitation*

It is unclear to what extent overriding mandatory provisions that originate in the *lex causae* can be applied. There is no doubt about the applicability of overriding mandatory provisions when the situation falls within its explicit scope of application[28] or about the inapplicability of overriding mandatory provisions when the situation falls outside its specific scope. French law remains unclear in this respect when the overriding mandatory provision is silent as to its scope of application.

Mayer and Heuzé argue that the minimum scope of application is not necessarily the maximum scope of application. The application of the rule might not be crucial for the state but the state is not necessarily hostile to seeing its interest applied. Overriding mandatory provisions that adequately regulate the situation without being linked to a certain economical or social goal can be applied. Overriding mandatory provisions that do not satisfy these criteria cannot be applied, even though the applicable law is French.[29] Hence, whenever a clear aim underlies the overriding mandatory provision and that aim is not at stake, the overriding mandatory provision cannot be applied. Mayer and Heuzé use as an example art. 112-1 *ff* of the Code monétaire et financier. These provisions regulate indexation clauses with the aim of avoiding the inflationary effect of such clauses, in order to protect the French economy. They should not be applied even if French law is applicable when the contract is performed outside of France and the inflationary effect therefore does not threaten the French economy. The approach of Mayer and Heuzé seems to have support in case-law. A similar approach can be discovered in the already discussed opinion of AG Guérin. The *loi relative à la sous-traitance* aimed at the protection of small construction companies operating on the French market. The law therefore only applies to contracts relating to building sites in France and is rendered inapplicable when the site is located outside of France.

3.1.3 *Foreign Overriding Mandatory Provisions*

The definition by Francescakis of *lois de police* favours the application of the overriding mandatory provisions of the *lex fori*, but gives no

[28] It has been argued that this also applies to loi de police that have an implicit field of application. Bureau/Muir Watt, *supra* note 2, pp. 569.
[29] Mayer/Heuzé, *supra* note 10, pp. 91–92.

guidance about the question when to apply overriding mandatory provisions that do not belong to the *lex fori*. In fact, according to Francescakis only overriding mandatory provisions belonging to the *lex fori* can be applied. That position has nowadays been abandoned by scholars and the courts alike. The two main arguments are that the application of overriding mandatory provisions should, in an era of choice of forum and law, not completely depend on the forum before which it is invoked.[30] Secondly, a liberal approach towards foreign overriding mandatory provisions might be rewarded by the application of French overriding mandatory provisions by foreign courts. France did not make a reservation towards art. 7 (1) of the Rome Convention and thus allowed a French judge to give effect to foreign overriding mandatory provisions. The application is dependent upon three conditions mentioned in art. 7 (1) Rome Convention. The criterion concerning the nature and purpose of the overriding mandatory provision is interpreted in the legal doctrine that the protected interest should be legitimate and the protection not excessive.[31] Because the French court is, when interpreting the foreign provision, in a substantially disadvantageous position, it should as a starting point follow the indications provided by the foreign legislator as interpreted in the foreign case-law.

Although the possibility of applying foreign overriding mandatory provisions is recognised in the literature, the Cour de Cassation has never actually applied a foreign overriding mandatory provision. Coming rather close, the Cour did in *Royal Dutch* accept the extraterritorial application of a Dutch regulation (in)validating the issuing of bonds by Dutch companies during the period of Nazi-occupation of the Netherlands in the Second World War.[32] The regulation was a purely public law instrument because it had as aim the invalidation of titles after they had been issued, and with invalidated bonds falling back to the State and not the issuing company. In any case, the application of foreign public law in domestic courts goes considerably further than the application of foreign overriding mandatory provisions. More

[30] Audit, *supra* note 10, pp. 676 ; Batiffol/Lagarde, *supra* note 3, pp. 428–430 ; Loussouarn, Y., *Droit international privé*, Dalloz, Paris, 8e édition, 2004, pp. 152–155 ; Mayer/Heuzé, *supra* note 10, pp. 93–96.

[31] Mayer/Heuzé, *supra* note 10, pp. 94.

[32] Cour de Cassation, 25 January 1966, *Revue Critique de Droit International Privé*, 238 (note Francescakis)

recently, in 2010, the Cour de Cassation quashed a decision of the Cour d'Appel d'Angers on the grounds that it failed to consider the application of a Ghanaian trade embargo under art. 7 (1) Rome Convention.[33] The Cour de Cassation did not address the question whether the Ghanaian overriding mandatory provision should have been applied against the French governing law, but held that a plea of the parties to that effect should at least have been considered, and referred the question back to a lower court.

A handful of cases of lower courts demonstrate that a French court does not out of principle refuse to give effect to foreign overriding mandatory provisions. In *Expand Afrique Noir* the Cour de Cassation held that a Senegalese overriding mandatory provision could be applied to an employment contract (the applicable law was French) concluded in France between a French company and a French employee, but executed in Dakar. The Senegalese overriding mandatory provisions was finally not applied because it operated to the detriment of the employee.[34] In addition to the conditions for the application of foreign overriding mandatory provisions that are laid down in the literature and the Rome Convention, the application of foreign overriding mandatory provisions must not be to detriment of the position of the weaker party.

The Paris Cour d'Appel similarly qualified an Algerian exchange control provision as an overriding mandatory provision. It held that it could be applied on a territorial basis to all payments made on its territory and thereby limit the autonomy of the private parties. Although the contract of rent related to an immovable located in Algeria, the payment was made in France. According to the principle that the place of payment determines the currency, the Cour d'Appel refused to apply the Algerian overriding mandatory provision.[35] The Cour d'Appel apparently considered the application of exchange controls to payments made outside the State's territory excessive.

The Paris Cour d'Appel did, in 1975, give effect to a foreign overriding mandatory provision. A Vietnamese ordonnance required governmental consent prior to the transfer of an immovable to a foreigner. The French State bought in 1956 a piece of land situated in South-Vietnam from a French citizen, Roux. The contract was

[33] Cour de Cassation, 16 March 2010, no 330 FS-P+B.
[34] Cour de Cassation, 31 May 1972
[35] Cour d'Appel de Paris, 10 June 1967

presumably governed by French law; Vietnamese law was at least not the *lex causae*. Neither of the parties sought the required approval. The French State did not pay the price and Roux sought to enforce the contract. The Cour d'Appel held that the ordonnance constituted an overriding mandatory provision which applied to all transfers of immovables situated in South-Vietnam. The non-observation of the ordonnance rendered the contract null and void. The Cour d'Appel subsequently refused to enforce the contract.[36]

The application of overriding mandatory provisions in France is, both in case-law and legal writing, a well-considered issue. Emphasis is usually placed on the territorial application of laws that were originally seen as clauses of positive *ordre public*. In addition, French courts are not reluctant to resort to overriding mandatory provisions for the protection of a weaker party. Consequently, the conception of national overriding mandatory provisions is rather wide. The effects can be slightly reduced by only accepting the applicability of overriding mandatory provisions towards the interest they seek to protect. Although French case-law is unclear whether it follows this approach, the option is favoured in the literature. Foreign overriding mandatory provisions are in principle eligible for application and were actually applied once in 1975 by the Paris Cour d'Appel.

3.2 *Germany*

The contemporary German Private International Law system is still heavily inspired by the work of Friedrich Carl von Savigny. In the spirit of Von Savigny, the conflict of laws rules are still based on a rather rigid division between public and private law. Conflict of laws norms have as their primary focus the parties rather than the State and are neutral, or rule blind. The ideas of Von Savigny have however been modernised. According to Kegel, one of the most influential modern scholars, the ultimate goal of PIL is the quest for justice. This should not be understood as an abandonment of the neutral character of PIL. Justice in PIL should be contrasted with justice in the substantive norms of private law. Justice is undivisible but has multiple features. Whereas the material (substantive) justice is deducted from normative rules, justice in PIL must be established beforehand. It is objectively impossible in PIL

[36] Cour d'Appel de Paris 15 May 1975

to establish which law is *sachlich* (substantively) the better law, but justice can realised by applying the spatially (*räumliche*) better law. The *räumliche* better law is the law of the place of the territory whose people have a close connection to the situation involved.[37] Justice will then often coincide with the 'Sitz' of a legal relationship.

When the strict separation between public and private law of Von Savigny and Kegel is taken to an extreme, private law becomes a *Freiraum* for private parties. The subdivision made by Kegel of interests that underlie PIL is indeed not concerned with interests of the state. Kegel distinguished between *Parteiinteressen, Verkehrsinteressen* and *Ordnungsinteressen.*[38] *Parteiinteressen* are the interests of individuals to see a law applied with which they are familiar, *Verkehrsinteressen* are the interests of all the market participants in a simple and predictable PIL system, and finally *Ordnungsinteressen* are the interests of society to see unitary and coherent laws. *Staatinteressen* can only be applied in exceptional cases through either the *ordre public* exception or through overriding mandatory provisions. Also Von Savigny acknowledged that some rules were law of a strictly positive and of an imperative nature that carried vital policies for the state and could never be displaced by foreign law.[39] However Von Savigny was of the opinion that due to the growing liberalisation of human relations, and decreasing unilateralism, these rules were bound to disappear.

The distinction made by Kegel is not universally accepted. Several authors have tried to move away from the value free conflict of laws system in favour of a system based on the American governmental interest analysis. For example, Flessner argues that both the interest-based private international law doctrine of Kegel and the governmental interest analysis (Currie) have been without effect. The reason is that the conceptualisation of interests creates abstract and surreal fictions that are in legal practice subordinate to considerations such as reasonableness, suitability and legal certainty.[40] Kropholler also does not refer to Kegel's distinction, but without referring to any specific theory, nontheless recognises that also the State has an interest in seeing its own

[37] Kegel, G., and K. Schurig, *Internationales Privatrecht*, Verlag C.H. Beck, München, 8. Auflage, 2001, pp. 114.

[38] Kegel/Schurig, *supra* note 37, pp. 117–130.

[39] Von Savigny, F., System des Heutige Römische Recht,, VIII System, § 349.

[40] Flessner, A., Interessenjurisprudenz im IPR, Mohr Siebeck, Tübingen, 1990, pp. 44–46.

laws applied.[41] Although PIL in Germany is still primarily focussed on the parties, State interests do play a (limited) role.[42]

The strong emphasis on the private parties creates a strong predominance of the possibility of a choice of law. The Rome Convention was implemented in Germany as part of the Einführungsgesetz zum Bürgerlichen Gesetzbuche (EGBGB) in 1986,[43] but both theory and legal practice had already recognised the possibility of a choice of law. Courts would traditionally only fall back on the objective connecting factors when parties had not made an explicit or implicit choice of law and no hypothetical *Parteiwille* could be established.[44] In the period between the Second World War and the introduction of the Rome Convention the subjective establishment of the *Parteiwille* was more and more abandoned in favour of an objective establishment.[45] Until the Rome Convention, the choice of law that parties could make was however restricted to the related legal systems.[46] Art. 27 (1) EGBGB provides for the possibility of a choice of law when the contract has a connection with a foreign State. The article does not prevent parties from opting for a non-state body of laws. It has been argued that parties therefore have the possibility to choose, for example, the Unidroit principles to govern their contract. However, for some issues, parties have to fall back on a state body of law to the extent that the UNIDROIT principles do not regulate a specific issue (e.g. prescription).[47]

---

[41] Kropholler, J., *Internationales Privatrecht*, Mohr Siebeck, Tübingen, 5. Auflauge, 2004, pp. 32.

[42] Michaels, R., "Two Economists, Three Opinions? Economic Models for Private International Law – Cross-Border Torts as Example", J. Basedow and T. Tono (eds.) *An Economic Analysis of Private International Law,* Mohr Siebeck, Tübingen, 2006, pp. 143–186. Nilsen, J., and R. Michaels, "Private Law and the State Comparative Perceptions and Historical Observations", *RabelsZ*, Vol. 71, 2007, pp. 345–397.

[43] The Einführungsgesetz zum Bürgerlichen Gesetzbuch contains the rules implementing the Rome Convention in Germany.

[44] The difference between an implicit choice of law and a hypothetical choice of law is that in the former the judges tries to ascertain by objective characteristics the existence of a choice of law (exclusive choice of forum clause or the fact that both parties based all their submissions upon a single law). In the latter the judge tries to find the applicable law by answering the question which law reasonable acting parties would have chosen if the question of a choice of law would have come up.

[45] Rammeloo, S., *Das Neue EG-Vertragskollisionrecht*, Carl Heymanns Verlag KG, Köln, 1992, pp. 26–42.

[46] Von Hoffmann, B., "Inländische Sachnormen mit zwingendem internationalem Anwendungsbereich", *IPRax*, vol. 9, 1989, pp. 261–272.

[47] Siehr, K., *Internationales Privatrecht: Deutsches und europäisches Kollisionsrecht für Studium und Praxis*, C.F. Müller Verlag, Heidelberg, 2001, pp. 118–126.

The combination of a rigid distinction between public and private law and the liberal possibility of a choice of law presupposes an interchangeability of private laws. This interchangeability is one of the preconditions for a bilateral PIL system. Already in 1941 and 1942 Wengler[48] and Zweigert[49] criticised the functioning of the bilateral conflict rules with regard to semi-public law. If foreign semi-public provisions were part of the *lex causae*, their application was frequently refused on the grounds of *ordre public*. Wengler and Zweigert proposed a second connection, to be applied in parallel to the normal conflict of laws rule, based on the claimed scope of application of the semi-public law. In their original theory a sufficient close connection and the safeguard of the interests of the forum were only used as a corrective of an excessive scope of application.[50] The independent connection of semi-public law is referred to as 'Sonderanknüpfung'.

Sonderanknüpfung gained increasing ground in the seventies when academics realised that the bilateral choice of law rules were inadequate to conceptualise the increasing state intervention in private law in PIL.[51] The conception of private law as a *Freiraum* of private parties could no longer be maintained and PIL was unable to recognise the interplay between the state and private parties.[52] The result was a paradigm shift. The conflict that PIL had to solve was no longer restricted to a conflict between private interests, but could also involve a conflict of state interests that tried to pursue their own socio-economical goal.[53] The acceptance of a second connection gave German courts the possibility of maintaining their sharp distinction between public and private law.

The theory of *Sonderanknüpfung* therefore not only relates to overriding mandatory provisions; it refers as well to connecting factors which are aimed at the protection of weaker parties. Art. 6 and 8 Rome I may also lead to the application of semi public law. The common

---

[48] Wengler, W., "Die anknüpfung des zwingenden Schuldrechts im IPR", *ZVergRWiss*, 1941, pp. 168–212

[49] Zweigert, K, "Nichterfüllung auf Grund auslandischer Leistungsverbote", *RabelsZ*, 1942, pp. 283–307.

[50] Fetsch, J., *Eingriffsnormen und EG-Vertrag*, Mohr Siebeck, Tübingen, 2002, pp. 27–28.

[51] Specfiically with regard to competition law: Joerges, C., "Die klassische Konzeption des Internationalen Privatrechts und das Recht des unlauteren Wettbewerbs", *RabelsZ*, Vol. 36, 1972, pp. 421–491.

[52] Basedow, J., "Wirtschaftskollisionsrecht", *RabelsZ*, Vol. 52, 1988, pp. 8–40.

[53] Fetsch, *supra* note 50, pp. 23.

element of those norms is the ability to override the normal, party autonomy based, conflict of laws rules.[54]

The overriding mandatory provisions were, prior to the date of application of Rome I, at a national level covered by art. 34 EGBG:[55]

> Dieser Unterabschnitt berührt nicht die Anwendung der Bestimmungen des deutschen Rechts, die ohne Rücksicht auf das auf den Vertrag anzuwendende Recht den Sachverhalt zwingend regeln.[56]

It is noteworthy that the notion of *Eingriffsnormen* already appeared in the literature in the seventies but has only become popular relatively recently.[57] The heading of art. 34 EGBGB and of art. 7 of the Rome Convention refers to 'zwingende Vorschriften', which can be translated as mandatory provisions. The English language version of the proposal for a Rome I referred in art. 8 (1) to mandatory provisions, this was changed in the final version of the Regulation into 'overriding mandatory provisions' because it could give rise to confusion about the relationship with the mandatory provisions of art. 3 Rome I. Such a confusion has not taken place in Germany.

Overriding mandatory provisions were prior to the explicit recognition in the EGBGB recognised in legal writing and applied by courts. Art. 34 EGBGB therefore only confirmed what was already perceived in the case-law as self-evident.[58] The starting point was the *ordre public* exception in the old EGBGB. This provision read:

> Die Anwendung eines auslandischenn Gesetzes ist ausgeschlossen wenn die Anwendung gegen die guten Sitten oder gegen den Zweck eines deutschen Gesetzes verstossen würde[59]

---

[54] Von Hoffmann, *supra* note 46. Von Bar/Mankowski refer to the connection of overriding mandatory provisions as 'Sonderanknüpfung von Eingriffsrecht' and to art. 5 and 6 Rome Convention as 'besonderer Anknüpfung; Von Bar, C., and P. Mankowski, *Internationales Privatrecht, Band I: Allgemeine Lehren*, Beck'sche Verlagsbuchhandlung, München, 2. Auflage, 2003, pp. 269.

[55] Gesetz (Law) of 24 September 2009, no. I 3145 repeals the provisions insofar they are in the scope of the Rome I Regulation.

[56] 'Nothing in this subsection shall restrict the application of those provisions of German law, which govern the subject matter irrespective of the law otherwise applicable to the contract.' Translation of the Bundesministerium der Justiz http://bundesrecht.juris.de/englisch_bgbeg/englisch_bgbeg.html, as of 15 March 2011.

[57] Neuhaus, P., *Die Grundbegriffe des Internationalen Privatrechts*, Mohr Siebeck, Tübingen, 2. Auflage, 1976, pp. 136–140.

[58] Von Bar, C., *Internationales Privatrecht, Erster Band: Allgemeine Lehren*, Beck'sche Verlagsbuchhandlung, München, 1987, pp. 232.

[59] The application of a foreign law is excluded when the application would be incompatible with the good morals or the aim of a German law.'

The *ordre public* exception was divided into a positive and a negative function.[60] As in France, the negative function of the *ordre public* refused to give effect to foreign laws whose effects of application would be manifestly against the public policy of the forum whereas the positive function gave effect to domestic laws claiming application notwithstanding a foreign applicable law.[61] On the occasion of the implementation of the Rome Convention, overriding mandatory provisions were separated from *ordre public* and given their own article. It is assumed that the *ordre public* has since the introduction of art. 34 EGBGB no longer a positive function and that that function is now completely covered by the *Eingriffsnormen*.[62]

Although the Bundesgerichtshof[63] applies, at least with regard to overriding mandatory provisions of the forum, *Sonderanknüpfung*, the approach is not universally accepted in the legal doctrine. The *Schuldstatuttheorie* still believes that the conflict of laws rules are absolute and designate a comprehensive law. Whether a provision is caught by the conflict of laws rules depends on the question whether the rule is from a public or private nature. Since no satisfying distinction can be found all private rules aimed at the protection of a public interest should be applied when part of the *lex causae*.[64] On the other side of the spectrum is the *Machttheorie*. The *Machttheorie* does not consider overriding mandatory provisions to be part of PIL, but of public law. Overriding mandatory provisions can only be applied on the basis of the principle of territoriality. A court can only take foreign overriding mandatory provisions into account when the foreign state is able to enforce its overriding mandatory provisions, for example when the private party has property in the foreign state.[65]

---

[60] Firsching, K., and B. von Hoffmann, *Internationales Privatrecht: einschließlich der Grundzüge des Internationalen Zivilverfahrensrechts*, Beck'sche Verlagsbuchhandlung, München, 4. Auflage, 1995, pp. 240.

[61] Spickhoff, A., *Der ordre public im internationalen Privatrecht ; Entwicklung – Struktur – Konkretisierung*, Alfred Metzner Verlag, Neuwied, 1989, pp. 130–132.

[62] Kropholler, *supra* note 39, pp. 242–243.

[63] Bundesgerichtshof 19 March 1997, Bundesgerichtshof 1 December 2005 III ZR 191/03.

[64] Mann, F., "Eingriffsgesetze und Internationales Privatrecht", Klaus Müller (ed.), *Festschrift für Eduard Wahl zum siebzigsten Geburtstag*, Universität Heidelberg, Heidelberg, 1973, pp. 139–160.

[65] Kegel, G., "Zum Territorialitätsprinzip im internationalen öffentlichen Recht", A. Heldrich, D. Henrich and H. Sonnenberger (eds.), *Konflikt und Ordnung; Festschrift für Murad Ferid zum 70. Geburtsdag*, C.H. Beck'sche Verlagsbuchhandlung, München, 1978, pp. 233–278.

A relatively new theory has been developed by Schurig, the *Bündelungsmodell*[66] which has already found several adherents in German legal writing.[67] The model criticises the distinction between multilateral and unilateral conflict of laws rules. It presupposes that every substantive norm can be attributed its own conflict of laws norm. The model approaches US conflict of laws theories by focusing on the interest behind the rule. It assumes that the all inclusive conflict of laws norm is, in essence, nothing more than set of bundled individual norms that underlie the same conflict of laws interest. Since the substantive norms share the same conflict of laws interest a more or less automatic connection can be established. The bundling of the national substantive rules with a similar *Tatbestand* is referred to as vertical bundling. The conflict of laws norm that is attached to the group of norms may potentially refer to every legal system in the world (horizontal bundling). If a specific substantive rule underlies a different conflict of laws interest it cannot be bundled. It then sets its own conflict of laws rule. 'Traditional' unilateral conflict of law rules are merely unbundled legal rules and are not an inherently different way of determining the applicable law. Overriding mandatory provisions are then the smallest vertical unit. The difference between unilateral and multilateral conflict of rule laws rules is thus already reflected at the *Bündelungszustand.*[68] A more horizontal solution would lead to the application of a single legal system. For example, the legal consequences of the death of an Italian testator are determined by Italian law.[69] A more vertical solution would lead to the applicability of multiple legal systems. The content and the protected interest of the substantive rule only play a subsidiary role in the sense that it may influence the *kollisionsrechtlichen Interessen*, but is not in itself decisive. The *Bündelungsmodell* places a strong emphasis

---

[66] Schurig, K., *Kollisionsnorm und Sachrecht: zu Struktur, Standort und Methode des internationalen Privatrechts*, Duncker & Humblot, Berlin, 1981, pp. 89–106.

[67] Wördemann, N., *International zwingende Normen im internationalen Privatrecht des europäischen Versicherungsvertrages: Eine kollisionsrechtliche Untersuchung zur Bedeutung und Tragweite des Art. 7 ABS. 2 zweite Ri Schadenv sowie des Art. 4 ABS. 4 zweite Ri LEBV*, Verlag Versicherungswirtschaft, Karlsruhe, 1997, pp. 100–105; Fetsch, *supra* note 438, pp. 37– 40; Wiese, V., *Der Einfluss des EG-rechts auf das internationale Sachenrecht der Kulturgüter*, Mohr Siebeck, Tübingen, 2004, pp. 184–185. Vasthoff, C., *Kollisionsrechtliche Qualifikation von Personengesellschaftskonzernen*, 2006, pp. 30–34, electronically available at: http://w3.ub.uni-konstanz.de/v13/volltexte/2006/1881//pdf/Diss_Vasthoff.pdf, as of 15 March 2011.

[68] Nojack, J., *Exclusivnormen im IPR: Interessenanalyse, dogmatische Einordnung und Anwendungsprobleme*, Mohr Siebeck, Tübingen, 2005, pp. 139–141.

[69] Fetsch, *supra* note 50, pp. 37–40.

on the national classification of groups of *Sachnormen* and their *kollisionsrechtlichen Interessen*.

3.2.1 *Classification*

Art. 34 EGBGB describes the core element of overriding mandatory provisions: they can be applied regardless the law that governs the contract. It does not however define what an overriding mandatory provision is. A normative definition can also not be found in German doctrine or case-law. Art. 9 (1) Rome I thus introduces a novelty.

Recently the German legislator started indicating whether a specific provision should be classified as overriding mandatory and thus falls within the scope of art. 34 EGBGB.[70] For example par. 449 (1) Handelsgesetzbuch (HGB) declares some provisions of the HGB with respect to consumers mandatory. One of those provisions is par. 425 HGB establishing the liability of the freighter for delay caused by the loss or damaging of the shipped good. Par. 449 (3) HGB provides that the first limb of that provision applies even when the contract is governed by a foreign law when the place of acceptance and delivery of the good is located in Germany. The rule aims to guarantee a normative result, rather than the resolution of a conflict of laws, and would under Dutch doctrine be classified as a scope rule.

Despite the lack of a normative definition, the literature and case-law have developed a set of criteria to assess in the absence of a scope rule whether a provision triggers the application of art. 34 EGBGB. It is very controversial whether provisions aimed at the protection of the weaker party can also be applied. Von Bar and Mankowski have advocated that art. 7 Rome Convention does not cover the second generation overriding mandatory provisions.[71] Consumers and employees are, as weaker parties, already protected in art. 5 and 6 Rome Convention by means of a correcting connecting factor. Kropholler also maintains that the relationship between the protective connecting factors and overriding mandatory provisions is mutually exclusive; a provision either primarily protects the interest of a state, or an individual interest, but not both.[72]

---

[70] Von Bar/Mankowski, *supra* note 54, pp. 269.
[71] Von Bar/Mankowski, *supra* note 54, pp. 269–270.
[72] Kropholler, *supra* note 39, pp. 493–496.

Fetsch has argued that the problem is actually a non-issue. The root of the confusion lies in the assumption that the overriding mandatory provisions must be based on a statutist conflict of laws mechanism. According to Fetsch that is not necessarily true. On the basis of the *Bündelungsmodell* he argues that the *'kollisionsrechtlichen Interessen einer Norm'* are decisive for a special connection rather than the public interests that may underlie the substantive rule. The solution is thus no longer sought on a substantive level, but on a private international law level. The question then becomes whether the *kollisionsrechtlichen Interessen einer Norm* of a substantive rule are already adequately addressed by the normal conflict of laws rules. If the answer is in the negative, the *Eingriffsnorm* becomes a unilateral connecting factor. If the answer is in the affirmative, there is no place for a special connection. Overriding mandatory provisions protecting the employee can therefore only be applied on the basis of art. 34 EGBGB when the underlying interest is not already protected by art. 30 EGBGB.[73] An overriding mandatory provision is thus merely the smallest unit of *Sachnormen*. This approach might be attractive if one considers that overriding mandatory provisions developed as a correction to the conflict of laws system since the emergence of a welfare state, and the resulting interest of a State in seeing its private law applied, could not be adequately conceptualised in the system of Von Savigny. It does however not solve the issue. It merely shifts the focus from qualification of a provision as overriding mandatory to conditions of its application and assumes, but does not explain that the primary aim of protection of the weaker party is a valid *kollisionsrechtlichen Interesse*.

The Bundesgerichtshof held in 2005 that the application of overriding mandatory provisions should at least serve a public interest. A German consumer borrowed a sum of about 100.000 Swiss francs from a Swiss bank in order to finance the acquisition of a house. The amount was due in ten years but the contract could be renewed for a period of another five years. The bank reserved in the contract, which contained a choice of law in favour of Swiss law, the right to alter after the expiry of the initial ten years the terms of the contract. After the expiry the bank proposed to renew the contract but raised the interest. The German consumer did not accept the raise of interest and the bank subsequently sought repayment. The German consumer invoked as

[73] Fetsch, *supra* note 50, pp. 41.

overriding mandatory provisions certain articles of the German *Verbraucherkreditgesetzes* (consumer credit law) alleging nullity of the obligation of repayment in case of dispute between the parties about the terms of renewal. The Bundesgerichtshof held that:

> Die Regelungen des Verbraucherkreditgesetzes seien aber nicht zwingend im Sinne des Art. 34 EGBGB, weil sie primär die individuellen Interessen des Verbrauchers schützten, während der auf internationaler Ebene maßgebliche Schutz der Gemeinwohlinteressen in den Hintergrund trete.[74]

The word 'primär' (primarily) in the quote is slightly misleading. From the decision as a whole, it becomes apparent that it is not necessary to apply a strict separation between provisions that protect primarily the weaker party or provisions that protect primarily the interest of the state. What is required is that a provision at least protects a public interest. The public interest protected should not be subsidiary or ancillary to the protection of the individual interest, but a goal in itself. What is the consequence of the literal interpretation of art. 34 EGBGB on the interpretation of art. 7 of the Rome Convention and art. 9 (1) of the Rome I? Rome I leaves the classification of a provision as overriding mandatory to the Member State concerned. It is for Germany to define what it considers to be crucial for the functioning of the German state.[75] Germany should therefore remain free to consider provisions that only protect an individual interest, without aiming to realise a public aim, to be excluded from the concept of overriding mandatory provisions.[76] However the division between the national courts is based upon the relationship between overriding mandatory provisions and protective

---

[74] Bundesgerichtshof 13 December 2005 XI ZR 82/05. Translation: 'The provisions of the Consumer Credit Law are however not mandatory within the meaning of art. 34, because they primarily protect the individual interests of the consumer, while the protection of public interests on the international plane step into the background'. The Bundesarbeitsgericht had previously already held that in order for art. 34 to bite a provision must not exclusively be directed at the individual interests but must also serve a public interest. Bundesarbeitsgericht 13 December 2001 5 AZR 255/00: 'Erforderlich ist, daß die Vorschrift nicht nur auf den Schutz von Individualinteressen der Arbeitnehmer gerichtet ist, sondern mit ihr zumindest auch öffentliche Gemeinwohlinteressen verfolgt werden' (par. 36). See also: Bundesarbeitsgericht 24 August 1989, *IPRax* (1991), 407.

[75] Plender, R., and M. Wilderspin, *The European Private International Law of Obligations*, Sweet & Maxwell, London, Third Edition, 2009, pp. 338.

[76] At least those overriding mandatory provisions that are not the implementation of Union law.

connecting factors. If the ECJ were to adopt the German position, it would prevent French courts from classifying rules that equalise the strength between the private parties as overriding mandatory provisions. Similarly, were the ECJ to rule that the relationship is not exclusive, a strong argument could be in Germany to reconsider the case-law of the Bundesgerichtshof.

The interpretation given by the French and German courts are mutually exclusive and it would, in the light of uniform application of the Rome I be desirable to ask the European Court of Justice on the earliest occasion for clarification. It must therefore be seen as a missed opportunity that the Bundesgerichtshof recently reconfirmed its position, without asking the ECJ for a preliminary ruling.[77]

In order for art. 34 EGBGB to bite on its current interpretation the provision must thus at least protect a public interest. The public interest at stake must justify the *Sonderanknüpfung*. Moreover the situation must fall within the scope of the protected interest and there should be a sufficient close link. The provision must not assume an exorbitant scope of application and finally application of the overriding mandatory provision should not contravene EU law.[78] It is interesting to observe that contrary to the French courts, German courts do specifically address the issue whether application of an overriding mandatory provision is contrary to Union law, and in particular the free movement provisions.[79]

3.2.2 *Self Limitation*

The result of the *Sonderanknüpfung* is that a German overriding mandatory provision can find application regardless the applicable law, but on the other hand the fact that German law is applicable does not necessarily result in the application of German overriding mandatory provisions. *Sonderanknüpfung* renders the debate about the minimum or maximum scope of application of overriding mandatory provisions unnecessary. The fact that an overriding mandatory provisions originates in the *lex causae* is not sufficient to justify application and the overriding mandatory provision has to separately justify its own application. The overriding mandatory provision can therefore not be

---

[77] Bundesgerichtshof 9 July 2009 XA ZR 19/08.

[78] Sonnenberger, H., "Eingriffsrecht – Das trojanische Pferd im IPR oder notwendige Ergänzung?", *IPRax*, 2003, pp. 104–116.

[79] Bundesgerichtshof 27 February 2003 VII ZR 169/02.

applied outside its own scope of application. *Sonderanknüpfung* thus automatically leads to a maximum scope of application.

3.2.3 *Foreign Overriding Mandatory Provisions*

Art. 34 EGBGB only refers to German overriding mandatory provisions and the EGBGB contains no reference to the application of foreign overriding mandatory provisions. Germany is due to a reservation under art. 22 (1a) not bound to art. 7(1) of the Rome Convention. German courts principally refuse to apply foreign public law.[80] This does not mean, however, that foreign overriding mandatory provisions cannot have effect in German courts. The fact that an overriding mandatory provision cannot be applied directly does not mean its factual consequences should be ignored. Foreign overriding mandatory provisions may be classified as an operation of fact and not of law.[81]

German authors make a distinction between the normative and the factual application of a rule.[82] Normative application of the provision as such is used to establish the immorality of the contract (par. 138 BGB). Factual application is not concerned with the norm itself, but rather with its practical effects. Normative application of a rule might not be contrary to the German *ordre public*, but that foreign norm may nevertheless generate criminal responsibility outside of Germany. The *Iranian Beer Supply Contract* case concerned the export of German beer to Iran. After Ayatollah Khomeini came into power, the import of beer to Iran was criminalised and violators could be sentenced to death. The Bundesgerichtshof concluded, in the light of the criminal liability, that the parties were mutually freed from their obligations.[83] In general, the factual consequences of foreign overriding mandatory provisions have been accepted as a defence to defaulting on the obligations due to objective impossibility.[84]

---

[80] Zimmer, D., "Auslandisches Wirtschaftsrecht vor deutschen Zivilgerichten: Zur Unterscheidungg zwischen einer normativen Berücksichtigung fremder zwingender Normen und einer bloßen Beachtung ihrer tatsachlichen Folgen", *IPRax*, 1993, pp. 65–69.

[81] Reithmann, C., und D. Martiny, *Internationales Vertragsrecht: das Internationale Privatrecht der Schuldvertrage*, Verlag Dr Otto Schmidt KG, Köln, 1988, pp. 346.

[82] Zimmer, *supra* 80; Kuckein, M., *Die 'Berüksichtigung' von Eingriffsnormen im deutschen und englischen internationalen Vertragsrecht*, Mohr Siebeck, Tübingen, 2008, pp. 72–83.

[83] Bundesgerichtshof 8 February 1984 VII ZR 254/82, NJW 1984, 1746.

[84] Brüning, S., *Die Beachtlichkeit des fremden ordre public*, Duncker & Humblot, Berlin, 1996, pp. 126–142.

An example of normative application is the *Nigerian Masks* case where a Nigerian company had concluded an insurance contract with a German insurer for the transportation of cultural items.[85] When some of the items did not arrive at their destination the Nigerian company claimed compensation. According to Nigerian law the cultural goods could only be exported with prior approval. The Nigerian company had not obtained such approval. The Bundesgerichtshof held that the Nigerian export regulation could not as such be applied to a contract governed by German law but that the disregard of an export regulation of the country of origin constituted a *Verstoß gegen die guten Sitten* and was therefore contrary to par. 138 BGB.

Foreign overriding mandatory provisions could also be applied if they are part of the *lex causae*. The *Schuldstatutstheorie* does not distinguish between general private law and overriding mandatory provisions. It thus favours the application foreign overriding mandatory provisions that are part of applicable law provided that they do no conflict with the *ordre public*. When the connecting factor refers to, for example, Swedish law it also refers to Swedish overriding mandatory provisions.[86] One can find cases where courts have applied foreign overriding mandatory provisions that originated in the *lex causae*. For example, the Oberlandesgericht Schleswig-Holstein applied Austrian law to a credit agreement between two Austrian nationals. To answer the question whether the agreement was null and void the OLG applied the par. 3 of the Austrian Devisengesetzes (1946).[87] Similarly, the OLG Hamburg applied Russian monetary law to decide on the nullity of a performance to a contract governed by Russian law.[88] The case-law is however far from consistent and no general conclusion can be reached.[89]

The reservation made by Germany to art. 7 (1) of the Rome Convention was therefore not due to an absolute impossibility of applying foreign (semi) public law but rather the fear that the possibility of applying overriding mandatory provisions might lead to too much legal uncertainty.[90] Art. 9 (3) Rome I introduces a limited possibility for

[85] Bundesgerichtshof 22 June 1972, BGHZ 59.
[86] Habermeier, S., *Neue Wege zum Wirtschaftskollisionsrecht*, Nomos, Baden-Baden, 1997.
[87] Oberlandesgericht Schleswig-Holstein IPRspr. 1954/55, 463.
[88] Oberlandesgericht Hamburg *IPRspr*. 1930, 43 (Bruning *supra* note 84).
[89] For example : Bundesgerichtshof 7 December 2000, *NJW* (2001), 1936.
[90] Drucksache[n] des Deutschen Bundestages, 10/504, 100.

courts to apply foreign overriding mandatory provisions. Since there is no obligation, courts are free to refuse direct application and turn to national private law. Art. 9 (3) Rome I does therefore not necessitate a change in the German approach.

The general German conflict of laws rules place a heavy emphasis on the private parties and the strict separation between public and private law. The concept of overriding mandatory provisions has been a hotly debated topic in German legal doctrine. German overriding mandatory provisions are subject to a *Sonderanknüpfung*. Their application is independently assessed from the applicable law. Consequently, Germany adheres to a maximalist approach. A similar treatment towards foreign overriding mandatory provisions does not exist. German courts are reluctant in the application of foreign public law. A solution however exists outside of PIL; effect may be given to foreign overriding mandatory provisions via general clauses in substantive private law.

3.3 *The Netherlands*

Arts. 6, 7 and 10 of the law on general provisions of regulation of the Kingdom (1829) contain some conflict of laws rules.[91] Art. 6 and 10 are still in force and art. 7 was only repealed in May 2008. The law is based on the Dutch statutist approach and strongly underlines the principle of territoriality. The provisions only regulated very limited PIL issues[92] and until the second half of the 20th century Dutch PIL was primarily based on case-law. Since the beginning of the eighties one can observe the start of a process of national codification. The codification process has not yet been completed and the consolidation of conflict of laws rules in an additional book to the Civil Code is currently pending in Parliament.[93]

---

[91] Wet van 15 mei 1829 houdende algemeene bepalingen der wetgeving van het Koningrijk

[92] Art. 6 provides that the laws on the privileges, status and capacity are binding upon Dutch nationals even if they reside abroad; art. 7 provided for the *lex rei sitae* rule and art. 10 provides that the form of legal acts is to be assessed according to the place where the legal act occurred.

[93] Vaststelling en invoering van Boek 10 (Internationaal privaatrecht) van het Burgerlijk Wetboek (Vaststellings- en Invoeringswet Boek 10 Burgerlijk Wetboek), Tweede Kamer Vergaderjaar 2009–2010, 32 137 no. 2. Book 10 would apply to all matters insofar not covered by EU regulations.

Belgium, the Netherlands and Luxembourg have, however, already attempted several times since the late forties to codify PIL on the Benelux level. A Benelux Convention on Private International Law was accepted by the governments in 1951 and revised in 1969 but never ratified.[94] The Dutch government finally withdrew its proposal for ratification pending in parliament in 1976. The official reason was the development of PIL within the framework of the EEC, but few government officials will have mourned the definitive end of the Benelux codification.

Until the entry into force of the Rome Convention case-law represented also in international contracts the main source of conflict of laws rules. Lower courts heavily relied on legal doctrine. Legal doctrine was divided between proponents of multilateral and unilateral conflict of laws rules. The former were represented by Asser who advocated legal certainty through international uniformity. The latter was most prominently represented by Josephus Jitta and emphasised the development of unilateral rules through gradual national codification. The view of Asser ultimately prevailed and was further elaborated upon by Koster, who inspired by Von Savigny, developed what was at that time referred to as the 'Bible of Dutch Private International Law'.[95] The strong influence of legal doctrine can be explained by the fact that the Hoge Raad (Supreme Court) could until 1963 only to a limited extent decide upon PIL issues. After that year, the case-law of the Hoge Raad gained increasing importance due the expansion of its general review powers.[96]

The question of what legal system should be applicable to an international contract has been a cause of division amongst Dutch scholars for a very long time.[97] The theory of the most characteristic performance

---

[94] Tractatenblad 1951, no. 125; Tractatenblad 1969, no. 167; Meijers, E., "The Benelux Convention on Private International Law", *American Journal of Comparative Law*, Vol. II, No. 1, 1953, pp. 1–11.

[95] For further discussion and references: Boele-Woelki, K., C. Joustra and G. Steenhoff, "Dutch Private International Law at the end of the 20th Century: Pluralism of Methods, Netherlands Reports to the Fifteenth International Congress of Comparative Law", S. Symeonides (ed.), *Private International Law at the End of the 20th Century: Progress or Regress?*, Kluwer Law International, Deventer, 2000, pp. 203–227.

[96] A decision of a lower court could now also quashed for a violation of unwritten principles of law. This was in the light of its uncodified nature extremely important for PIL. See: Bloembergen, A., (et al.), *De Hoge Raad der Nederlanden: De plaats van de Hoge Raad in het huidige staatsbestel*, Tjeenk Willink, Zwolle, 1988, pp. 79–81.

[97] Strikwerda, L., *De overeenkomst in het IPR*, Kluwer, Deventer, 2004.

as introduced by De Winter in Dutch legal writing gradually gained acceptance in case-law.[98] The test of the most characteristic performance, borrowed from Swiss PIL and later incorporated in art. 4 of the Rome Convention, results in the application of the law of the place of establishment of the party that has to deliver the most characteristic performance.[99] For example, a contract for the sale of a good primarily focuses on the delivery of the good, rather than the counter performance – the payment of the purchase price. The most characteristic performance is therefore the sale of the good and consequently the law of the place of the residence of the seller will be applicable. Under the Rome Convention, however, the test only creates a presumption. Despite the place of residence of the seller it is possible that the situation is more closely connected to a different legal system. When interpreting the Rome Convention the Hoge Raad confirmed in 1992 that the test of the most characteristic performance is the main rule but that particular circumstances of the situation may lead to a different conclusion, although it held that the exceptions to the test of the most characteristic performance must be interpreted narrowly.[100]

The test of the most characteristic performance becomes relevant only in the absence of a choice of law. Contrary to the situation in Germany before the introduction of the Rome Convention, Dutch PIL required an explicit choice of law and did not have a doctrine of an implicit or hypothetical choice of law.[101] The question whether parties should be allowed the possibility of a choice of law had been subject of a long controversy.[102] It was perceived that the principle of a choice of law was hard to conceptualise in Dutch PIL and that parties should not

---

[98] De Winter, L., "Enige Beschouwingen over de Wet van de Karakteristieke Prestatie", *Met eerbiedigende werking, opstellen aangeobden aan prof. Hijmans van den Bergh*, Kluwer, Deventer, 1971, pp. 367.

[99] Rammeloo, S., *Das Neue EG-Vertragskollisionrecht*, Carl Heymanns Verlag KG, Köln, 1992, pp. 286–318.

[100] Hoge Raad 25 September 1992, *Nederlandse Jurisprudentie* (1992), 750 (Balenpers). More recently: Hoge Raad 17 October 2008 LJN: BE7201 (Embrica). The position of the Hoge Raad can however no longer be maintained in the light of Case C-133/08 *Intercontainer Interfrigo (ICF) SC v Balkenende Oosthuizen BV and MIC Operations BV* [2009] ECR I-9687.

[101] Van Rooij, R., and M. Polak, *Private International Law in the Netherlands*, Kluwer, Deventer, 1987, pp. 121; De Boer, Th., "Subjectieve verwijzing: anomalie of grondbeginsel?", *Partij-invloed in het international privaatrecht; Vier opstellen ter gelegenheid van het 25-jarig bestaan van het Centrum voor Buitenlands Recht en Internationaal Privaatrecht aan de Universiteit van Amsterdam*, Deventer, Kluwer, 1974, pp. 47–72.

[102] Deelen, J., *Rechtskeuze in het Nederlands internationaal contractenrecht*, W.L.G. Lemaire, Amsterdam 1965.

be given the ability to place themselves above the objectively applicable law.[103] It was maintained that parties should not be allowed to prevent the application of mandatory laws and could therefore only choose in the non-mandatory substantive law, not in PIL. The Hoge Raad only took a clear stand in favour of the possibility of a choice of law in the famous *Alnati* decision.[104]

In a contract for the carriage of potatoes from Antwerp (Belgium) to Rio de Janeiro (Brazil) a choice of law in favour of Dutch law was made. The contract excluded the liability of the carrier for damage or loss of the cargo. Such a clause would be void under art. 91 of the Belgian Code of Commerce. The Hoge Raad confirmed that the principle of party autonomy entailed that parties to an international contract could exclude the otherwise applicable law, including the mandatory rules as long as this does not conflict with the law. The Hoge Raad referred here to Dutch overriding mandatory provisions and conflict of laws rules that exclude a choice of law. The Hoge Raad continued and observed that a foreign State may have such an interest in the observance of its mandatory rules outside its territory that these rules have to be respected by a Dutch court. Contracting parties can thus not exclude these rules, not even by a choice of law. In this particular case, the Hoge Raad ruled that the connection with Belgium was not sufficiently close to warrant the application of Belgian mandatory rules.[105]

It is in the Alnati case important to keep the national background in mind. The decision came only three years after the Hoge Raad was, through an expansion of its review powers, made capable of providing active guidance in PIL issues. It had to make two principle decisions at once: first of all whether parties could validly select a law other than the law that would have been applicable according to the objective connecting factors and secondly, whether (foreign) rules could independently warrant application. The acceptance of a special category of mandatory rules partially met the objection raised by legal writers that parties should not be allowed to place themselves above the (objective) applicable law, while on the other hand it honoured the desire of

[103] Bervoets, Th., "Een rechtstheoretisch onderzoek naar het beginsel van rechtskeuze", *Partij-invloed in het international privaatrecht; Vier opstellen ter gelegenheid van het 25-jarig bestaan van het Centrum voor Buitenlands Recht en Internationaal Privaatrecht aan de Universiteit van Amsterdam*, Deventer, Kluwer, 1974, pp. 31–45.

[104] Strikwerda, L., *Inleiding tot het Nederlandse Internationaal Privaatrecht*, Kluwer, Deventer, 2005, pp. 171.

[105] Hoge Raad 13 May 1966, *Nederlandse Jurisprudentie* (1967), 3 (Alnati).

autonomy for market participants in commercial dealings. Accepting the possibility of application of foreign overriding mandatory provisions maintained the multilateral flavour of Dutch conflict of laws rules and worked towards international uniformity. The Hoge Raad seized the Alnati case as an opportunity to take a stand on the core principles of the Dutch conflict of laws system.

The concept of overriding mandatory provisions, referred to in Dutch as 'voorrangsregels', was introduced in the Netherlands by De Winter. He recognised the applicability to international contracts of a Dutch mandatory provision '*when it fulfils an important socio-economic function and if it flows from its purpose that the rule should be applied in the case concerned.*'[106] Overriding mandatory provisions gained ground because Dutch scholars did not accept the preposition of Von Savigny that private law can be found in society. Legal rules, even strict private law rules, are issued by the legislator to shape and adjust society.[107]

Dutch legal writing was initially reluctant to countenance recognition of semi-public law in the conflict of laws rules. In the beginning of the 19th century, semi public law was perceived to be positive *ordre public* and therefore subject to the principle of territoriality. Proponents of this territorial theory were supported by a decision of the Hoge Raad in 1907 where it declared the Dutch rules on divorce to be *ordre public* norms. Every Dutch court confronted with a divorce had to apply Dutch law, regardless of the fact whether the divorce had connections with other jurisdictions.[108] The territorial approach was gradually replaced by a *lex causae* approach. It was thus assumed that the conflict of laws rules referred both to the 'pure' private law as well as to semi public rules. The basic notion was that a judge should decide a foreign case in an identical way to the foreign judge. All semi-public rules of the *lex causae* had therefore to be applied. The neutral Savignian conflict of laws rules are, however, not adequately equipped to deal with semi-public law, and the *lex causae* approach therefore had to allow for more and more exceptions, ultimately making it untenable.[109]

---

[106] De Winter, L., "Dwingend recht bij internationale overeenkomsten", *Nederlands Tijdschrift voor Internationaal Recht*, 1964, pp. 329–365. Translated from Dutch by Boele-Woelki/Joustra/Steenhoff, *supra* note 95, pp. 203–227.

[107] Strikwerda, L., *Semipubliekrecht in het conflictenrecht: Kruispunt van methoden*, Tjeenk Willink, Alphen a/d Rijn, 1978, pp. 131.

[108] Hoge Raad 13 December 1907, W. 8636 (Boon-Schmidt)

[109] Strikwerda, *supra* note 104, pp. 68–75.

3.3.1 *Classification*

The consequence of *Alnati* is the 'bijzondere aanknopingsleer'. An overriding mandatory provision is not automatically applicable but its applicability has to be separately assessed. The approach has strong similarities with *Sonderanknüpfung* in Germany. Just as in Germany, the discussion about the minimum or maximum scope of application abounds. The content, function and regulatory interest may merit the application of a rule otherwise outside the *lex causae*, but overriding mandatory provisions originating in the *lex causae* are not necessarily applied. Whereas purely private laws remain subject to the Savignian approach, that is to say the applicable law deduced from the situation, the applicability of semi-public rules is deduced from the rule itself. The dual approach is referred to as 'tweesporigheid'.[110]

Art. 7 of the book 10 draft provides for a definition of overriding mandatory provisions that is nearly identical to art. 9 (1) Rome I. The second subparagraph deals with the application of Dutch overriding mandatory provisions:[111]

> De toepassing van het recht waarnaar een verwijzingsregel verwijst, blijft achterwege, voor zover in het gegeven geval bepalingen van Nederlands bijzonder dwingend recht toepasselijk zijn..[112]

The provision does not differ in effect from art. 9 (2) Rome I. According to the prevailing opinion in Dutch doctrine overriding mandatory provisions can be aimed both at the safeguard of public interests as well as the safeguard of a private interest.[113] The acceptance of second

---

[110] Van Hoek, A., "De Bilaterisering van de Voorrangsleer in Europa", Th. de Boer (ed.), *Voorkeur voor de lex fori; Symposium ter gelegenheid van het afscheid van Prof. Th. de Boer*, Kluwer, Deventer, 2004, pp. 5–36

[111] The concept mainly relates to areas of conflict of laws that have not yet been harmonised on a Community level. It is specifically provided that the concept would apply to contracts in so far they are not covered by Rome I (art. 154). Vaststelling en invoering van Boek 10 (Internationaal privaatrecht) van het Burgerlijk Wetboek (Vaststellings- en Invoeringswet Boek 10 Burgerlijk Wetboek), Tweede Kamer, Vergaderjaar 2009–2010, 32 137, no. 2.

[112] 'The application of the law that is applicable according to a conflict of laws rule shall not be forthcoming, in so far as in the case concerned provisions of Dutch overriding mandatory provisions are applicable'.

[113] Strikwerda, *supra* note 104, pp. 72. Similair: Bertrams, R., and S. Kruisinga, *Overeenkomsten in het internationaal privaatrecht en het Weens Koopverdrag*, Kluwer, Deventer, 2007, pp. 58. Contra: Roelvink, H., "Artikel 6:2 BW en het Nederlandse IPR, in: Grensoverschijdend Privaatrecht", *Opstellen aangeboden aan J. Rijn van Alkemade*, Kluwer, Deventer, 1993, pp. 219–230 (224).

generation overriding mandatory provisions is however rather theoretical and application is rare.[114] Strikwerda argues that due to the emergence of protective connecting factors the second generation has lost a part of its relevance. The difference in power between the parties in labour and consumer contracts has already been equalised in the connecting factor.

Dutch courts do not easily classify a national provision as overriding mandatory. The general provision on fair dealings was for example not considered as an overriding mandatory provision.[115] The same applied to the mandatory employment rules laid down in book 7 Title 10 Civil Code. These rules are only mandatory in a domestic sense. On the other hand, the provisions on the attachment of earnings and the indexation of the minimum amount of pay with inflation are considered to be overriding mandatory provisions[116] as well on the law on employee participation.[117]

Outside the field of labour and consumer law a handful of provisions have been classified as overriding mandatory.[118] The Explanatory Memorandum to the proposed book 10 mentions as examples the Mededingingswet (Dutch competition law) and exchange controls.[119] Several examples may also be found in the case-law. A testator with Monegasque nationality (the law of Monaco was therefore applicable to the legacy) bequeathed several art objects and paintings to the Bredius Museum, a Dutch body of public law, on the condition that the art works could never leave the museum. After visitor numbers dropped the city council sought to relocate the museum and art works, but this was contrary to the legacy. The city council requested a Dutch court to change the legacy pursuant to the Museumwet in order to allow for permanent exposition on a different location. The Hoge Raad held that since the legacy was made to a Dutch public law body and the art works

114 Van Hoek, A., *Internationale mobiliteit van werknemers: Een onderzoek naar de interactie tussen arbeidsrecht, EG-recht en IPR aan de hand van de detacheringsrichtlijn*, SDU, Den Haag, 2000, pp. 129

115 Opinion AG Strikwerda in Hoge Raad 18 May 1998, *Nederlandse Jurisprudentie* (1999), 169

116 Polak, M., *Arbeidsverhoudingen in het Nederlandse internationaal privaatrecht*, Kluwer, Deventer, 1988, pp. 120–122.

117 Wet op de Ondernemingsraden.

118 Staatscommissie voor het Internationaal Privaatrecht, Rapport Algemene Bepalingen Wet Internationaal Privaatrecht (2002), par. 56.

119 Memorie van Toelichting, Vaststelling en invoering boek 10, Tweede Kamer, vergaderjaar 2009–2010, 32 137, no. 3.

were permanently exhibited in the Netherlands there was a sufficient close link with Dutch general interest to warrant the application of the Museumwet.[120]

Also art. 6 (now: 7) of the law on the supervision on stock transactions (1995) was held to be an overriding mandatory provision.[121] Art. 6 required a broker that operated on the Dutch market to have a licence. The Amsterdam Court of Appeal therefore refused to enforce a contract nominating German law between a German broker that operated on the Dutch market and a Dutch non-professional stockholder due to the lack of a licence of the operator.[122]

Also the Dutch legislator often attempts to simplify the task of the judge of establishing which norms should be classified as overriding mandatory by indicating the international field of application of a rule. An example can be found in art. 6:247 of the Civil Code. This provision stipulates that section 3 of title 5 of book 6 on general terms is applicable, regardless of the applicable law to contracts between professional traders that are both established in the Netherlands, but not applicable regardless the applicable law when one of the parties is not established in the Netherlands.

3.3.2 *Self Limitation*

Looking back, the first hint of the decision of the Hoge Raad in *Alnati* and the *bijzondere aanknopingsleer* could already be observed in *Melchers*.[123] Art. 6 of the Buitengewoon Besluit Arbeidsverhoudingen (Labour Relations Decree, BBA) requires prior approval of dismissal by the Director of the District Employment Office. The BBA is primarily aimed at the protection of the Dutch labour market.[124] The Hoge Raad held, however, that the fact that Dutch law was applicable to the labour relationship did not necessarily mean that the interests were so much related to the Dutch labour market that application of the BBA was required. Because the dismissal would not have any impact on the Dutch labour market, the Hoge Raad refused to apply art. 6 BBA. Had

---

120 Hoge Raad 16 March 1990, *Nederlandse Jurisprudentie* (1991), 575. Forder, C., "The Bredius Museum Case: Public Interest and Private International Law", *International Journal of Cultural Property*, vol. 2, 1993, pp. 117–126.

121 Wet toezicht effectenverkeer 16 november 1995.

122 Hof Amsterdam 14 January 1999, *Nederlands Tijdschrift voor het Internationaal Privaatrecht*, 1999, pp. 152

123 Hoge Raad 5 June 1953, *Nederlandse Jurisprudentie* (1953), 613 (Melchers)

124 Polak, *supra* note 116, pp. 100.

the Hoge Raad followed the *lex causae* approach it would have resulted in the automatic application of the BBA. To assess the applicability of art. 6 BBA courts nowadays use the test whether it is reasonable to expect that the employee would, after termination of the employment contract, fall back on the Dutch labour market. A US citizen being posted by a US company for a period of five years in The Hague was for example not likely to fall back on the Dutch labour market.[125] No prior approval of dismissal was therefore necessary.

3.3.3 *Foreign Overriding Mandatory Provisions*

The Hoge Raad in *Alnati* explicitly confirmed the possibility of applying foreign overriding mandatory provisions. The Netherlands also did not make a reservation against art. 7 (1) Rome Convention. The possibility of applying foreign overriding mandatory provisions is recognised in art. 7 (3) of the draft book 10:

> Bij de toepassing van het recht waarnaar een verwijzingsregel verwijst, kan gevolg worden toegekend aan bepalingen van bijzonder dwingend recht van een vreemde staat waarmee het geval nauw is verbonden. Bij de beslissing of aan deze bepalingen gevolg moet worden toegekend, wordt rekening gehouden met hun aard en strekking alsmede met de gevolgen die uit het toepassen of het niet toepassen van deze bepalingen zouden voortvloeien.[126]

The formulation of art. 7 resembles much more 7 (1) Rome Convention than art. 9 (3) Rome I. The application of foreign overriding mandatory provisions is not limited to the country where an obligation has to be performed. In part, that can be explained from the fact that book 10 would apply to the whole area of PIL and not just contractual obligations (that fall outside the scope of Rome I). Reference to the law of the place where the contract has to be performed is not then appropriate. Another feature is that art. 7 (3) does not distinguish between overriding mandatory provisions that are part of the *lex causae* and overriding mandatory provisions that are not. The explanatory memorandum explicitly holds that foreign overriding mandatory provisions are due

---

[125] Hoge Raad 23 oktober 1987, *Nederlandse Jurisprudentie* (1988), 842 (Sorensen)

[126] When applying under a conflict of laws rule the law of a country, effect may be given to the overriding mandatory provisions of the law of a foreign State with which the situation has a close connection. In considering whether to give effect to these mandatory rules, regard shall be had to their nature and purpose and to the consequences of their application or non-application.

to the bijzondere aanknopingsleer not automatically part of the governing law.[127] Their application has to be assessed separately from the application of the governing law. Naturally, this can only occur under art. 7 (3) of the draft book 10 or art. 9 (3) Rome I. The Hoge Raad has so far never made use of the possibility of applying foreign overriding mandatory provisions.

A striking example of the unwillingness to give effect to foreign overriding mandatory provisions is the *Sewrajsingh* case.[128] Mr. Sewrajsingh sold and conveyed his matrimonial home without the permission of his wife to his brother, a Surinam resident. The property was situated in the Netherlands Antilles and that law applied. Mrs. Sewrajsingh tried to nullify the contract on the basis that the brother did obtain prior governmental authorisation as required by the Surinam Exchange Regulation (1947) for the acquisition of property outside Surinam. The Hoge Raad held that the interest of the Netherlands Antilles of upholding real estate transactions in general outweighed the interest of Suriname (prevention of excessive outflow of Surinamese currency) since nullifying the contract would not significantly promote the Surinamese interest. This is quite interesting. The Surinamese law attaches strong importance to the place of residence of the parties. In fact, it is a literal copy of the Dutch Exchange Decree (1945), which operated on the same principle. The operation of the Suriname Exchange Regulation would be severely jeopardised if contracts for the acquisition of foreign property were enforceable abroad without prior authorisation.[129] Moreover, the Hoge Raad did not at all address Art. VIII Sec. 2 (b) Bretton Woods that stipulated that: '*exchange contracts which involve the currency of any member and which are contrary to the exchange control regulations of that member maintained or imposed consistently with this Agreement, shall be unenforceable in the territories of any member.*'[130]

Lower courts also seem reluctant to apply foreign overriding mandatory provisions. During the Turkish occupation of Cyprus four icons

[127] Memorie van Toelichting, *supra* note 119, 16.

[128] Hoge Raad 12 January 1979 *Nederlandse Jurisprudentie* (1980), pp. 526.

[129] Jessurun d'Oliveira, H., "Eigen huis is vreemde valuta waard", *Ars Aequi*, Vol. 29, No. 4, 1980, pp. 254–262. Critical: Schultsz, J., "Annotation to *Sewrajsingh*", *Nederlandse Jurisprudentie*, No. 42, 1980, pp. 1700–1702.

[130] It can of course be doubted whether the contract at issue constitutes an exchange contract: Madsen-Mygdal, N., "The Bretton Woods Agreement Article VIII, Sec. 2 (b)", *Nordic Journal of International Law*, Vol. 25, No. 1, 1955, pp. 63–78.

disappeared from a Greek orthodox church. The icons resurfaced in the Netherlands and were bought in the seventies by a Dutch collector. The church claimed it had remained owner on the basis of Cypriot Antiquities Law and art. 27 of the Cypriot Sale of Goods Law and that these provisions should be applied regardless the applicability of Dutch law. The District Court Rotterdam simply stated that the Cypriot provisions could not be classified as overriding mandatory.[131] The Rotterdam court arrived at that conclusion rather easily. The protection of cultural items, especially in armed conflicts, is an aim recognised by the international community.[132] Application of the *lex rei sitae* rule automatically leads to application of the law of place where the object resurfaces and a subsequent real right is established. Cypriot legislation can therefore only effectively protect Cypriot artefacts if legislation such as the Cypriot Antiquities Law can be applied regardless of the applicable law. The principle refusal to classify the Cypriot provisions as overriding mandatory is, in light of the already described *Bredius* case, remarkable. Although in theory the concept of overriding mandatory provisions is multilateral, one cannot escape the conclusion that domestic mandatory provisions enjoy a preferential position as opposed to foreign overriding mandatory provisions.

Is the acceptance of the possibility to apply foreign overriding mandatory provisions in *Alnati* then merely a feint made by the Hoge Raad to maintain the dogmatic multilateral approach? That conclusion would be too pessimistic. In 2000, the Hoge Raad quashed a decision of the Court of Appeal of 's Gravenhage that had failed to investigate the argument made by one of the parties that the Belgian law on provisions relating to the supervision of insurance companies (1975) led to the nullity of the insurance agreement.[133] It is true that courts are very reluctant in the application of foreign overriding mandatory provisions, but the fact that they are considered demonstrates that the possibility is not a dead letter.

---

[131] Rechtbank Rotterdam 4 February 1999, *Nederlands Internationaal Privaatrecht*, 1999, no 159.

[132] See for example: Convention on the protection of Cultural Property in the event of armed conflict (1954).

[133] Hoge Raad 24 March 2000, LJN: AA5259. The case was referred to the Amsterdam Court of Appeal which concluded that in fact no insurance contract was ever concluded, making the question towards the Belgian overriding mandatory provision superfluous.

The District Court Maastricht did apply a Belgian overriding mandatory provision.[134] The facts of the case fell outside the temporal scope of the Rome Convention and was therefore tried under old Dutch PIL. In an employment contract between Wittevrongel (the employee) and Vadotex a choice of law in favour of Dutch law had been made. Wittevrongel had Belgian nationality and the employment contract was to be performed in Belgium. In 1993, Vadotex terminated in accordance with Dutch law the employment contract. Belgian labour law provided for a longer termination period and Wittevrongel lodged a claim for the recovery of wage payable over the Belgian termination period. The Maastricht court ruled that the labour provision constituted an overriding mandatory provision in the sense of art. 3 of the Belgian Civil Code and should therefore be applied by a Dutch court. The decision has been criticised because the court did not establish the relevance of the application of the rule to the Belgian public policy, but seemed to have blindly accepted the binding effect of the Belgian classification.[135]

Also the Dutch civil code contains a provision that leads to the nullity of legal acts that are contrary to the law, public order or good morals (art. 3:40 BW). The foreign overriding mandatory provision can as such not be applied, since art. 3:40 only refers to Dutch law.[136] In certain limited circumstances the violation of a foreign (overriding mandatory) provision may violate good morals, for example when parties violate foreign legislation in bad faith.[137]

The development of overriding mandatory provisions in the Netherlands thus strongly coincided with the grant of the autonomy to private parties to choose the applicable law. In *Alnati* the Hoge Raad accepted that both Dutch and foreign overriding mandatory provisions

---

[134] Rechtbank Maastricht, 7 March 1996, NIPR 1996, no. 240.

[135] Van der Plas, C., *De taak van de rechter en het IPR: een verkenning van de grenzen van de taak van de Nederlandse rechter bij de toepassing van vreemd privaat- en publiekrecht*, Kluwer, Deventer, 2005, pp. 253–255.

[136] Hoge Raad 22 February 1924, *Nederlandse Jurisprudentie* (1924), p. 488. Hartkamp, A., *Mr. C. Asser's Handleiding tot de Beoefening van het Nederlands Burgerlijk Recht: Verbintenissenrecht: Deel II Algemene leer der overeenkomsten*, Tjeen Willink, Deventer, 10e druk, 1997, pp. 230.

[137] Hoge Raad 16 November 1956, *Nederlandse Jurisprudentie* (1957), 1. In this case the defendant was entitled to exchange under a favourable exchange rate Indonesian rupiahs for Dutch guilders, while the plaintiff was not. The parties agreed that the defendant would under false pretences approach the Indonesian authorities and exchange rupiahs to guilders for the plaintiff, thereby violating the Indonesian exchange law. The Hoge Raad held the contract unenforceable as contrary to good morals.

could form a restriction on the choice of law. Overriding mandatory provisions are assessed independently on their application. The Savnigian conflict of rule approach is replaced by a neo-statutist approach. The PIL division between private law and semi-public law is referred to as *bijzonder aanknoping* and leads to *tweesporigheid*. Overriding mandatory provisions do have the character of an exception in the Netherlands. Although in principle provisions primarily aimed at the protection of the weaker party can also be classified as overriding mandatory, their application is rare in practice. Despite the formal acceptance of the possibility to apply foreign overriding mandatory provisions, only one Dutch court has made use of this possibility.

3.4 *The United Kingdom*

If one desires to provide a national perspective on overriding mandatory provision within the European Union the United Kingdom is a must. Not only is English law often selected in choice of law clauses, the common law tradition is inherently different from the continental Member States compared. Although the English and Scottish legal systems of PIL do not differ as much as they do on many substantive issues, the present analysis will be limited to English law. In English doctrine conflict of laws is sometimes referred to as choice of law, whereas PIL relates to conflict of jurisdictions. This analysis will maintain the Continental (French/Dutch) conception of PIL.[138]

Whereas Bartolus de Saxoferrato (1313-1357) already laid the foundations of the continental PIL in the fourteenth century, English lawyers were not aware of the problem until the eighteenth century and the first comprehensive treatise on PIL written by an Englishman was only published in 1858.[139] The problem was avoided by applying to contracts with an international dimension the general law of the merchant common to European nations. The growing commercial and social intercourse between England, its colonies and the Continent in the nineteenth century accelerated the development of English PIL.

[138] Private International Law thus refers to the three branches in the French/Dutch tradition (jurisdiction, applicable law and recognition of judgements). The system of rules that designates the applicable law will be referred to as conflict of laws.

[139] Westlake, J., *A Treatise on Private International Law*,W. Maxwell, London, 1858. See: North, P., and J. Fawcett, *Cheshire and North Private International Law*, Butterworths, London, Eleventh edition, 1987, pp. 23.

The absence of a PIL tradition made the continental theories influential when in courts the *lex mercatoria* was increasingly abandoned in favour of PIL solutions.[140] The work of Von Savigny has also been influential upon the first English scholars, but mainly as means of establishing the proper law in absence of an explicit choice of law.[141]

The Savignian conception of PIL as the law of the nations and the interchangeability of private laws has not been very popular. Dicey refused to give an autonomous status to private law norms and was principally against giving effect to the laws of a foreign sovereign.[142] PIL was traditionally seen as a branch of national law. It gave courts the possibility to maintain the idea of national sovereignty and the superior status of English law in England.[143]

The preference to classify PIL as a part of the national legal system rather than forming part of international law can perhaps be explained by an interesting feature of English PIL. It does not only have to solve international conflicts, but internal conflicts as well. Deciding whether the law of England or Scotland applies is just as relevant as deciding whether the law of France or Germany applies. Scottish law is in that sense as foreign as French or German law. Classifying the law that determines the applicable law in cases with an English and Scottish element as international law would undoubtedly make the hearts at the headquarters of the Scottish National Party beat faster.

Just as in the Continental countries case-law was until the middle of the twentieth century the primary source of conflict of laws rules in England. The implementation of international conventions and some very important law reforms prepared by the Law Commission made statutes gradually replace case-law.[144] Also the conflict rules in

---

[140] Sack, A., "Conflict of Laws in the History of English Law", *Law: A Century of Progress 1835–1935*, New York Vol. III, 1937, pp. 342–454 (375–377).

[141] Nadelmann, K., "Private International Law: Lord Fraser and the Savigny (Guthrie) and Bar (Gillespie) Editions", *International and Comparative Law Quarterly*, Vol. 20, No. 2, 1971, pp. 213–222.

[142] Cutler, C., Private Power and Global Authority: Transnational Merchant Law in the Global Political Economy, Cambridge University Press, Cambridge, 2003, pp. 48–49.

[143] Lord Mansfield in *Holman v Johnson* (1775) 1 Cowp 341 'Every action here must be tried by the law of England, but the law of England says that in a variety of circumstances, with regard to contracts legally made abroad, the laws of the country where the cause of action arose shall govern.' Hood, K., *Conflict of Laws within the UK*, Oxford University Press, Oxford, 2007, pp. 30.

[144] North/Fawcett, *supra* note 139, pp. 11.

international contracts were prior to the implementation of the Rome Convention, part of the common law.[145]

The starting point of the common law was that every contract was governed by its 'proper law'. The notion proper law was introduced by Westlake and is 'the law of country with which the contract has its most real connection'.[146] The proper law governs a specific legal issue.[147] Dicey's theory was that the proper law was established by an express choice of law, alternatively an implied choice of law, or in the lack of both alternatively the closest and most real connection gained the upper hand.[148] The principle that parties may choose the law that governs the contract has been established since 1796.[149] There has been considerable discussion as to whether parties could choose a law that was unconnected to the situation.[150] Being the dominant law, English law was and is often chosen although no concrete link with England exists. In the *Vita Food Case* the Privy Council upheld a choice in favour of English law, despite the fact that the situation had no factual connection with England whatsoever.[151] English courts will however not uphold a choice of law that is not bona fide or that is against public policy. Bona fide means that parties cannot choose to contract under one law in order to validate an agreement that has its closest connection manifestly with another law, under which the contract would be invalid.[152] The choice of law is determined at the date of the making of the contract, but parties are allowed to change the proper law by

---

[145] Briggs, P., *The Conflict of Laws*, Oxford University Press, Oxford, 2002, pp. 147. The Rome Convention was implemented by the Contracts (Applicable) Law Act (1990).

[146] Westlake, J., A Treatise on Private International Law, W. Maxwell, London, 1858, 2

[147] Different parts of the contract could therefore be governed by different laws. Collins, L., *et al* (eds.), *Dicey, Morris and Collins on the Conflicts of Laws Volume II*, Sweet Maxwell, London, Twelfth Edition, 1993, pp. 1206 (with further references). The starting point is however that a contract has only one proper law and that varying the proper law is an exception.

[148] Morris and North, *Cases and Materials on Private International Law*, 1984 [John Morris also published *Cases on Private International Law* 4th ed., 1968, 276

[149] *Gienar v Meyer* (1796) 2 Hy Bl 603

[150] Williams, P., "The EEC Convention on the Law Applicable to Contractual Obligations", *International and Comparative Law Quarterly*, Vol. 35, 1986, pp. 1–31 (11–12).

[151] *Vita Food Products Inc. v. Unus Shipping Co. Ltd.*, [1939] A.C. 277 (P.C.)

[152] English courts have fallen short of elucidating this point: North/Fawcett, *supra* note 139, pp. 454; Briggs, P., *Agreements on Jurisdiction and Choice of Law*, Oxford University Press, Oxford, 2008, pp. 382.

agreement. The conduct of parties after contracting, however, may not be taken into account in determining the proper law.[153]

When parties have made no explicit choice of law, courts may determine that an implied choice of law has been made. The choice of jurisdiction was probably conclusive for an implied choice of law if not substantially all the other factors would point to the applicability of a different law.[154] The existence of an exclusive jurisdiction clause is also according to Rome I, a strong indication that a tacit choice of law has been made.[155]

Only if no explicit choice was made and no implicit choice could be inferred would the courts then seek to establish with which legal system the contract had its closest and most real connection. The distinction was in practice applied less rigidly. Inferring a choice of law often was an objective test, not to elicit an in intention but rather to impute an intention and many courts moved immediately from the first to the third test.[156] The influence of Von Savigny is notable. Cheshire & North propose with regard to the criteria in order to ascertain the closest most real connection:

> On an objective view of the matter, every term of the contract, every detail affecting its formation and performance, every fact that points to its *natural seat* (emphasis added) is relevant[157]

Also German PIL would only resort to the localisation of the natural seat of the legal relationship in case no choice of law was made and no implicit or hypothetical choice could be deducted. From the outset the English and German conflict of laws mechanisms with regard to international contracts had a lot in common. The reign of the proper law is, however, far more absolute than that of the applicable law in Germany. Proper law determines the obligations under a contract. English law does not know the rigid distinction between public and private law,[158] but English courts do refuse to enforce foreign penal and revenue

[153] North, P., *Essays in Private International Law*, Clarendon Press, Oxford, 1993, pp. 54–55.

[154] Briggs, *supra* note 152, pp. 160.

[155] Giuliano-Lagarde Report 14–15, recital 14 to the Rome I Regulation

[156] Collins, L., *et al* (eds.), *Dicey, Morris and Collins on the Conflicts of Laws*, Sweet Maxwell, London, fourteenth edition, Volume II, 2006, pp. 1540.

[157] North/Fawcett, *supra* note 139, pp. 464.

[158] Allison, J., "Variation of View on English Legal Distinctions between Public and Private", *Cambridge Law Journal*, Vol. 66, No. 3, 2007, pp. 698–711.

law.[159] With regard to other public laws, there is no '*general principle that this country will not entertain an action whose object is to enforce the public law of another State*'.[160] The issue of excluding beforehand rules of a semi-public nature that are part of the *lex causae* does therefore not arise in English case-law or legal writing. Rather it should be assessed in each individual case whether a special ground of English public policy would require the (public) law in question not to be enforced.[161]

3.4.1 *Classification*

Was the rule of the proper law then absolute and was deviation only possible in a case of violation of the (negative) English public policy? In contrast to the Continental legal systems, mandatory rules are relatively novel to the English legal system. English lawyers were therefore not overenthusiastic about art. 7 Rome Convention.[162] However prior to the Rome Convention a further limitation on the proper law could be found in overriding English statutes. If the situation enters into the scope of applicability of an overriding statute, the statute will push, on that point, the proper law aside.[163] The special status of statutes lets itself be explained from the position statutes traditionally take in English law. Statutory intervention is not frequent but, as constitutional rule, prevails over common law rules and previous legislation. A statute is therefore not necessarily subject to the ordinary conflict of laws rules; it has the power to alter them.[164]

In *Hollandia* the plaintiff shippers shipped a road-finishing machine on board a vessel belonging to the defendant carriers for carriage to Bonaire in the Dutch West Indies. The parties had made a choice of law in favour of Dutch law and subsequently the parties limited the carriers

---

[159] House of Lords, *In re Visser* [1928] 1 Ch. 877, 884 (Ch.D), but the principle is not without criticism: Collier, J., *Conflict of Laws*, Cambridge University Press, Cambridge, 3rd edition, 2001, pp. 369; Hewitt, E., "The exclusion of foreign revenue claims", *Cambridge Student Law Review*, Vol. 3, No. 4, 2008, pp. 289–299.

[160] Court of Appeal, *Government of the Islamic Republic of Iran v. The Barakat Galleries Ltd.*, [2008] 1 All E.R. 1177, par. 151.

[161] Staughton J.; House of Lords *A.-G. of New Zealand v. Ortiz* [1982] 1 Q.B. 349.

[162] Mann, F., "Contracts: Effects of Mandatory Rules", Lipstein, K., (ed.), *Harmonisation of Private International Law by the E.E.C.*, Chameleon Press Limited, London, 1978, pp. 31–37.

[163] Collins *et al* (eds.), *supra* note 156, pp. 24–29.

[164] Hartley, T., "Mandatory Rules in International Contracts", *Recueil des Cours*, Vol. 266, 1997, pp. 337- 431 (354).

liability to fl. 1250 (approx. GBP 250). During the unloading of the ship at Bonaire the machine got severely damaged. The damage amounted to GBP 22.000. While the United Kingdom was party to the Hague-Visby rules, the Netherlands was not. The plaintiff brought proceedings in England. Art. 8 III of the Carriage of Goods by Sea Act (1971), implementing the Hague-Visby rules in the United Kingdom, rendered the clause limiting liability void. Art. X (b) of the Carriage of Goods by Sea Act provided that the Act would apply when the carriage departed from a port in a contracting State. The House of Lords held that art. X alone determined whether the Act comes into play. Allowing the parties to contract out of the Act by a choice of law would undermine the effectiveness of the Hague-Visby rules. The Act thus applied regardless of Dutch law being the proper law.[165]

Also s 27 (2) of the Unfair Contract Terms Act and (1977), s 288 and 289 of the Trade Union and Labour Relations (Consolidation) Act (1992) and s 204 (1) of the Employment Rights Act (1996) indicate the international field of application of the respective act.[166] After s 288 limits the possibility to contract out of the Trade Union and Labour Relations (Consolidation) Act, s 289 provides: 'For the purposes of this Act it is immaterial whether the law which (apart from this Act) governs any person's employment is the law of the United Kingdom, or of a part of the United Kingdom, or not'.

The doctrine of overriding English statutes achieves with regard to statutes the same effect as the recognition of overriding mandatory provisions of the forum. When the statute is unclear it is a matter for statutory construction to establish whether the rule is deemed to apply even when the proper law is foreign (true construction).[167] There is no general set of criteria to determine the potential application of these generally worded statutory provisions,[168] but in general one should presume that an Act of Parliament is not intended to have extraterritorial

[165] *Owners of Cargo on Board the Morviken v Owners of the Hollandia* [1983] 1 A.C. 565

[166] McClean, D., and K. Beevers, *The Conflict of Laws*, Sweet & Maxwell, London, Sixth edition, 2006, pp. 359–361.

[167] Plender, R., *The European Contracts Convention : The Rome Convention on the Choice of Law for Contracts*, Sweet & Maxwell, London, 1991, pp. 156

[168] Whincop, M., and M. Keyes, "Statutes' Domains in Private International Law: An Economic Theory of the Limits of Mandatory Rules", *Sydney Law Review*, Vol. 20, 1998, pp. 435–456; Keyes, M., "Statutes, Choice of Law, and the Role of Forum Choice", *Journal of Private International Law*, Vol. 4, No. 1, 2008, pp. 1–33.

effect.[169] The theory is in any case limited to statutes and does however not cover common law rules. England did not draw the same conclusions as Germany from the adoption of art. 7 (2) Rome Convention. The application of English overriding mandatory provisions originating in common law is still perceived to be a positive operation of public policy.[170]

Outside the field of contracts overriding mandatory provisions also seem to gain recognition. With regard to tort and delicts art. 14 (4) of the Private International Law Miscellaneous Provisions Act (1995) provides that a choice of law shall not prejudice 'the operation of any rule of law which either has effect notwithstanding the rules of private international law applicable in the particular circumstances or modifies the rules of private international law that would otherwise be so applicable'.

The strong reliance on statutes has made the issue of classification less pressing than on the continent. There is no debate whether overriding mandatory provisions that primarily protect the interests of the weaker party are in principle eligible for application. If Parliament were to enact such a statute, English courts would follow its claimed scope of application.

3.4.2 *Self Limitation*

The principal of a close connection is in Brussels I save for cases of special and exclusive jurisdiction not of major concern. Parties may choose a forum that has no, or barely any, relations with the contract.[171] Rome I allows parties to an international contract to choose a completely unconnected legal system. English courts are often chosen to solve a contractual dispute applying the law of England. That position could be endangered if English semi public law would be applied to contracts that have no links with the United Kingdom whatsoever.

Art. 27 (1) of the Unfair Contract Terms Act and (1977) provides:

> Where the [law applicable to] a contract is the law of any part of the United Kingdom only by choice of the parties (and apart from that choice would be the law of some country outside the United Kingdom) sections

---

[169] Kuckein, M., *Die 'Berüksichtigung' von Eingriffsnormen im deutschen und englischen internationalen Vertragsrecht*, Mohr Siebeck, Tübingen, 2008, pp. 184–185.

[170] Hartley, *supra* note 164, pp. 351; Kuckein, *supra* note 169, pp. 175–181.

[171] Tang, Z., "The Interrelationship of European Jurisdiction and Choice of Law in Contract", *Journal of Private International Law*, Vol. 4, No. 1, 2008, pp. 35–82.

> 2 to 7 and 16 to 21 of this Act do not operate as part [of the law applicable to the contract].

The reason for the insertion of this clause was exactly that it was thought not be desirable to impose the Unfair Contract Terms Act (1977) on purely international contracts with no links to the United Kingdom because it might discourage foreign businessmen from agreeing to arbitrate in England.[172] The fact that the proper law is English is in itself not sufficient to trigger the application of English public order law. Such a provision is perceived as the opposite of an overriding statute and referred to as a self-denying statute.[173] Translated into Continental language: overriding mandatory provisions are not automatically applied because they originate in the *lex causae*. This inapplicability is however limited to self-denying statutes and no general conclusions with regard to the semi-public provisions of the proper law can be drawn. Hartley argues that public policy is usually not applied to international contracts unless there is an impact on the forum.[174] In the light of the commercial interests at stake, that assumption would for at least English overriding mandatory provisions hold ground.

3.4.3 *Foreign Overriding Mandatory Provisions*

Until now, the focus has been on English overriding mandatory provisions. The United Kingdom has made a reservation against art. 7 (1) Rome Convention. Accepting the possibility of applying foreign overriding mandatory provisions was perceived as a 'dangerous novelty for judges' and a 'source of uncertainty for litigants'.[175] The United Kingdom, in the process of drawing up the Rome Convention, adopted a very sceptical view towards foreign overriding mandatory provisions.[176] The refusal to apply foreign overriding mandatory provisions is however not absolute. The old common law with regard to foreign overriding mandatory provisions still stands.[177]

A contract is, regardless the *lex causae* or proper law, invalid if the performance is unlawful according the *lex loci solutionis* (the law of the

---

172 North/Fawcett, *supra* note 139, pp. 464. With further references.
173 Collins, L., *et al* (eds.), *supra* note 156, pp. 29.
174 Hartley, *supra* note 164, pp. 352.
175 Briggs, *supra* note 152, pp. 167
176 North, *supra* note 153, pp. 46.
177 *Akai Pty. Ltd. v. People's Insurance Co. Ltd.* [1998] 1 Lloyd's Rep. 90, 100; *Caterpillar Financial Services Corporation v. SNC Passion* [2004] EWHC 569.

place where the contract has to be performed).[178] In *Ralli v Naviera* a charter contract for the transportation of goods from India to Spain and governed by English law provided for payment of the freight upon arrival in Spain. During the voyage a Spanish decree entered into force that introduced a statutory limit on the rate payable. The statutory limit was lower than the agreed rate. The parties would be liable for criminal proceedings if the contract was performed according to its terms. The Court of Appeal gave effect to the Spanish decree by holding the contract was frustrated insofar the obligation to pay freight exceeded the statutory limit.[179] The rule that the proper law is displaced in so far as the performance of the contract is unlawful by the law of the place of performance is now widely accepted.[180] It is considered to be an implied term that the act leading to the performance of the contract is lawful according the law of the place where that act is performed. However, the scope of *Ralli* is limited. It is restricted to (1) obligations required by a contract (2) whose performance would be illegal, which is a higher threshold than overriding mandatory provisions whose non-observance not necessarily makes the performance illegal, (3) according the *lex loci solutionis*.

Next to the *Ralli* principle a second, partly overlapping principle was developed. In *Foster v Driscoll* the House of Lords held that a contract for the smuggling of whiskey into the USA, in the era of the US prohibition of alcohol, for unenforceable. Similarly, in *Regazzoni* the House of Lords refused to uphold a contract for the export of jute from India (that had prohibited export to South-Africa) to Genoa since the parties could only have envisaged to re-export the jute to South-Africa.[181] English public policy prevents upholding a contract that obliges to violate the laws of a friendly State. The *Regazzoni* principle is narrower in the sense that it requires a wilful breach of foreign law (parties acting in bad faith), but more wide in the sense that overriding mandatory provisions of jurisdictions other than a strictly defined *lex loci solutionis* can be applied as long there is a strong link with that jurisdiction.[182]

---

178 Plender, R., *The European Contracts Convention : The Rome Convention on the Choice of Law for Contracts*, Sweet & Maxwell, London, 1991, pp. 153.

179 *Ralli v Naviera* [1920] 2 K.B. 287.

180 Mann, F., "The Proper Law in the Conflict of Laws", *International & Comparative Law Quarterly*, Vol. 36, 1987, pp. 437–453.

181 *Foster v Driscoll* [1929] 1 K.B. 470; *Ragazzoni v Sethia* [1958] AC 301; see also: *Euro-Diam v Bathurst* [1990] QB 1.

182 Kuckein, *supra* note 169, pp. 269.

Indian law did not prohibit the contract to the extent that it obliged the parties to ship the jute to Genoa. The interest of India lay only in the prohibition of the subsequent reshipment to South-Africa. Indian law was therefore strictly speaking not the *lex loci solutionis.*

It is uncertain whether the parties to a contract have to explicitly plead the illegality of the contract under the *lex loci solutionis* or that the English courts are *ex officio* obliged to establish the illegality,[183] but foreign law has to be pleaded and proved as question of fact.[184]

As already described in the English tradition, some authors still perceive the operation of the latter rule as an operation of the public policy exception or even as a principle of customary international law.[185] Public policy would require English courts not to encourage or require parties to act in contravention with criminal law of the place where the act has to be performed.[186] Be that as it may, English public policy does not itself classify a certain act as criminal but is completely dependedant and ancillary to the foreign rule and its protected interest.

A second possibility for applying foreign overriding mandatory provisions originates in the common law not making the distinction between public and private law, as most notably is done in Germany. The common law conflict of laws rules designate a law that should completely govern the situation and is not concerned with the public or private law nature of a law. This means that English courts are also willing to apply the overriding mandatory provisions of the *lex causae* or proper law even if the *lex causae* is not English law.[187] This might, in cases where the overriding mandatory provisions are part of the *lex causae*, yield the same results as allowing the forum to give effect to foreign overriding mandatory provisions. Foreign overriding mandatory provisions may thus be applied when they are part of the *lex loci solutionis* or the *lex causae.*

---

[183] Fentiman, R., *Foreign Law in English Courts: Pleading, Proof and Choice of Law*, Oxford University Press, Oxford, 1998, pp. 107–113.

[184] Hartley, T., "Pleading and Proof of Foreign Law: The Major European Legal Systems Compared", *International & Comparative Law Quarterly,* Vol. 45, 1996, pp. 271–292.

[185] Mann, F., *Foreign Affairs in English Courts*, Clarendon Press, Oxford, 1986, pp. 155.

[186] Stone, P., *EU Private International Law : Harmonization of Laws*, Edward Elgar, Cheltenham, 2006, pp. 306–307.

[187] Max Planck Institute for Foreign Private and Private International Law, Comments on the European Commission's Proposal for a Regulation of the European Parliament and the Council on the law applicable to contractual obligations (Rome I), *RabelsZ*, Vol. 71, 2007, pp. 225–344.

English PIL had a slow start and was, from its coming into existence, heavily influenced by Continental theories. The introduction of the notion mandatory law via the Rome Convention in England was a novelty. The doctrine of overriding English statutes however reaches, with regard to statutes, the same results as domestic overriding mandatory provisions. The international field of application does necessarily have to be expressly provided for by the statute but can also be derived from its content and purpose. The lack of a distinction between public and private law means that the conflict of law rules attribute the situation as a whole to an applicable legal system. That thus also includes the overriding mandatory provisions. However, this effect is, for English statutes, limited by self-denying provisions. These provisions only have effect within their claimed scope of application. There is no general possibility for applying foreign overriding mandatory provisions against the *lex causae*. Courts have accepted that the proper law is displaced in so far as the performance of the contract is unlawful by the law of the place of performance. Overriding mandatory provisions of the *lex loci solutionis* are therefore eligible for application.

3.5 *Comparative Conclusions*

The emergence of overriding mandatory provisions is subject to the peculiarities of the national conflict of laws system. The harmonisation of the connecting factors in the area of contracts raises the question whether Member States should not adapt their conception of overriding mandatory provisions to the functioning of Rome I. Whereas in France and Germany overriding mandatory provisions were initially perceived as positive operations of the *ordre public* exception, the overriding mandatory provisions were in the Netherlands principally aimed as correction to the autonomy of private parties. The renowned *Alnati* decision is outside the Netherlands mostly famous for accepting the formal possibility of applying foreign overriding mandatory provisions, but in the Netherlands of much more practical relevance because the Hoge Raad for the first time clearly accepted the possibility for parties to choose the applicable law. English law, prior to the introduction of the Rome Convention, was not familiar with the notion 'mandatory' rules. However, with regard to statutes, the same effect was reached by the doctrine of English overriding statutes.

In France the concept of overriding mandatory provisions is interpreted in a much wider manner. Substantial sections of labour law are classified as overriding mandatory. This is a striking difference with the Netherlands where, save for the provisions laid down in art. 3 (1) of Directive 96/71 only a few labour provisions are given that status. Where the Cour de Cassation held in 1999 that the *loi sur le crédit de consommation* had to be classified as overriding mandatory, the Bundesgerichtshof held in 2005 that this was not the case for the *Verbraucherkreditgesetz.*

The wide French perception of overriding mandatory provisions is maintained in the debate whether overriding mandatory provisions must primarily protect a state interest or could also be primarily aimed at the protection of the interests of the weaker party. The Cour de Cassation applies these so-called 'second generation' overriding mandatory provisions even to legal persons. The limited interest of the state is demonstrated by the fact that a court is not supposed to raise the application of overriding mandatory provisions of its own motion. The theoretical possibility of applying second generation rules exists in the Netherlands, but application is rare in practice. It is assumed that second generation overriding mandatory provisions have lost much of their importance due to the introduction of protective connecting factors (e.g. art. 5-8 Rome I). In England, the issue has not generated much attention since the emphasis is placed on statutory intent.

Both *Sonderanknüpfung* and *bijzondere aanknoping* entail an autonomous test to establish the applicability of semi-public law. Overriding mandatory provisions of the the *lex causae* are not automatically applied, but overriding mandatory provisions that do not originate in the *lex causae* are also not automatically excluded from application. *Sonderanknüpfung* is contrary to the Dutch understanding of *bijzondere aanknoping* not restricted to overriding mandatory provisions, but refers as well to the protective connecting factors. The common element is their ability to override the normal, party autonomy based, conflict of laws rules. France does not have a clear dogmatic approach. It is subsequently necessary to establish whether the claimed scope of application is the minimum or maximum claimed scope. There is no clear answer to this question. In England the doctrine of English overriding statutes only applies to English statutes. England does not traditionally make a rigid distinction between public and private law as made in Germany. If the overriding mandatory provisions are part of the *lex causae* or, proper law, they are in principle eligible for application. The doctrine of self denying statutes, the opposite of overriding statutes, is used to limit the application of English public order provisions when the protected public interest is not at stake.

Both France and the Netherlands have the formal possibility of applying foreign overriding mandatory provisions against the *lex causae*. Extremely few precedents may be found in decisions of lower courts. Germany and the United Kingdom have made a reservation against art. 7 (1) Rome Convention and therefore do not have the formal possibility to give effect to foreign overriding mandatory provisions. Germany has found a solution in national private law; disregard of a foreign regulation may under certain circumstances be contrary to the good morals. Also England gives effect to foreign provisions via national law; it is considered to be an implied term that a contract is lawful according to the law of the place where it has to be performed. A clause in a contract is unenforceable insofar it obliges or incites a party to perform an act that is illegal in the country where the act has to be performed. With regard to overriding mandatory provisions that originate in the *lex loci solutionis* the same effect is realised as by applying art. 7 (1) Rome Convention. The English solution forms the basis for art. 9 (3) Rome I. Where Member States have lost the possibility to make a reservation against art. 9 (3), the provision only foresees in the possibility of applying foreign overriding mandatory provisions of the *lex loci solutionis* insofar as it would render the performance of the contract unlawful.

3.5.1 *The Necessity for a Preliminary Reference*

Despite the principle of uniform interpretation of the Rome Convention and the competence of the ECJ it has been demonstrated that with regard to art. 7, major differences of interpretation exist at the national level. National courts have interpreted the Rome Convention in the light of pre-existing national practices. In principle Rome I does not harmonise the content of overriding mandatory provisions. It leaves it to the Member States to define whether the application of a provision is crucial for the safeguard of its political, social or economical organisation. Questions such as whether second generation overriding mandatory provisions are covered by art. 9 (1) or the circumstances under which an overriding mandatory provision belonging to the *lex fori* or *lex causae* does not require application should left to be determined by the Member State concerned. It would feel rather odd if the ECJ were to oblige German courts to apply a German provision primarily protecting the weaker party, because the ECJ considerd such a provision to be crucial for the functioning of the German public order.[188]

The matter is however not that simple.[189] The ECJ exercises a negative control over the public policy exception of the Member States. The Court could therefore find that a French rule affording protection to the weaker party is not essential for the safeguard of public interests of a state. Moreover, even if the ECJ refrained from interfering in a positive manner in the public policy of Member States it is doubtful whether the French and German position can continue to exist in parallel. Rules of Union law could potentially be classified as overriding mandatory provisions. It does not appear that neither the ECJ nor the Union legislator adheres to the doctrine that overriding mandatory provisions should protect a public interest in a strict sense.[190] If what is considered to be crucial for the safeguard of the political, social or economical organisation of a Member State is left to the Member States, what is crucial for the safeguard of the political, social or economical organisation of the Union should be left to the Union. It would of course be possible for a German court to distinguish in the application of art. 9 between Union rules, or provisions implementing them, and strictly German provisions, but one may wonder whether that would promote the coherency of rules in the German legal order. Even if German courts found such a position to be feasible, it could not be condoned by the ECJ. The German position is founded on the perception of a mutual exclusive relationship between art. 6 and 8 on the one hand and art. 9 on the other hand. A provision is either aimed at the protection of a weaker party or at the protection of a public interest. French, Dutch and English courts have taken a different approach towards the hierarchy and relation of art. 9 to the other provisions of Rome I. Although the ECJ should refrain from defining the public policy of the Member States, the question of the relationship and hierarchy between the provisions in Rome I should be answered by the Court.

The solution preferred here is not to interpret the relationship between art. 6/8 and art. 9 in a rigid manner. A provision aimed at

---

[188] In this sense: Plender, R., and M. Wilderspin, *The European Private International Law of Obligations*, Sweet & Maxwell, London, 2009, pp. 388.

[189] Kuipers, J. and S. Migliorini, Qu'est-ce que sont les lois de police ? Une controverse franco-allemande, in: *European Review of Private Law*, vol. 18, No. 2, 2011, pp. 187–207.

[190] Case 381/98 *Ingmar* [2000], ECR I-9305.

equalising the economic strength of parties could may also contribute to the realisation of a public aim. Drawing the dividing line between the provisions will be difficult and risks becoming arbitrary. It cannot be excluded that a state would consider the observation of a provision primarily protecting the weaker party to be crucial for the safeguard of its political, social or economical organisation. The ECJ should therefore leave the possibility open for Member States to apply on the basis of art. 9 provisions that primarily protect the weaker party.

CHAPTER 4

THE SCOPE OF SECONDARY UNION LAW: A MATTER FOR ROME I?

The interrelationship between Union law and Private International Law goes beyond positive harmonisation or the modification of PIL concepts to accommodate the structure of the internal market. As every legal order the Union will be confronted with the need to delimit its scope of application. Two options are available: the Union could fall back on the conflict of laws rules of the Member States; or it could autonomously set its own scope of application. From a Union perspective, it is seems normal to assume that the international field of application of a legal order *sui generis* cannot be made depended upon the diverging conflict of laws norms of its Members States. However, the unification of conflict of laws norms at the Union level may necessitate a change in point of view.

From the outset, it must be observed that the scope of application of Union law is generally limited to the territory of the Member States (art. 355 TFEU). In the area of competition law, however, the Court has adopted the implementation doctrine.[1] When a practice or agreement is implemented in the Union, it could potentially affect the trade between the Member States. The Court held that the Union competition rules would therefore apply to practices or agreements between foreign private parties when they are implemented in the Union.[2] The boundaries of the implementation doctrine are drawn rather widely. An agreement is for example implemented in the Union when the goods of the foreign producers are sold in one of the Member States.[3] The scope of application is thus deducted from the aim and purpose of the rule involved rather than from the perspective of the legal relationship. The implementation doctrine also gives no guidance about the

[1] Dabbah, M., *The Internalisation of Antitrust Policy*, Cambridge University Press, Cambridge, 2003.

[2] Case 114/85 *Wood Pulp* [1988] ECR 5193.

[3] Griffin, J., "Extraterritoriality in US and EU Antitrust Enforcement", *Antitrust Law Journal*, Vol. 67, No. 1, 1999, pp. 159–200.

question when to apply foreign competition law. In PIL terminology, the Court therefore adopted with regard to competition law a unilateral approach.

A similar unilateral approach can be perceived in other areas of primary law. The free movement of goods applies to products produced in a third country when the products have lawfully entered the Union: Moroccan oranges benefit from free circulation to France once they have entered Spain. The free movement of services and the freedom of establishment apply to undertakings established in the Union. If a French company lawfully employs third country nationals in France, it can within the framework of the freedom to provide services, temporarily post those workers to Luxembourg.[4] It would be a restriction of the freedom to provide services if an employer would be obliged to apply for a working permit in Luxembourg, if the workers are already lawfully employed in France. The scope of the free movement of capital is deduced slightly different since art. 63 TFEU explicitly provides that it also applies to capital movements between a Member State and a third country.[5] What underlies these interpretations is the need for a single market without any internal frontiers. Union law should be applied if its application promotes the realisation of that goal, but does not require application when its goals are not served.

PIL instruments, even when adopted on the Union level, are not apt to delimitate the scope of primary Union law. Leaving aside the difficulties in conceptualising the public interests that underlie the Treaties in the traditional conflict of laws norm, a hierarchal argument comes into play: a regulation cannot limit the scope of application of a Treaty provision. Different methods must therefore be sought to co-ordinate the application of Union law on the international level with other sovereigns.[6] Whereas the hierarchy between Union law and the specific characteristics of the free movement provisions and competition law call for an autonomous delimitation, the situation may be different in cases concerning secondary law. Not only is the hierarchal argument absent, secondary law often concerns the pure balancing of private

---

[4] Case C-445/03 *Commission v Luxembourg* [2004] ECR 1-10191.

[5] See in general : Fallon, M., "Libertés communautaires et règles de conflit de lois", A. Fuchs *et al* (eds.), *Les conflits de lois et le système juridique communautaire*, Dalloz, Paris, 2004, pp. 31–80.

[6] See for example: EU/US Competition Cooperation Agreement (1991) and (1998).

interests. The focus upon the perceived needs of the own legal order and the pursuance of (political) public aims is in these circumstances less appropriate.

After the Single European Act and the Maastricht Treaty, an increasing amount of secondary legislation was directly aimed at the interference with the relationship between two private parties. Whereas the directives until the early nineties collectively ignored the PIL question altogether, the Unfair Contract Terms Directive brought a change.[7] Mainly in the area of consumer law, directives started to indicate their international scope of application. The provisions differed in formulation and substance but underscored similar unilaterist thinking. The provisions only stipulated the scope of application of the specific instrument but remained silent about the application of foreign law. The PIL approaches that the Union has adopted in its instruments are, from the point of view of a conflict of laws lawyer, rather medieval.[8] It is strongly reminiscent of Bartolus de Sassoferrato (1314–1357) and subsequent legal scholars who all answered the question whether national law could be applied against foreigners residing in the relevant jurisdiction, and whether national law could be applied outside the territory of the relevant jurisdiction, on the basis of the nature of the rule concerned. It was only Friedrich Carl von Savigny (1779–1861) who overcame the difficulties of the statutist approach and deducted the applicable law from the point of view of the legal relationship rather than the rule. Taking the point of view of the legal relationship avoided the problems of interpreting the aim and purpose of a rule and better served the legitimate expectation of private parties. Moreover, taking the perspective of the private party made it possible to solve the problem when several laws competed for application or when no national law claimed application. PIL has, since Von Savigny, been wary of incorporation of political or social goals, rather favouring rule-blindness or neutrality towards the substantial result obtained. For PIL purposes it does not matter whether the conflict of laws norms lead to the designation of Estonian or Iranian private law.

---

[7] Kohler, C., "Verständigungsschwierigkeiten zwischen europäischem Gemein schaftsrecht und internationales Privatrecht", H. Mansel *et al* (eds.), *Festschrift für Erik Jayme Band I*, Sellier, München, 2004, pp. 445–459 (446–449).

[8] González Campos, J., "La Cour de Justice de Communautés Européennes et le non-Droit international privé", H. Mansel *et al* (eds.), *Festschrift für Erik Jayme Band I*, Sellier, München, 2004, pp. 261–275 (273).

In Germany, authors such as Kegel argued that private law was an area free of state interference and the state had therefore principally no interest in seeing its laws applied.[9] It was only with the emergence of the modern welfare state that the interest of states in PIL gradually reappeared.

The multilateral conflict of laws rule remains one of the most important conflict of laws mechanisms in the Rome I Regulation. The rule that in absence of a choice of law a contract is governed by the law of the place where the party that has to render the most characteristic performance is established is in principle not concerned with the realisation of interests underlying the potentially applicable rules of the forum, but with advancing the interests of international commerce by providing legal certainty and foreseeability. Hence whereas PIL regulations follow the traditional European conflict of laws norms, secondary law resorts to a different methodological framework than was pre dominant in the Member States. If Union directives systematically took prevalence over Rome I, and hence its provisions on the possibility to choose the applicable law, party autonomy would come under severe pressure.

The unilateral approach does therefore not appear to fit well in Rome I. In this chapter, the provisions in secondary law indicating the desired scope of application on the international level will first be analysed. Since the unilateral approach as adopted by the Union focuses upon the realisation of Union objectives, the content and purpose of Union law in the area of consumer and labour law will be briefly assessed. After all, if one desires to establish the scope of secondary legislation autonomously the goal and purpose of that legislation becomes crucial. The areas of consumer and labour law are chosen because it is in these fields that the interplay between national private law, PIL and Union law has become the most apparent. Subsequently the role of Rome I in these areas will be analysed, aiming for a more thorough analysis of the method of delimiting the scope of secondary Union law.[10]

---

[9] Kegel. G., and K. Schurig, *Internationales Privatrecht*, Verlag C.H. Beck, München, 8. Auflage, 2001, pp. 117–130.

[10] An elaborate analysis is carried out by: Francq, S., *L'applicabilité du droit Communautaire dérivé au regard des méthodes du droit international privé*, Bruylant, Brussels, 2005.

4.1 *Private International Law in Secondary Union Law Instruments*

PIL may feel confident that even if at a certain point in time the Union were to completely replace the private law of the Member States, conflict of laws rules could still fulfil a function. The international scope of application of the common rules remains to be established. Whereas the international application of primary Union law has exclusively to be determined by those provisions themselves, the situation is different with regard to secondary law. That applies in particular to directives, since they require implementation in the national legal order and cannot be directly relied upon.[11] In principle one could adopt two different approaches. Either one determines the scope of secondary Union law autonomously, taking into account the aim and content of the relevant measure or one can delimit the scope of secondary Union law by resorting to traditional conflict of laws mechanisms. The dichotomy between an autonomous approach and a conflict of laws approach represents up to a certain extent the juxtaposition between a unilateral and a multilateral conflict of laws rule. An autonomous approach based upon the aim and content of a directive would establish the reach of a directive, without at all addressing the potential application of foreign law.

Certain instruments will by definition be limited to the internal market. Roaming is the use of a mobile telephone or other device by a roaming customer to make or receive phone calls while in a Member State other than that in which his home network is located. Before the intervention of the Union legislator, consumers paid very high charges for the use of their mobile phone in a different Member State. The Roaming Regulation (717/2007) set a maximum on the retail charge which a home provider may levy from its roaming customer as well as a maximum that the operator of the visited network may levy from the roaming operator of the customer's home network. Some provisions relate directly to contract law: art. 4 (4) for example provides for the right of a consumer to switch to or from a Eurotariff. Any switch must be made within one working day of receipt of the request, must be free

[11] Bertoli, P., "The Court of Justice and Private International Law", *Yearbook of Private International Law*, Vol. 8, 2006, pp. 375–412 (402–3). Fallon does not attribute any relevance to the requirement of transposition. Fallon, M., "Le principe de proximité dans le droit de l'Union Européenne", *Mélanges en l'honneur de Paul Lagarde ; Le droit international privé : esprit et méthodes*, Dalloz, Paris, 2005, pp. 241–262 (252).

of charge, and it may not entail conditions or restrictions pertaining to other elements of the subscription. Because the definitions of 'home network', 'visited network' and 'roaming customer' all relate to a provider or consumer established in the territory of one of the Member States, the application of the Regulation is necessarily limited to intra-Union situations. The relationship to conflict of laws is not directly clear. It might be possible to deduce an implicit conflict of laws rule, determining that the Regulation will apply whenever a consumer makes use of his mobile phone network in another Member State. On the other hand, one could argue that it concerns a situation internal to the Union and that therefore the application of the law of a third country may not set aside the application of mandatory Union law, including the Regulation. A third possibility would be to argue that since a regulation does not need to be transposed by the Member States and confers direct rights and obligations upon an individual which can be invoked in a purely horizontal relation, the Regulation concerns uniform Union private law which would prevail over the conflict of laws norms.[12] Hence, though the desired scope of application of the instrument is clear, such instruments leave uncertainty as to their conceptualisation in the conflict of laws process.[13]

Little doubt will exist about the conceptualisation of an instrument in the conflict of laws process when the instrument itself contains an explicit provision claiming a certain international field of application. Art. 23 Rome I provides that the regulation '*shall not prejudice the application of provisions of Union law which, in relation to particular matters, lay down conflict-of-law rules relating to contractual obligations*'. However, art. 23 does no more than codify the principle that the *lex specialis* takes precedence over the *lex generalis*. Until the early nineties the question of the international scope of directives remained largely untouched, but the introduction of the Rome Convention

---

[12] This type of regulation is relatively rare, it has been observed: 'This type of direct intervention by the Community to protect consumers (...) can hardly serve as a model for other sections of consumer law, especially in the contractual field, where national differences rather suggest other methods of Community intervention'. Stuyck, J., "The Consumer Law Compendium, A New Era for European Consumer Law?" *European Business Law Review*, Vol. 20, 2009, pp. 377–382 (379).

[13] The author recognises that for all three positions reasonable arguments can be advanced but would propose to follow the second option since it does not cause disturbance in conflict of laws process without jeopardising the attainment of the objectives of Union law.

brought a conceptual change.[14] From the Unfair Contract Terms Directive onwards directives, although mainly in the area of consumer law, started to indicate their own field of application.

4.1.1 *Data Protection Directive*

The provisions in secondary legislation are not always equally clear, however. Even when a specific provision seems to stipulate the desired international scope of application of a directive, one may raise doubts as to whether it really concerns a conflict of laws rule. The application of the Data Protection Directive (95/46 EC, DPD) is in art. 4 made dependent upon the establishment of the controller on the territory of a Member State, or if the controller is not established in the Union, on the use of equipment by the controller on the territory of a Member State.[15] The delimitation of the scope of the DPD in the international arena is difficult since data protection is at the dividing line between public and private, as traditionally deployed by Member States. The Directive contains both public and private elements. Perhaps a uniform solution cannot be reached for the instrument as a whole. For example, art. 8 requires Member States to prohibit the processing of personal data which reveals racial or ethnic origin, political opinions, religious or philosophical beliefs, trade-union membership, and the processing of data concerning health or sex life, and art. 25 requires Member States to prohibit the transfer of data to a third country if that country does not guarantee an adequate level of protection. Those provisions of the DPD address the supervision of data processors and places Member States under a duty to apply their national legislation. Those provisions have a strong public character.

Art. 7 (a) provides that data may, *inter alia*, only be processed when the data subject has given his express consent. The consent required

---

[14] Fallon, M., and S. Francq, "Towards Internationally Mandatory Directives for Consumer Contracts?", J. Basedow *et al* (eds.) *Private Law in the International Arena: Liber Amicorum Kurt Siehr*, T.M.C. Asser Press, The Hague, 2000, pp. 155–178 (161).

[15] Bygrave, L., "Determining Applicable Law pursuant to European Data Protection Legislation", *Computer Law & Security Report*, Vol. 16, 2000, pp. 252–257 (252); Poullet, Y., "Transborder Data Flows and Extraterritoriality : The European Position", electronically available at: http://www.europarl.europa.eu/meetdocs/2004_2009/documents/dv/poullet_/poullet_en.pdf, as of 15 March 2011; Stalla-Bourdillon, S., "Re-allocating horizontal and vertical regulatory powers in the electronic marketplace: what to do with private international law", F. Cafaggi and H. Muir Watt (eds.), *The Regulatory Function of European Private Law*, Edward Elgar, Chelthenham, 2009, pp. 290–342 (330).

directly governs the private law relationship. Any claim for the process of data without consent of the data subject would, even if the right to privacy is considered to be a fundamental right, still have to be shoehorned in a civil claim.[16] The requirements to be fulfilled to establish consent may vary from jurisdiction to jurisdiction. It would appear that the question to determine which law should be applied to ascertain whether the consent of the data subject has been obtained should be left to be determined by PIL. A literal interpretation of art. 4 would lead to the conclusion that a Member State is obliged to enforce its definition of consent when the data processor is established on its territory or when it has no establishment in the Union but operates equipment on the territory of the Member State involved. The consent of a European data subject would thus not be governed by the DPD when the data processor is established in the US and has no equipment in one of the Member States. The protection offered to European data subjects would be severely undermined if the standards of the DPD applied to a data transfer to data processors in a third country but not to data collection. Especially on the internet, information circulates with a lot of ease. Maintaining a strict notion of consent against European professionals, would lose much of its effect if information collected by an American data processor, under a supposedly laxer standard of consent, could freely circulate on the web. A solution would be to interpret art. 4 DPD as referring to rules which concern administrative authorisations, prudential supervision or product quality, but not to rules governing the purely horizontal relation between the parties inter se.[17]

That solution would fit in the reasoning of the ECJ in *Alpine Investments*.[18] In that case, the Netherlands made the award of a licence to operate as a financial agent conditional upon the promise of the

---

[16] See in this respect a decision of the English Court of Appeal, *Douglas v Hello!*, [2005] EWCA Civ 595.

[17] However according to the Data Protection Working Party art. 4 DPD is a conflict of laws rule based on the country of origin principle. This reasoning fails to persuade, in particular when the situation involves links with third countries. Art. 29 Data Protection Working Party, Working document on determining the international application of EU data protection law to personal data processing on the Internet by non-EU based web sites, 5035/01/EN/Final WP 56, 6. Kuner even maintains that art. 4 exclusively deals with conflict of laws: Kuner, C., Internet Jurisdiction and Data Protection Law: An International Legal Analysis, 2009, available at SSRN: http://ssrn.com/abstract=1496847, as of 15 March 2011.

[18] Case C-384/93 *Alpine Investments* [1995] ECR I-01141.

agent not to engage into unsolicited calling of potential clients (cold calling) even if it was directed to other Member States. The Court held that '[t]he Member State from which the telephone call is made is best placed to regulate cold calling. Even if the receiving State wishes to prohibit cold calling or to make it subject to certain conditions, it is not in a position to prevent or control telephone calls from another Member State without the cooperation of the competent authorities of that State.'[19] The enforcement of public law or licence requirements outside the territory of the enacting jurisdiction is factually very difficult, and often even impossible. The fact that the licensing and enforcement of the attached conditions would be most effective if it were conducted by the Member State in whose territory the operator was situated, however, does not settle the law applicable between the operator and the consumer. The 'best regulator' does not necessarily have the greatest proximity to the contract. It is beyond any doubt that in *Alpine Investments*, in the absence of a choice of law, the law applicable to a contract concluded after cold calling between Alpine Investments and a consumer established in Belgium would have been Belgian.[20]

Art. 4 would thus mean that Member States are not obliged to ensure the public enforcement of the directive or the powers of the supervisory authority to controllers established outside the Union or having no equipment in the territory of that Member State. That limitation makes sense. As recognised by the ECJ in *Alpine Investments* it will be very hard to enforce legislation over a subject that is physically not present or has no assets in the relevant jurisdiction. The limitation of the enforcement of the Data Protection Directive by Member States does not, however, resolve the question of the private law applicable to the relationship between a third country controller and an EU data subject. That question should left to be governed by PIL. Although the DPD itself does not provide for further indication, one could argue that in the light of the crucial function that the interpretation of consent plays in the protection of the right to privacy of the EU data subject, it should apply regardless the applicable law. The protection of the data subject, one of the objectives of the directive,

---

[19] *Alpine Investments*, *supra* note 18, par. 48.

[20] A Dutch court would thus have applied Belgian consumer law (Art. 5 Rome Convention on the Law Applicable to Contractual Obligations (1980)).

would thus require the classification of art. 7 (a) as an overriding mandatory provision.

4.1.2 *Return of Cultural Objects Directive*

Outside the area of contracts another potential conflict of laws rule in the grey area between public and private is art. 12 of the Return of Cultural Objects Directive. The provision lays down a multilateral conflict of laws rule. 'Ownership of the cultural object after return shall be governed by that law of the requesting Member State.' The provision does however not delimit the scope of application of the directive, but rather determines the national law applicable to the question of ownership. It thus harmonises on this specific point the conflict of laws rule of the Member States, rather than constituting a specific conflict of laws rule delimiting the scope of an instrument of secondary law.[21] Art. 12 aims to avoid problems of characterisation rather than indicating the territorial reach of the Return of Cultural of Objects Directive. The introduction of a harmonised conflict of laws rule is necessary in order to facilitate the operation of the procedure for the return of cultural items that is established by the Directive.

4.1.3 *Timeshare Directive*

On first sight, a better example of a unilateral conflict of laws rule would be art. 12 of the Timeshare Directive (2008/122). It provides that if the immovable property is situated within the territory of a Member State, Member States '*shall take the measures necessary to ensure that, whatever the law applicable may be, the purchaser is not deprived of the protection afforded by this Directive*'. In addition to art. 9 of the original Timeshare Directive (94/47), art. 12 (2) of the revised Timeshare Directive provides: '*where the applicable law is that of a third country, consumers shall not be deprived of the protection granted by this Directive, as implemented in the Member State of the forum if* (1) *any of the immovable properties concerned is situated within the territory of a Member State, or,* (2) *in the case of a contract not directly related to immovable*

---

[21] Jayme, E., "Globalization in Art Law: Clash of Interests and International Tendencies", *Vanderbilt Journal of Transnational Law*, Vol. 38, 2005, pp. 927–945; Jakubowski, A., "Return of Illicitly Trafficked Cultural Objects Pursuant to Private International Law: Current Developments", A. Vrdoljak and F. Francioni, *The Illicit Traffic of Cultural Objects in the Mediterranean*, EUI Working Paper Law, 2/2009, pp. 137–148.

property, the trader pursues commercial or professional activities in a Member State or, by any means, directs such activities to a Member State and the contract falls within the scope of such activities'.

The directive is restricted to purchasers who are natural persons acting outside their profession. The scope is wider than art. 6 of Rome I since the professional seller does not need to undertake any commercial activities directed towards the place of habitual residence of the consumer. In fact, art. 12 Timeshare Directive does not have any similar limitation as regards the type of contracts or the circumstances under which it is concluded. This also applies to the rules of art. 6 (2) of the Unfair Contract Terms Directive, art. 12 (2) of the Distance Selling Directive and art. 12 (2) of the Financial Services Directive. These rules read: '*Member States shall take the necessary measures to ensure that the consumer does not lose the protection granted by this Directive by virtue of the choice of the law of a non-Member country as the law applicable to the contract if the latter has a close connection with the territory of the Member States*'.

4.1.4 *Unfair Contract Terms Directive*

Art. 6 (2) Unfair Contract Terms Directive does not specify which law should be applied. The Directive does not give any indication whether the law of the Member State where the consumer or where the professional is established should apply or whether one should fall back on the minimum standards of the Directive. Art. 6 (2) also does not preclude the law of a third country from applying, as long as the consumer does not lose the protection granted by the Directive. Rather than resolving a conflict of laws, art. 6 (2) is concerned with the safeguard of a substantive result, being the protection of the consumer. It is also difficult to construe the directive on the basis of art. 6 (2) as a set of overriding mandatory provisions. Overriding mandatory provisions override the otherwise applicable law. Because of the substantive interest that underlies the rule, the otherwise applicable law is overridden regardless of whether the applicable law was established on the basis of a choice of law or upon the objective operation of connecting factors. However, art. 6 (2) applies when a choice of law has led to the deprivation of the protection afforded by the Directive, but does not prevent a loss of protection when the applicable law has been established in the absence of a choice of law. Consequently the consumer will lose the protection of the Directive if he travels to another Member State and concludes a contract for the sale of goods with a professional established in a third country. Art. 4 (1a) Rome leads to the application of the law of the place where the third country professional has his central place of administration.

Art. 6 (2) can neither be read as a unilateral conflict of laws rule nor as an overriding mandatory provision. A unilateral conflict of laws rule aims to resolve a conflict of laws, whereas an overriding mandatory provision aims to promote a specific forum interest.[22] The fact that the directive does not resist the application of the law of a third country as long as its meets the level of protection of the Directive, means that art. 6 (2) is concerned with the protection of a specific forum interest, the protection of the consumer, rather than at resolving a conflict of laws. On the other hand, it is difficult to classify art. 6 (2) as an overriding mandatory provision since it only addresses the consequences of a choice of law, but does not prevent the application of the law of a third country on the basis of the operation of the objective connecting factors.

Regardless of the construction of the provision in the conflict of laws methodology, art. 6 (2) aims to protect the mobile consumer. The mobile consumer will also fall under the protection of these directives, even if a choice of law for a legal system of a third country has been made, when the professional has his central place of administration in one of the Member States. It was the specific purpose of the Directive to complement the protective connecting factor in the Rome Convention by filling the gaps it leaves in consumer protection.[23] It is illustrative in this regard that the ECJ held that Spain erred in implementation of art. 6 (2) Unfair Contract Terms Directive by restricting its scope to art. 5 Rome Convention.[24] The Court thus held that the mobile consumer is also covered by the consumer *acquis*. Art. 6 Rome I is thus not able to ensure the application of the aforementioned directives in all circumstances. If one desires to incorporate these provisions in PIL terminology, national courts cannot do other than resort to art. 9. Classifying the provisions as overriding mandatory would be the only way of guaranteeing the application of the provisions in

---

[22] Par. 2.4.1.3.

[23] Tenreiro, M., and J. Karsten, "Unfair Terms in Consumer Contracts: Uncertainties, contradictions and novelties of a Directive", H. Schulte-Nölke (ed.), *Europäische Rechtsangleichung und nationale Privatrechte*, Nomos Verlagsgesellschaft, Baden-Baden, 1999, pp. 223–276 (247–253).

[24] Case C-70/03 *Commission v Spain* [2004] ECR I-9657.

all cases regardless the applicable law.[25] The classification of these directives as overriding mandatory requires a broad interpretation of international public policy and goes considerably further than the protection offered to consumers within the framework of this concept than in most Member States.

4.1.5 *Relationship to the Conflict of Laws Process*

The rules in the directives create a lot of disturbances in the conflict of laws process. An example is the requirement of a 'close connection' which was not used in traditional PIL. The Unfair Contract Terms Directive does not specify what a close connection with the territory of one of the Member States means.[26] The definition was left deliberately vague in order to make it possible to take account of various ties depending on the circumstances of the case.[27] Does it for example mean that the directive does not rule out a choice of law in all circumstances, even if it would lead to the application of a body of law that is less favourable to the consumer?[28] The directive might have functioned in an equally satisfying way had the criterion of close connection been left out. Art. 6 Rome I would have declared the Unfair Contract Terms Directive applicable when the consumer is approached by the professional in his home jurisdiction, while in the case of active consumers, as a result of the test of characteristic performance, the directive would only have been applicable when the professional was established in a Member State.

The notion of 'close connection' may, however, have been introduced in order to protect professionals in the Union. It prevents Union professionals operating outside the Union from being forced to comply with the consumer protection standards applicable within the Union. On the basis of an objective operation of the conflict of laws norms the law applicable to a contract between a Union professional and a consumer established outside the Union could be the law of the Member

[25] The initial draft of the Timeshare directive seemed however to be inspired more by art. 5 of the Rome Convention. Jayme, E., and C. Kohler, "L'interaction des règles de conflit contenues dans le droit dérivé de la Communauté européenne et des conventions de Bruxelles et de Rome", *Revue Critique de Droit International Privé,* Vol. 84, No. 1, 1995, pp. 1–36 (18). For a detailed analysis of the function of PIL in consumer law: Francq, *supra* note 10, pp. 281–372.

[26] Fallon, *supra* note 11, pp. 255–261.

[27] *Commission v Spain*, *supra* note 24, par. 32.

[28] Francq, *supra* note 10, pp. 315.

State. Supposedly, art. 6 (2) would not resist a choice of law in favour of the law of the habitual residence of the consumer, since in such circumstances no close connection with the Union would exist. If that were the objective of 'close connection', it had been preferable if a parallel would have been sought with art. 3 (3) Rome Convention, which stipulates that a choice of law may not lead to a deprivation of the norms applicable in a country that cannot be deviated from by contract, when all relevant connections are with that country.

The *lex rei sitae* rule in the Timeshare Directive differs from the *lex rei sitae* traditionally employed. The German legislation implementing the original Timeshare Directive provided that it applied when the immovable was situated on the territory of a Member State.[29] Hence, a German court would apply the German implementing law to a contract between a Belgian consumer and a French undertaking concerning a property located in Spain. Application of the *lex rei sitae* would thus not necessarily lead to the application of the law of the place where the immovable was situated, but of the directive as implemented by the forum if the immovable was situated in the territory of one of the Member States. Although that approach promotes procedural economy since it saves the forum from ascertaining how another Member State had implemented the directive, the French approach seemed preferable. It laid down the *lex rei sitae* and only provided for the application of the French implementing legislation in absence of implementation of the Timeshare Directive in the *lex rei sitae*.[30] It feels rather odd to apply German implementing legislation to a contract that has no real connection with Germany. Nevertheless the German approach prevailed in art. 12 (2) of the new Timeshare Directive.[31] Under certain circumstances, the applicability of the law of a third country may not deprive the consumer of the protection of the directive, as implemented in the law of the forum. The emphasis on the application of the directive, instead of the application of the law of the place where the immovable is situated, in combination with the fact that the law of the forum will only step in when the consumer would otherwise be deprived of his protection, strengthens the impression that what is at stake is not

[29] Directive 2008/122 repealing directive 94/47 makes clear in art. 12 (2) that a choice of law may under circumstances not deprive the consumer of the protection of the directive, as implemented in the law of the forum.

[30] Example borrowed from: Fallon/Francq *supra* note 14, pp. 166.

[31] As well as art. 3 (4) Rome I which guarantees the application of mandatory Union rules 'where appropriate as implemented in the Member State of the forum'.

the application of the directive as such, but rather the interest it seeks to protect. It is therefore difficult to conceptualise art. 12 as a unilateral conflict of laws rule since it does not aim to resolve a conflict of laws, but rather the protection of a substantive value.

When the delimitation of secondary Union law is at stake, the Union legislator has given preference to a unilateral method of PIL. The specific choice of law provisions thus only describes the circumstances in which an instrument applies and remains silent about the application of foreign law. The Member States expressed, upon ratification of the Rome Convention, the desire for the adoption of conflict of law norms in future secondary law compatible with the Rome Convention.[32] As argued above, this has not happened in practice. Directives that contain an explicit provision stipulating its international field of application use a different conflict of laws mechanism compared to the Rome instruments. Moreover, since the directive has to be transposed into national law the risk of different interpretations exists. The use of vague concepts such as a 'close connection' adds significantly to that risk. It has therefore been submitted that these scope rules do more harm than good.[33]

However, the example of the Unfair Contract Terms Directive and the Data Protection Directive leads us to question whether all provisions in directives that address the international field of application of an instrument are really conflict of laws rules. Art. 4 DPD does probably not address private international law and could be read as not affecting the determination of the applicable law between a data processor and a data subject. Art. 6 (2) Unfair Contract Terms Directive is aimed at the safeguard of a substantive result rather than the resolution of a conflict of laws and is limited to situations involving a choice of law. The provision can therefore neither be read as an unilateral conflict of laws rule nor as an overriding mandatory provision. As will be argued below, the provision should instead be read as laying down a scope rule, which ensures the applicability of that directive when all elements are connected to the Union.

---

[32] Jayme, E., and C. Kohler, "Das Internationale Privat- und Verfahrensrecht der EG 1993 – Spannungen zwischen Staatsverträgen und Richtlinien", *IPRax*, Vol. 13, No. 6, 1993, pp. 357–371 (358).

[33] Commission Green Paper Rome I Regulation COM (2002) 654 final, 17.

4.2 *An Autonomous Approach in the Consumer Acquis?*

The examples of provisions indicating the international scope of application of secondary legislation demonstrate that even though Rome I maintains the traditional multilateral conflict of laws rule, the aim, content and the context of the directive in the general framework of Union law becomes relevant. Before analysing whether, and if so how, consumer directives should be incorporated in the framework of Rome I, the general context and objectives of EU consumer law have to be discussed. Consumer law is characterised by a high degree of harmonisation. The Maastricht Treaty introduced art. 153 on consumer policy,[34] which has been renumbered into art. 169 TFEU.[35] Before the introduction of an autonomous competence, art. 111 TFEU (95 EC) was taken as a legal basis.[36] The EU Consumer Policy Strategy 2007 - 2013 identifies three main goals of the Commission consumer policy. The first is to empower EU consumers through accurate information, market transparency and the confidence that stems from effective consumer protection, while the second is to enhance consumer welfare in terms of price, choice, quality and safety. The Commission considers that consumer welfare is at the heart of well-functioning markets. The final objective is to protect consumers effectively from serious risks and threats. The underlying aim is to achieve by 2013 a more effective and integrated internal market. With consumer spending representing 58% of the EU GDP, it is not surprising that the Commission is keen on reducing the differences in legal regime between the Member States and create the largest retail market in the world.[37] Consumer protection becomes then intertwined with the establishment of an internal market. It is therefore not surprising that the Commission still does not present consumer protection measures as laws aimed at the protection of the weaker

[34] Howells, G., and T. Wilhelmsson, *EC Consumer Law*, Ashgate, Darmouth, 1997, pp. 6–13; Poillot, E., *Droit Européen de la Consommation et Uniformisation du Droit des Contrats*, LGDJ, Paris, 2006, pp. 42–64.

[35] Reich, N. and G. Woodroffe (eds.), *European Consumer Policy after Maastricht*, Kluwer, Deventer, 1994; Howells, G., and R. Schulze (eds.), *Modernising and Harmonising Consumer Contract Law*, Sellier, München, 2009.

[36] Reich, N., *Europäisches Verbraucherschutzrecht: Binnenmarkt und Verbraucherinteresse*, Nomos Verlagsgesellschaft, Baden-Baden, 1993, pp. 29–33; Weatherhill, S., *EU Consumer Law and Policy*,: Elgar European Law, Cheltenham, 2005.

[37] EU Consumer Policy Strategy 2007 –2013

party, but rather as measures to prevent distortion of the market (market correction).[38]

The high level of consumer protection that the Union strives for is understood as necessary for consumer confidence in the internal market.[39] Equivalent rights and equivalent remedies throughout the Union, regardless of the place where the transaction was made, are, in their turn, the pillars of the consumer confidence. The second aim of EU consumer policy, to ensure the competitiveness of enterprises, is supposed to be ensured by a more predictable regulatory environment in order to decrease their compliance costs and allow for easy access to consumers in other Member States.[40] The protective connecting factor and second generation overriding mandatory provisions are not concerned with ensuring a high level of consumer protection. They merely prevent that a choice of law lead to a lower standard of protection. Internal market considerations are not of primary concern; on the contrary, the application of the protective connecting factor and the second generation overriding mandatory provisions maintains the divergent standards within the internal market and thereby impose a burden upon intra Union trade.

Within the area of consumer law the following instruments have been enacted:

- Product Liability Directive (EEC 85/374)
- General Product Safety Directive (EEC 92/59)
- Unfair Contract Terms Directive (EEC 93/13)
- Misleading Advertising Directive (EEC 84/450)
- Doorstep Selling Directive (EEC 85/577)
- Consumer Credit Directive (EEC 87/102)
- Package Travel Directive (EEC 90/314)
- Distance Selling Directive (EC 97/7)
- Price Indication Directive (EC 98/6)
- Consumer Sales Directive (EC 99/44)
- Electronic Commerce Directive (2001/31)

[38] Cafaggi, F., and H. Muir-Watt, "The Making of European Private Law: Regulation and Governance Design", European Governance Paper N-07-02, 2007, 9.

[39] The legal basis for enhancing consumer confidence may however be doubtful: see: Roth, W., Case C-168/00, *Leitner v TUI Deutschland GmbH & Co. KG*, Judgment of 12 March 2002 (Sixth Chamber), ECR 2002, I-2631, *Common Market Law Review*, Vol. 40, 2003, pp. 937–951 (944).

[40] Poncibò, C., "The Challenges of EC Consumer Law", EUI Working Paper MWP No. 2007/24.

- Late Payments Directive (2000/35)
- Distance sales of financial services (EC 2002/65)
- Unfair Commercial Practices Directive (EC 2005/29)
- Consumer Protection Cooperation Regulation (EC 2006/2004)
- Time Share Directive (EC 2008/122)
- Injunctions Directive (EC 2009/22)

These directives take art. 114 TFEU as their legal basis, reducing the significance of art. 169.[41] One of the reasons might be that as a result of art. 169 (4) the specific competence for consumer protection only allows for minimum harmonisation. Another reason for taking art. 114 as the legal basis is that the Commission mainly focuses its harmonisation efforts upon the national consumer legislation admissible under negative harmonisation. Thus under the internal market rationale, if a barrier to trade is allowed to persist, the consumer norms should at least be uniform throughout the Union. Consumer measures then serve the internal market by harmonising legitimate obstacles to trade.[42] It is not possible here to discuss the substance of these directives,[43] but it is worth drawing attention to their sectoral and fragmentary nature. Differences in implementation and interpretation lead to a divergent application between Member States and consequently to divergent levels of 'minimum protection'. Member States attempt to fill gaps left by directives with national law.[44] The directives are moreover based on the principle of minimum harmonisation. Member States are free to introduce, and have widely done so, norms that afford a higher level of protection to consumers, but the higher level of

---

[41] The TFEU allocates consumer protection measures taken in the context of the promotion of the internal market to art. 114, whereas art. 169 is the legal basis for measures which support, supplement and monitor the policy pursued by the Member States.

[42] Unberath, H., and A. Johnston, "The Double-Headed Approach of the ECJ concerning Consumer Protection", *Common Market Law Review*, Vol. 44, 2007, pp. 1237–1284 (1239–1242).

[43] See: Reich, N., and H. Micklitz, *Europäisches Verbraucherrecht*, Nomos, Baden-Baden, 2003; Weatherhill, S., "An Ever Tighter Grip: The European Court's Pro-Consumer Interpretation of the EC's Directives Affecting Contract Law", M. Andenas *et al* (eds.) *Liber Amicorum Guido Alpa*, British Institute of International and Comparative Law, London, 2007, pp. 1037–1069.

[44] Schulte-Nölke, H., (ed.), EC Consumer Law Compendium: Comparative Analysis, 2008, electronically available at http://ec.europa.eu/consumers/rights/docs/consumer_law_compendium_comparative_analysis_en_final.pdf, as of 15 March 2011.

protection is subject to the scrutiny of free movement provisions.[45] The higher level of protection constitutes the rules on consumer protection that cannot be deviated from by contract and it remains therefore necessary to establish which consumer law of what Member State should be applied.

Unberath and Johnston have demonstrated a double bias in the case-law of the ECJ.[46] In relation to negative harmonisation, the court displays a bias in favour of free trade and is sceptical to national measures founded on consumer protection. The Court has used the principle of proportionality to come up with creative alternative consumer protection measures which are less restrictive to the internal market; even considerations of public health often failed to convince the Court that restrictions were justified. The Court tested national measures against the standard of a reasonable and well-informed consumer. With regard to positive harmonisation the ECJ has granted directives a wide scope of application, enhancing their regulatory and interventionist potential. In cases of ambivalent wording, the Court opts for the most consumer-friendly interpretation, ignoring pleas of Member States for the increase of legal certainty and the confinement of interventionist legislation. One may wonder what the reasonable and well-informed consumer would have thought if he had been invited by the Court to comment upon its case-law relating to positive harmonisation.[47]

The fragmented nature of the directives was perceived to be unfeasible since it imposed legal and other compliance costs upon undertakings in order to make sure that they conformed to the appropriate level of consumer protection in the country of destination.[48] The proposal for a Directive on Consumer Rights is an attempt to remedy the problems resulting from divergent interpretation and divergent standards by reviewing the Consumer Sales Directive, the Unfair Contract Terms Directive, the Distance Selling Directive and the Doorstep Selling

[45] Case C-20/03 *Burmanjer* [2005] ECR I-4133; Case C-441/04 *A-Punkt Schmuckhandels* [2006] ECR I-2093.

[46] Unberath/Johnston, *supra* note 42.

[47] Unberath/Johnston, *supra* note 42, pp. 1282.

[48] Impact assessment report, p 8. Consumer protection becomes here the protection of consumer interests. Since companies have to pass on the incurred costs on the end user, consumers will ultimately be confronted with higher prices or the refusal of undertakings to engage in cross border transactions. From this perspective, consumer protection increases consumer welfare.

Directive on the basis of maximum harmonisation.[49] The principle of maximum harmonisation was also used in the Unfair Commercial Practices Directive.[50] The Commission seems to link the divergence resulting from minimum harmonisation in the Member States with a negative effect on consumer confidence.[51] The scope of the directive is, however, mainly limited to sales and leaves, for example, out hire or hire purchase agreements and contracts for the supply of a digital content.[52]

The idea behind full harmonisation is that the consumer is guaranteed the same level of protection throughout the Union. In the harmonised area, it should therefore not matter whether the law of the Czech Republic or that of France is applicable. The consumer no longer requires protection against the too harsh consequences of a choice of law since a choice of law for Czech law cannot deprive him of the mandatory consumer protection offered by French law. Art. 6 (2) Rome I then becomes superfluous. The situation is different when Russian instead of Czech law is chosen. Art. 43 of the proposal then falls back on Rome I;[53] the Consumer Rights Directive constitutes a set of provisions that are mandatory in the domestic sense. A choice of law in favour of Russian law may therefore not deprive the French consumer from the mandatory protection offered to him by Union law. The consumer *acquis*, therefore, mainly aims to enhance the confidence of the consumer in the internal market by conferring equivalent rights upon him regardless of whether he contracts in his own, or in another Member State. The choice of art. 114 TFEU as the legal basis implies that the high level of protection afforded to weaker party is a means to establish a larger degree of consumer confidence in the internal

[49] Mak, V., "Review of the Consumer Acquis: Towards Maximum Harmonization", *European Review of Private Law*, Vol. 17, No. 1, 2009, pp. 55–73.

[50] Art. 3(5) Unfair Commercial Practices Directive.

[51] Micklitz, H., and N. Reich, S. Whittaker, "Joint response of the Society of Legal Scholars and the Northern Commercial Law Group and the Consumer Academic Network ('Joint Response')" electronically available at: http://ec.europa.eu/consumers/cons_int/safe_shop/acquis/index_en.htm, as of 15 March 2011, 6.

[52] Twigg-Flesner, C., "No Sense of purpose or direction? The modernisation of European Consumer Law", *European Review of Contract Law,* 2007, pp. 198–213 (211).

[53] See recital 59 to the proposal: 'The consumer should not be deprived of the protection granted by this Directive. Where the law applicable to the contract is that of a third country, Regulation (EC) No 593/2008 of the European Parliament and of the Council on the law applicable to contractual obligations (Rome I) should apply, in order to determine whether the consumer retains the protection granted by this Directive.'

market, rather than a goal in itself. One may therefore doubt the function of an autonomous approach in cases with a foreign element. Will the consumer really lose confidence in the internal market when he is deprived of the minimum protection as afforded to him by Union law when he enters into a contract with an undertaking established in the US?

The internal market rationale has penetrated the methodological framework of the provisions indicating the international scope of application of consumer directives: neither art. 43 of the proposal for a Consumer Rights Directive nor art. 6 (2) Unfair Contract Terms Directive provide any protection in the event that the consumer contracts with a professional established in a third country. In the co-ordination of the conflict of laws of rules for consumer protection, a slight gap occurs: when a French consumer physically travels to the Czech Republic and is targeted by a professional established in a third country, the parties can validly opt-out of the EU consumer *acquis*. The French consumer will lose his protection, even though he has not left the Union. However, if the third country professional had contracted with a Czech consumer, the choice of law would not lead to a deprivation of the Czech standards that cannot be deviated from by contract. The French consumer is thus, as compared to a Czech consumer in a disadvantageous position when he travels to the Czech Republic. That consequence is hard to relate to the idea of enhancing the confidence in the internal market. Although the problem is relatively small, it plays a role in particular with regard to tourists, who are physically present in concentrated areas in other Member States. A professional could targets tourists in such an area without being bound by the EU consumer *acquis*. As will be argued below, a solution could be found in giving a flexible interpretation to the notion 'country'.[54]

4.3 *Autonomous Determination of the International Scope of Application of Secondary Law*

Whereas in cases where secondary legislation contains a provision indicating the desired international scope of application of the instrument concerned, the actual meaning of that provision might be ambiguous, the international scope of application of instruments that remain

[54] Par. 4.6.3.

silent about their effect in the international arena is even more uncertain. Determining the scope of a directive autonomously can occur in subtle different ways. One could simply ignore conflict of laws altogether or try to fit an autonomous approach into Rome I. In other words, one could determine the international scope of application of secondary legislation on the basis of a (implicit) unilateral conflict of laws rule or try to fit the harmonised rules in art. 9 Rome I.

The classification of the harmonised field, on the basis of its object and purpose, as a set of overriding mandatory provisions would in fact also entail an autonomous approach. Despite using the framework of Rome I to accommodate secondary legislation, the object and purpose of the directive would still be decisive for the international scope of application of a directive. Despite the restrictions upon the qualification and application of overriding mandatory provisions, party autonomy would still be at risk if directives were systematically classified as overriding mandatory. The harmonised field would apply regardless the law chosen by the parties or designated by the conflict of laws rules. The readiness of the ECJ to resort to overriding mandatory provisions – as compared to national courts – in order to ensure the applicability of directives is illustrated by a decision of the French Cour de Cassation. The Cour de Cassation refused to classify the French provisions implementing art. 17–19 of the Agency Directive as overriding mandatory. The provisions were domestically mandatory, but not internationally (overriding) mandatory.[55] However, only nine days earlier, the ECJ held in *Ingmar* that arts. 17–19 of the Commercial Agents Directive were mandatory to the degree that they were applicable regardless the applicable law.[56] The question arose in a dispute relating to an agency contract concluded between a Californian principal and an UK agent. A choice of law in favour of Californian law had been made. When the principal terminated the agency agreement the agent sought compensation on the basis of the relevant articles. The Agency Directive contained no provisions indicating its international field of application but was found by the ECJ to be applicable, regardless the choice of law.

---

[55] Cour de Cassation, 28 November 2000, No. 98 – 11.335. The District Court Arnhem (The Netherlands) already held on 11 July 1991 that an internationally mandatory nature does not follow from the Agency Directive, *Nederlands Internationaal Privaatrecht*, Vol. 10, 1992, pp. 100.

[56] Case 381/98 *Ingmar* [2000], ECR I-9305.

4.3.1 *Ingmar as Authority for an Autonomous Approach*

It is certainly remarkable that the ECJ did not refer to the Rome Convention when establishing the international field of application of the Commercial Agents Directive, but rather relied on the nature and purpose of the Directive. Did the ECJ however have to refer to the Rome Convention at all? It should be kept in mind that not only did the facts of the case fall outside the temporal scope of the Rome Convention; the ECJ also did not yet possess the competence to interpret the Rome Convention. The referring court asked:

> Under English law, effect will be given to the applicable law as chosen by the parties, unless there is a public policy reason, such as an overriding provision, for not so doing. In such circumstances, are the provisions of Council Directive 86/653/EEC, as implemented in the laws of the Member States, and in particular those provisions relating to the payment of compensation to agents on termination of their agreements with their principals applicable when:
>
> (a) a principal appoints an exclusive agent in the United Kingdom and the Republic of Ireland for the sale of its products therein; and
> (b) in so far as sales of the products in the United Kingdom are concerned, the agent carries out its activities in the United Kingdom; and
> (c) the principal is a company incorporated in a non-EU State, and in particular in the State of California, USA, and situated there; and
> (d) the express applicable law of the contract between the parties is that of the State of California, USA?'[57]

The English court already stipulated the consequences of an affirmative answer of the ECJ. If the ECJ were to find the Commercial Agents Directive to be mandatory in that context it would, in line with the Rome Convention, be classified as overriding mandatory. The ECJ did not therefore have to rule on the relationship between art. 7 (2) and art. 20 Rome Convention. It consequently does not follow from *Ingmar* that the application of secondary legislation should be tested outside the framework of the Rome Convention, but rather that the mandatory nature of a provision should be established in the light of the instrument itself. The Court surpassed the argument, put forward by the Commission and the United Kingdom government, that the territorial scope of the Directive was a question of Union law, and who subsequently alleged that upon a construction of the objectives pursued by

[57] Case 381/98 *Ingmar* [2000], ECR I-9305, par. 13.

the Directive it required to be applied to all commercial agents established in a Member State, irrespective of the nationality or the place of establishment of their principal.[58] Instead the Court followed the argument put forward by the German government that in the absence of any express provision in the Directive as regards its territorial scope, it is for the court of a Member State seised to decide whether the applicable national rules are to be regarded as mandatory rules for the purposes of PIL.[59] The necessity that the degree of mandatoriness is assessed in the light of the Directive is not shocking; the degree of mandatoriness of purely national legislation is also answered in the light of the nature and purpose of the rule involved.

Accordingly, it is not the methodological framework that is used by the Court to assess the degree of international mandatoriness of the Directive that has been criticised. The Court held the application of the directive to the dispute was, in the light of its purposes, essential for the Union legal order, those purposes being the elimination of restrictions on the carrying-out of the activities of commercial agents, the unification of conditions of competition within the Union and the increase of security in commercial transactions.[60] That reasoning is far from convincing. Was the imposition of the Directive in these circumstances really necessary for the functioning of the internal market? Imagine that if, due to the fear of losing the protection of his home Member State, the agent had refrained from contracting with the firm established in the US. Would the decision not to conclude a contract with an US principal really have impacted upon the Union market? The reasoning of the Court is more concerned with the parallel uniform application of Union law in international cases and the protection of the weaker party, whose protection has become an objective as such.[61]

---

[58] *Ingmar*, par. 18.

[59] *Ingmar*, para. 19–20. Michaels/Kamann however seem to assume that the ECJ did not follow the submission of the German government but that of the Commission and UK government. Michaels, R., and H. Kamann, "Grundlagen eines allge meinen gemeinschaftlichten Richtlinienkollisionsrechts – "Amerikanisierung" des Gemeinschafts-IPR?", *Europäisches Wirtschafts- & Steuerrecht*, Vol. 12, No. 6, 2001, pp. 301–311 (304).

[60] *Ingmar*, par. 23 and 25. The difference with the reasoning of the Cour de Cassation nine days later is striking: Jacquet, J., Note sous CJCE 9 Novembre 2000, *Journal de droit international*, Vol. 128, 2001, pp. 517–523. Indeed from a PIL perspective the decision is criticisable, the Court for example did not refer at all to the Hague Agency Convention. Idot, L., Note sous CJCE 9 Novembre 2000, *Revue Critique de Droit International Privé*, Vol. 90, 2001, pp. 112–120.

[61] *Ingmar*, in particular par. 20. Staudinger, A., "Die ungeschriebenen kolli sionsrechtlichen Regelungsgebote der Handelsvertreter-, Haustürwiderrufs- und

A sufficiently close link with the Union apparently exists when the agent carries out his activities on the territory of one of the Member States.[62]

The second objection raised against the Courts reasoning is the distinction between mandatory and overriding mandatory provisions. If the criterion for international mandatoriness of a provision is that the provision should be aimed at the proper functioning of the internal market, nearly every directive would be classified overriding mandatory since every directive is in one way or the other aimed at the functioning of the internal market. The Court neglects the distinction between *ordre public* and *ordre public international*; in PIL not every mandatory provision is classified as overriding mandatory. Especially because overriding mandatory provisions limit private autonomy and may potentially lead to legal uncertainty, the category has to be interpreted narrowly. The observance of overriding mandatory provisions is crucial for the safeguard of the political, social or economical order of the jurisdiction involved. The protection of an agent to a transnational contract is not.[63] The ECJ attitude could be classified as slightly ambivalent: whereas it imposes a strict proportionality test upon national overriding mandatory provisions that potentially affect the functioning of the internal market, it is less reluctant to resort to the concept of overriding mandatory provisions to guarantee the application of Union law regardless the applicable law.[64]

The potential detrimental effects of *Ingmar* may go beyond overriding party autonomy or the objective applicable law. Does the reasoning of the ECJ also mean that if a choice of law clause is accompanied by a jurisdiction clause, Union courts will be required to strike the jurisdiction clause down in the light of the likelihood of non-application of the Agency Directive? After all, if parties had opted for the application of Californian law and arbitration before an American arbitrator it is unlikely that the arbitrator would have applied the Agency Directive. The Oberlandesgericht München answered that question, without

Produkthaftungsrichtlinie", *Neue Juristische Wochenschrift*, Vol. 54, 2001, pp. 1974–1978.

[62] Francq *supra* note 10, pp. 415–416.

[63] Dutch and French courts have ruled that the provisions protecting the agent are domestically mandatory, but not internationally mandatory. *Supra* note 55.

[64] Gaudemet-Tallon, H., "Le droit international privé des contrats dans un ensemble régional : l'exemple du droit communautaire", T. Einhorn and K. Siehr (eds.), *Intercontinental Cooperation through Private International Law: Essays in Memory of Peter E Nygh*, TMC Asser Press, The Hague, 2004, pp. 119–137.

asking the ECJ for a preliminary ruling, in the affirmative[65] and thereby departed slightly from pre-existing case-law in Germany. The decision of the OLG is detrimental for party autonomy in agency contracts and raises major issues from a legal certainty perspective. A party would not only see the Agency Directive partially modifying the applicable law, but could be surprised with proceedings before a foreign court despite an exclusive jurisdiction clause. The absence of a preliminary ruling should be regretted since the answer of the ECJ would not have been obvious.[66]

4.3.2 *An Autonomous Approach via Overriding Mandatory Provisions*

From the outset it must be observed that merely because the Member States have interpreted overriding mandatory provisions in a narrow way, that does not preclude the Union from giving a wider interpretation to that concept. The ECJ has consistently held that in case of the failure or incorrect transposition of a directive, the directive itself does not confer direct rights upon the individual and cannot be relied upon in purely horizontal situations.[67] One could argue that a directive is incorrectly transposed insofar as the conflict of laws norms do not guarantee the international scope of application as required by a construction of the aim and content of the relevant directive. National courts are under a duty of consistent interpretation.[68] National law, and not only the national law implementing the relevant directive, should be interpreted as far as possible in conformity with Union law and hence give as far as possible an interpretation that realises the purposes of the directive.[69] Consistent interpretation is able to ensure the full

---

[65] OLG München 17 May 2006 – 7 U 1781/06.

[66] Rühl, G., "Extending *Ingmar* to Jurisdiction and Arbitration Clauses: The End of Party Autonomy in Contracts with Commercial Agents?", *European Review of Private Law*, Vol. 15, No. 6, 2007, pp. 891–903.

[67] Case 41/74 *Van Duyn v Home Office* [1974] ECR 1337; Case 152/84 *Marshall* [1986] ECR 723; Case C-91/92 *Faccini Dori* [1994] ECR I-3325.

[68] Dougan, M., "The "Disguised" Vertical Effect of Directives", *Cambridge Law Journal*, Vol. 59, No. 3, 2000, pp. 586–612; Betlem, G., "The Doctrine of Consistent Interpretation; Managing Legal Uncertainty", J. Prinssen and A. Schrauwen (eds.), *Direct Effect: Rethinking a Classic of EC Legal Doctrine*, European Law Publishers, Groningen, 2001, pp. 79–105; Amstuz, M., "In-between Worlds: *Marleasing* and the Emergence of Interlegality in Legal Reasoning", *European Law Journal*, Vol. 11, No. 6, 2005, pp. 766–784.

[69] Case 18/83 *Von Colson* [1984] ECR 1891; Case C-106/89 *Marleasing* [1990] ECR I-4135; Case C-81/98 *Alcatel Austria* [1999] ECR I-7671; Joined Cases C-397-403/01 *Pfeiffer and others v Deutsches Rotes Kreuz* [2004] ECR I-8835.

effectiveness of Union law despite the absence of direct horizontal effect. Since the principle is inherent in the system of the Treaty, it would also apply to the margin of discretion that art. 9 (2) Rome I leaves to national courts.[70] Art. 9 (2) only states that the Regulation does not restrict the forum in the application of its overriding mandatory provisions and thus leaves the application of domestic overriding mandatory provisions in principle to national law. What is considered to be crucial for the safeguard of the political, social or economical organisation of a state has in principle to be determined by that state itself. The situation is different when a national rule is implementing a directive, since the application of the national doctrine of overriding mandatory provisions should achieve an outcome consistent with the objectives pursued by that directive.

The doctrine of consistent interpretation does not require a *contra legem* interpretation of national law,[71] nor does it determine or aggravate the criminal liability of persons acting in contravention of the directive.[72] However, the consistent interpretation does not necessarily have to be in conformity with pre-existing case-law.[73] The duty of consistent interpretation may thus require modification of the existing legal doctrines to ensure the attainment of the purposes of the directive. A Member State is after all prevented from relying upon 'provisions, practices or circumstances existing in its internal legal system in order to justify a failure to comply with its obligations under Union law'.[74] In that sense, the concept of overriding mandatory provisions may be interpreted more widely as traditionally understood by Member States, in order to guarantee the effective application of Union law. If what is to be considered crucial for the safeguard of the political, social or economical organisation of a state is in principle to be left to be determined by the state involved, what is to be crucial for the

---

[70] *Pfeiffer supra* note 69, par. 114. Previously, the legal basis lay in a combined reading of art. 10 and art. 249 (3) EC Treaty, see: Betlem, G., Beyond *Francovich*: Completing the Unified Member State and EU Liability Regime, D. Obradovic and N. Lavranos (eds.), *Interface between EU Law and National Law*, European Law Publishers, Groningen, 2007, pp. 297–309 (302).

[71] Case C-334/92 *Wagner-Miret* [1993] ECR I-6911; AG Colomer in C-397-403/01 *Pfeiffer and others v Deutsches Rotes Kreuz* [2004] ECR I-8835, par. 27.

[72] Case 80/86 *Kolpinghuis Nijmegen* ECR [1987] 3969; Case C-168/95 *Arcaro* [1996] ECR I-4705.

[73] Case C-215/97 *Bellone* [1998] ECR I-2191; AG Jacobs in: Case C-456/98 *Centrosteel* [2000] ECR I-6007, par. 5.

[74] Case C-5/89 *Commission v Germany* [1990] ECR I-3437, par. 18.

safeguard of the political, social or economical organisation of the Union should in principle be determined by the Union.

The context, objective and purpose of a national rule are also taken into account when assessing its mandatory nature on the international level. Also, overriding mandatory provisions originating in national law are often not accompanied by a scope rule and national courts deduct their implicitly claimed scope of application upon a construction of their aim and content. One could therefore only speak of an autonomous approach when the objective and purpose of the directive systematically prevail over a multilateral conflict of laws rule. Directives would as such be classified crucial for the safeguard of the political, social or economical organisation of the Union.[75] Such a classification would completely blur the distinction between mandatory and overriding mandatory law and would exclude private autonomy.

4.3.3 *An Autonomous Approach via (implicit) Unilateral Conflict of Law Rules*

The other line of reasoning to supports an autonomous approach to the international scope of application of the EU consumer *acquis* is that as, a consequence of *Ingmar* a directive should be assessed on its implicit claimed scope of application, a test outside the framework of art. 6 Rome I.[76] This claim is born out of a strict (German) separation whereby art. 6 refers to provisions aimed at strengthening the position of an individual weaker party, and art. 9 exclusively refers to provisions protecting state interests in a strict sense.[77] Overriding mandatory provisions would therefore only have limited effect with regard to consumer law, since consumer rules primarily aim to protect an individual interest rather than the protection of the society as a whole. *Ingmar* would, in this respect, pose problems, since at stake was the protection of the

[75] Reich, N., "EuGH: Handelsvertreterrichtlinie unabdingbar gegenüber Drittlandprinzipial", *Europäische Zeitschrift für Wirtschaftsrecht*, Vol. 12, 2001, pp. 50–52. 'Dies verlangt (wie im Wettbewerbsrecht), dass für eine Tätigheit in der Gemeinschaft auch die hier allgemein geltenden, durch die Mitgliedstaaten umzusetzenden Schutzregelungen des Handelsvertreter- Verbraucherschutz- und Arbeitsrechts als zwingende Vorschriften i.S. des Art. 34 EGBGB gelten'.

[76] Hoffmann, J., and V. Primaczenko, "Die kollisionsrechtliche Absicherung des Verbraucherschutzes in Europa: Zu Anerkennung ungeschriebenen Richtlinienkollisionrecht", *IPRax*, Vol. 27, No. 3, 2007, pp 173–179

[77] Mankowski, P., "Wichtige Klärungen im Internationalen Arbeitsrecht", *IPRax*, 1994, pp. 88–98.

individual interests of a weaker party rather than the protection of the society as a whole. The resort to art. 9 barred, reliance on an implicitly claimed scope of application appears to be logical. Courts in other Member States however, such as France and the Netherlands, have not limited the concept of overriding mandatory provisions to rules protecting the interest of a state in a strict sense. If one accepts that art. 9 only plays a role with regard to second generation overriding mandatory provisions if the weaker party has not been protected by art. 6 against the negative consequences of a choice of law, one sees that the German claim does not hold ground. The conclusion on the relationship between art. 6 and 8 on the one hand and art. 9 on the other would therefore affect the relationship between arts. 9 and 23. The relationship between art. 6/8 and art. 9 is however far from clear. As the French and Dutch position demonstrates, the protection of the individual interest of a weaker party can in principle be incorporated in the doctrine of overriding mandatory provisions.

Even if one accepts that the ECJ in *Ingmar* resorted to the public policy exception in the tradition of conflict of laws, an argument for testing the scope of the EU consumer *acquis* on its implied scope of application can still be made. Art. 23 Rome I only addresses the primacy of specific conflict of laws rules and does not address the position of secondary legislation in Rome I explicitly. In fact, Rome I does not prevent, or acknowledge, that the international scope of application of a directive should be tested upon an autonomous construction of its object and purpose. Having said that, it is hard to justify why the scope of application of the Injunctions Directive,[78] the E-Commerce Directive,[79] the Consumer Protection Cooperation Regulation[80] and the Services Directive,[81] which specifically provide that they do not lay down any additional conflict of laws rules and hence do not prejudice the application of Rome I, should be determined on the basis of Rome I, while the scope of consumer directives that neither contain a specific scope rule nor specifically state not to prejudice the conflict of laws rules should be determined autonomously on their implied scope of application.

[78] Art. 2 (2) Directive 98/27.
[79] Art. 1 (4) Directive 2001/31.
[80] Art. 2 (2) Regulation 2006/2004.
[81] Art. 3 (2) Directive 2006/123.

Nevertheless, one has to be reluctant to apply rules which, implicitly or explicitly claim, a specific international scope of application. The 40th recital to Rome I declares a situation of limited and dispersed conflict of laws rules to be undesirable. Art. 23 is an evolution of its predecessor, art. 20 Rome Convention, although they do not share the same problem. The relationship between Rome Convention, an international treaty, was fundamentally different from the relationship between the Regulation, a Union instrument, and Union law. Whereas supremacy of the Union legal order may require that the application of secondary law should not be made dependent upon an international convention, supremacy does not preclude making the application of Union law depended upon another Union instrument. The restrictive approach that the 40th recital takes with regard of delimiting the scope of application of secondary law outside the framework of Rome I is defensible. The evolution of the Rome Convention into a Regulation takes much wind out of the sails of the argument for incorporating the objective and purpose of a directive in the choice of law process.

Slightly different is the argument that the implicit rule on the scope of application should take precedence over a multilateral conflict of laws rule on the basis that the *lex specialis* takes precedence over the *lex generalis*.[82] The precedence of implicit scope rules in Union instruments therefore does not depend upon art. 23 Rome I or the supremacy of Union law but is set autonomously on the basis of a general principle of law. The transformation of the Rome Convention into Rome I therefore does not change the argument. Nonetheless, it is hard to imagine that every directive contains an unwritten scope rule. Does the Agency Directive really aim to lay down a conflict of laws rule relating to contractual obligations, or does it only aim to provide a substantive result (the protection of the agent)?[83] The implicit scope rule in the Agency Directive would then not be a unilateral conflict of laws rule, since its application cannot be set aside by a choice of law rule, but an overriding mandatory provision. The presumption that every directive

---

[82] Franq, S., "The Scope of Secondary Union Law in the Light of the Methods of Private International Law – or the Other Way Around?", *Yearbook of Private International Law*, Vol. 8, 2006, pp. 333–374 (354–355).

[83] Verhagen, H., "Het spanningsveld tussen de vrijheid van rechtskeuze en het communautaire harmonisatie-proces", *Nederlands Internationaal Privaatrecht*, Vol. 19, No. 1, 2001, pp. 27–33 (30); Verhagen, H., "The tension between party autonomy and European Union law: some observations on Ingmar", *International Law and Comparative Law Quarterly*, Vol. 51, 2002, pp. 135–154 (139).

contains an unwritten scope rule is untenable. Some directives exclusively aim to lay down a substantive norm without being accompanied by an explicit or implied scope rule.

Establishing the international scope of application of a directive is fundamentally different from establishing the international scope of application of primary law. Secondary law cannot limit the application of primary law. There is however no principal objection why a regulation could not determine, and limit, the scope of application of another secondary law instrument. Moreover, a directive has to be implemented in the national legal order of the Member States. After transposition the directive becomes an intrinsic part of the national legal order. Implementing rules are not always clearly identifiable and its different treatment in a conflict of laws case as opposed to a purely national rule could generate a lot of legal uncertainty for the parties.

It is submitted that unilateral determination of the international field of application of a directive on the basis of an autonomous test raises serious difficulties of interpretation and it should therefore be preferred, in the lack of an explicit conflict of laws rule, to making the application of secondary law subject to Rome I.[84] The substantive rules contained in directives, are after implementation, absorbed into the national legal system and undergo the same conflict of laws process in international cases.[85] If one were to establish the scope of application of secondary legislation outside the scope of Rome I, one want also render the provision on the choice of law inapplicable. The principle of party autonomy would therefore be severely undermined if secondary legislation would systemically prevail over Rome I.[86]

---

[84] Similar : Jayme, E., and C. Kohler, "L'interaction des règles de conflit contenues dans le droit dérivé de la Communauté européene et des conventions de Bruxelles et de Rome", *Revue Critique de Droit International Privé*, Vol. 84, No. 1, 1995, pp. 1–40 (16). 'L'exigence de respecter l'unité fonctionnelle de la réglementation conflictuelle se reflète également au niveau de l'*interprétation* des dispositions du droit dérivé. Elle aussi doit se faire ‹en harmonie› aves les règles conventionnelles et essayer de parvenir, sur le fondement d'une présomption de conformité d'inspiration et de princes, à des résultats compatibles avec le système en général.'

[85] Fallon, M., "Les conflits de lois et de juridictions dans un espace économique intégré.", *Recueil des Cours*, Vol. 253, 1995, pp. 13–281 (185–186) ; Verhagen, *supra* note 83.

[86] AG Léger in case 381/98 *Ingmar* [2000], ECR I-9305, par. 72. See as well: Schwarz, S., "Das international Handelsvertreterrecht im Lichte von "Ingmar" – Droht das Ende der Parteiautonomie im Gemeinschaftsprivatrecht?", *Zeitschrift für Vergleichende Rechtswissenschaft*, Vol. 101, 2002, pp. 45–74.

4.4 *Ingmar – A Judgment Open for Revision?*

It remains to be seen whether the ECJ will give wider application to *Ingmar*, or whether in subsequent decisions will adopt a more restrictive approach towards international public policy. The issue of determining the scope of application of a rule on the basis of public policy has until now not reappeared before the ECJ, although the Court has been confronted on several occasions with the question whether recognition or enforcement of an arbitral decision should be refused on the basis of public policy, the alleged violation constituting the non-observation of a mandatory Union rule. The first case was decided prior to *Ingmar*, where the Court held in *Eco Swiss* that art. 101 TFEU (81 EC) constituted a fundamental provision which is essential for the accomplishment of the tasks entrusted to the Union and, in particular, for the functioning of the internal market.[87] The Court equated the status of competition law with that of national public policy.[88] Member States were obliged to set aside an arbitral award in case of non-observation of art. 101 TFEU, if courts would be obliged to refuse recognition in similar circumstances on the grounds of public policy.

In *Mostaza Claro* the Court was confronted with the recognition of an arbitral award, where the choice of jurisdiction in the contract would have constituted an unfair clause under the Unfair Contract Terms Directive.[89] *Asturcom* concerned similar factual circumstances, but the national court only first heard the case at the enforcement stage.[90] Both cases concerned Spanish consumers and Spanish telecom operators. In that sense *Mostaza Claro* and *Asturcom* provide only limited guidance about *Ingmar*, since both contracts were completely internal to Spain.[91] However, in these judgments the court explicitly

---

[87] Case C-126/97 *Eco Swiss* [1999] ECR I-3055, par. 36.

[88] The language of the ECJ makes it not clear in what context public policy is used. The emphasis on the 'failure to observe rules of public policy' raises the impression that the ECJ is discussing public policy in the context of overriding mandatory provisions and not of public policy in the context of refusing to enforce an arbitral award. Shelkopylas, N., *The Application of EC Law in Arbitration Proceedings*, European Law Publishing, Groningen, 2003, pp. 128.

[89] Case C-168/05 *Mostaza Claro* [2006] ECR I-10421.

[90] Case C-40/08 *Asturcom* [2009] ECR I-9579.

[91] The classification of the UFCT Directive as public policy in *Mostaza Claro* and *Asturcom* therefore does not say anything about the international scope of application of the directive. Private parties may not evade the mandatory norms applicable

sought a connection to the public policy exception of the Member States.[92] Did the Court here draw a difference between the two concepts of public policy? Should the provision be of a fundamental nature, or in other words, should its observation be crucial for the safeguard of the social, political or economical organisation of the Union to be classified as part of the international public policy and does the mandatory characteristic of consumer law suffice for public policy in a wider sense? Although the reasoning of the Court is rather confusing,[93] it could be argued that the Court brought this hierarchy into Union law.[94] The same impression becomes apparent from the proposal of the Consumer Rights Directive. Although it is beyond doubt that its provisions would be mandatory when all connections are with the Union, the 59th recital makes it clear that is not necessarily the case where the law applicable to the contract is that of a third country. According to that recital it should be left to Rome I to determine whether the consumer retains the protection granted by this Directive. These provisions on consumer protection therefore appear in principle not to be part of the international public policy.

Although the decision in *Ingmar* is to be regretted because the ECJ has interpreted the concept of overriding mandatory provisions significantly more widely than Member States have traditionally done, it does not follow that every directive has to be assessed autonomously on its implied scope of application. On the contrary, by following the submission of the German government, the ECJ sought a connection with the PIL of national Member States. The Court simply followed the logical conclusion; the degree of mandatory nature of a national rule implementing a directive should be assessed in the light of the object and purpose of the directive.

---

in a country, by means of a choice of law or choice of court, when the contract is exclusively connected to that country (art. 3 (3) Rome Convention, Rome I Regulation not yet applicable to these cases).

[92] *Mostaza Claro*, *supra* note 89, par. 35. Although it should be admitted that in the light wording the consequences of this distinction are somewhat mitigated, see: Ebers, M., "From *Océano* to *Asturcom*", *European Review of Private Law*, Vol. 18, 2010, pp. 823–846.

[93] Stuyck, J., Case Note to *Pannon* and *Asturcom*, *Common Market Law Review*, Vol. 47, 2010, pp. 879–898.

[94] Schebesta, H., "Does the national Court know Union Law? A note on ex-officio application after Asturcom" *European Review of Private Law*, Vol. 18, 2010, pp. 847–880 (864).

4.5 *The Legislative History of art. 23 Rome I Regulation*

A restrictive reading of *Ingmar* is confirmed by the legislative history of art. 23 Rome I. In the light of the controversy it would have been very welcome if the Regulation had brought more clarity as to the relationship between Rome I and the consumer directives. The Commission proposal did in art. 22 attempt to clarify that relationship and referred to an annex in which directives that laid down choice of law rules with respect to contractual obligations in particular matters were listed. Only four directives featured on this list: the Return of Cultural Objects Directive (EC 7/93); the Posted Workers Directive (EC 71/96); the Second non-life insurance Directive (EC 49/92) and the Second life assurance Directive (EEC 619/90). Although it is debatable whether the list was meant to be exhaustive, the absence of consumer directives is striking. It could perhaps be explained by the proposed choice of law rule in consumer contracts: the law of the place of habitual residence would apply and no choice of law was possible. Specific choice of law rules in consumer contracts were thus no longer warranted.[95] Although some evidence for this position can be retrieved from the preparatory documents,[96] this line of reasoning only holds limited ground. As argued earlier, the Union consumer *acquis* protects a wider group of consumers than art. 6 Rome I.[97] A choice of law would thus still be possible in situations involving for example mobile consumers while art. 6 would not contain any safeguards for the application of mandatory Union law. The explanation that consumer directives were omitted from the annex as corollary of the proposed connecting factor for consumer contracts is therefore inadequate. Perhaps the Commission considered that the consumer directives did not lay down additional conflict of laws rules.

The proposed art. 22 was substantially modified and the annex deleted. The reason for the modification was not disagreement about

---

[95] Max Planck Institute for Foreign Private and Private International Law, Comments on the European Commission's Proposal for a Regulation of the European Parliament and the Council on the law applicable to contractual obligations (Rome I), *RabelsZ*, Vol. 71, 2007, pp. 225–344 (340).

[96] The Proposal of the Portuguese (check March 2007) for a Rome I Regulation, 6935/07 JUSTCIV 44 CODEC 168, 24 explicitly holds that amendment might be necessary if a new article on consumer protection is inserted.

[97] *Commission v Spain, supra* note 24.

its content, but the European Parliament[98] desired a better alignment with the Rome II Regulation on non-Contractual Obligations. That is a pity, because art. 27 Rome II[99] was undoubtedly inspired by art. 20 Rome Convention. The intention of the Commission was exactly the clarification of this provision. Although it should be regretted that the proposal did not become law, the legislative history of art. 23 Rome I pleads against an expansive interpretation of that article. Only four directives that laid down clear conflict of laws rules were listed as taking precedence over Rome I. Establishing the degree of mandatory nature in the light of the object and purpose of the directive for the purpose of the classification of the provision as international public policy is something different from autonomously delimiting the scope of that directive. The legislative history and the 40th recital of the preamble to Rome I indicate that the international scope of application of secondary legislation should therefore, in the absence of an explicit conflict of laws rule, be tested within the framework of Rome I.

Confirmation of the central role of Rome I in establishing the international field of application of secondary law can be found outside Rome I as well. The new Timeshare Directive also recognises that the instrument does not contain a unilateral conflict of laws rule that takes

---

[98] European Parliament Report on COM(2005) 650, A6-0450/2007, amendment 58.

[99] The provision itself was a subject of controversy. In particular the European Parliament had in the past advocated a broader application of art. 27. Art. 23 of the proposal (COM 2003 427, final) read:

1. This Regulation shall not prejudice the application of provisions contained in the Treaties establishing the European Communities or in acts of the institutions of the European Communities which:
   - in relation to particular matters, lay down choice-of-law rules relating to non-contractual obligations; or
   - lay down rules which apply irrespective of the national law governing the non-contractual obligation in question by virtue of this Regulation; or
   - prevent application of a provision or provisions of the law of the forum or of the law designated by this Regulation.
2. This regulation shall not prejudice the application of Community instruments which, in relation to particular matters and in areas coordinated by such instruments, subject the supply of services or goods to the laws of the Member State where the service-provider is established and, in the area coordinated, allow restrictions on freedom to provide services or goods originating in another Member State only in limited circumstances.

See: Dickinson, A., "Cross-Border Torts in EC Courts – A Response to the proposed 'Rome II' Regulation", *European Business Law Review*, Vol. 13, 2002, pp. 369–388 (379); Kramer, X., "The Rome II Regulation on the Law Applicable to Non-Contractual Obligations: The European private international law tradition continued", *Nederlands Internationaal Privaatrecht*, Vol. 26, 2008, pp. 414–424 (417).

precedence over Rome I. The 17th recital provides that although it should be avoided that the applicability of the law of a third country leads to the deprivation of the protection afforded by the directive, the law applicable to a contract should be determined in accordance with the Union rules on private international law and makes an explicit reference to Rome I. A similar recital was not included in the original Timeshare Directive.

Art. 27 (1b) Rome I contains a review clause requiring the Commission to submit by 17 June 2013 'an evaluation on the application of Article 6, in particular as regards the coherence of Union law in the field of consumer protection.' Several delegations proposed to incorporate the specific applicability provisions in consumer directives also in Rome I, as was done with regard to insurance contracts. Due to lack of time and the desire to reach a compromise in the first reading the issue was left out. The review clause might be a reason for the Commission to address the wider issue of relationship between secondary law and PIL. As will be argued below, the incorporation of provisions from specific consumer directives in Rome I is not the obvious solution.

4.5.1 *Transformation into Rome I: The Wider Perspective*

It is certainly true that the Rome Convention had serious shortcomings in conceptualising the particularities of Union law. It treated a cross border situation as international regardless of whether all contacts were located within the Union, or not. The *Gran Canaria* cases decided in German courts provide for an excellent illustration.[100] German consumers went on holiday to Spain and were there approached by Spanish professionals established formally on the Isle of Man. Once back in Germany, the consumers sought to withdraw from the contract on the basis of the Doorstep Selling Directive. Germany had implemented the directive properly, but the contract contained a choice of law in favour of the law of the Isle of Man. The *Bundesgerichtshof* refused to apply

[100] Taupitz, J., "Kaffeefahrten deutscher Urlauber auf Gran Canaria: Deutscher Verbraucherschutz im Urlaubsgepäck?", *Betriebsberater*, 1990, pp. 642–652 ; Mäsch, G., *Rechtswahlfreiheit und Verbraucherschutz ; Eine Untersuchung zu den Art. 29 I, 27 III und 34 EGBGBI*, Duncker & Humblot, Berlin 1993, pp. 114–125 ; Rauscher, T., "Gran Canaria — Isle of Man — Was kommt danach", *Europäische Zeitschrift für Wirtschaftsrecht*, vol.7 (1996), 650-3.

art. 5 Rome Convention since the commercial activities of the provider were not directed against the home Member State of the consumer and saw no other possibility to apply the Doorstep Selling Directive. It explicitly held that the provisions in the Doorstep Selling Directive were not overriding mandatory provisions. Although the contract had exclusive connections with the Union, a German consumer being approached by a Spanish professional in Spain, the consumer could not rely on the minimum protection of the Directive. Interpretations like these undermine the effective application of Union law and are detrimental for the confidence of consumers in the internal market. The problem is not limited to the Doorstep Selling Directive: consider for example the possibility of circumventing the E-Commerce Directive by choosing US law in a contract between a German consumer and a provider established in the United Kingdom.

The impossibility as perceived by German courts of applying the Doorstep Selling Directive demonstrates quite well the difficulties that some traditional PIL lawyers have in conceptualising the specific characteristics of the Union. An international contract is international, regardless of whether the contract is exclusively connected to the Union or not. From this traditional PIL perspective, a contract with connections to both France and Germany is as international as a contract with connections to France and the US. A more satisfying outcome could have been reached by following the ECJ's case-law with regard to the recognition and enforcement of judicial decisions in civil proceedings. The ECJ held that for the purposes of the Brussels Convention the territories of the Member States may be regarded as forming a single entity.[101] Subsequently, an analogy could have been sought with art. 3 (3) Rome Convention, stipulating that the fact that the parties have chosen a foreign law shall not, 'where all the other elements relevant to the situation at the time of the choice are connected with one country only, prejudice the application of rules of the law of that country which cannot be derogated from by contract.'

The resort to an alternative approach in the sense that a directive should be applicable in cases with a very close connection to the Union, but not necessarily with one Member State in particular,[102] can perhaps

---

[101] Case C-398/92 *Mund & Fester* [1994] ECR 1-467, par. 19.

[102] Advanced by: Joustra, C., "Europese Richtlijnen en internationaal privaatrecht", *Weekblad voor het Privaatrecht Notariaat en Registratie,* 1999, pp. 664-670. In this approach, a directive is applicable when it concerns a 'Union case'.

be understood with the *Gran Canaria* cases in the back of our minds.[103] To what extent can Union law be blamed for the preference to establish its own scope of application or to widen the application of the doctrine of overriding mandatory provisions if the national conflict of laws norms seem not be apt for dealing with its specific features? As a legal order *sui generis*, the application of Union law on the territory of the Union cannot be made dependent upon the operation of national conflict of laws mechanisms. However, the fact that an additional guarantee is necessary in order to ensure the application of mandatory Union law when a situation has connections with exclusively two or more Member States does not as such justify an unilateral approach of autonomously fixing the international scope of application of directives. Art. 3 (4) Rome I demonstrates that it is possible to accommodate the special status of Union law in a multilateral conflict of laws rule.[104] The deficiency in the Rome Convention with regard to situations that are wholly internal to the Union thus now has been cleared. The application of directives, or at least the minimum protection they offer, cannot be avoided if all connections are within the Union.

4.6 *Contracts Involving a Link with a Third Country*

The situations where the effect of Union legislation in the internal market is at stake is however intrinsically different from *Ingmar* situations, since in the latter there exists a strong connection with the legal system of a third country. The two situations underlie a different logic.[105]

> Denn es ist etwas anderes, ob ein Gesetzgeber seine Überzeugungen innerhalb der eigenen Rechtsordnung durchsetzt, wo er allein normsetzungsbefugt ist, oder ob er das auch gegenüber einer anderen Rechtsordnung mit einem ebenso souveränen Gesetzgeber tut.[106]

---

[103] The Green Paper (on the conversion of the Rome Convention of 1980 on the law applicable to contractual obligations into a Union instrument and its modernisation COM (2002) 654 final) refers, although implicitly, to the Gran Canaria cases, 21

[104] From the mandatory application of Union law it follows that when a situation has all connections with the Union, but with several Member States, only the minimum in the directive falls in the scope of art. 3 (4) and not the national clauses that go beyond that protection. See: Grundmann, S., "Binnenmarktkollisionsrecht – vom klassischen IPR zur Integrationsordnung", *RabelsZ*, Vol. 64, 2000, pp. 457-477, (471-476).

[105] Poillot Peruzzetto, S., "Ordre Public et loi de police dans l'ordre communautaire", Travaux du Comité Français de Droit International Privé 2002-2004, 65-106.

[106] Michaels/Kamann *supra* note 59, 305. 'It is however something else, when a legislator pushes through his convictions in his own legal order, where he is the sole

Although the insistence upon the application of Union law within the territory of the Union is understandable, what justifies the application of a directive at the expense of the application of rules of other sovereign legal orders? The principle of supremacy of Union law applies to the relationship between Union law and national law.[107] Member States have for the purpose of the establishment of the internal market given up part of their sovereignty. The Union has, albeit within limited fields, become the sovereign.[108] In cases of conflict between national and Union law the latter should therefore prevail. In *Ingmar* situations, however, there is a conflict between Union law and the law of a third country. By applying supremacy of substantive norms over the national conflict of laws norms, the Union controls the application of foreign law. On the international plane EU private law lifts off the internal market and finds its equal with other sovereigns, for example Canadian or Chinese private law. The preferential position of Union law towards the law of the Member States cannot be held against Canada or China. The traditional arguments in favour of a multilateral conflict of laws rule and private autonomy therefore reappear. Establishing the applicable law from the perspective of the legal relationship instead of the national rule better serves the expectations of the private parties, a legislator should exercise self-restraint when it is not the sole competent creator of norms, and the ability to choose the applicable law promotes legal certainty and economic efficiency. The scope of application, and the resulting non-application of secondary law, must therefore determined by the classical conflict of laws norms.[109] This self-restraint should not be seen as a limitation on the sovereignty of the EU legal order, but rather as the proper exercise of it.

Legal certainty would benefit from such an approach. Not only is the question addressed under what circumstances national law should be applied, but also under what conditions foreign law should be ap plied. It would also avoid the often difficult exercise of finding the intention of the legislator. The quest of finding the most closely

competent creator of laws, or when he does so against another legal order with an equally sovereign legislator.'

[107] Craig, P., and G. de Búrca, *EU Law : Text, Cases and Materials*, Oxford University Press, Oxford, fourth edition, 2008, pp. 344-378.

[108] Case 6/64 *Costa v ENEL* [1964] ECR 585.

[109] Verhagen, H., "Het spanningsveld tussen de vrijheid van rechtskeuze en het communautaire harmonisatie-proces", *Nederlands Internationaal Privaatrecht*, Vol. 19, No. 1, 2001, pp. 27-33 (32).

connected, or most affected legal system is better able to respect the legitimate expectations of the private parties. In transnational contracts, that often raise complicated conflict of laws questions, parties may avoid the uncertainty by establishing the applicable legal system in advance. It should be borne in mind that legal certainty and legitimate expectations are also general principles of EU law.[110] Moreover, the acceptance that Union law might give way to the application of the laws of a third country significantly facilitates its interaction with other legal systems.

If conflict of laws rules were to be concentrated in a single document rather than dispersed over several directives, Union law would benefit from increased legal simplicity and clarity. Even if the directives were interpreted in a manner so as to be as much as possible in conformity with the Rome I,[111] the parties to a contract would still be confronted with the burdensome task of testing every directive individually on their implicitly or explicitly claimed scope of application. Since directives do not cover the applicable law fully, parties would subsequently still have to settle the applicable law. Contracting parties would thus be faced with a dual burden. Moreover, scattered conflict of laws provisions might lead to contradictory results. It was exactly those considerations[112] that led to the incorporation of the conflict of laws norms laid down in the First and Second Non-life Insurance Directive in art. 7 Rome I.

Making directives subject to the conflict of laws norms in the Rome instruments is able to ensure the effective application of EU law. Under the doctrine of effective application, national courts cannot make the enforcement of Union law practicably impossible or excessively difficult.[113] It is important not to forget that parties have the possibility of a choice of law. In *Ingmar* the agent had voluntarily given up its protection by opting for Californian law. The Union legal order is based on individual freedom and responsibility; it leaves the decision to the individuals themselves how to best safeguard their interests which require

---

[110] Case T-115/94 *Opel Austria* [1997] ECR II-39, see: Chalmers, D., *et al*, *European Union Law*, Cambridge University Press, Cambridge, 2006, pp. 454-455.

[111] Klauer, S., *Das europäische Kollisionsrecht der Verbraucherverträge zwischen Römer-EVÜ und EG-Richtlinien*, Mohr Siebeck, Tübingen, 2002.

[112] Par. 2.7.2 and 4.10.

[113] Case C-142/87 *Belgium v Commission* [1990] ECR I-959; Case C-5/89 *Commission v Germany* [1990] ECR I-3437.

protection.[114] Where consumers and employees have to be protected against the negative consequences of a choice of law because they might see such a clause imposed upon them, the need for protection of agents is less obvious since it often involves better-informed and experienced professionals.

4.6.1 *Americanisation or Unfamiliarity with Conflict of Laws?*

Michaels and Kamann conclude on the basis of *Ingmar* that the Union insists more on the application of its semipublic law than the Member States have traditionally done. They perceive in the emphasis the Courts places upon the international limits of a law rather than on the principle of closest connection and the invalidation of a choice of law clause an Americanisation of European PIL.[115] This Americanisation originates in the heavier emphasis on *Marktordnung* in European private laws as compared to national private laws, the apparent transposition of a rationale of guaranteeing the effect of directives from *intra* Union situations to international situations and the traditional preference of the ECJ to exclusively set the scope of Union law.

The authors warn against the adoption of American principles that are no longer undisputed in the US. The restrictive approach towards party autonomy in the US is subject to increasing criticism and the conflict of laws systems indeed favour more and more party autonomy.[116] The role of party autonomy has also gained an important place in recent EU codifications, and has actually gone beyond what has been traditionally recognised by Member States. As has been demonstrated, good reasons exist to allow parties to choose the law applicable to their contract; it enhances legal certainty and it promotes efficiency.[117] In any case, it would be feasible for the ECJ to adhere to the increasing importance of party autonomy as translated by the Union legislator in its recent codifications of PIL and to serve better 'justice' to those who PIL actually concerns: namely private parties.

---

[114] AG Trstnjak in: Case C-331/05 *Internationaler Hilfsfonds v Commission* [2007] ECR I-05475, par. 93.

[115] Michaels/Kamann *supra* note 59, 311.

[116] Rühl, G., "Party Autonomy in the Private International Law of Contracts: Transatlantic Convergence and Economic Efficiency", CLPE Research Paper 4/2007, Vol. 03 No. 01, 2007, with furher references.

[117] Par. 2.3.3.

It is rather debatable whether the Court really aimed to transplant American conflict of laws principles into the European legal order. Union private law reacts in a similar way to foreign laws as national private law did with the emergence of PIL. When confronted with increasingly trans-jurisdictional issues, courts were initially occupied with the questions under which conditions domestic law could be applied against foreigners residing in the relevant jurisdiction and in what circumstances national law could be applied outside the territory of the relevant jurisdiction. Also in Europe, PIL long evolved around the proclaimed application of the rule and only slowly accepted the possibility of a choice of law. It was only in the 19th century that perspective shifted to private parties and their legitimate expectations became the cornerstone of PIL. The question was turned around: the applicable legal system should not be determined upon the pretention of the rule, but rather from the perspective of the legal relationship.[118] It may be hoped that the present unilateral approach in Union law is indeed only an 'infancy problem' and that the Union legislator will soon address the application of foreign law while the ECJ will allow national courts more leeway to forego application of Union law to promote conflict of laws justice and legal certainty in international trade. The unilateral determination of the applicability of the rules of the forum would be a step back in time of 700 years.

The legislative process of transforming the Rome Convention into a Regulation might give a reason for the ECJ to reconsider the degree of mandatory nature of the Agency Directive it established in *Ingmar*. Art. 7 of the proposal for the conversion of the Rome Convention into a Regulation contained a special connecting factor for agents.[119] The law governing the contract between the principal and the agent would have been the law of the country in which 'the agent has his habitual residence, unless the agent exercises or is to exercise his main activity in the country in which the principal has his habitual residence, in which case the law of that country shall apply'. Art. 7 (1) however reconfirmed the existence of the possibility of a choice of law.[120]

---

[118] Par. 2.1

[119] Proposal for a Regulation on the Law applicable to contractual obligations, COM (2005) 650 final.

[120] Max Planck Institute for Foreign Private and Private International Law, Comments on the European Commission's Proposal for a Regulation of the European Parliament and the Council on the law applicable to contractual obligations (Rome I), *RabelsZ*, Vol. 71, 2007, pp. 225-344 (298-312).

A choice of law would be rather useless if it only applied to default rules, since the freedom of contract does in a national context already allow for the avoidance of such rules.[121] Art. 7 was however deleted from the final text of the instrument since a special regime for agency contracts was not deemed necessary.[122] The Courts willingness to align the degree of mandatory nature in Union law provisions to the public policy conception of the Member States with regard to the recognition and enforcement of arbitral awards, is a positive indicator for better aligning the applicability of Union law to international cases with national public policy as regards the establishment of the applicable law.

4.6.2 *A Possible Solution to the 'Gran Canaria Problem'*

It is admitted that art. 3 (4) Rome I does not, in relation to third countries, cover the effective application of Union law completely. A typical example would be the version of *Gran Canaria* cases where the provider was established in a third country. According to art. 3 (4) parties could, without any reservation, lawfully choose the application of the law of the Island of Man. The effectiveness of EU consumer law would be undermined if a professional established in a third country could target EU consumers who temporarily reside in the territory of another Member State without being bound by EU consumer law. Even if second generation overriding mandatory provisions were included in the definition provided by art. 9 (1), not every provision of consumer law can be classified as crucial for the safeguard of the political, social or economical order. The solution does not lie, however, in autonomously delimiting the scope of, for example the Doorstep Selling Directive, but rather to adopt a flexible interpretation of the protective connecting factor for consumers. Whereas Rome I, compared to the Rome Convention, already places a stronger emphasis upon the actions of the professional, that professional can reasonably foresee he will be bound by EU consumer law when he targets his business activities to the territory of the Union. Making entitlement to the minimum EU consumer protection dependent upon the criterion of residence in a specific Member State seems incompatible with the general principle of

[121] Michaels/Kamann *supra* note 59, 305.

[122] UK Ministry of Justice, Rome I – should the UK opt in?, Consultation Paper CP05/08, 31. This is illustrated by the fact that the Hague Agency Convention has only been ratified by three Member States (France, the Netherlands and Portugal).

non-discrimination. In order to optimise the aim of enhancing the confidence of consumers in the internal market, the notion of 'country' in art. 6 Rome I should be interpreted so as to include the Union.[123] The rationale behind the targeting requirement of art. 6 is to prevent the professional from being taken by surprise and bound to comply with requirements of consumer protection under a foreign law. Therefore what is at stake in art. 6 is not so much a country as defined by rules of public international law, but rather the rules enacted by a specific jurisdiction. For the purposes of application of legislation implementing directives, the territories of the Member States of the Union should be seen as a single jurisdiction.[124] Whenever a professional targets his activities to one of the Member States of the Union, it cannot contract out of the minimum Union standards, regardless the question in which Member State the consumer is domiciled.

4.7 *Unilateral Conflict of Law Rules in Secondary Law Reconsidered*

The deficiency in the Rome Convention, which offered no guarantee for the application of mandatory Union rules analogous to a choice of law in a purely internal situation, has been cleared. From a PIL perspective, the current situation is not intrinsically different from a classical conflict of laws issue involving the laws of a Member State and a third country. As already stated, the role of party autonomy in private law in Europe is increasingly being acknowledged. Private parties should in principle be allowed to choose the law they wish to be subject to. Private law differs in this respect from other areas of law; it would, for example, be considered downright absurd for a defendant in a criminal proceeding with connections to several jurisdiction to request to the court to adjudicate his case according to the criminal laws of another jurisdiction.

With regard to private law, not every provision that uses territorial criteria is necessarily a unilateral conflict of laws rule. A provision indicating the material scope of a directive on the basis of territorial criteria does not necessarily define an international field of application. Material conditions of application say something about the interest of legislation to be applied to a certain case. In international situations,

[123] The position that 'country' also refers to rules of Union law has already been made with regard to art. 9 (1) Rome I. See par. 2.4.2.3.

[124] With regard to the Brussels Convention: *Mund & Fester*, *supra* note 101, par. 19.

the convictions of the legislator cannot have the same force since there are multiple sovereigns. Material conditions for the applicability of a rule provide for the applicability of that rule once the legal system in which it originates is found to be the governing law, but do not necessarily interfere in the conflict of laws process.

The real question boils down to the exclusion of party autonomy. What the directives have been doing prior to the introduction of art. 3 (4) Rome I is not so much setting their conditions of applicability but rather indicating the degree of mandatory nature of the instrument concerned. The directives filled the gaps created by the conflict of laws rules.[125] In this interpretation the legislator would, by specifying that the directive is applicable when a close connection to the territory of the Union exists, try to find an analogy with art. 3 (3) Rome Convention by indicating that the directive is mandatory within that specific context and, thereby excludeing party autonomy. Support for this interpretation could be found in for example art. 6 (2) of the Unfair Contract Terms Directive: '*Member States shall take the necessary measures to ensure that the consumer does not lose the protection granted by this Directive by virtue of the choice of the law of a non-Member country as the law applicable to the contract if the latter has a close connection with the territory of the Member States*'.[126]

Art. 6 (2) only comes into play if a choice of law has been made in favour of the laws of a third country. A Slovakian company and a 'mobile' Romanian consumer will therefore not be restricted to choose the law of Malta, but may be restricted in opting for Russian law. Supposedly, the application of the Unfair Contract Terms Directive would be guaranteed if the applicable law were Maltese, but not necessarily if it were Russian. The Unfair Contract Terms Directive will not be applicable if, on the basis of an objective connection, the law of a third country is designated. If the company were not Slovakian, but Russian, the applicable law would in our example be Russian. Under traditional PIL, an overriding mandatory provision would be

[125] Fourtoy, F., *L'impact du droit communautaire secondaire sur le droit international privé français*, EUI Thesis, 2003, 249.

[126] The recital states: 'Whereas there is a risk that, in certain cases, the consumer may be deprived of protection under this Directive by designating the law of a non-Member country as the law applicable to the contract; whereas provisions should therefore be included in this Directive designed to avert this risk'. Admittedly, it would have been easier to adopt art. 3 (3) Rome Convention in the Unfair Contract Terms Directive.

applicable regardless the applicable law and it would not matter whether the otherwise applicable law is established by a choice of law or upon an operation of the objective conflict of laws norms. Moreover, the parties will not be restricted in their choice of law if the situation does not have a close connection to the territory of the Member States. For example, it is not likely that a close connection to territory of the Member States exists when the contract was concluded and performed in Moscow. For the purpose of the directive, the territory of the Union become a single jurisdiction.[127] A similar argument would apply to art. 12 (2) Distance Selling Directive, art. 7 (2) Consumer Sales Directive and art. 12 (2) Distance Sales of Financial Services Directive.

Although art. 3 (3) Rome Convention sets a higher threshold, namely that all elements should be connected with one country rather than the existence of a close connection, the analogy is striking. Party autonomy may not displace mandatory rules when a qualified connection exists with a single jurisdiction. If policy considerations lead to the conclusion that, with regard to a specific rule, party autonomy is not feasible, it could be excluded in two different degrees: domestic and internationally mandatory norms. Accordingly, if provisions could be set aside by private parties by a mere choice of law, why maintain the mandatoriness in the conflict of law process in the absence of a choice of law? Although the desire of the Union to guarantee the universal application of its mandatory rules throughout its territory is quite understandable, the same does not hold true when this approach is maintained in relation with third countries. The Union is not the sole sovereign. The proper exercise of sovereignty requires some restraint. The interest of the Union in establishing an internal market is hardly at stake when one of the parties is established outside the territory of the Union.

PIL being unable to draw a formal distinction between intra-Union situations and truly international situations, the only mechanism left for the Union was to guarantee the application of mandatory EU law regardless the law designated by the conflict of laws rules. In the Netherlands, rules that guarantee the scope of application of specific law are referred to as scope rules.[128] General conflict of law rules and

---

[127] The ECJ held for the purposes of the Brussels Convention the EC to be a single jurisdiction. *Mund & Fester, supra* note 101, par. 19.

[128] Strikwerda, L., *Inleiding tot het Nederlandse Internationaal Privaatrecht*, Kluwer, Deventer, 2005, pp. 74. Strikwerda however describes scope rules as a unilateral conflict of laws rule, but coupled to a specific instrument. The theory of 'règles d'applicabilité'

applicability criteria (scope rules) thus fulfil two different functions. The former is concerned with the designation of the applicable law, while the latter tries to ensure the effective application of secondary Union law. Trying to ensure the effective application of Union law, the Union legislator used a special applicability rule referring to the frontiers of its own legal system. The technique is not so much different from overriding mandatory provisions.[129]

Where the Union legislator would in art. 6 (2) Unfair Contract Terms Directive, art. 12 (2) Distance Selling Directive, art. 7 (2) Consumer Sales Directive and art. 12 (2) Distance Sales of Financial Services Directive indicate that the provisions are domestically mandatory since they cannot be avoided by a mere choice of law when a qualified link with the Union exists, Art. 12 Timeshare Directive would, by stipulating that the purchaser is not deprived of the protection afforded to him by the directive regardless the applicable law when the immovable is situated within the Union, indicate that the Timeshare Directive is overriding mandatory.[130] Art. 12 (2) delimits the circumstances in which the directive can be applied when the governing law is that of a third country. The distinction between mandatory and overriding mandatory provisions can therefore also be retrieved from Union law. If this interpretation would be followed it would not be necessary to include the 'conflict of laws norms' laid down in consumer directives in Rome I since the directives can already be accommodated in the framework of Rome I. The explicit applicability criteria should thus not be understood as unilateral conflict of laws rules, rather the provisions

---

can also be found in Belgian PIL: Rigaux, F., and M. Fallon, *Droit International Privé*, 3rd edition, Larcier, Brussels, 2005, pp. 131.

[129] Fallon, M., and S. Francq, "Towards Internationally Mandatory Directives for Consumer Contracts?" J. Basedow *et al* (eds.) *Private Law in the International Arena: Liber Amicorum Kurt Siehr*, T.M.C. Asser Press, The Hague, 2000, pp. 155-178 (165).

[130] Duintjer Tebbens, H., "Les règles de conflit contenues dans les instruments de droit dérivé", A. Fuchs *et al* (eds.), *Les conflits de lois et le système juridique communautaire*, Dalloz, Paris, 2004, pp. 101-115 (108). The Polish delegation has submitted both in process of deliberation on Rome I and to the Working Party on Consumer Protection and Information the opinion that art. 8 of the old Timeshare Directive should not be classified as a conflict of laws rule but as an overriding mandatory provision. The Polish submission was supported by several other delegations, but did not appear in the final document in order to preserve the parallel with Rome II. Interinstitutional File 2005/0261 (COD) 13515/07 JUSTCIV 256 CODEC 1030. The position is however defended that the new provision is a 'full-fledged conflict rule'. Downes, N., "More about Timeshare: A Revised Directive of a Regulation? Incidents of Other Instruments of Consumer Protection", *European Review of Private Law*, Vol. 16, 2008, pp. 607-625 (617).

should be understood as scope rules facilitating the task of the judiciary to establish in what sense a mandatory provision is mandatory.

Would this explain the absence of consumer directives on the list of directives that laid down specific conflict of laws rules? Did the Commission try to indicate that art. 12 Timeshare Directive was not a unilateral conflict of laws rule in the strict sense, but a scope rule? Prevalence over the multilateral conflict of laws rule in Rome I would then not be based upon art. 23, but as overriding mandatory provisions upon art. 9. Since the directives do not lay down conflict of laws norms it is for the purpose of ensuring simplicity and coherency not even preferable to incorporate those provisions in Rome I.

4.7.1 *Exclusion of Private Autonomy*

If one assumes that the rationale behind the provisions in the consumer directives was the exclusion of private autonomy, one has to ask the question to what extent private autonomy was excluded. Is the aim of the provision to exclude private autonomy in a domestic or international sense? The application of art. 23 would then be reserved for rules that cannot be incorporated in either art. 3 (4) or 9 Rome I Regulation.[131]

Because of the unclear drafting of the scope rules, establishing its precise meaning will always depend up to a certain extent upon speculation. Support for the reading of the provisions in the consumer *acquis* as scope rules rather than unilateral conflict of laws rules could be found in the proposal for a Consumer Rights Directive. Art. 43 provides: '[i]f the law applicable to the contract is the law of a Member State, consumers may not waive the rights conferred on them by this Directive.' It must first be noted that the provision removes the close connection requirement as maintained by the scope rules in the Consumer Sales Directive, the Unfair Contract Terms Directive and the Distance Selling Directive. For the purpose of our argument, more importantly, the text of the provision is placed under the heading 'imperative nature'. It indicates that is should be resistant against a choice of law, placing the Consumer Rights Directive in the category of domestic public policy.

It is admitted that the scope rule of the Consumer Rights Directive still does not reach the same result as art. 3 (4) Rome I. The Consumer

[131] An example would be art. 4 Regulation on Rail Passengers Rights and Obligations 1371/2007. See par. 4.10.

Rights Directive ensures that a choice of law cannot evade its application, while art. 3 (4) Rome I provides that a choice of law may not lead to non-application of mandatory Union rules when all contacts are exclusive to the Union. Art. 43 Consumer Rights Directive goes beyond ensuring the applicability of the directive when all connections are exclusive with one or more Member States. If a professional established in Sweden would enter into a contract with a consumer established in Florida, in the absence of a choice of law, Rome I would in certain circumstances lead to the applicability of Swedish law. Subsequently, the Consumer Rights Directive would be applicable as part of Swedish law. If the parties decided to make the contract subject to the law of the place of the habitual residence of the consumer, the Florida consumer would because of the choice of law be deprived of the protection of the Consumer Rights Directive. The deletion of the requirement of 'close connection' would eliminate the escape clause, tying the hands of the court. Art. 43 Consumer Rights Directive thus confers a competitive disadvantage upon the Union undertaking. Why should a professional established in the Union not be allowed to offer consumer contracts to consumers outside the Union on the basis of the local standard of consumer protection? In that sense, art. 43 does more harm than good, and it would be preferrable if the article referred directly back to art. 3 (4) Rome I.

4.8 *Interim Conclusions*

In the light of the difference in interest pursued between PIL and Union law and their respective methodological framework it may be understandable that Union law and PIL developed in isolation. The gradual awareness of the potential extra-territorial scope of the treaties and the delimitation of the international scope of application of private law directives beginning in the early nineties did temporally not coincide with the introduction of art. 65 in the Treaty of Amsterdam (now: art. 81 TFEU). The Union could therefore not introduce a comprehensive conflict of laws rule, but was forced to adopt a case by case approach. The Brussels and Rome Convention were drafted albeit within the framework of the EU, but by national PIL experts. Consequently, the particular interest and characteristics of Union law cannot really be found in the Conventions. Union law can hardly be blamed for taking matters into its own hand and guaranteeing its own application.

The introduction of the Rome Convention caused a paradigm shift: directives in the area of consumer law started to lay down criteria for their application in the international arena. The growing awareness of PIL probably also led to the observation that the Rome Convention had been unable to accommodate the specific characteristics of Union law. In specific instruments the Union therefore ensured the applicability of the instrument concerned regardless the conflict of laws rules. On a proper construction these rules were not unilateral conflict of laws rules, but instead constituted scope rules. It was perceived to be unfeasible that the connecting factors in some cases led to the inapplicability of an instrument, even where all connections were exclusively with one or more Member States or that parties could evade the application of an instrument laying down mandatory minimum protection by a mere choice of law. The deficiency in the Rome Convention has in the transformation of the Convention into a Regulation now been repaired. With the effective application of consumer directives ensured in *intra* Union situations, there is on a dogmatic level no reason to prevent the application of secondary Union law from depending on the (harmonised) conflict of laws rules. The legislative history of Rome I suggests that the applicability of Union consumer directives should not be assessed outside the framework of Rome I. Equally the Union consumer *acquis* cannot be classified as a whole as overriding mandatory provisions, although it is very plausible that specific rules in those instruments should be considered to be so.

On a closer inspection, *Ingmar* also does not provide the authority for the preposition that the international field of application of secondary Union law is tested outside the framework of Rome I. On the contrary, by following the submissions of the German government, the ECJ sought connection with the PIL systems of the Member States. The ECJ did not challenge the determination of the applicable law by the English courts as such, but required that the degree of mandatoriness of a national provision implementing a directive should be assessed in the light of the aim and purpose of the directive. The Court did not depart from the methodological framework traditionally used by Member States that took all relevant considerations into account in assessing whether a purely national provision was mandatory in the sense that it applied regardless the applicable law. What has to be criticised is that the ECJ established rather lightly the international mandatory nature of the directive and used a formula that could potentially be applied to nearly every directive. The Court thereby put a heavy pressure upon the principle of private autonomy and jeopardised the principles of legal certainty and legitimate expectations. If the Union genuinely desires to become a major actor in private law, it would be preferable to emphasise more the desire and intention of the private parties.

It seems that there is a conflict going on within the Commission between the DG Justice and Home Affairs, which pushes for codification of conflict of laws in Union instruments that follow in main lines the national PIL traditions, and DG Internal Market which tries to adopt the country of origin principle also in the area of private law.[132] This clash within the Commission might reflect the deeper tension between private international specialists and Union law specialists. The former believe that Member States will always have differences, up to a certain degree, between their respective legislation and should be left with sufficient leeway to manoeuvre and perceive their own discipline to be most adequately equipped to deal with multiple claims of application. Union lawyers on the other hand do not seem to acknowledge any role for PIL and reason on the basis of equivalence: the application of the law of one Member State can be replaced by the application of the laws of another Member State. The precise content of the law does not matter, since the laws of the Member States should be substantially similar. Mutual recognition is thus used to oil the functioning of the internal market.[133] The case-law with regard to the Brussels Convention and Brussels I Regulation supports the DG Internal Market. The ECJ is more concerned with preserving the mandatory nature of the Regulations rather than to look at the reasonable interests of the parties involved.[134] That is a pity; traditional PIL, that even on the Continent was not always codified, allowed for much more flexibility. Party autonomy being the cornerstone of Rome I, the ECJ should adopt at least with regard to the law applicable to contractual obligations a more party orientated approach. Union lawyers should be careful not to

---

[132] Basedow, J., "European Private International Law of Obligations and Internal Market Legislation – A matter of Coordination", J. Erauw *et al* (eds.), *Liber Memorialis Petar Šarčević: Universalism, Tradition and the Individual*, Sellier, München, 2006, pp. 13–24 (18).

[133] Kessedjian, C., "Le droit international privé et l'intégration juridique européene", T. Einhorn and K. Siehr (eds.), *Intercontinental Cooperation through Private International Law: Essays in Memory of Peter E Nygh*, TMC Asser Press, The Hague, 2004, pp. 187–196.

[134] See par. 1.5.1.

make the same mistake made by the postglossators, and only address in which circumstances their own law should be applied, when for the first time confronted with the PIL question.

4.9 *An Autonomous Approach in Labour Law?*

The analysis of the scope of directives in Union consumer law can in principle also be applied to directives in other harmonised areas. In the lack of an explicit scope rule, the international sphere of application has to be determined by the normal conflict of laws rules whereby the degree of mandatoriness of the directive on the international plane is established in the light of the directive itself. In the next section it shall be assessed how this rationale can be applied to the area of labour law. To assess the purpose of a directive, it is useful to first briefly touch upon the general objectives of EU labour law, which is by itself already a rather complex issue. It was only the Maastricht Treaty that introduced the social and labour market policy as an independent policy area. The drafters of the EEC Treaty were of the opinion that higher social standards would automatically follow from the increased welfare as a result of the introduction of the internal market. Social policy was therefore decoupled from the internal market and left to be governed by Member States.[135] Social and labour matters were only dealt with in the Social Action Programmes following the Paris Declaration of the Heads of State or Government (1972).[136] More important was perhaps the decision of the ECJ in *Defrenne II* and the directives which followed on equal treatment and equal pay that gave a large impetus to the non-discrimination principle.[137] Arts. 146 – 150 TFEU provide the Union with very limited competences on employment policy. The Union shall encourage, and if necessary, complement national strategies aimed at the realisation of a high level of employment. Arts. 151 – 154 TFEU provide the Union with competence in the social sphere. In order for '*the promotion of employment, improved living and working conditions,*

[135] Scharpf, F., "The European Social Model: Coping with the Challenges of Diversity", *Journal of Common Market Studies*, Vol. 40, No. 4, 2002, pp. 645–670; Syrpis, P., "Should the EU be attempting to harmonise national systems of labour law?", *European Business Law Review*, Vol. 21, 2010, pp. 143–163.

[136] Nielsen, R., *European Labour Law*, DJØF Publishing, Copenhagen, 2000, pp. 43–46.

[137] Case 43/75 *Defrenne II* [1975] ECR 455.

so as to make possible their harmonisation while the improvement is being maintained, proper social protection, dialogue between management and labour, the development of human resources with a view to lasting high employment and the combating of exclusion'[138] art. 153 TFEU calls for measures supporting and complementing the policies of the Member States. On the policy fields listed in art. 153 (1) the Union may, by means of directives, adopt minimum requirements for the gradual implementation of social policy.

The Union has made use of its harmonisation powers in following areas:[139]

- Health and Safety Framework Directive (EC 89/391)
- Employment Conditions Directive (EC 1991/533)
- Posted Workers Directive (EC 96/71)
- Collective Redundancies Directive (EC 1998/59)
- Race and Ethnic Origin Directive (EC 2000/43)
- Employment Discrimination Framework Directive (EC 2000/78)
- TUPE Directive (EC 2001/23)
- Worker Participation General Framework Directive (EC 2002/14)
- Working Time Directive (EC 2003/88)
- Equal Treatment Directive (EC 2006/54)
- European Works Council Directive (2009/38)

And with regard to specific groups of workers:

- Pregnant Workers Directive (EC 92/85)
- Parental Leave Directive (EC 96/34)
- Young Workers Directive (EC 94/33)
- Fixed Term Work Directive (EC 99/70)
- Temporary Agency Work Directive (2008/104)

The diversity amongst welfare states, expressed in the ability to pay for social transfers and services as well as in the political ambitions and institutional structures has proven to be an effective block against a uniform European social policy beyond low minimal standards that were acceptable to all Member States.[140] The European Employment Strategy and the Open Method of Coordination have therefore become

---

[138] Art. 136 (1) EC.

[139] De Vos, M., *European Union Employment and Labour Law : Law and Cases*, Knops Publishing, Herentals, 2007.

[140] Scharpf, *supra* note 135, pp. 645.

important 'soft' policy tools to contributing to the goals laid down in art. 151 TFEU.[141] From a Union perspective harmonising labour laws is less interesting than harmonising consumer law. If a Member State guarantees both a high level consumer and labour protection the former has potentially a far more intrusive effect upon the functioning of the internal market. The costs of the high labour standards will be borne by the national industry who is confronted with higher labour costs. The costs of consumer protection are on the other hand not only borne by national producers, but also averted to foreign producers who desire to sell their product on that specific market. The additional costs constitute a barrier to entry for the foreign producer. Labour costs only become relevant if the foreign producer decides to produce in the relevant territory. Where there are strong internal incentives to lower labour costs to enhance competitiveness *vis-à-vis* producers from other Member States, such incentives may not necessarily be there in consumer law where the additional costs may also form a barrier to shield off the national market from foreign producers. Because the costs of the high labour standards are primarily born by the Member State itself, labour law is a less likely candidate for anti-integrationist behaviour by Member States.[142]

This is not the place to discuss either the soft policy strategies or to fully discuss EU labour law,[143] but instead attention will be drawn to the interesting features for private international law. Interestingly enough, the Commission already advanced in the seventies the need

[141] Commission of the European Communities, Working together, working better: A new framework for the Open Method of Coordination of social protection and inclusion policies in the European Union, COM (2005) 706 final; Porte (de la), C., "Is the Open Method of Coordination Appropriate for Organising Activities at European Level in Sensitive Policy Areas?" *European Law Journal*, Vol. 8, 2002, pp. 38–58; Szyszczak, E., "Experimental Governance: The Open Method of Coordination", *European Law Journal*, Vol. 12 No. 4, 1996, pp. 486–502; Braams, B., "Equal Opportunities between Men and Women and Gender Mainstreaming under the European Employment Strategy (EES) and the Open Method of Coordination (OMC) – A New Policy Approach to Combat Gender Discrimination?", *European Integration online Papers*, Vol. 11, 2007.

[142] For example the requirement that beer can only be marketed under the name 'beer' if it is brewed in accordance with a traditional national recipe may officially have the aim of protecting public health and/or consumers from confusion, but is rather suspicious since it mostly prevents foreign beer from being marketed as such. Case 178/84 *Commission v Germany* [1987] ECR 1227 (*Reinheitsgebot*).

[143] See for example: Bercusson, B., *European Labour Law*, Butterworths, London 1996; Teyssié, B., *Droit européen du travail*, Litec, Paris, 2e edition, 2003; Barnard, C., EC Employment Law, Oxford University Press, Oxford, 3rd edition, 2006.

for a regulation dealing with the applicable law to employment contracts. The proposal for a regulation, that would have taken the free movement of workers as legal basis, was however withdrawn after the adoption of the Rome Convention.[144] A quick glance at the directives already reveals that labour law is, in common with consumer law, quite fragmented, just as, until recently, in consumer law the favoured technique has been minimum harmonisation.[145]

Moreover, provisions such as art. 3 (1) Posted Workers Directive, 10 (3) Young Workers Directive and art. 16 Working Time Directive leave Member States a large amount of discretion with regard to the required minimum standard. The fragmented nature of the directives and the diverging standards renders it necessary to establish which mandatory law of what Member State is applicable. In the national context, it will often be impossible to contract out of those provisions; the harmonised minimum standards should be considered as mandatory in the sense of art. 8 (2) Rome I. Whereas the Rome Convention has led in consumer law to general more awareness of PIL questions, even more recently adopted instruments in the field of labour law, such as the Young Workers Directive or the Fixed Term Work Directive, remain silent about their international their scope of application. An example of a clear unilateral conflict of laws rule would be art. 2 of Regulation 561/2006 on the harmonisation of certain social legislation relating to road transport.[146] However several directives contain hints about

---

[144] Houwerzijl, M., *De Detacheringsrichtlijn: Over de inhoud, achtergrond en implementatie van Richtlijn 96/71/EG*, Kluwer, Deventer, 2005, pp. 381.

[145] Provisions allowing Member States to introduce more favourable terms are laid down in art. 7 Employment Conditions Directive, art. 3 (10) Posted Workers Directive, art. 5 Collective Redundancies Directive, art. 6 Race and Ethnic Origin Directive, art. 8 Employment Discrimination Framework Directive, art. 8 TUPE Directive, art. 15 Working Time Directive, art. 27 Equal Treatment Directive, art. 1 (3) Pregnant Workers Directive, clause 4 Parental Leave Directive and clause 8 Fixed Term Work Directive. Furthermore, provisions such as art. 9 (4) Worker Participation General Framework Directive state that its implementation may not lead to a regression in existing rights.

[146] Art. 2 (2). This Regulation shall apply, irrespective of the country of registration of the vehicle, to carriage by road undertaken:

(a) exclusively within the Community; or
(b) between the Community, Switzerland and the countries party to the Agreement on the European Economic Area.
(3) The AETR shall apply, instead of this Regulation, to international road transport operations undertaken in part outside the areas mentioned in paragraph 2, to:
(a) vehicles registered in the Community or in countries which are contracting parties to the AETR, for the whole journey;

their international scope of application, but do not address PIL either fully or directly.

4.9.1 *The TUPE Directive*

An example of an unclear relationship with PIL is art. 1 (2) TUPE Directive[147] which provides that the directive shall apply 'where and in so far as the undertaking, business or part of the undertaking or business to be transferred is situated within the territorial scope of the Treaty.' Regardless of the law that governs the employment relationship the directive thus requires application whenever the undertaking to be transferred is situated in one of the Member States.

The French[148] and Dutch[149] implementing legislation do not contain a requirement that the undertaking be established on their respective territories. On the other hand, the Transfer of Undertaking Regulation,[150] which implements the TUPE Directive in the United Kingdom, expressly provides it applies to transfers of undertakings where the undertaking to be transferred is established in the United Kingdom. Sections 18 contains a provision on the prevention of contracting out, which provides that any clause seeking to exclude or limit the operation of any part of the Regulation shall be void. In this respect, the application of the directive does not seem to be guaranteed when the application of the Regulation is not avoided by a choice of

---

(b) vehicles registered in a third country which is not a contracting party to the AETR, only for the part of the journey on the territory of the Community or of countries which are contracting parties to the AETR.

The provisions of the AETR should be aligned with those of this Regulation, so that the main provisions in this Regulation apply, through the AETR, to such vehicles for any part of the journey made within the Community.

Directive 2002/15 subsequently makes its scope of application in art. 2 depend upon the predecessor of Regulation 561/2006 (Regulation 3820/85).

147 Van Straalen, P., *Behoud van rechten van werknemers bij overgang van onderneming*, Kluwer, Deventer, 1999.

148 Loi n°83-528 du 28 juin 1983. The TUPE Directive is implemented in arts. L1224-1 - L1224-4 Code du Travail.

149 Uitvoering van de Richtlijn 98/50/EG van de Raad van de Europese Unie van 29 juni 1998 tot wijziging van de Richtlijn 77/187/EEG inzake de onderlinge aanpassing van de wetgevingen der lidstaten betreffende het behoud van de rechten van de werknemers bij overgang van ondernemingen, vestigingen of onderdelen van ondernemingen of vestigingen, Staatsblad 215 (2002). The TUPE Directive is implemented in arts. 7:662- 7:666 Civil Code.

150 The Transfer of Undertakings (Protection of Employment) Regulations 2006, no. 246.

law, but by the operation of the objective connecting factors.[151] In practice, it will be less problematic since the objective connecting factors will lead to the application of the law where the employee habitually carries out the performance of the employment contract. Problems might arise though when the place of establishment of the undertaking does not correspond with the place where the employee habitually carries out his obligations.

More problematic is that the Directive does not indicate according to which law the rights of the worker under the employment contract have to be guaranteed.[152] Suppose a factory is relocated from Sweden to Lithuania with the subsequent transfer of a group of Swedish workers to Lithuania. If in the employment contract no choice of law was made, the applicable law would change from Swedish to Lithuanian since the workers would start habitually carrying out their activities in Lithuania. If the Swedish workers were to argue that the transferral led to a regression in old-age benefits, should that claim be answered on the basis of the Lithuanian or Swedish legislation implementing the directive? The question becomes extremely important if one considers that it is in the discretion of Member States to apply the principle of the transferral of rights under an employment contract also to old-age benefits (art. 3 (4)).[153] The Directive does not provide for a solution and it might cause a rush to the courts since the application of the retention of rights clause would depend upon the court who decides the case. What the provision aims at is not the resolution of a conflict of laws, but rather the protection of a substantive result.

---

[151] In such circumstances the employee would not be protected by *national* employment law and therefore fall outside the scope of the directive (art. 2(d)).

[152] More clear is the Protection of Employees in case of Insolvency Directive (2008/94). It deals with the situation when an undertaking has employees in more than one Member State (but is unfortunately silent with regard to third countries). The Member State in which the employee habitually carries out his work shall be the Member State responsible for safeguarding the employee rights. According to art. 9 (2) the extent of employees' rights shall be determined by the law governing the competent guarantee institution.

[153] The argument that only the minimum core in the Directive can be classified in an EC context seems in these circumstances less feasible since the situation is intrinsically different from a minimum harmonisation clause. The Directive leaves MS a choice with regard to a specific issue and even provides for a mandatory alternative when MS decide not to introduce the transferral clause with regard to old-age benefits.

4.9.2 *The Worker Participation General Framework Directive*

Though not related to contract law, better formulated is the Worker Participation General Framework Directive. It applies to a 'public or private undertaking carrying out an economic activity, whether or not operating for gain, which is located within the territory of the Member States' and to establishments located within the territory of a Member State.[154] Supposedly, the Directive shall apply even if the *lex societas* is that of a third country. In fact, it approaches a solution similar to *re Compagnie des Wagons-lits*, where the French Cour de Cassation held that the Ordonnance on worker participation committees also applied to the establishments in France of a company with its primary establishment in Brussels and governed by Belgian law.[155] The relevant provisions of the Ordonnance were to be classified as overriding mandatory. In analogy, the Worker Participation General Framework Directive should be classified as overriding mandatory. A similar argument could be made towards criteria for the material scope of application of the European Works Council Directive (EWCD). *A fortiori* art. 3 (6) lays down a unilateral conflict of laws rule for the classification of the concept 'controlling undertaking. It reads:

> The law applicable in order to determine whether an undertaking is a 'controlling undertaking' shall be the law of the Member State which governs that undertaking.
>
> Where the law governing that undertaking is not that of a Member State, the law applicable shall be the law of the Member State within whose territory the representative of the undertaking or, in the absence of such a representative, the central management of the group undertaking which employs the greatest number of employees is situated.

Similarly to the Return of Cultural Objects Directive, the EWCD addresses a particular issue and aims to avoid problems of characterisation rather than giving any guidance about the international scope of application of the directive. The classification whether for the purpose of the EWCD an undertaking is controlling will thus always be made on the basis of the national laws of one of the Member States.[156] An American undertaking therefore cannot submit that according to

---

[154] Art. 1 Worker Participation General Framework Directive (EC 2002/14).

[155] Conseil d'État 29 juin 1973, *Journal de droit international privé* 1975, 538 (note M. Simon-Depitre).

[156] Case C-62/99 *Betriebsrat der bofrost** [2001] ECR I-2579 (information to be provided to establish controlling undertaking).

American law it would not be classified as a controlling undertaking. The establishment of the controlling undertaking outside the territory of the Member States does not set aside the application of the EWCD. According to art. 4 (2), the central management's representative agent in a Member State, or in absence the central management of the establishment in the Member State with the largest number of employees, shall take on the responsibility to establish a works council. If the central management in the third country refuses to provide information necessary to set up a works council, that task shall be incumbent upon the central management under art. 4 (2). The latter central management shall request the information from the undertakings established in other Member States. Those undertakings are, when they are in possession of the information or are in a position to obtain it, under an obligation to provide the information.[157]

4.9.3 *Ordre Public*

In labour law the question of the applicability of Union directives does not only come into play at the stage of determining the applicable law, but also influences upon the public policy of Member States. First, the Race and Ethnic Origin Directive provides that it shall apply, within the competences of the Union, to all persons, as regards both the public and private sectors, specifically including public bodies (art. 3 (1)). The provision is, rather than indicating the material scope of application of the directive, giving its formal scope. From a PIL perspective a more interesting provision is perhaps art. 14 (b) which requires 'any provisions contrary to the principle of equal treatment which are included in individual or collective contracts or agreements, (..) are or may be declared, null and void or are amended'. The Directive requires courts in Member States to resort to the *ordre public* exception in the case of discrimination on the grounds of race or ethnic origin if a case would come up before it even though the law governing the employment relationship is that of a non Member State. The same would apply on the basis of art. 16 (b) to Employment Discrimination Framework Directive to discrimination on the grounds of religion or belief, disability, age or sexual orientation as regards employment and occupation and a similar clause was introduced with regard to discrimination on

[157] Case C-440/00 *Kühne & Nagel* [2004] ECR I-0787, par. 64; Case C-349/01 *Anker* [2004] ECR I-6803.

the basis of gender in art. 23 (b) Equal Treatment Directive. The idea that a violation of the non-discrimination principle is manifestly incompatible with the public policy of Member States would fit into the 'fundamentalisation' of the equal treatment principle,[158] as is reflected in art. 21 (1) of the Charter of Fundamental Rights, which, as envisioned by the Treaty of Lisbon, would give the non-discrimination principle the status of fundamental right.[159]

Although labour law directives contain hints about their degree of mandatoriness, contrary to consumer law they lack clear indicators. The directives do not provide for the consequences which follow when, on the basis of a choice of law or the operation of the objective connecting factors the directive is not part of the governing law. The lack of explicit provisions and the potentially different ways of interpreting the material conditions of application of the directives, as well as, the inadequacy of implicit international applicability criteria for attaining the objectives of the instrument involved add to a need to find an appropriate uniform manner for establishing the international field of application of labour directives.[160]

4.9.4 *Posted Workers Directive*

It does not appear that PIL considerations were taken into account in the process of drafting the directives discussed previously. The exception is the Posted Workers Directive,[161] which seems to be equipped with a scope rule. It makes the Directive even more interesting since

[158] Besson, S., "L'Égalité de Traitement entre Particuliers en Droit Communautaire", F. Werro (ed.), *L'Européanisation du Droit Privé*, Editions Universitaires Fribourg, Fribourg, 1998, pp. 51–96 ; Bell, M., *Anti-Discrimination Law and the European Union*, Oxford University Press, New York, 2002; Sargeant, M., "The Employment Equality (Age) Regulations 2006: A Legitimisation of Age Discrimination in Employment", *Industrial Law Journal*, Vol. 35, No. 3, 2006, pp. 209–227; Jans, J., "The Effect in National Legal Systems of the Prohibition of Discrimination on Grounds of Age as a General Principle of Union Law", *Legal Issues of Economic Integration*, Vol. 3, No. 1, 2007, pp. 53–66; Basedow, J., "Der Grundsatz der Nichtdiskriminierung im europäischen Privatrecht", *Zeitschrift für Europäisches Privatrecht*, 2008, pp. 230–251.

[159] The general interaction between EU law, PIL and human rights is explored by: Van den Eeckhout, V., "Promoting Human Rights within the Union: The Role of European Private International Law", *European Law Journal*, Vol. 14, No. 1, 2008, pp. 105–127.

[160] Moreau, M., "Le détachement des travailleurs effectuant une prestation de services dans l'Union européenne", *Journal de droit international*, Vol. 123, No. 3, 1996, pp. 889–908 ; Francq *supra* note 10, pp. 383–384.

[161] The other exception, the EWCD has already been discussed.

posted workers are explicitly excluded from the protection afforded by art. 6 Rome I. Recitals 6 - 10 make an express reference to the Rome Convention, and in particular to art. 6 and 7 thereof. The Posted Workers Directive applies to undertakings established in a Member State, which temporarily employs workers on the territory of another Member State, in the framework of the transnational provision of services. The directive is in fact less concerned with labour law than with PIL,[162] since it rather aims to fill the gap that is created by art. 6 Rome Convention. The overall aim of the Posted Workers Directive is to reconcile the interest in the protection of workers with the needs of the internal market. For that purpose, Art. 3 (1) lays down a set of mandatory rules, such as a minimum wage requirement, that have to be observed by a foreign service provider regardless the applicable law.

The directive does however not require the introduction of a minimum wage requirement nor does it set a specific standard. The directive only requires that if a minimum wage requirement is applicable on the territory of a Member State, it must also be made compulsory for posted workers, regardless the applicable law. Art. 3 (1) Posted Workers Directive therefore declares that provision to be overriding mandatory.[163] By indicating its mandatory nature in a conflict of laws situation, the Directive differs from other directives in labour law, which refer to 'undertakings established on the territory of a Member State' or 'employment conditions governed by the law of a Member State'. Art. 3 (1) thus lists the overriding mandatory provision a Member State may impose upon a labour contract where the service provider is established in another Member State.

Art. 3 (1) is therefore not really a specific choice of law rule that would take precedence over Rome I.[164] Rather, it indicates the mandatory nature of the provisions listed. One can therefore doubt whether the Posted Workers Directive should have been included in the list of directives in the Commission's proposal for Rome I that as specific conflict of laws rule would have taken precedence over Rome I on the basis of the proposed art. 22. The precise reasons for its inclusion

---

[162] Francq *supra* note 10, pp. 374.

[163] Similar: Van Hoek, A., *Internationale mobiliteit van werknemers: Een onderzoek naar de interactie tussen arbeidsrecht, EG-recht en IPR aan de hand van de detacheringsrichtlijn*, SDU Uitgevers, Den Haag, 2000, pp. 543–546. Houwerzijl argues that art. 3 96/71 constitutes a concretisation of art. 7 Rome Convention, *supra* note 144, pp. 161.

[164] Brière, C., "Le Droit International Privé Européen des Contrats et la Coordination des Sources", *Journal du Droit International*, Vol. 136, No. 3, 2009, pp. 792–807 (796).

cannot be found, but that should not change the principle that art. 3 (1) identifies a set of overriding mandatory provisions whose status can be accommodated in Rome I via art. 9. That is precisely the meaning of the 34th recital to Rome I, which provides that the rule on individual employment contracts should not prejudice the application of the overriding mandatory provisions of the country to which a worker is posted in accordance with PWD. The PWD therefore does not lay down a specific choice of law rule in the sense of art. 23 Rome I.

4.10 *Unilateral Conflict of Law Rules in Insurance Contracts and Contracts of Carriage*

The best examples of unilateral conflict of laws rules are not to be found in consumer or labour law, but rather in insurance. For example, art. 32 of the Life Insurance Directive 2002/83 declared the law of the Member State of commitment to govern the insurance contract.[165] Also art. 7 of the Second Non-Life Insurance Directive laid down connecting factors to establish the law applicable to the insurance contract. As already described, the conflict of laws rules dispersed over the several instruments required a contract to be distinguished on the basis whether it

---

[165] Article 32 (1). The law applicable to contracts relating to the activities referred to in this Directive shall be the law of the Member State of the commitment. However, where the law of that State so allows, the parties may choose the law of another country.

(2). Where the policy holder is a natural person and has his/her habitual residence in a Member State other than that of which he/she is a national, the parties may choose the law of the Member State of which he/she is a national.

(3). Where a State includes several territorial units, each of which has its own rules of law concerning contractual obligations, each unit shall be considered a country for the purposes of identifying the law applicable under this Directive.

A Member State in which various territorial units have their own rules of law concerning contractual obligations shall not be bound to apply the provisions of this Directive to conflicts which arise between the laws of those units.

(4). Nothing in this Article shall restrict the application of the rules of the law of the forum in a situation where they are mandatory, irrespective of the law otherwise applicable to the contract.

If the law of a Member State so stipulates, the mandatory rules of the law of the Member State of the commitment may be applied if and in so far as, under the law of that Member State, those rules must be applied whatever the law applicable to the contract.

(5). Subject to paragraphs 1 to 4, the Member States shall apply to the assurance contracts referred to in this Directive their general rules of private international law concerning contractual obligations.

concerned a life or non-life insurance, whether the non-life risk was small or large and whether the risk was situated in a territory of a Member State or not. Depending on the answer to the questions, a different conflict of laws rule would be applied. Moreover, the possibility of a choice of law could be enlarged depending on the Member State whose law was declared to be applicable. The situation was highly complex and did not contribute to legal certainty. With some modification the conflict of laws rules of the insurance directives were incorporated in Rome I.[166] Art. 23 Rome I now specifies that art. 7 Rome I supersedes the conflict of laws rules in the individual directives. For the question of international the international scope of application of insurance directives, the specific unilateral conflict of laws norms have lost their relevance.

In contracts of carriage the existence of unilateral conflict of laws rules is less clear. In any case, the introduction of the special connecting factor for contracts of carriage has not superseded any potential unilateral conflict of laws norm laid down in secondary legislation.[167] However, similar to consumer and labour law it can be doubted to what extent a provision that indicates the international scope of application of a provision is a unilateral conflict of laws rule. An example of an instrument which lays down a particular conflict of laws rule the Regulation on Rail Passengers Rights and Obligations (1371/2007). The Regulation provides an extract of the uniform rules contained in the Convention concerning International Carriage by Rail (1980) that lays down detailed rights and obligations between the carrier and the passenger. Art. 2 (1) provides that the Regulation shall apply to all rail journeys and services throughout the Union provided by one or more railway undertakings licensed in accordance with Directive 95/18 on the licensing of railway undertakings. A unilateral conflict of laws rule

---

[166] See par. 2.7.2.

[167] Also Regulation 392/2009 on the liability of carriers by sea lays down a conflict of law with regard to rules on liability in the event of accidents liability and insurance for the carriage of passengers by sea, but does not affect contract law.

Art. 2: 'This Regulation shall apply to any international carriage within the meaning of point 9 of Article 1 of the Athens Convention and to carriage by sea within a single Member State on board ships of Classes A and B under Article 4 of Directive 98/18/EC, where:

(a) the ship is flying the flag of or is registered in a Member State;
(b) the contract of carriage has been made in a Member State; or
(c) the place of departure or destination, according to the contract of carriage, is in a Member State.'

is laid down in art. 4; the conclusion and performance of a transport contract and the provision of information and tickets shall be governed by the provisions of Title II and Title III of Annex I to the Regulation.

4.10.1 *The Denied Boarding Regulation*

An example of a unilateral conflict of laws rule could be art. 3 (1) of the Denied Boarding Regulation (261/2004).[168] Art. 3 (1) lays down territorial criteria[169] whereas art. 12 provides that the Regulation shall apply without prejudice to a passenger's rights to further compensation. A higher level of protection could be afforded under the law of a third country. The fact that a foreign law leads to a higher level of protection does not lead to the non-application of the Regulation, but the compensation granted under the Regulation can be deducted from the further compensation. The Regulation thus envisages that it will apply in parallel with the foreign law. On the other hand, one of the territorial criteria of art. 3 (1) contains a limitation concerning passengers flying with a Community carrier departing from an airport located in a third country to an airport situated in the territory of a Member State, namely, that the passenger should not have received benefits or compensation and assistance in that third country, if the operating air carrier of the flight concerned is a Community carrier. That limitation creates the impression that what is at stake is not the resolution of a conflict of laws, but rather the guarantee of a substantive value: the protection of the passenger. From that perspective, it would be more likely that art. 3 (1) is a scope rule indicating in which circumstances the Regulation should be applied regardless the applicable law.

If the Regulation were to be classified as a set of overriding mandatory provisions, a forum in a Member State would, due to the detailed scope rule, have no discretion in applying the Regulation. For the passenger it is immaterial whether he receives the protection afforded

[168] Diederiks-Verschoor, I., and M. Butler, An introduction to air law, Kluwer, Deventer, 8th edition, 2006, pp 92

[169] Art. 3 (1) provides:
'This Regulation shall apply:
(a) to passengers departing from an airport located in the territory of a Member State to which the Treaty applies;
(b) to passengers departing from an airport located in a third country to an airport situated in the territory of a Member State to which the Treaty applies, unless they received benefits or compensation and were given assistance in that third country, if the operating air carrier of the flight concerned is a Union carrier.'

under the Regulation on the basis that the unilateral conflict of laws rule supersedes Rome I (art. 23 Rome I) or whether it is classified as a set of overriding mandatory provisions and will apply regardless the applicable law (art. 9 Rome I). However, because an overriding mandatory provision reflects a fundamental policy of the forum the non-observation of that rule by a foreign court could be ground for the forum not to recognise or enforce that judgment. That principle is incorporated in art. 15 (2) of the Denied Boarding Regulation; if a derogation or restrictive clause in a contract shall be applied the passenger shall still be entitled to take the necessary proceedings before the competent courts or bodies in order to obtain additional compensation. When an arbitral tribunal or a court established in a third country does not apply the Regulation, the passenger is not prevented from initiating fresh proceedings in a Union court.

4.10.2 *The Cabotage Transport Regulation*

The Regulation on common rules for access to the international road haulage market (1072/2009) lays down rules relating to cabotage. Most of its provisions relate to a Community licence or the qualifications of the driver. The Regulation does not therefore seem to directly affect contract law. However, art. 9 (1a) also lays down a rule on the conditions governing the transport contract. The same applies to art. 4 (1a) of the Cabotage Transport of Passengers Regulation (12/98) and art. 3 (1a) of the Cabotage by Waterways Regulation (3921/91). The law applicable to such matters is the law of the host Member State. If parties do not choose the applicable law, that solution would correspond to art. 5 (1) Rome I since by definition in a cabotage transport the carrier will not be established in the host Member State and the contractual place of delivery will be in the host Member State. However a choice of law is under Regulation 1072/2009 not possible. The exclusion of private autonomy is not justified in instrument. Moreover, art. 9 is subject to the limitation 'save as otherwise provided by Community legislation'. Despite the Regulations 1072/2009 being the *lex specialis,* the question of applicable law has to be determined according to Rome I.

The only clear examples of unilateral conflict of laws rules are mainly thus to be found in insurance law. The relationship between rules indicating the field of application of a secondary instrument and conflict of laws in the area of transport law is far less clear. It is striking that it was exactly in the area of insurance law where strong critique to the incoherent and arbitrary functioning of the conflict of laws rules led to the incorporation of those rules in Rome I. The 'situation where conflict-of-law rules are dispersed among several instruments and where there are differences between those rules should be avoided'.[170]

4.11 *Conclusions*

The relationship between instruments of secondary law and conflict of laws norms is often very vague. It is hoped that the adoption of Rome I will be an impetus for better co-ordination between secondary law and PIL. The traditional argument that conflict of laws norms are not apt to deal with the particularities of the Union legal order because an international contract is treated as an international contract, regardless its connections to the Union, is no longer valid. Art. 3 (4) Rome I Regulation provides that a choice of law does not prevent the application of mandatory rules of Union when all connections point exclusively to two or more Member States. Rome I thereby prevents a situation, such as in the notorious *Gran Canaria* cases, whereby a choice of law in favour of the law of a third country led to the setting aside of mandatory consumer rules in a contract between a Spanish professional and German consumer concluded in Spain.

It would be preferable in absence of a specific unilateral conflict of laws rule to make, to make the application of secondary Union private law dependent upon the traditional conflict of laws mechanisms. Abiding by a single choice of law rule would enhance legal certainty and the coherency of Union law. If directives systematically took precedence over Rome I, and its provisions on the possibility of choosing the applicable law to a contract, party autonomy would be severely undermined.

The provisions in the directives indicating the international scope of application of the relevant directive that were introduced after the entry into force of the Rome Convention should therefore be understood as remedying *Gran Canaria* type of situations. Hence, instead of providing for a unilateral conflict of laws rule, provisions such as art. 6 (2) Unfair Contract Terms Directive and art. 12 Timeshare Directive should be understood as scope rules, indicating the degree of mandatory nature of the instrument. Whereas art. 6 (2) UCTD

[170] 40th recital of the Preamble to Rome I.

would therefore indicate that the directive is mandatory when all connecting factors are located in the Union, art. 12 Timeshare Directive would be classified as overriding mandatory. Art. 23 Rome I should be left for those rules whose effect cannot be accommodated in the normal conflict of laws rules. The fact that only four directives featured on the list of directives containing explicit choice of law rules that would supersede Rome I does suggest art. 23 should be construed narrowly. This reading may be confirmed by the fact that the 17th recital to the new Timeshare Directive explicitly stipulates the law applicable to a timeshare contract has to be determined on the basis of the conflict of laws rules contained in Rome I.

That conclusion is not in any way affected by *Ingmar*. *Ingmar* does not provide authority for the proposition that the international scope of application of directives has to be established outside Rome I. It should be recalled that the facts of *Ingmar* fell outside the scope of material application of the Rome Convention and the ECJ did not yet possess the power of interpretation. In fact, the Court followed a methodological framework not different from that traditionally used by the Member States. The ECJ merely required that the degree of mandatory nature of a directive has to be established in the light of the context of that directive. What is worrying about *Ingmar* is thus not so much the conceptual point of view, but rather the lightness of the reasoning that the Court employs to qualify art. 17–19 of the Agency Directive as overriding mandatory. The Courts reasoning is capable of being applied to nearly every directive. If a similar case would come up before the ECJ today, it cannot be excluded that the Court would decide differently. That the Court does possess the power of interpretation and the status of Rome I as part of the *acquis communautaire* is beyond doubt. In *Renault v Maxicar, Mostaza Claro* and *Asturcom*, the Court sought closer alignment with the public policy conception of the Member States.

The preference for an integrated Rome I approach applies to all the areas scrutinised alike. The fact that labour directives are not as explicit as consumer directives in indicating their degree of mandatory nature on the international plane does not alter the conclusion drawn in the general analysis. The international field of application of directives is in principle subject to the general conflict of laws rules, which are in the field of contracts, laid down in Rome I. Only an explicit conflict of laws rule takes precedence over the general multilateral conflict of laws rule. Just like national rules, Union law may contain rules laid down in directives that protect fundamental policies and should be applied regardless the applicable law. Although it is certainly true that the Union adopts a lower threshold for the imperativeness of directives than Member States with regard to their domestic laws, that does not change the argument that the supremacy of Union law can only be held against the Member States. On the international plane, the Union enjoys sovereignty for its harmonised private rules in the same way Member States use to enjoy their sovereignty. Similarly, there is nothing intrinsically new in the approach that the degree of mandatory nature of a rule (as laid down in a directive) on the international plane should established in the light of the rule itself.

CHAPTER 5

THE HARMONISATION OF CONTRACT LAW BY THE UNION

The previous chapter has analysed the role and function of the Rome I Regulation in the international arena. However, the majority of international contracts in Europe have exclusively connections with two or more Member States. The ongoing process of harmonisation of substantive law raises the question of the future role of PIL in the internal market. The convergence between the European legal systems mitigates their mutual differences and thereby reduces the function of conflict of laws. There would be no need for PIL when all law would be uniform. The future role of PIL on the internal market thus depends much upon the competence of the Union to harmonise private law.

It must first be observed that only a complete unification of contract law, being the replacement of the legal systems of the Member States by a European one, would render Rome I obsolete. The unification of contract law would constitute a deep intrusion in the sovereignty of the Member States. It has therefore been submitted that the co-ordination of private law is the only option available that would take European legal pluralism seriously.[1] A compelling argument in favour of PIL could indeed be made. The European Union is neither a state nor a traditional federation. It consists of nation states that have kept sovereignty in all but specifically enumerated domains. The common interest in, and the commitment to maintain a proper functioning internal market has thus continuously to be balanced against the normative preferences that are expressed in the national legal systems of the Member States.[2] Where harmonisation of conflict of laws rules is able to take away an obstacle to the internal market it should be preferred over the harmonisation of substantive laws. In the former possibility Member States remain able to pursue their local policies. Harmonisation of substantive law should therefore constitute the means of last resort.

---

[1] Joerges, C., "The Challenges of Europeanization in the Realm of Private Law: A Plea for a New Legal Discipline", *Duke Journal of Comparative and International Law*, Vol. 14, 2004, pp. 149–193.

[2] Joerges, *supra* note 1, pp. 167.

Local legislators are the most capable at identifying local values. If regulation is the expression of diverging local preferences (heterogeneous preferences), regulation at the de-central level is more beneficial than a unified standard. In this chapter it will be argued that the Union should not exhaustively replace the private law systems of the Member States and that in fact, conflict of laws should be re-considered in areas that were destined for harmonisation.

5.1 *The Harmonisation of Contract Law*

The harmonisation of private law has already been on the agenda for many years. The 1980 Lando Commission was set up with the aim to find common European rules through comparative research. Repetitive calls of the European Parliament in favour of the creation of a European Civil Code spurred a lively academic debate.[3] During the nineties working groups were set up throughout Europe in order to develop common principles that could contribute to the further harmonisation of European contract law. Without striving for completeness the Pavia group, the Study Group on a European Civil Code (Von Bar Group) and the Research Group on EC Private Law (Acquis Group) must be mentioned.

The Lando Commission published in 1995 Part I of the Principles of European Contract Law (PECL), Part II was published in 2000 and Part III in 2003.[4] The principles are a set of non-binding rules that can be chosen as applicable (neutral) law by the parties involved, but may equally provide for a model for legislators, or can serve as a tool for the

[3] OJ C 158 [1989], 400; OJ C 205, [1994], 518; OJ C 140 E, [2002], 538; OJ C 76 E, [2004], 95. On the debate: McKendrick, E., "The State We Are In, in: The Harmonisation of European Contract Law; Implications for European Private Laws, Business and Legal Practice", S. Vogenauer and S. Weatherill (eds.), Hart Publishing, Portland, 2006, 5–29; Hondius, E., "CISG and a European Civil Code: Some Reflexions", *RabelsZ*, Vol. 71, 2007, pp. 99–114; Collins, H., *The European civil code : the way forward*, Cambridge University Press, Cambridge, 2008; Grundmann, S., "Grand European Code Napoléon or Concise Uniform Contract Law? : Defining the Scope of a Common Frame of Reference", A. Somma (ed.), *The politics of the draft common frame of reference*, Kluwer, Alphen a/d Rijn, 2009, pp. 19–37; Micklitz, H., "Failures or Ideological Preconceptions?: Thoughts on two Grand Projects: the European Constitution and the European Civil Code", S. Sankari (ed.), *The Many Constitutions of Europe*, Ashgate, Farnham, 2010, pp. 109–140.

[4] Commission on European Contract Law, Lando, O., *et al* (eds.), *Principles of European Contract Law*, Kluwer Law International, The Hague, 2003.

EU institutions when drafting legislation and stand model for a European Code of Contracts.[5] The method of comparative analyses between the various national legal systems however means that the PECL is limited to the traditional private law existing in the Member States at the exclusion of rules of the *acquis communautaire*. The PECL therefore form an incomplete and partly inadequate picture of European Contract law.[6] The Aqcuis Group published in 2008 the Principles of Existing EC Contract Law (ACQP). The aim of the ACQP was a restatement and critical revision of the existing *aqcuis communautaire*. The ACQP thus filled the gap that was left open by the PECL. The existing laws were taken as a basis for the formulation of principles and rules in the field of contract law.[7]

Meanwhile, the Commission launched in 2001 a consultation paper inviting stakeholders to express their views on the possible harmonisation of contract law.[8] The follow up, 'A More Coherent European Contract Law – An action plan', was published by the Commission in February 2003 identifying the responses of the stakeholders.[9] The majority preferred a combination of promoting the development of common principles of contract law and to improve the quality of legislation already in place, instead of the adoption of new comprehensive legislation at the Union level. The Commission responded in two ways. The first aimed to remedy the deficiencies in the consumer directives,[10] which ultimately led to a Proposal for a Directive Rights consolidating four existing directives.[11] Secondly, the Commission called for the

---

[5] Smits, J., "The Principles of European Contract Law and the Harmonisation of Private Law in Europe", Antoni Vacquer (ed.), *La Tercera Parte de Los Principios de Derecho Contractual Europeo*, Tirant, Valencia, 2005, pp. 567–590.

[6] Basedow, J., "Anforderungen an eine Europäische Zivilrechtsdogmatik", R. Zimmermann, R. Knütel and J.P. Meincke (eds), *Rechtsgeschichte und Privatrechtsdogmatik*, C.F. Müller, Heidelberg, 1999, pp. 81–82.

[7] Art. 1:101 (1) ACQP. Critically: Jansen, N., and R. Zimmermann, "Restating the Acquis? A critical examination of the 'Principles of the existing European Contract Law", *Modern Law Review*, Vol. 71, No, 4, 2008, pp. 505–534.

[8] Communication from the Commission to the European Parliament and the Council on European Contract Law, COM (2001) 398 final, OJ 2001, C 255/01.

[9] Communication from the Commission to the European Parliament and the Council, A More Coherent European Contract Law – An Action Plan, COM (2003) 68 final, OJ 2003, C 63/01.

[10] Green Paper on the Review of the Consumer Acquis, COM (2006) 744, final.

[11] Proposal for a Directive on Consumer Rights, COM (2008) 614 final. See: Reich, N., and H. Micklitz,"Crónica de una muerte anunciada: The Commission Proposal for a 'Directive on Consumer Rights", *Common Market Law Review*, Vol. 46, No. 2, 2009, pp. 471–519; Lévay-Fazekas, J., "Connection between the CFR and the

adoption of a Common Frame of Reference (CFR) that would not only help to improve the existing EU legislation on contract law, but also assist arbitrators in finding unbiased solutions, be a source of inspiration for the ECJ, could be incorporated in Commission contracts and potentially contribute to an optional EU instrument on contract law. With such high ambitions it is not surprising that the scope of the instrument should be wide. According to the Commission, the CFR ought to cover fields that go to the root of the contract law system including the definition of a contract, the way how a contract is concluded, remedies, assignment and prescription.[12]

In 2005, the efforts of the von Bar and the Acquis group were merged with the aim of completing a CFR on an academic level. After an interim outline version,[13] the Academic Draft Common Frame of Reference was published in February 2009. It includes not only model rules but also comments and notes in a format similar to the Principles of European Contract Law (PECL). The scope of the DCFR is however much wider and covers a wide range of subjects including contract law, non-contractual obligations, transfer of movables and security rights in movable assets.[14] Although the DCFR should be distinguished from the CFR called for by the Commission in its Action Plan on a More Coherent European Contract Law, the DCFR is unquestionably a comprehensive body of rules systematically covering the field of contract law. If one includes all the comments and comparative notes, the work covers no less than 6.100 pages. The DCFR thus goes far beyond the present *aqcuis* and the aim of creating a 'tool-box' for legislators but

---

Proposal for a Directive on Consumer Rights", R. Schulze, *Common frame of reference and existing EC contract law*, Sellier, Münich, 2009, pp. 309–313; Rott, P., and R. Terryn, "The Proposal for a Directive on Consumer Rights : No Single Set of Rules", *Zeitschrift für europäisches Privatrecht*, Vol. 17, 2009, pp. 456–488; Beale, H., "The Draft Directive on Consumer Rights and UK Consumer law: Where now", G. Howells and R. Schulze (eds.), *Modernising and harmonising consumer contract law*, Sellier, München, 2009, pp. 289–302.

[12] Commission's Communication on 'European Contract Law and the Revision of the Acquis: The Way Forward', COM (2004) 651 final, OJ 2005, C14/05.

[13] Von Bar, C., E. Clive, H. Schulte-Nölke *et al.* (eds.), *Principles, Definitions and Model Rules of European Private Law: Draft Common Frame of Reference. Interim Outline Edition*, (DCFR), Sellier, Munich, 2008.

[14] Von Bar, C., "Coverage and Structure of the Academic Common Frame of Reference", *European Review of Contract Law*, Vol. 3, 2007, pp. 350–361; Beale, H., "European Contract Law: The Common Frame of Reference and Beyond", C. Twigg-Flesner, *The Cambridge Companion to European Union Private Law*, Cambridge University Press, Cambridge, 2010, pp. 116–130.

resembles more a national code. Instead of common principles, the project lays down in a systematic manner detailed rules on European private law. Even according to one of its drafters, the DCFR is a European Civil Code in all but its name.[15] However, other drafters have continued to adhere to the view that the DCFR is nothing more than an academic project producing insights and providing for a reference for a discussion on European contract law.[16] Be it as it may, the DCFR has received fierce criticism. Core of that critique is that the discussion on the future orientation of European contract law should not yet revolve around individual rules, concepts, doctrinal arguments, or even individual parts of the DCFR. The DCFR lacked a sufficiently broad and thorough discussion on the pro and cons of the solutions proposed. If the DCFR would have been intended as a starting point of an academic discussion in Europe, the drafters should have refrained from adopting a closed and comprehensive system.[17]

The DCFR is another milestone on the road towards a larger convergence between the European legal systems. It is however unclear where that road will lead to. The future orientation of European contract law still has to be decided. For that purpose the Commission established an Expert Group on the Common Frame of Reference in the area of contract law.[18] The main task of that Expert Group is to assist the Commission in the preparation of a proposal for a Common Frame of Reference in the area of European contract law by restructuring, revising and supplementing the Draft Common Frame of Reference relating to contract law and by taking into consideration other research work conducted in this area as well as the Union *acquis*. The Expert Group is

[15] Hesselink, M., "The Common Frame of Reference as a Source of European Private Law", *Tulane Law Review*, Vol. 83, 2009, pp. 919, 923.

[16] The drafters have in this way somehow tried to legitimise their work. One must not forget that the motivation for this project was the European Commission's desire for a revision and improvement of the existing European directives in the field of private law and not create the European equivalent of a national code. See: Smits, J., Editorial: "The Draft-Common Frame of Reference for a European Private Law; Fit for its purpose?" *Maastricht Journal of International and Comparative Law*, Vol. 15, 2008, pp. 145–148.

[17] Eidenmüller, H., *et al*, "Der Gemeinsame Referenzrahmen für das Europäische Privatrecht – Wertungsfragen und Kodifikationsprobleme –", *Juristenzeitung*, Vol. 63, 2008, pp. 529–550. Jansen, N., and R. Zimmermann, "'A European Civil Code in all but name "Discussing the nature and purposes of the Draft Common Frame of Reference", *Cambridge Law Journal*, Vol. 69, 2010, pp. 98–112.

[18] Commission Decision of 26 April 2010 setting up the Expert Group on a Common Frame of Reference, OJ L (2010), 105.

part of a wider initiative to explore the policy options leading towards a Europeanisation of contract law. In July 2010, the Commission launched a Green Paper inviting stakeholders to comment upon several possibilities such as a model law, a toolbox for EU lawmakers, a Contract Law Recommendation, an optional instrument, harmonisation via secondary law or a civil code.[19] Evidently the improvement of the drafting and internal coherence between European directives would not affect the conflict of laws mechanism. Only the policy options of harmonisation via secondary law or a civil code would significantly limit the role of Rome I. The next sections will therefore analyse the limits upon the competence of the Union to act in the area of contract law and subsequently explore the feasibility of harmonisation in contract law. A prediction shall be made with regard to which sort of rules harmonisation will prove to be feasible.

5.2 *The Issue of Competence*

There is no explicit legal basis in the TFEU empowering the Union to act in the area of contract law. Therefore, a potential European Civil Code or Contract Code has to be based upon a general law making competence. Art 114 (1) TFEU allows the Union to adopt 'measures for the approximation of the provisions laid down by law, regulation or administrative action in Member States which have as their object the establishment and functioning of the internal market.' Art. 114 could thus provide a legal basis, insofar the adoption of a European Civil Code would be necessary for the functioning of the internal market. However, in *Germany v European Parliament and Council* the ECJ denied a too broad interpretation of art. 114. The mere finding of disparities between national rules and the abstract risk of obstacles to the exercise of fundamental freedoms or of distortions liable to result there from was not sufficient. On the other hand, art. 114 would offer a legal basis if the aim of the measure would be the prevention of the emergence of future obstacles to trade resulting from multifarious development of national laws and the measure in question was aimed at the prevention the obstacles that would be likely to

[19] Green Paper on policy options for progress towards a European Contract Law for consumers and businesses, COM (2010) 348, final.

emerge.[20] The ECJ nuanced its position in *British American Tobacco*. Art. 114 may serve as a legal basis as long as the directive is genuinely aimed to improve market conditions and it actually contributes to the elimination or prevention of existing or future obstacles to free movement. It does not matter that the measure is based upon other decisive considerations, such as public health.[21]

The argument goes that differences between the private law systems in general could constitute a barrier for companies to do business in other Member States. Companies would need advice from local lawyers before they could enter the relevant market. These burdens would, relatively speaking, weigh heavier on Small and Medium sized Enterprises (SME's), because their incurred legal costs could not be spread out over a high number of transactions.[22] In particular with regard to consumers, it has been argued that only a harmonized contract law would create the sufficient degree of confidence to engage in cross-border shopping.[23] Even rules that would be condoned by the ECJ under negative harmonisation could thus constitute, for the purposes of positive harmonisation an obstacle to the smooth functioning of the internal market. Political arguments equally come into play;[24] a European Civil Code has a symbolic value[25] or is an excellent way to guarantee social standards.[26]

---

[20] Case C-376/98 *Germany v European Parliament and Council* [2000] ECR I-8419, par. 84.

[21] Case C-491/01, *British American Tobacco* [2002] ECR I-11453. Slater, D., "The Scope of the EC harmonising powers: The ECJ Tobacco Case", *German Law Journal*, Vol. 4, 2003, pp. 137–148.

[22] Lando, O., *Principles of European Contract Law*, Kluwer Law International, The Hague, 2000, pp. 61.

[23] Reich, N., "Der Common Frame of Reference und Sonderprivatrechte im 'Europäischen Vertragsrecht'", *Zeitschrift für Europäisches Privatrecht*, Vol. 15, 2007, pp. 161–179 (172).

[24] Van den Berg, P., *The Politics of European Codification. A History of the Unification of Law in France, Prussia, the Austrian Monarchy and the Netherlands*, European Law Publishing, Groningen, 2007.

[25] Collins, H., "Why Europe Needs a Civil Code: European Identity and the Social Model", M. Andenas *et al* (eds.), *Private Law Beyond the National Systems: Liber Amicorum Guido Alpa*, British Institute for International and Comparative Law London, 2007, pp. 259–269. For a discussion: Schäfer, B., and Z. Bankowski, "Mistaken Identities: The Integrative Force of Private Law", M. van Hoecke and François Ost (eds.), *The Harmonisation of European Private Law*, Hart Publishing, Oxford, 2000, pp. 21–45.

[26] Mattei, U., "Hard Code Now!", *Global Jurist Frontiers*, Vol. 2, No. 1, 2002, article 1; Hesselink, M., *et al*, "Social Justice in European Contract Law: a Manifesto", *European Law Journal*, Vol. 10, No. 6, 2004, pp. 656–674.

The general consensus seems to be that the Union lacks the competence to undertake a comprehensive codification.[27] Sector specific codes dealing exclusively with contract law, or even limited to consumer contracts, have been proposed.[28] Although the introduction of a consumer code is more likely than a comprehensive codification of private law it is questionable whether codification would be necessary for the functioning of the internal market at all.[29] In some countries legal differences, and thus barriers between parts of the country exist, while this has barely any effect on the trade between those parts of the country. For example, in Spain the autonomous regions of Catalonia and Navarra have their own contract codes without this having a major impact on trade between the regions. Also in the United Kingdom there is no evidence to suggest that differences between the English and Scottish legal system have a significant impact on trade within the United Kingdom.[30] Moreover, empirical studies have demonstrated that private actors do not really perceive differences in private law to be a genuine obstacle to cross border trade.[31] Finally, the privative

[27] In general see: Vogenauer, S., and S. Weatherill, "The EC's Competence to Pursue Harmonisation", S. Vogenauer and S. Weatherill (eds.), *The Harmonisation of European Contract Law; Implications for European Private Laws, Business and Legal Practice*, Hart Publishing, Portland, 2006, pp. 105- 148; Nadaud, S., *Codifier le droit civil européen*, Larcier, Brussels, 2008. One can debate whether the Union lacks competence since art. 114 TFEU only allows for harmonisation when necessary for the internal and harmonisation of substantive law would not be necessary when the obstacle to trade can be taken away by PIL, or whether the principle of subsidiarity prevents harmonisation. In favour of the latter: Grundmann, S., *Europäisches Schuldvertragsrecht* 1999, pp. 36.

[28] Hesselink, M., "European Contract Law: A Matter of Consumer Protection, Citizenship, or Justice?" *European Review of Contract Law*, Vol. 15, No. 3, 2007, pp. 323–348; Rutgers, J., and R. Sefton-Green, "Revising the Consumer *Acquis*: (Half) Opening the Doors of the Trojan Horse", *European Review of Private Law*, Vol. 16, No. 3, 2008, pp. 427–442.

[29] Van den Bergh, R., "Uneasy Case for Harmonising Consumer Law", K. Heine and W. Kerber, *Zentralität und dezentralität von Regulierung in Europa*, Lucius Lucius, Stuttgart, 2007, pp. 183–206; Weatherill, S., "Maximum or Minimum Harmonisation: What Kind of 'Europe' do we want?", K. Boele-Woelki and W. Grosheide (eds.), *The Future of European Contract Law*, Wolters Kluwers, Alpen a/d Rijn, 2007, pp. 133–146.

[30] Cámara Lapuente, S., Opinion on Communication on European Contract Law, http://ec.europa.eu/consumers/cons_int/safe_shop/fair_bus_pract/cont_law/comments/5.28.pdf, as of 15 March 2011.

[31] Vogenauer/Weatherill, *supra* note 27; Low, G., "How and Why We Are (Not) Bothered By the Costs of Legal Diversity - A Behavioural Approach to the Harmonization of European Contract Law", Tilburg Institute of Comparative and Transnational Law Working Paper No. 2009/8; Low, G., "The (Ir)Relevance of Harmonization and Legal Diversity to European Contract Law: A Perspective from Psychology", *European Review of Private Law*, Vol. 18, 2010, pp. 285–305.

codification will not be necessary for the functioning of the internal market if the potential obstacles to trade can be prevented or eliminated by a measure that would not require the replacement of national laws.

5.2.1 *Optional Instrument*

The exhaustive regulation of private, contract or consumer law on the European level is therefore not likely to occur within the next decades. As the Commission has identified, codification may well occur in different forms. One possible alternative identified in the Commissions' Green Paper is the development of a European private law system parallel to that of the Member States. The European codification would function as a 28th legal system. Parties could opt-in, or depending upon the chosen form opt-out, whenever they engage in cross-border trade. Precisely because an optional code would not replace the national legal systems but rather complement them, the question of legal basis would be different.[32] The ECJ found that art. 114 TFEU could not provide a legal basis for a measure which leaves unchanged the different national laws already in existence, but instead creates an additional system, since that measure cannot be regarded as being aimed at the approximation the laws of the Member States.[33]

Art. 81 or art. 352 TFEU, either individually or combined, could provide an alternative legal basis. The possibility and form of such an optional instrument has been discussed at length.[34] In fact, the answer to the competence question depends much upon the form and content of the optional code. The proposal for Rome I contained the possibility

---

[32] Max Planck Institute for Comparative and International Private Law, "Policy Options for Progress Towards a European Contract Law", in: *RabelsZ* (forthcoming, 2011)

[33] Case C-436/03 *European Parliament v Council* [2006] ECR I-3733, par. 44.

[34] Staudenmayer, D., "Un instrument optionnel en droit européen des contrats", *Revue trimestrielle de droit* civil, 2003, pp. 629–644; Huber, P., "European Private International Law, Uniform Law and the Optional Instrument", *ERA Forum*, Vol. 4, No. 2, 2003, pp. 85–98; Kerber, W., and S. Grundmann, "An optional European contract law code: Advantages and disadvantages", *European Journal of Law and Economics*, Vol. 21, No. 3, 2006, pp. 215–236; Hesselink, M., J. Rutgers and T. De Booys, "The Legal Basis for an Optional Instrument on European Contract Law", Centre for the Study of European Contract Law Working Paper no. 2007/04; Schulte-Nölke, H., "The way forward in European consumer contract law: optional instrument instead of further deconstruction of national private laws", C. Twigg-Flesner, *The Cambridge Companion to European Union Private Law*, Cambridge University Press, Cambridge, 2010, pp. 131–146.

for parties to choose a non-state body of law, recognised internationally or by the Union,[35] but this provision was ultimately deleted. However, the preamble to Rome I explicitly provides that in the event that the Union were to adopt rules of substantive contract law, including standard terms and conditions, such instrument may provide that the parties can choose to apply those rules.[36] The effects of the choice of law are uncertain. One the one hand, it could be argued that the 28th regime would merely be another law parties could stipulate to apply. The choice in favour of the optional code would be subject to the same limitations as the choice in favour of any national law. However, one could also construe the optional code as an alternative to Rome I. The application of Rome I would then be prevented, including the resort to the special protection awarded to consumers and employees in the conflict of laws process.[37]

The possibility of the optional code preventing the application of Rome I would evidently be favoured by the frequent trader. If the optional instrument would be merely an alternative to the election of the laws of a Member State, its added value would be somewhat limited. A professional can already insist upon choosing the law of a specific Member State to prevent making his contracts subject to different laws. Will a professional really be inclined to choose an optional European instrument instead of the laws of his own Member State? However, if the optional instrument were to supersede Rome I professionals could avoid having to deal with different national rules on consumer protection, by opting in to the optional instrument. Contract law rules would then comprehensively be offered on the central and Member State level.[38] The optional instrument might in such circumstances defeat the 'critical mass' argument. Private parties may not opt for the applicability of a legal instrument unless other private parties have already opted for that instrument and a sufficient amount of

[35] Art. 3 (2) Proposal Rome I.

[36] Recital 14 of the preamble to Rome I.

[37] Rutgers, J., "An Optional Instrument and Social Dumping", Centre for the Study of European Contract Law Working Paper Series no. 2006/03; Hertel, C., "Preventive Consumer Protection in an Optional Instrument - A Practitioner's View", *ERA Forum*, Vol. 4, No. 2, 2003, pp. 70–84.

[38] Sinai, A., "Inclusion of Mandatory Rules in an Optical EC Contract Law Instrument", *European Business Law Review*, Vol. 15, 2004, pp. 41–72; Heiss, H., and N. Downes, "Non-optional elements in a Optional European Contract Law. Reflections from a Private International Perspective", *European Review of Private Law*, Vol. 13, 2005, pp. 693–712.

case-law has been generated, ensuring legal certainty. However, in the light of the efforts in Rome I to protect consumers in choice of law cases it is rather difficult to imagine that Member States would agree to an instrument which would bypass the specific rules on consumer protection.[39] It will be decisive in such circumstances what level of protection the optional instrument would afford to the weaker party.

Art. 352 TFEU provides the Union with power to adopt measures for the attainment of one of the objectives set out in the Treaties, if the Treaties have not provided the Union with the necessary powers. Art. 352 is therefore a legal basis of last resort. A potential legal basis for an optional instrument would be art. 81 TFEU. However, it has been argued that art. 81 TFEU only provides a legal basis for the approximation of private international law, and not for substantive law.[40] Moreover, the aims that a measure may pursue for the promotion of judicial cooperation of civil matters are laid down in art. 81 (2). On first sight, none of the aims would allow the adoption of an optional instrument. However, as long as the measure adopted is aimed at the development of judicial cooperation in civil matters, there is nothing in art. 81 to suggest that the harmonisation of substantive law would be excluded from its scope.

The scope of 81 is broader than art. 114. On the basis of art. 81, for the purposes of enhancing judicial cooperation in civil matters, the Union *may* include the adoption of measures for the approximation of the laws and regulations of the Member States. The competence is therefore not necessarily restricted to measures which approximate the laws of the Member States. A measure adopted on the basis of art. 81 could therefore leave the legal systems of the Member States intact.

The question of competence depends therefore much upon the aim and purpose of the potential instrument. It is established case-law that if a measure pursues 'a twofold purpose or that it has a twofold component and if one of these is identifiable as the main or predominant purpose or component whereas the other is merely incidental, the act must be based on a single legal basis, namely that required by the main or

---

[39] Lando takes the view that a choice of a non-state body of law will not set aside the mandatory provisions in the sense of private international law. See: Lando, O., "Have the PECL been a success or a failure?" *European Review of Private Law*, Vol. 17, 2009, pp. 367–375.

[40] Staudenmayer, D., "Un instrument optionnel en droit européen des contrats?", *Revue trimestrielle de droit civil*, Vol. 102, 2003, pp. 629–644 (640).

predominant purpose or component'.[41] Although by exception a dual legal basis is possible when the primary component cannot be identified, the optional code requires a single legal basis since the procedures laid down by art. 81 and 352 are mutually exclusive.[42] Denmark cannot be bound by a measure adopted on the basis of art. 81, while Ireland and the United Kingdom enjoy the privilege of an opt-in. If the primary aim would be to enhance the confidence of professionals and consumers in the internal market, art. 352 should serve as a legal basis. If the primary aim would be to promote the compatibility of the rules applicable to cross-border contracts, art. 81 would seem more appropriate. In particular when the application of the optional code would depend upon party autonomy, would only be eligible for selection by the parties to cross-border contacts and would set aside the protective mechanisms in the conflict of laws process, the optional code would factually be a conflict of laws rule in disguise. In such circumstances, since art. 352 is a legal basis of last resort, art. 81 should prevail.

The choice of art. 81 TFEU as a legal basis has however some severe political drawbacks. Although the applicable legislative procedure would be on the basis of qualified majority voting, whereas art. 352 requires unanimity, any optional instrument would not bind all Member States. The United Kingdom and Ireland will enjoy a significant amount of political leverage because of their privilege of an opt-in. The unanimity requirement of art. 352 is however not very appealing either. In the light of these political obstacles, it would not come as a surprise if the Union legislator would attempt to use art. 114 as legal basis.

5.2.2 *Redundancy of Private International Law*

The competence of the Union to harmonise the private laws of the Member States, and the form such harmonisation should take therefore remain open to speculation. The political momentum seems to be in favour of an optional instrument.[43] Although there is still a lot of

---

[41] Case C-338/01 *Commission v Council* [2004] ECR I-4829, par. 55.

[42] Joined Cases C-164/97 and C-165/97 *Parliament* v *Council* [1999] ECR I-1139, par. 14.

[43] Reding, V., "Warum Europa ein Optionales Europäisches Vertragsrecht benötigt", *Zeitschrift für Europäisches Privatrecht*, Vol. 19, 2011, pp. 1–6.

mystery surrounding the optional code, in any constellation it would only create an additional legal system and leave the private law systems of the Member States intact. Consequently the Union would still be confronted with 27 different national legal orders. Differences between the legal systems will continue to exist. Rome I will therefore remain its pertinence. However, the piece meal approach to harmonisation of private law would probably be continued. Directives may provide for a large amount of harmonisation in specific areas.[44] The gradual harmonisation of contract law diminishes the role of Rome I. Especially the apparent shift in preference of the Union legislator to move in consumer law from minimum harmonisation to maximum harmonisation, if pursued systematically, could lead to the gradual replacement of the national consumer policy by an EU *acquis*.

The next sections will demonstrate that on the basis of an economic argument the harmonisation of contract law is not only not necessary, but not even feasible. The idea of drawing the dividing line between Union and Member State regulation in commercial law on the basis of economic arguments is not new.[45] The competence of the Union to enact unified substantive law is after all interwoven with the creation of an internal market. The economic argument in favour of uniformity has been forcefully attacked on several occasions.[46] What will be argued in this section is that harmonisation of the conflict of laws norms is not merely a second best solution to the full harmonisation of contract law. On the contrary, the exercise goes beyond the application of the principle of subsidiarity. The unification of the conflict of laws norms is, from a normative point of view, to be preferred over the unification of substantive rules.

[44] Müller-Graff, P., "EC Directives as a Means of Private Law Unification", A. Hartkamp and E. Hondius, *Towards a European Civil Code*, Kluwer Law International, Deventer, 2004, pp. 77–100; Johnston, A., and H. Unberath, "Law at, to or from the Centre? The European Court of Justice and the Harmonization of Private Law in the European Union", F. Cafaggi (ed.), *The Institutional Framework of European Private Law*, Oxford, University Press Oxford, 2006, pp. 149–190; Mak, V., "Harmonisation through 'Directive-Related' Case Law", *Zeitschrift fúr Europäisches Privatrecht*, Vol. 18, 2010, pp. 129–146.

[45] Buxbaum, R., and K. Hopt, *Legal Harmonization and the Business Enterprise*, Walter de Gruyter, Berlin, 1988, pp. 21.

[46] Schmidtchen, D., "Vereinheitlichung des Vertragsrechts in Europa – eine Lösung auf der Suche nach dem Problem?", T. Eger and H. Schäfer, *Ökonomische Analyse der europäischen Zivilrechtsentwicklung*, Mohr Siebeck, Tübingen, 2007, pp. 1–45.

5.3 *The Feasibility of Common Rules*

The gradual replacement of the national private law systems by European legislation has to be welcomed with restraint. The claim that a uniform law will enhance legal certainty often fails to acknowledge the effect of the conflict of laws rules.[47] Unification of conflict of laws rules has already generated legal certainty about the applicable law and has parties given the possibility to identify the applicable law in advance, reducing information costs. The advantages of market integration often tend to overstated, while the advantages of decentralisation and regulatory autonomy are often ignored.[48] Legal diversity is not necessarily a bad thing; Member States are better able to respond to local preferences. Schäfer has for example demonstrated that the efficiency of clear and precise rules as opposed to general principles decreases when a country reaches a higher degree of industrial development.[49] The preciseness of the rules acts as a substitute for a shortage in judicial skills. Countries that recently joined the Union could thus prefer to establish a high number of precise rules as contract default law, whereas some of the old Member States could prefer to establish general principles. There is also no European consensus on the adequate level of consumer protection, even not amongst the old Member States. For example, the distinction between consumers and commercial persons was not drawn in Germany before the introduction of a consumer policy by the European Union, and Scandinavian countries still prefer higher levels of consumer protection than provided for by Union legislation.[50] Local preferences may thus vary.

---

[47] Schmidtchen, *supra* note 46.

[48] Kerber, W., and R. van den Berg, "Mutual Recognition Revisited: Misunderstandings, Inconsistencies, and a Suggested Reinterpretation", *Kyklos*, Vol. 61, 2008, pp. 447–465 (455).

[49] Schäfer, H., "Direktiven als Ersatz für Humankapital: Empfehlen sich für Entwicklungs- und Transformationsländer präzisere Rechtsnormen als für hochentwickelte Staaten? " *RabelsZ*, Vol. 67, 2003, pp. 550–580.

[50] Wagner, G., "The Virtues of Diversity in European Private Law", *The Need for a European Contract Law: Empirical and Legal Perspectives*, European Law Publishing, Groningen, 2005, pp. 3–24 (6); Gomez, F., "The Harmonization of Contract Law through European Rules: a Law and Economics Perspective", *European Review of Contract Law*, Vol. 4, 2008, pp. 89–118; Rösler, H., "Schutz des Schwächeren im Europäischen Vertragsrecht", *Rabelsz*, Vol. 73, 2009, pp. 889–911 (901).

5.3.1 *Legal Innovation and Competition for the Best Legal System*

Decentralised regulation making is not necessarily a bad thing since that it allows for legal experiments aimed at developing innovative solutions.[51] A uniform law is impossible to change by an individual Member State and might become static. Not only will local preferences vary, desired norms and optimal standards will evolve overtime.[52] Maintaining diversity would incite Member States to come up with clever solutions better serving its citizens and private parties. If it is assumed that individuals know what is best for them and always act in the pursuit of their own interest, market participants could move to the Member State offering the most innovative solutions. Other Member States could decide to follow or promulgate even more efficient rules, which could lead to a race to the top.[53] Because Member States are forced to learn from each other, the most efficient legal structure will ultimately prevail.[54] Maintaining legal diversity thus does not necessarily lead to an unmanageable amount of diverging legal rules. It has been demonstrated that, on the contrary, contract law in Europe has been converging towards the most efficient solution.[55] However, that does not necessarily apply for the interventionist part of contract law because national preferences regarding the level of protection are likely to differ.

Competition for the best legal system assumes that consumers and producers have full mobility between the legal systems at marginal costs, that citizens enjoy perfect information about the legal systems in force in other Member States and can fully appreciate their costs and

[51] Hayek, F., "Der Wettbewerb als Entdeckungsverfahren", Kieler Vorträge N.S. 56, Kiel, 1968; O'Hara, E., and L. Ribstein, *The Law Market*, Oxford University Press, Oxford, 2009, pp. 32–33.

[52] Kraus, J., "Legal Design and the Evolution of Commercial Norms", *Journal of Legal Studies*, Vol. 26, No. 2, 1997, pp. 377–411.

[53] Kitch, E., "Business Organization law: State or federal?", Buxbaum *et al* (eds.), *European Business Law: Legal and Economic Analysis on Integration and Harmonization*, 1991, pp. 35–50.

[54] Posner, R., *Economic Analysis of Law*, Aspen Law & Business, New York, 5th edition, 1998; Cooter, R., and T. Ulen, *Law and Economics*, Pearson Addison Wesley, Boston, 3rd edition, 2000, pp. 167.

[55] Ogus, A., "Competition between National Legal Systems: A contribution of Economic Analysis to Comparative Law", *International and Comparative Law Quarterly*, Vol. 48, 1999, pp. 405–418; Wagner, G., "The Economics of Harmonization: the Case of Contract Law", *Common Market Law Review*, Vol. 39, 2002, pp. 995–1023 (1012).

benefits. Moreover, a sufficient number of communities should exist to generate actual choice. Those conditions are in reality not met in the EU. Costs of physical relocation are high, differences in language and culture exist between the Member States and consumers are typically ignorant of their rights, let alone the rights they would enjoy under the laws of another Member State. Whereas forcing market participants to physically relocate may form a strong barrier to avoid legislative competition, a choice of law may constitute a low cost substitute for physical movement.[56] The imposition of strict choice of law rules prevents turning to another legal system.[57] Determining the law applicable to a company on the criterion of where the company carries out its main centre of business prevents the company from benefiting from more efficient rules in other Member States. Whereas in an international contract parties can normally choose any law to govern their contract, without moving their place of business, overriding mandatory provisions are also imposed territorially. Their imposition cannot be avoided by a choice of law when its criteria for application are met. Overriding mandatory provisions and strict conflict of law rules may shield off parts of the national market from regulatory competition. In this respect, the case-law of the ECJ fulfils a crucial function. It is not open to the host Member State to second guess the application of the conflict of laws system of the home Member State. In that sense, the conflict of laws of boundaries to regulatory competition are not set by the state trying to shield off its market, but by the Member State producing the more efficient rules. What was decisive was that English law determined a company could be set up in its territory, even though a company did not carry out any business in England, rather than the Danish rule requiring a company that mainly pursued its business in Denmark to be set up in that Member State. Also in contract law, the control of the free movement provisions over the application of overriding mandatory provisions prevents the abuse of conflict of laws as barrier to regulatory competition.

A possible application of a race to the top could be observed in the area of company law. After the ECJ held in *Centros*[58] that Denmark was bound to recognise a company duly set up in the United Kingdom and

[56] Collins, H., *The European Civil Code: The Way Forward*, Cambridge University Press, Cambridge, 2008, pp. 66.

[57] Ogus, *supra* note 55, pp. 412.

[58] Case C-212/97 *Centros* [1999] ECR I-1459.

in *Inspire Art*[59] that the Netherlands could not impose any additional requirements to a company duly set up in the United Kingdom but carrying out all of its activities in the Netherlands, both countries started revising their company laws. Denmark and the Netherlands saw in the developments on the European level an incentive to make their company laws more internationally competitive by in general introducing more flexibility. Subsequent debates demonstrated that a minimum capital requirement was not very efficient for the protection of creditors since in case of bankruptcy the requirement was never sufficient to satisfy a substantial amount of claims. On the other hand, the minimum capital requirement constituted an obstacle to the setting up of a new company. Whereas Denmark significantly lowered its minimum capital requirement for private limited companies,[60] in the Netherlands it was proposed to abolish the requirement altogether.[61] The case-law of the ECJ thus constituted a reason for Denmark and the Netherlands to critically revise their company laws and to reconsider whether a minimum capital requirement was actually really needed.

The fear exists that instead of a race to the top, a race to the bottom is triggered. Wealthier Member States will lower their consumer and social standards to compete with Member States that have laxer standards. These Member States will on their turn lower their standards to remain competitive where ultimately the winner of the race to the bottom is the Member State with the lowest social standards. There is however little evidence to support the claim that Member States are using deregulation of consumer and labour standards as a tool of competition.[62] The reasons for a race to the bottom to fail to materialise are various. Legislators might find it difficult to locate and too costly to target legal areas with less stringent regimes that have little effect on the domestic market but significant cross border externalities.[63]

---

[59] Case C-167/01 *Inspire Art* [2003] ECR I-10155.

[60] Werlauff, E., "A 'Copenhagen Effect'?", *European Company Law*, Vol. 4, No. 4, 2009, pp. 160–168.

[61] Memorie van Toelichting, Wijziging van Boek 2 van het Burgerlijk Wetboek in verband met de aanpassing van de regeling voor besloten vennootschappen met beperkte aansprakelijkheid (Wet vereenvoudiging en flexibilisering bv-recht), Tweede Kamer der Staten Generaal 2006–2007, 31 058, no. 3. At the time of writing, the bill was still pending in the Tweede Kamer (House of Commons).

[62] Ross, G., "Assessing the Delors Era and Social Policy", S. Leibfried and P. Pierson (eds), *European Social Policy: Between Fragmentation and Integration*, Brookings Institution, Washington DC, 1995, pp. 357–388; Barnard, C., "Social Dumping and the Race to the Bottom", *European Law Review*, Vol. 25, 2000, pp. 57–78.

[63] Ogus, *supra* note 55, pp. 414–415.

There might also be an information problem on the consumer and producer side to assess the quality of legislation.[64] Another reason could be that it might actually be beneficial for companies to be established in a regime with stricter standards since the obligation to comply with higher standards might trigger technological improvements that would result in a competitive advantage for firms complying with them.[65]

5.3.2 *Varying Local Preferences*

The differences between the legal cultures of the Member States have been vigorously defended. One cannot harmonise legal rules if those rules constitute the expression of different legal mentalities. Convergence has not been taking place and will not take place.[66] Contrary to regulatory law, private law is deeply rooted in national legal culture.[67] In a less radical way, Van den Berg provides the example of the protection of consumers against unfair trade practices. The different values between the Member States can be expressed in different stands related to taste and decency. What is considered to be an unfair or aggressive trade practice may therefore vary from Member State to Member State. Although the Unfair Commercial Practices Directive (2005/29) recognises that the legal requirements related to taste vary widely among the Member States,[68] it presents in an annex practices that are deemed to be unfair or aggressive. Persistent and unwanted solicitations by phone, fax, e-mail or other remote media features on this list. It is doubtful whether these practices are really uniformly

---

[64] Some of the arguments used also reason against a race to the top. In fact, there is only limited knowledge about regulatory competition. The outcome depends on the specific kind of regulation and particular conditions. See: Sun, J., and J. Pelkmans, "Regulatory Competition in the Single Market", *Journal of Common Market Studies*, Vol. 33, 1995, pp. 67–89.

[65] Woolcock, S., "Competition Among Rules in the Single European Market", W. Bratton *et al* (eds), *International Regulatory Competition and Coordination: Perspectives on Economic Regulation in Europe and the United States*, Clarendon Press, Oxford, 1996, pp. 289–321 (318).

[66] Legrand, P., "European Legal Systems are not Converging", *International and Comparative Law Quarterly*, Vol. 45, 1996, pp. 52–81. Lando has however argued that the differences in legal culture should not prevent the adoption of a code: Lando, O., "Culture and Contract Laws", *European Review of Contract Law*, Vol. 3, No. 1, 2007, pp. 1–20.

[67] Van den Bergh, R., "Subsidiarity as an Economic Demarcation Principle and the Emergence of European Private Law", *Maastricht Journal of International and Comparative Law*, Vol. 5, 1998, pp. 129–152 (146–147).

[68] Recital 7 of the preamble to the UCPD.

disapproved in all Member States.[69] The *Alpine Investments* case could only arise before the ECJ because the Netherlands effectively prohibited cold calling, while Belgium did not.[70] The harmonisation of what is an aggressive trading practice has become an impediment for Member States to pursuing a consumer protection policy as preferred by their respective populations.

The varying local preferences constitute an obstacle for the creation of uniformity through the imposition of rules, even if harmonisation were pursued.[71] Smits has demonstrated that identical legal rules can only lead to uniformity in jurisdictions that have a comparable socio-economic constellation. That would mean, in the case of the European Union, that the rules that are directly related to the coming into being of a common market can be expected to remain the most uniform. However, harmonised rules that are not related to the common goal of creating the internal market will thus not necessarily lead to uniformity since the rule has to operate in different socio-economical contexts.[72]

It seems *prima facie* that the optimal level of regulation in a purely domestic context can best be determined by the Member State concerned. The length of a withdrawal period that a professional has to grant a consumer will depend upon the perception of fair commercial dealings in the jurisdiction as well as the degree of pro-activity that is expected from the consumer. If all contacts are internal to one Member State it is beyond doubt that length of the withdrawal period, and hence the probability that the consumer will make use of it, is best determined by the jurisdiction concerned.[73] The situation becomes more

[69] Van den Bergh, *supra* note 29, pp. 188.

[70] Case C-384/93 *Alpine Investments BV v. Minister van Financiën* [1995] ECR 1-1141.

[71] It appears that despite the maximum harmonisation of the Unfair Commercial Practices Directive the outcome of a particular case depends upon national courts and administrative authorities. Anagnostaras, G., "The Unfair Commercial Practices Directive in Context: From Legal Disparity to Legal Complexity", *Common Market Law Review*, Vol. 47, 2010, pp. 147–171.

[72] Smits, J., "How to predict the differences in uniformity between different areas of a future European private law? An evolutionary approach", A. Marciano and J. Josselin, (eds.), *The Economics of Harmonizing European Law*, Edgar Elgar, Cheltenham, 2002, pp. 50–70 (64).

[73] Tiebout, C., "A Pure Theory of Local Expenditures", *Journal of Political Economy*, Vol. 64, 1956, pp. 416–424. But Inman/Rubinfield draw a distinction between policies that have a high degree of spillover and those who have not. In the case of the former, the policy should not only strive for intrajurisdictional efficiency but also for inter-jurisdictional efficiency. Inman, R., and D. Rubinfeld, "Federalism", B. Bouckaert and G. de Geest (eds.), *Encyclopedia of Law and Economics, Volume V: The Economics of Crime and Litigation,* Edward Elgar Cheltenham, 2000, pp. 661–691 (676).

complex when the professional contracts with a consumer established in another Member State and the two Member States have different optimal levels of regulation. When is the setting of a harmonised standard beneficial overall, and what should that harmonised standard be? The lowest common denominator, the average, the toughest or even tougher than any previous national standard?[74] The answer to that question depends on the technology available and the heterogeneity of (consumer) preferences.[75] Moreover, the length of the withdrawal period has a redistributive effect. A longer withdrawal period will lead to the distribution of wealth between the pro-active and passive consumer since the professional will include the likelihood that a consumer makes use of his right of withdrawal in the price of the product. If it is assumed that the producer cannot *ex ante* distinguish between consumers, the extended length of the withdrawal period for the passive consumer will therefore be calculated in the price that is also charged to the pro-active consumer. In the light of the complexities both from an efficiency and distributive point of view it is difficult to draw general conclusions for contract law, or even consumer law. Rather a case by case approach is required, whereby in general in case of heterogeneity of preferences, minimum standards are to be preferred over a unified standard.[76] From this perspective it is hard to understand the recent proposal of the Commission in the Consumer Rights Directive to move from minimum to maximum harmonisation.[77] The

[74] Gomez, F., The Economics of Harmonized Law-Making in Private Law: Mechanisms, Modes and Standards, R. Brownsword *et al* (eds.), *Foundations of European Private Law*, Hart Publishing: Portland, 2010.

[75] Gómez, F., and J. Ganuza. "Optimal Harmonized Standards to Promote Cross-Border Trade", Universitat Pompeu Fabra Working Paper, 2008; Crettez, B., B. Deffains and R. Deloche, "On the optimal complexity of law and legal rules harmonization", *European Journal of Law and Economics*, Vol. 27, 2009, pp. 129–142; Kyriacou, A., "Decision rules, membership and political centralization in the European Union", *European Journal of Law and Economics*, Vol. 27, 2009, pp. 143–158.

[76] Grundmann, S., and W. Kerber, "European System of Contract Laws. A Map for Combining the Advantages of Centralised and Decentralised Rule-making", S. Grundmann and J. Stuyck (eds.), *An Academic Greenpaper on European Contract Law*, Kluwer Law International, The Hague, 2002, pp. 295–342; Kerber, W., "European system of private laws: an economic perspective", F. Cafaggi and H. Muir Watt (eds.), *Making European Private Law: Governance Design*, Edward Elgar, Cheltenham, 2008, pp. 64–97 (75); Gómez/Ganuza, *supra* note 75, pp. 10–13.

[77] Mak, V., "Review of the Consumer Aqcuis: Towards Maximum Harmonisation", *European Review of Private Law*, Vol. 17, No. 1, 2009, pp. 55–73; Smits, J., "Full Harmonization of Consumer Law? A Critique on the Draft Directive on Consumer Rights", *European Review of Private Law*, Vol. 18, 2008, pp. 5–14. Positive is:

replacement of the national standards by a uniform law in an area where such strong differences in preferences between the Member States exist will result in loss of welfare, and therefore be too costly. Even if a uniform standard constituted a more efficient solution, the presence of transaction costs when harmonising heterogeneous legal products might make the development of that unified standard an unviable option in practice.[78]

5.4 *Heterogeneous and Homogeneous Legal Products*

Ogus[79] draws in his analysis scrutinising the feasibility of harmonisation on the central level a distinction between homogeneous ('facilitative') and heterogeneous legal products ('interventionist').[80] The former tries to support the free exchange between private parties by saving transaction costs.[81] In the case of facilitative law, the assumed preference is the minimisation of legal costs consistent with ensuring the outcomes desired by those involved in the transactions, while interventionist laws protect defined interests and/or supersedes voluntary transactions. Whereas in case of homogeneous legal products spontaneous convergence could be expected, competition between national systems will not necessarily lead to a convergence of 'interventionist' law. Ogus is in general reluctant about a more pro-active harmonisation, but in cases of heterogeneous legal products even more than in cases of homogeneous legal products.

Hondius, E., "The Proposal for a European Directive on Consumer Rights: A Step Forward", *European Review of Private Law*, vol. 18, 2010, pp. 103–127. Hondius underlines that the political momentum should be seized.

78 In Law and Economics this problem is referred as the Coase Theorem. In the absence of transaction costs (drafting of uniform legislation, training judges) a uniform standard would have been the first best solution but the presence of massive transaction costs to pursue harmonization makes it unsuitable in the real world so that the second best option is preferable. In legal harmonisation: Herings, J., and J. Kanning, "Unifying Commercial Laws of nation-states, Coordination of Legal Systems and Economics Growth", METEOR Working Paper no. 027, 2002; Crettez, B., and R. Deloche, "On the unification of legal rules in the European Union", *European Journal of Law and Economics*, Vol. 21, 2006, pp. 203–214.

79 Ogus, *supra* note 55.

80 Ogus calls the latter 'interventionist law' but it does not become clear to what extent it can be placed against 'facilitative law'. It is unclear whether Ogus refers to mandatory or choice of law mandatory rules.

81 Transaction costs are being saved by providing for a legal framework to enforce contracts and to create a standard legal solution (default rules).

Mandatory rules are not necessarily the expression of a heterogeneous preference. A distinction should be drawn between mandatory information rules and mandatory substantive rules. The first promote economic efficiency by curing market failures, such as asymmetrical information problems, but do not interfere with the freedom of contract as such. The latter strive for the attainment of additional aims, such as wealth redistribution. In pursuance of social aims, they restrict the freedom of private parties to contract. They constitute the expression of heterogeneous preferences in the Member States. The Union legislator has, particularly in the area of consumer law, refrained from enacting mandatory substantive rules but has rather emphasised information obligations.[82] This approach does not only respect the freedom to contract for private parties but equally respects the regulatory authority of the Member States in rules that constitute the expression of heterogeneous preferences. A case can be made for harmonisation of the mandatory information requirements on the European level, since the preferences of the Member States only vary with regard to the information that has to be provided about the product and not with regard to the product or contract itself. Parties remain free to contract as they see fit.[83]

Ogus assumes that with regard to heterogeneous legal products 'the costs as well as the benefits of legal protection are internalised to citizens within the boundaries of the national jurisdiction'.[84] In absence of transboundary effects the costs of a high level of consumer protection are born by the national society as a whole. Replacing, even exclusively in transfrontier cases, the national standards by a uniform standard would lead to welfare losses. Imagine that the Union were to harmonise on the basis of maximum harmonisation the length of a withdrawal period in consumer contracts, with the uniform standard set at ten days, and suppose that previously the withdrawal period in Member State A was twelve days and in Member State B fourteen days. In a contract between a consumer resident in Member State A and an undertaking in Member State B both states will contract below their optimal level. The welfare loss could be prevented by adopting appropriate conflict of laws norms or mutual recognition.[85] The solution proposed by

---

[82] Kerber/Grundmann, *supra* note 34, pp. 223.
[83] Grundmann/Kerber *supra* note 76.
[84] Ogus, *supra* note 55, pp. 414.
[85] Leebron, D., "Lying Down with Procrustes: An Analysis of Harmonization Claims", J. Bhagwati and. R. Hudec, *Fair Trade and Harmonization*, Vol. 1, 1996, pp. 41–117.

Ogus would be 'to offer to those affected in the receiving jurisdiction the level of protection which would meet their preferences if they had to pay the increased costs of complying with that standard.' The sale of consumer goods on the territory of a Member State would thus be governed by the laws of that Member State. Professionals would calculate the likelihood of application of the protective standard of that Member State in the price of the product.

However, the fact that a rule is interventionist does not necessarily mean it is represents a social concern. Examples include mandatory requirements to safeguard the genuine expression of the will of the parties. These rules do not distribute welfare, but promote economic efficiency by guaranteeing that a meeting of minds took place. In very general terms production regulations, restrictions upon the conclusion of a contract or rules on how to approach potential clients are meant to enhance the efficient working of the system as a whole or to control negative externalities to third parties. By contrast, a minimum wage requirement or the check on unfair contract terms aims to equalise the difference in economic strength between two parties.[86] They protect a specific standard of social justice in a Member State[87] and fulfil a more distributive role.

5.4.1 *Homogeneous and Heterogeneous – Efficiency and Welfare Distribution*

A strong case for harmonisation would thus exist in case of homogeneous preferences, but less with heterogeneous preferences. Homogeneous and heterogeneous preferences can roughly be divided along the lines of rules promoting efficiency and rules redistributing social welfare. There is no general agreement in Law and Economics about the precise meaning of efficiency. 'A society is considered to be efficient if, and only

[86] Secondary Union law seems to prefer information requirements over substantive conditions. Information requirements have next to a distributive function also a strong efficiency function. Grundmann, S., "Information, Party Autonomy and Economic Agents", *Common Market Law Review*, Vol. 39, 2002, pp. 269–293.

[87] Lurger, B., "The Future of European Contract Law between Freedom of Contract, Social Justice, and Market Rationality", *European Review of Contract Law*, Vol. 1, No. 4, 2005, pp. 442–468; Lando, O., "Liberal, Social and 'Ethical' Justice in European Contract Law", *Common Market Law Review*, Vol. 43, 2006, pp. 817–833. Together the authors list as instruments to promote social justice five categories that intervene in the horizontal relation (information duties, withdrawal, mandatory intervention in the contractual stipulations, burden of proof and liability for statements made by suppliers) and only one (formal requirements) instruments to promote justice and fairness in European contract law.

if, under the given endowments it is no longer possible to improve the welfare of any individual and at the same time no individual has been made worse off'.[88] It is assumed that contracts concluded by two fully informed parties will be profit-maximising in the sense that they confer gains on each party.[89] Efficiency is hence about reaching the optimal level of overall welfare, or to put it in another way, to a situation where allocation of the resources initially available has led to the highest possible level of utility. The efficiency argument does not proclaim that an efficient society is a just one. Whereas Member States can legitimately differ on what a just outcome is, reaching consensus about the most efficient outcome will be less difficult. In principle the contract laws of every Member State will be aimed at maximising economic efficiency. Supposedly economic efficiency is best served by minimising legal costs. Although Member States might initially pursue the maximisation of economic efficiency by different methods, their aim does not vary. There will not be a wide divergence in local preferences. In the distinction of Ogus, efficiency rules will often be classified as homogeneous legal products. Because market mechanisms do not lead to a fair distribution of societal wealth a certain degree of redistribution is necessary in order to reach an outcome that better fits our concerns of social justice.[90] The redistribution of local wealth is made up of choices based on local preferences. In the distinction of Ogus they will often be classified as heterogeneous legal products. Distributive rules should not be understood as rules meant to compensate the loser of every efficiency rule, nor should efficiency losses be simply accepted as a necessary consequence of distributive justice. Economists often argue that redistribution could, instead of fixing a minimum or a maximum price, be achieved by taxation.[91]

---

[88] Schäfer, H., and C. Ott, *The Economic Analysis of Civil Law*, Edward Elgar, Cheltenham, 2004, 8.

[89] Schillig, M., "The Contribution of Law and Economics as a Method for Legal Reasoning in European Private Law", *European Review of Private Law*, Vol. 17, 2009, pp. 853–893 (860).

[90] Smorto, G., "Efficiency and Justice in European Contract Law", *European Review of Private Law*, Vol. 16, No. 6, 2008, pp. 925–948.

[91] Kaplow, L., and S. Shavell, "Why the Legal System Is Less Efficient Than the Income Tax in Redistributing Income", *Journal of Legal Studies*, Vol. 23, 1994, pp. 667–681; Sanchirico, C., "Taxes Versus Legal Rules as Instruments for Equity, A More Equitable View", *Journal of Legal Studies*, Vol. 29, 2000, pp. 797–820; Kaplow, L., and. S. Shavell, "Should Legal Rules Favor the Poor? Clarifying the Role of Legal Rules and the Income Tax in Redistributing Income", *Journal of Legal Studies*, Vol. 29, 2000, pp. 821–836; Eidenmüller, H., "Party Autonomy, Distributive Justice and the

The distinction between efficiency and distributive rules might in some instances be hard to draw,[92] in particular because a rule might have both efficiency and distributive elements. A typical example where one might think that by definition redistribution takes place is consumer law. The consumer is compensated for the stronger bargaining position of the professional. This does not however adequately reflect what is meant in Law & Economics by distribution rules. The improvement of the position of the consumer is incorporated in the price the consumer has to pay for the product or service. The apparent conflict between the interests of the professional and the consumer could be reformulated into a conflict between consumer interests. The consumer is confronted with either higher prices, but low protection standards or lower prices but higher protection standards. As long as consumers prefer higher standards over lower prices and the market is not able to answer to this preference in the general terms of sale, consumer protection rules promote economic efficiency.[93]

An example of a rule that has both efficiency as well distributive elements is the prohibition on discrimination in employment matters on the basis of gender, religious beliefs, racial origins or sexual preferences. It does not correspond with our ideas about a modern society that private employers refuse to hire women or pay them a lower amount of remuneration.[94] However, one could easily frame the argument in efficiency terms; discrimination on the basis of gender is inefficient per se and the market failure has to be corrected since it leads to the appointment of less qualified employees.[95]

5.5 *Reintroducing Conflict of Laws*

Empirical data thus suggests that, although there are information costs, market participants do not really see differences in private law as

Conclusion of Contracts in the DCFR", *European Review of Contract Law*, Vol. 5, No. 2, 2009, pp. 109–131 (119), but see: Rich, W., and W. Burress, "Economic Analysis and Distributive Justice", *Research in Law and Economics*, Vol. 18, 1997, pp. 15–64.

[92] Waldron, J., "Locating Distribution", *Journal of Legal Studies*, Vol. 32, 2003, pp. 277–302; Kaplow, L., and S. Shavell, "Fairness versus Social Welfare: Notes on the Pareto Principle, Preferences and Distributive Justice", Harvard Discussion Paper no. 411, 2003, pp. 17.

[93] Schäfer/Ott, *supra* note 88, pp. 9.

[94] Nuener, J., "Protection Against Discrimination in European Contract Law", *European Review of Contract Law*, Vol. 2, No. 1, 2006, pp. 35–50.

[95] Schäfer/Ott, *supra* note 88, pp. 9–10.

constituting a genuine barrier to cross border trade, while law and economics demonstrates that the optimal level of regulation is not necessarily on the central level and legal diversity might be beneficial. Law and Economics teaches us that 'the legislative powers should be vested in local, regional or national political institutions unless there is a compelling reason to invest them at a higher level of government.'[96] In particular with regard to rules which are the expression of a heterogeneous preference, a strong argument for maintaining the legal diversity in substantive contract law could thus be made, provided that an alternative is offered that deals with the realities of a common European justice area. Grundmann has argued that '[e]ven though substantive rules are to be found in several jurisdictions and on several (at least two) levels – in order to enhance, for instance, the advantages of regulatory competition – the framework for such competition (the set of rules for the game) have to be uniform.'[97] Mutual recognition combined with a country of origin principle do not provide an adequate framework. It merely results in the non-application of the law of the host Member State if it is more restrictive than the law of the home Member State. The applicable law is necessarily restricted to that of either the home or the host Member State. That would narrow the choice of private parties since in PIL a choice of law in favour of the law of a Member State that has no connections with the relevant legal relationship may be made. The internal market thus requires a combination between mutual recognition and conflict of laws whereby in principle the determination of the relationship between horizontal parties should be left to be governed by conflict of laws norms.

The underlying presumption in the claim that plurality in private law generally, and in contract law in particular, is in essence a good thing is private autonomy. In order for regulators to start a race to the top, market participants should be completely free to navigate to the most favourable legal system. It should be left to the parties to decide which legal system serves their interests best.[98] Private autonomy will

---

[96] Wagner, *supra* note 55, pp. 1002.

[97] Grundmann, S., "Internal Market Conflict of Laws…", A. Fuchs *et al* (eds.), *Les conflits de lois et le système juridique communautaire*, Dalloz, Paris, 2004, pp. 5–29 (16).

[98] Carbonara, E., and F. Parisi, "Choice of Law and Legal Evolution: Rethinking the Market for Legal Rules", University of Minnesota Law School Legal Studies Research Paper Series no. 07–38, 2007.

therefore constitute the only available connecting factor.[99] To what extent does the present analysis add anything? Contract law should not be exhaustively unified by the Union, rather in order to co-ordinate the application of the various national laws uniform conflict of laws rules should be adopted, and those on the basis should be private autonomy. Replacing the national legal systems of the Member States is within the coming decades not a viable option, the Rome I Regulation provides for uniform conflict of laws rules and the possibility of choosing the applicable law is its cornerstone. However, as the diversity argument has demonstrated, the optimal level of regulation is not always at the Union level. Instead of harmonising more contract or consumer law, it should be considered to reintroduce the conflict of laws in fields which might have been mapped out for unification.[100] The proposed maximum harmonisation of the Consumer Rights Directive stands as a very good example.

Instead of discussing more harmonisation of private law, it should be critically assessed whether private law harmonisation has not already gone too far. Conflict of laws offers a viable alternative. By guaranteeing mobility between the legal systems, conflict of laws would function as a quasi-federal framework. If conflict of laws had a federal function, party autonomy would be elevated to the constitutional level. Competition between legal orders has already long been regarded as a paradigm of Union law, albeit with the reservation of preserving a certain set of socio-economic values.[101] The framework of the Union might prove to be a very fruitful soil for legal experiments and regulatory competition. As described by Wagner: 'With some exaggeration it may be said that federalism creates a market for governments, with all the virtues a market has: it allows individuals to satisfy their widely differing preferences, it is a means to explore new solutions to common

[99] Muir Watt, H., "Choice of Law in Integrated and Interconnected Markets: A Matter of Political Economy", *Columbia Journal of European Law*, Vol. 9, 2003, pp. 383–409.

[100] Muir Watt, H., "The Challenge of Market Integration for European Conflicts Theory", A. Hartkamp and. E. Hondius, *Towards a European Civil Code*, Kluwer Law International, Deventer, 2004, pp. 191- 204 (197–8), in the same sense: Kerber/Van den Bergh, *supra* note 48.

[101] Reich, N., "Competition Between Legal Orders: A New Paradigm of EC Law", *Common Market Law Review*, Vol. 29, 1992, pp. 861–896; Kerber, W., "Interjurisdictional Competition within the European Union", *Fordham International Law Journal*, Vol. 23, 2000, pp. 217–249; De Lima Pinheiro, L., "Competition between Legal Systems in the European Union and Private International Law", *IPRax*, Vol. 28, 2008, pp. 206–213.

problems and it works as a device to identify the most efficient of the different solutions that have been developed and deployed by the different entities'.[102] The question remains, however, as to what scope that quasi-federal framework should have.

5.6 *What Role for Private International Law?*

The acceptation that conflict of laws should be reintroduced in areas that have been mapped out for unification or even the acceptation that some areas of private law should be left at the national level acknowledges that differences between the legal orders on the internal market will persist. The coordination of the different legal orders requires a combination between mutual recognition and PIL. How should such a combination take shape? By instinct one would apply mutual recognition to public law and PIL to private law. However, the dichotomy between public and private whereby PIL comprehensively and exclusively determines the applicable private law has become untenable. The line that divides public from private is increasingly fading. Not only have many private laws been equipped with socio-economical values, but public legislation increasingly affects private law. Examples include environmental regulations prohibiting the process of waste originating from other regions,[103] or the prohibition of cold-calling.[104] Although these regulations do not become part of the applicable law as such, they affect the validity or modality of how a contract can be concluded. One way of dealing with this problem is to make these regulations also subject to the conflict of laws norms, thus extending the area of private international law to areas that used to be perceived as public.[105] The primary justification lies in a normative argument born out economic interdependence. States have, by opening up their markets, denounced exclusive regulatory authority over a cross-border contract and assumed a duty to contribute to global regulation.[106] Competition for

[102] Wagner, *supra* note 55, pp. 1003.

[103] Case C-2/90 *Commission v Belgium (Belgian Waste)* [1992] ECR I-4431.

[104] *Alpine Investments, supra* note 818.

[105] Muir Watt, *supra* note 99, pp. 402; Kitch does not rely on conflict of laws but pleads in favour of extending choice to public goods: Kitch, E., "Business Organization law: State or federal?" Buxbaum *et al* (eds.), *European Business Law: Legal and Economic Analysis on Integration and Harmonization*, 1991, pp. 35–50.

[106] Muir Watt, *supra* note 99, pp. 402; Muir Watt, H., "Aspects économiques du droit international privé", *Recueil des Cours*, Vol. 307, 2004, pp. 25–384.

the most attractive legal order would then also take place in the public domain.

Joerges has gone one step further and classified Union law as a new species of conflict of laws.[107] Although the normative argument of economic interdependence and globalisation lies at the bottom of his argument he observes that the extra-territorial effects of legislation are unavoidable. The imposition of a minimum wage requirement in Sweden artificially raises the price of labour, which deprives a Latvian worker of a competitive advantage that he would have enjoyed when he entered the Swedish market. The extra-territorial burdens cannot be easily justified by a democratic process internal to one Member State. Although affected, the Latvian worker does not have a say in the Swedish legislation. He perceives therefore the need for a model of 'deliberative supranationalism', founded upon the obligation of a Member State to give voice to foreign concerns and interests even within the national polity.[108] The framework established to control the extra-territorial effects and co-ordinate the application of laws is in essence based on conflict of laws norms and principles. For Joerges, EU law is conflict laws and should apply a conflict of laws methodology.[109]

It should first be observed that the fundamental freedoms have done an outstanding job in bringing down outdated or discriminatory national legislation.[110] PIL should not try to replace or reconceptualise it, but rather to complement it. There is certainly merit in Joerges argument insofar as it considers the extra-territorial externalising of cost. The free movement provisions only trigger the obligation not to apply the law of host Member State, and have difficulties in conceptualising a check on the extra-territorial effects of the laws of the home Member

[107] Joerges, C., "The Europeanization of Private Law as a Rationalisation Process and as a Contest of Disciplines – an Analysis of the Directive on Unfair Terms in Consumer Contracts", *European Review of Private Law*, Vol. 3, 1995, pp. 175–191; Joerges, C., "Working through "Bitter Experiences" towards Constitutionalisation. A Critique of the Disregard for History in European Constitutional Theory", EUI Working Paper Law No. 2005/14

[108] Joerges, C., "The Challenges of Europeanization in the Realm of Private Law: A Plea for a New Legal Discipline", EUI Working Paper Law No. 2004/12, pp. 43–47.

[109] Joerges, C., "Rethinking European Law's Supremacy", EUI Working Paper Law, No. 2005/12. Joerges does not present the new species of conflict of laws as a mechanism for establishing the appropriate rule on the basis of a pre-existing framework, but rather 'a response to legal diversity that ensures compatibility with Union concerns while respecting the autonomy of democratically legitimated actors.'

[110] See in particular: Weiler, J., "The Transformation of Europe", *Yale Law Journal*, Vol. 100, No. 8, 1991, pp. 2403–2483.

State, nor can it incorporate foreign concerns in national law. It is however doubtful whether conflict of laws, or conflict of laws principles would form an appropriate tool.[111]

The proposed function PIL could assume in a common European justice area proposed here is therefore the opposite one: narrowing the scope of traditional PIL to determine the law that governs the horizontal relations between private parties. Rules of administrative authorisations, prudential supervision or product quality may very well be framed in private law terminology or classified as private by Member States, but do not become part of the applicable law as such. The private law framework of those rules does however not change the territorial nature of the rule. They are therefore better dealt with under mutual recognition. The next chapter will further explore how the mix between mutual recognition and conflict of laws should take shape.

[111] In a certain way it can be said that Joerges' claim underlies the same claim as subsidiarity: the Union must show respect for the national legal autonomy, while the Member States must temper that autonomy. 'The problem is that this says everything and nothing'. Corkin, J., "European Law as <Conflicts Law>: The Implications for Individual Autonomy", A. Furrer (ed.), *Europäisches Privatrecht im wissenschaftlichen Diskurs*, Stämpfli Verlag, Bern, 2006, pp. 391–415.

CHAPTER 6

FREE MOVEMENT AND THE DETERMINATION OF THE APPLICABLE LAW

The previous chapter has demonstrated that the Union only enjoys limited competence to harmonise substantive contract law. Moreover, the comprehensive and exhaustive regulation of contract at the Union level would not be feasible. A mix between mutual recognition and conflict of laws should be used to prevent the emergence of obstacles to trade due to divergence of contract laws. This chapter will attempt to provide a more detailed interpretation of that mix. For that purpose, the analysis should be broader than contract law. It will first be assessed whether the combined application of a conflict of laws rule and the substantive law declared applicable may result in a restriction of one of the fundamental freedoms. On the basis of examples in the area of company and surname law it will be argued why rules concerning administrative authorisations, prudential supervision and product quality should be approached differently from rules meant to govern horizontal relations. Returning to the main field of contract law, it will then be concluded that whereas the possibility for choosing the substantive law applicable to a contract in general places contract law outside the scope of the free movement provisions, this does not apply to overriding mandatory provisions. The application of overriding mandatory provisions therefore becomes subject to the scrutiny of the fundamental freedoms. The hypothesis developed in this chapter will be used to formulate an answer to the question whether the E-Commerce Directive lays down an additional conflict of laws rule.

6.1 *Private Parties and the Free Movement Provisions*

Art. 34 TFEU guarantees the free movement of goods. The article prohibits quantitative restrictions on imports and all measures having equivalent effect. The Spaak Report suggested that the predecessor of art. 34, art. 28 EC, should be confined to measures having an obvious protectionist intent and effect. The Court, however, has ruled otherwise. In the famous *Dassonville* decision it held that art. 34 applied to 'all trading rules enacted by Member States which are capable of hindering directly or indirectly, actually or potentially intra-Union trade are to be considered as measures having an effect equivalent to quantitative restrictions'.[1] It does not require a very skilled lawyer to argue that a national rule may potentially or indirectly affect intra Union trade. Of crucial importance is that art. 34 requires a restriction and not necessarily a discrimination. However, the effect of a national provision which authorises the collector of direct taxes to seize goods found on the property of the taxpayer even though the goods were delivered under a retention of title clause by a supplier established in another Member State was too uncertain and indirect to warrant the conclusion that it might impede the trade between Member States.[2] The same applied to a pre-contractual duty of information[3] and the restriction of a special procedure for summary payment to creditors established in that Member State.[4]

A national measure, such as a technical regulation, does not necessarily have to be aimed at giving preferential treatment to domestic producers at the expense of producers from other Member States. Indeed a technical regulation requiring all electrical plugs to have three pins bars all two-pin plugs from the market.[5] Although it may not have been the intention of the national legislator, it insulates national markets. A German requirement aimed at the protection of fairness of the commercial transactions providing that liquor sold within Germany should contain an alcohol percentage of at least 25% applied to both domestic and foreign products alike.[6] A French producer seeking to sell on the German market was however confronted with a dual burden since it had to comply with both German and French legislation, while the German producer only had to comply with German law.[7] The Court

[1] Case 8/74 *Procureur de Roi v Dassonville* [1974] ECR 837, par. 5.

[2] Case C-69/88 *Krantz* [1990] ECR I-583.

[3] Case C-93/92 *CMC Motorradcenter*[1993] ECR I-5009.

[4] Case C-412/97 *ED v Fenocchio* [1999] ECR I-3845.

[5] Chalmers, D., *et al*, *European Union Law*, Cambridge University Press, Cambridge, 2006, pp. 675.

[6] Case 120/78 *REWE-Zentral v Bundesmonopolverwaltung für Branntwein (Cassis de Dijon)* [1979] ECR 649.

[7] One could argue that double regulation is in itself already a discrimination. Equal treatment requires that equal situations should be tread equal and unequal situations unequal. In favour: Marenco, G., "Pour une interprétation traditionnelle de la notion de mesure d'effet équivalent à une restriction quantitative", *Cahier droit européen*, Vol. 20, 1984, pp. 291–326 ; Jarass, H., "Elemente einer Dogmatik der Grundfreitheiten", *Europarecht*, 1995, pp. 202–226 (214). Against : Roth, W., "ECJ Case Law on Freedom to Provide Services : Keck", M. Andenas and W. Roth, *Services and Free Movement in EU Law*, Oxford University Press, Oxford, 2002, pp. 1–24 (13).

did not consider whether the German legislation was intended to limit export from France, but concentrated rather on the effects that the legislation could have.

The Court took a considerably different starting point with regard to the freedom to provide services, the free movement of workers and the freedom of establishment. The freedom to provide services was framed in a discrimination test.[8] However in *Säger* the Court added that art. 56 also applied to measures that apply 'without distinction to national providers of services and to those of other Member States, when it is liable to prohibit or otherwise impede the activities of a provider of services established in another Member State where he lawfully provides similar services'.[9] The approach to the free movement of workers and the freedom of establishment is similar: the starting point is a discrimination test with a restriction test only used in particular circumstances.[10] The restriction prohibition approach is left to be mainly applied to regulations that relate to the access of markets of other Member States.[11]

The wide *Dassonville* formula in the free movement of goods triggered a vast amount of case-law wherein traders challenged nearly every trading rule possible. The surge in workload could, it was feared, undermine the effectiveness of the ECJ. Moreover, it was believed that rules were not the property of the Court and the plurality of actors in the definition of what the law ought to be required some judicial restraint.[12] The Court therefore sought in *Keck* to re-examine and clarify its case-law.[13] The ECJ drew a distinction between product requirements and selling arrangements. The rationale is that the check on the compositional quality of the product will already have been carried out by the home Member State. Selling arrangements however do not relate to the characteristics of a product. As such, they do therefore not prevent the marketing of a product but rather specify the conditions in

---

[8] Case 33/74 *Van Binsbergen* [1974] ECR 1299; Case 15/78 *Koestler* [1978] ECR 1971.

[9] Case C-76/90 *Säger* [1991] ECR I-4421, par. 12.

[10] Case C-415/93 *Bosman* [1995] ECR I-4921; Case C-281/98 *Angonese* [2000] ECR I-4139; Case C-190/98 *Graf v Filzmoser* [2000] ECR I-493; AG Maduro in Case C-438/05 *Viking* [2007] ECR I-10779.

[11] Roth, *supra* note 7, 23.

[12] Maduro, M., "Harmony and Dissonance in Free Movement", Andenas, M. and W. Roth, *Services and Free Movement in EU Law*, Oxford University Press, Oxford, 2002, pp. 41–68.

[13] Joined Cases C-267/91 *Keck and Mithouard* [1993] ECR I-6097, par. 14.

which the product can be marketed. Product requirements will therefore always be covered by art. 34, while a selling arrangement will fall outside its scope provided that those provisions 'apply to all affected traders operating within the national territory and provided that they affect in the same manner, in law and in fact, the marketing of domestic products and of those from other Member States'.[14] The importance of *Keck* to burdens created by PIL is therefore limited. PIL only comes into play in a cross-border context and does thus not affect purely national situations and intra-Union situations in the same way.[15]

Although the *Keck* exception was criticised[16], the substance was welcomed in general.[17] The line between whether a selling arrangement affects in similar manner domestic and foreign products alike or not is sometimes rather thin. The Greek requirement that processed milk for infants could only be sold in pharmacies supposedly treated domestic and imported products alike,[18] but the requirement that bakers, butchers and grocers could not make sales on rounds in an administrative district unless they had an establishment there did not.[19] Local butchers did not have to set up an establishment, while foreign butchers did. The same argument would seem to be valid for Greek pharmacies. If a Bulgarian company would want to sell baby milk in Greece it could presumably not sell the milk via the internet but would have to open an establishment in Greece even though it already has an establishment in Bulgaria.[20]

It has been submitted that there is no convincing rationale for the different approaches of the ECJ towards the fundamental freedoms.[21]

---

[14] *Keck*, *supra* note 13, par. 16.

[15] Israël, J., *European Cross-Border Insolvency Regulation*, Intersentia, Antwerpen, 2005, pp. 109–113.

[16] AG Lenz in: Case C-391/92 *Commission v Greece* (Greek Milk) [1995] ECR I-1621 and in: Case C-387/93 *Banchero* [1995] ECR I-4663.

[17] Weatherill, S., "After *Keck*: Some thoughts on How to Clarify the Clarifcation", *Common Market Law Review*, Vol. 33, 1996, pp. 885–906; Enchelmaier, S., "The Awkward Selling of a Good Idea, or a Traditionalist Interpretation of *Keck*", *Yearbook of European Law*, Vol. 22, 2003, pp. 249–322 (with further references).

[18] *Greek Milk*, *supra* note 16.

[19] Case C-254/98 *Schutzverband gegen unlauteren Wettbewerb v TK-Heimdienst* [2000] ECR I-151.

[20] In similar vein: Case C-322/01 *Deutscher Apothekerverband* [2003] ECR I-1488.

[21] Snell, J., and M. Andenas, "Exploring the Outer Limits: Restrictions on the Free Movement of Goods and Services", M. Andenas and W. Roth, *Services and Free Movement in EU Law*, Oxford University Press, Oxford, 2002, pp. 69–139 (75).

On the basis of recent case-law[22] some authors have suggested that *Keck* has been replaced by a 'market access test'.[23] In any case, the prohibition to restriction test in the area of services and *Keck* in the area of goods have resulted in a larger convergence of the fundamental freedoms.[24] Since the Court has never adopted a wide restriction-based approach with regard to the freedom to provide services, there is to be no need for a *Keck* doctrine in art. 56.[25] The Court might have hinted in *Mobistar* to a possible application of *Keck* in the area of services.[26] However, applying the reading of the Keck doctrine that the ECJ adopted in *Mobistar* to services would go too far. A more plausible reading is that ECJ holds the opinion that not every obstacle to trade is able to constitute a restriction upon the internal market.[27] Since the ambit of application of the free movement of goods is still drawn wider than with regard to the freedom to provide services it shall, in the present analysis, be assumed that if a measure falls under the prohibition of restriction doctrine under art. 56, it would also have fallen in the scope of art. 34 if a link with the free movement of goods would have existed.

---

[22] Case C-110/05 *Commission v Italy* [2009] ECR I-519; Case C-142/05 *Mickelsson and Roos* [2009]; ECR I-4273.

[23] Spaventa, E., "Leaving Keck behind? The free movement of goods after the rulings in Commission v Italy and Mickelsson and Roos", *European Law Review*, Vol. 34, 2009, pp. 914–932; Barnard, C., "Trailing a new approach to free movement of goods?", *Cambridge Law Journal*, Vol. 68, 2009, pp. 288–290; Snell, J., "The Notion of Market Access: A Concept or a Slogan", *Common Market Law Review*, Vol. 47, 2010, pp. 437–472. But see: Weatherhill, S., "Current developments", *International and Comparative Law Quarterly*, Vol. 58, 2009, pp. 985–992; Wenneras, P., and K. Boe Moen, "Selling Arrangments, keeping Keck', *European Law Review*, Vol. 35, 2010, pp. 387–400.

[24] Maduro, *supra* note 12; Jarass, H., "A Unified Approach to the Fundamental Freedoms", M. Andenas and W. Roth, *Services and Free Movement in EU Law*, Oxford University Press, Oxford, 2002, pp. 141–162; Snell, J., "The Notion of Market Access: A Concept or a Slogan", *Common Market Law Review*, Vol. 47, 2010, pp. 437–472.

[25] It is worth drawing attention to the different rationale behind regulatory competition that might prevent the transposition of Keck to services: Snell, J., *Goods and Services in EC Law*, Oxford University Press, Oxford, 2002, pp. 70–128. AG Fenelly proposed to apply *Keck* also to the free movement of workers: Case C-190/98 *Volker Graf v Filzmoser Maschinenbau GmbH* [2000] ECR 1-493, para. 18–20; Schulte Westenberg, H., *Zur Bedeutung der Keck-Rechtsprechung für die Arbeitnehmerfreizügigkeit*, Mohr Siebeck, Tübingen (2009).

[26] Joined Cases C-544/03 and C-545/03 *Mobistar and Belgacom Mobile* [2005] ECR I-7723, par. 31. Tobler, C., "Endlich "Keck" im Freien Dienstleistungsverkehr", *Jus & News*, 2005, pp. 159–171.

[27] Hatzopoulos, V., "Legal Aspects in Establishing the Internal Market for services", College of Europe, Research Papers in Law, no. 6. 2007, pp. 10.

The prohibition of restrictions doctrine, or market access, does not exclusively apply to incoming goods or services but equally to outgoing ones. In *Alpine Investments*, the Dutch Ministry of Finance only issued licences on the condition that the undertaking would not engage in the unsolicited approaching of clients (cold calling).[28] The licence was also necessary when Alpine Investments wished to approach clients outside the Netherlands from its establishment within the Netherlands. The ECJ accepted a restriction on art. 56 since the prohibition prevented a rapid and direct technique for marketing and accessing the market in other Member States. Within the framework of the free movement of goods, art. 35 covers quantitative restrictions to exports or measures having equivalent effect. In *Gysbrechts*, Belgian legislation prohibited a supplier in a distance sale contract from requiring from consumers an advance or any payment before expiry of the period for withdrawal.[29] In a cross-border context, the measure was caught by art. 35 since it prevented the supplier from using an efficient enforcement mechanism.[30] In the light of the obstacles to bringing legal proceedings in other Member States, especially when dealing with relatively small sums, the prohibition might have the effect that suppliers would refrain from dealing with consumers in other Member States.

6.1.1 *Justification*

If a measure is caught by one the free movement provisions, it does not necessarily mean the measure is incompatible with it. A restriction on the free movement can be justified provided that it pursues a legitimate aim and that the measure is suitable and necessary to the realisation of its objective.[31] The principle thus not only tests whether the measure is proportionate to the interest pursued, but also checks the instrument.[32]

---

[28] Case C-384/93 *Alpine Investments BV v. Minister van Financiën* [1995] ECR 1-1141.

[29] Case C-205/07 *Gysbrechts* [2008] ECR I-9947.

[30] There is however not a full convergence between art. 34 and art. 35 TFEU, see: Szydło, M., Export Restrictions within the Structure of the Free Movement of Goods. Reconsideration of an old paradigm, *Common Market Law Review*, Vol. 47, 2010, pp. 753–789.

[31] Case C-19/92 *Kraus* [1993] ECR I-1663, par. 32; Case C-55/94 *Gebhard* [1995] ECR I-4165, par. 37; Case C-272/94 *Guiot* [1996] ECR I-1905, paras. 11 and 13

[32] De Búrca, G., "The Principle of Proportionality and its Application in EC Law", *Yearbook of European Law*, Vol. 13, 1993, pp. 105–150; Tridimas, T., "Proportionality in Union law: searching for the appropriate standard of scrutiny", E. Ellis (ed.), *The Principle of proportionality in the laws of Europe*, Hart Publishing, Oxford, 1999,

Proportionality not only entails that the measure should be proportionate to the realisation of the aim and does not go beyond what is necessary, but also that measure must be the least restrictive on intra Union trade as possible. Measures that directly distinguish between foreign goods or services can only be justified on narrow public policy grounds.[33] The Court developed outside the framework of the explicit treaty provisions a mandatory requirements doctrine for the justification of indistinctly applicable measures.[34] Just as the public policy grounds for the application of overriding mandatory provisions, the list is non-exhaustive. Member States have a wider array of public policy grounds, including the protection of the environment,[35] consumer protection[36] or the coherence of fiscal regime[37] with which to justify a restriction. The rule of reason can be invoked with regard to all fundamental freedoms.[38]

Suitability in the mandatory requirements doctrine means that the measure must be effective. What is tested is not whether the measure concerned is the most effective, but rather whether it contributes to ascertaining the interest it seeks to protect. When the Court assesses whether no less restrictive national measure is available, it focuses upon the effects of the restriction rather than on a comparison between the different national measures of Member States.[39] The core of the mandatory requirements doctrine essentially entails the exercise of the proportionality test,[40] which implies mutual recognition.[41] It would go

pp. 65–84; Jans, J., "Proportionality Revisited", *Legal Issues of Economic Integration*, Vol. 27, No. 3, 2000, pp. 239–265; Hös, N., "The Principle of Proportionality in the *Viking* and *Laval* cases: An Appropriate Standard of Judicial Review", EUI Working Paper Law, no. 6, 2009.

[33] Art. 30, art. 39 (3), art. 46 (1), art. 55 EC. The measure may however in no circumstances arbitrarily discriminate against imports. See: case 4/75 *Rewe Zentralfinanz GmbH v Landwirtschaftskammer Bonn* [1975] ECR 843.

[34] O'Leary, S., and J. Fernández-Martin, "Judicially-Created Exceptions to the Free Provision of Services", M. Andenas and W. Roth, *Services and Free Movement in EU Law*, Oxford University Press, Oxford, 2002, pp. 163–195.

[35] Case C-2/90 *Commission v Belgium* (Belgian Waste) [1992] ECR I-4431.

[36] Case C-448/98 *Guimont* [2000] ECR I-10663.

[37] Case C-300/90 *Commission v Belgium* [1992] ECR I-305.

[38] Chalmers, *supra* note 5, pp. 833.

[39] Tridimas, T., *The General Principles of EU Law*, Oxford University Press, Oxford, 2nd edition, 2006, pp. 214–215.

[40] Proportionality is referred to as the legal meta-principle of EU law. Von Danwitz, T., "Der Grundsatz der Verhältnismäßigkeit im Gemeinschaftsrecht", *Europäisches Wirtschafts & Steuerrecht*, Vol. 14, No. 9, 2003, pp. 393–402.

[41] Commission Communication - COM(1999) 299 final; Regulation 764/2008 laying down procedures relating to the application of certain national technical rules to

beyond what is necessary for the protection public health if the host Member State were to require laboratory tests that have already been carried in the home Member State.[42] Mutual recognition does not require that the protected standard is equivalent, but that the home Member State already took into account the interest that the host Member State seeks to protect. A Member State will thus be prevented from imposing consumer safety measures even if the home Member State provides for significantly laxer standards but not if the home Member State does not address consumer safety at all.

From a Union law perspective there is thus nothing that would exclude *a priori* rules of private law from the scope of the free movement provisions.[43] It is however not entirely certain to what extent private parties can rely in a dispute upon one of the fundamental freedoms. The ECJ has recognised the applicability of art. 45[44] and 49 TFEU[45] in a purely private dispute. Whether the freedom to provide services can be relied upon against a private individual, or whether that private actor should be factually a quasi-public organisation or an association exercising a regulatory task and having quasi-legislative powers is not entirely clear.[46] Despite case-law suggesting the contrary,[47] doubts have arisen whether also the freedom to provide goods can be invoked in a

---

products lawfully marketed in another Member State; Weiler, J., "The Transformation of Europe", *Yale Law Journal*, Vol. 100, No. 8, 1991, pp. 2403–2483; Kostoris Padoa Schioppa, F., *The Principle of Mutual Recognition in the European Integration Process*, Palgrave Macmillan, New York, 2005.

42 Case 272/80 *Frans-Nederlandse Maatschappij voor Biologische Producten* [1981] ECR 3277.

43 Roth, W., "Die Freiheiten des EG-Vertrages und das nationale Privatrecht", *Zeitschrift für Europäisches Privatrecht*, Vol. 2, No. 1, 1994, pp. 5–33.

44 *Bosman; Angonese supra* note 10. See: Van den Bogaert, S., "Horizontality: The Courts Attacks?", C. Barnard (ed.), *The Law of Single European Market*, Oxford University Press, Oxford, 2002, pp. 123–152.

45 Case C-438/05 *Viking* [2007] ECR I-10779.

46 In favour: Wyatt,D., "Horizontal Effect of Fundamental Freedoms and the Right to Equality after Viking and Mangold, and the Implications for Union Competence", Oxford Legal Studies Research Paper No. 20/2008; Reich, N., "The Public/Private Divide in European Law", H. Micklitz and F. Cafaggi, *European Private Law after the Common Frame of Reference*, Edward Elgar, Cheltenham, pp. 56–89. More cautious: Hartkamp, A., "The Effect of the EC Treaty in Private Law: On Direct and Indirect Effects of Primary Community Law", *European Review of Private Law*, Vol. 18, 2010, pp. 527–548.

47 Joined Cases 177 and 178/82 *Criminal proceedings against van de Haar and Kaveka de Meern* [1984] ECR 1797; Case 58/80 *Dansk Supermarked* [1981] ECR 181; Case 311/85 *Vereniging van Vlaamse Reisbureau's v. Sociale Dienst van de Plaatstelijke Gewestelijke Overheidsdiensten* [1987] ECR 3821, par. 30.

purely private context.[48] Private parties seem however to be able to rely on Union law to set aside national legislation incompatible with the free movement provisions. When interpreting a directive guaranteeing the free movement of goods the Court in *Unilever* prevented a private party from invoking a national measure incompatible with Directive 98/34 on the notifications of technical regulations to argue non-performance on the part of the other contracting party.[49] In similar vein in *CIA Securities*, a private party could not rely on a national technical regulation that was not notified in accordance with Directive 98/34 in a claim against a competitor to cease unfair commercial practices.[50]

The practical relevance of the impossibility of relying upon the fundamental freedoms against another private actor in a purely private dispute is somewhat limited. The duty of loyal cooperation as enshrined in art. 4 TEU places Member States under a positive duty to guarantee the effective application of the free movement provisions.[51] A claim for damages suffered as a result of repetitive attacks against foreign products[52] or the blocking of a highway[53] would then not be made against the other private party directly, but against the Member State involved for the failure to ensure the free movement of goods.

6.2 *Free Movement and Contract Law*

In *Koestler* the ECJ was confronted with a claim by a French bank against a German national arising out of a contract classified by German courts as a wagering contract. Such claims were as a matter of public policy not actionable in Germany. The Court held that a rule that determines that debts arising out of a wagering were not actionable cannot be regarded as discrimination against a person providing services established in another Member State if the same limitation applies to

---

[48] *Viking, supra* note 45, par. 62. The Court claims to find support for attributing horizontal effect to the freedom of establishment in its case-law regarding the free movement of goods.

[49] Case C-443/98 *Unilever* [2000] ECR I-7435. See: Weatherill, S., "Breach of directives and breach of contract", *European Law Review*, Vol. 26, 2001, pp. 177–186.

[50] Case C-194/94 *CIA Security v Signalson and Securitel* [1996] ECR I-2201

[51] Though the duty of loyal cooperation in art. 10 EC has been repealed by the Lisbon Treaty, it has been replaced in substance by art. 4 TEU.

[52] Case C-265/95 *Commission* v. *France (Spanish Strawberries)* [1997] ECR I-6959.

[53] Case C-112/00 *Schmidberger* [2003] ECR I-5659.

any person providing the service within the territory of the same state when that person claims payment of a debt of the same kind.[54] The ECJ held in *CMC Motorradcenter* that the effects of a pre-contractual information duty were too indirect and uncertain to warrant the conclusion that it might impede the trade between Member States.[55] However, the Court has implied in *Leitner* that the existence in some Member States but not in others of an obligation to provide compensation for non-material damage would cause significant distortions of competition.[56] Although the facts of *Leitner* were particular to that case since the Court was interpreting a provision in the directive exactly aimed at eliminating the disparities between the Member States, and a divergent interpretation would have undermined the uniform application of that instrument, the growing amount of secondary legislation in private law measures suggests that private law can constitute a barrier to intra-Union trade.[57] However given that after *Cassis de Dijon* the Commission has concentrated on the harmonisation of obstacles to trade that were admissible under the criteria of the Court,[58] the growing amount of harmonising measures could thus also be understood as indication that the harmonised national provisions would have been compatible with the fundamental freedoms. In any case, a general exemption for private law would go too far. It is debatable whether private law would constitute a selling arrangement, or with regard to the freedom to provide services would not have such an effect of preventing market access. Every area of private law, and even every individual private law rule, would then have to be assessed on whether it constituted a selling arrangement or had the effect of impeding market access.[59] Contract law is strongly centred around the individual. The possibility for

[54] *Koestler, supra* note 8, par. 5.

[55] *CMC Motorradcenter, supra* note 862.

[56] Case C-168/00 *Leitner v TUI Deutschland* [2002] ECR I-2631.

[57] Fallon, M., and J. Meeusen, "Private International Law in the European Union and the Exception of Mutual Recognition", *Yearbook of Private International Law*, Vol. 4, 2002, pp. 37–66 (49).

[58] Communication from the Commission concerning the consequences of the judgment given by the Court of Justice on 20 February 1979 in Case 120/78 ('Cassis de Dijon') OJ C 256/2. 'The Commission's work of harmonization will henceforth have to be directed mainly at national laws having an impact on the functioning of the common market where barriers to trade to be removed arise from national provisions which are admissible under the criteria set by the Court.'

[59] Klauer, I., *Die Europäisierung des Privatrechts*, Nomos Verlagsgesellschaft, Baden-Baden, 1997, pp. 74–98.

private parties of choosing the law applicable to their contract is the cornerstone of Rome I. However before one analyses whether the *Keck* exception applies, one has to analyse whether the rule concerned is caught by the free movement provisions. Does *CMC Motorradcenter* have any wider application for contract law? To answer that question one has to go back into the rationale behind mutual recognition.

6.2.1 *The Absence of a Favor Offerentis*

The question in essence aims to ascertain whether private law, or in particular contract law is caught by the principle of mutual recognition. The principle of mutual recognition could contain a hidden conflict of laws rule.[60] Basedow in particular has argued that the fundamental freedoms imply a *favor offerentis*.[61] He incorporates a functional element in conflict of laws; the law that is the most favourable to the Union trade of goods should be applied. Since it are producers and traders that are the real engine of European integration, the fundamental freedoms require application of the least restrictive law to a foreign trader (*Günstigkeitsprinzip, favor offerentis*). The principle of mutual recognition would then become a conflict rule also affecting private law relations. Grundmann takes it one step further and advocates the introduction of a *Binnenmarktkollisionsrecht*.[62] The scope of Rome I would be limited towards situations involving a conflict of laws with a third country. The applicable law should, both in harmonised and unharmonised areas, be determined on the basis of autonomous internal market conflict of laws. Whereas the autonomous conflict of laws rule in unharmonised areas is based upon the free movement provisions, Member States have lost in the harmonised areas, even in

[60] Bernard, P., "Cassis de Dijon und Kollisionsrecht – am Beispiel des unlauteren Wettbewerbs", *Europäisches Zeitschrift für Wirtschaftsrecht*, Vol. 14, 1992, pp. 437–438.

[61] Basedow, J., "Der kollisionsrechteliche Gehalt der Produktfreiheiten im europäischen Binnenmarkt: favor offerentis", *RabelsZ*, Vol. 95, 1995, pp. 1–55. Critical: Wilderspin, M., and X. Lewis, "Les relations entre le droit communautaire et les règles de conflits de lois des Etats membres", *Revue Critique de Droit International Privé*, 2002, pp. 1–37 ; Heuzé, V., "De la compétence de la loi du pays d'origine en matière contractuelle ou l'anti-droit Européen", *Le droit international privé : esprit et méthodes ; Mélanges en l'honneur de Paul Lagarde*, Dalloz, Paris, 2005, pp. 393–415.

[62] Grundmann, S., "Binnenmarktkollisionsrecht – vom klassichen IPR zur Integrationsordnung", *RabelsZ*, Vol. 69, 2000, pp. 457–477; Grundmann, S., "Internal Market Conflict of Laws…", A. Fuchs *et al* (eds.), *Les conflits de lois et le système juridique communautaire*, Dalloz, Paris, 2004, pp. 5–29; Schilling, K., *Binnenmarktskollisionsrecht*, De Gruyter, Berlin, 2006.

cases of minimum harmonisation, the ability to ability to impose more stringent rules in cross border cases.[63]

A Polish plumber that renders a service in Germany and in performance of the plumbing contract and causes collateral damage to the house should thus be sued for damages according to Polish law. Similarly one could argue that one has to answer the question whether a duty of care has been breached by an Italian truck driver causing an accident with a pedestrian in Copenhagen according to Italian law. It is hard to imagine that Union law would require such an outcome.[64] The Italian truck driver will most likely have an Italian driving license. Union law would require the recognition by the Danish authorities of that driving license.[65] Denmark may not verify whether it would have given in similar circumstances the Italian driver a Danish driving license;[66] in that sense it may not challenge the capability of the Italian driver. The fact that the Italian truck driver can lawfully drive around in Denmark, similarly as the Polish plumber can lawfully render services as plumber in Germany, does not say anything about the private law applicable. The relation that a foreign service provider or producer of goods has, *vis-à-vis* the host Member State, to be distinguished from the relationship he has with the citizens of that Member State. The question of which privileges an individual can invoke against a Member State should be separated from the question of applicable law to a horizontal relationship.

The debate preceding the adaptation of the Services Directive quite strongly indicates that private laws are only to a limited extent covered by the principle of mutual recognition. The original Commission draft (Bolkestein proposal) contained the country of origin principle. The country of origin principle is not identical to mutual recognition, but goes further. Mutual recognition requires a host Member State to take the legislation of the home Member State into account. A host Member State cannot apply its own legislation when the same issue is already governed by the home Member State. The country of origin principle is

---

[63] Grundmann, *supra* note 62, 22–23. Member States are not allowed to impose more stringent provisions since harmonisation has also selected the public policy reasons that can hinder inter Member State trade. However, the ECJ has allowed Member States to impose standards that go beyond minimum harmonisation also to cross-border cases. Case C-441/04 *A-Punkt Schmuckhandels* [2006] ECR I-2093, par. 11.

[64] Tison, M., *De interne markt voor bank- en beleggingsdiensten*, Intersentia, Antwerpen, 1999, pp. 792.

[65] Article 1(2) of Directive on Driving Licenses (EC 91/439).

[66] That obligation goes quite far: Case C-476/01 *Kapper* [2004] ECR I-5205.

not subject to that limitation and, for example, a foreign service provider may insist upon the overall application of the laws of the home Member State.[67] The Bolkestein proposal went in this respect thus considerably further than the case-law of the ECJ.

Art. 16 of the Bolkestein proposal contained the country of origin principle with a direct reference to the requirements governing contract and providers' liability. It appeared therefore that the contractual and non-contractual liability of the service provider had to be established according to the laws of the home Member State. One may doubt whether it was really the intention of the Commission to lay down a choice of law rule.[68] The consequences were at least not well thought through. In so far as one can deduce that the country of origin principle would also govern the material content of the applicable law, instead of the formal requirements for concluding a contract, it was severely criticised. The single applicability of the laws of the country of origin was not considered to be very promising for success. A country of origin conflict of laws rule would have contradicted many PIL instruments adopted on the Union level. Instead it was argued that contract law should as a whole be exempted from the scope of application of the services directive.[69] However, the country of origin principle as a whole was severely criticised and came under pressure.[70] Fears of the 'Polish plumber' led many worried citizens take to the streets in Brussels. Subsequently, the country of origin principle was dropped and replaced by the principle of mutual recognition. The Services Directive (2006/123) exempts in art. 3 (2) 'rules of private international law, in particular rules governing the law applicable to contractual and non

[67] Drijber, B., "The country of origin principle", Hearing before the Committee Internal Market and Consumer Protection on the Proposed Directive on Services in the Internal Market, 11 November 2004, http://www.europarl.europa.eu/hearings/20041111/imco/contributions_en.htm, as of 15 March 2011; De Witte, B., "Setting the Scene: How did Services get into *Bolkestein* and Why?", EUI Working Paper Law, no. 20, 2007.

[68] De Schutter, O., and S. Franq, "La proposition de directive relative aux services dans le marché intérieur: reconnaissance mutuelle et conflits de lois dans l'Europe élargie", *Cahiers de droit Européen*, 2005, pp. 603–660 (640).

[69] Basedow, J., "Dienstleistungsrichtlinie, Herkunftslandprinzip und Internationales Privatrecht", *Europäisches Zeitschrift für Wirtschaftsrecht*, Vol. 15, 2004, pp. 423–424. Mankowski, P., "Wieder ein Herkunftslandprinzip für Dienstleistungen im Binnenmarkt", *IPRax*, Vol. 24, No. 5, 2004, pp. 385–395.

[70] The sense and non-sense of the criticisms is discussed by: Pelkmans, J., "Deepening Services Market Integration: A critical assessment", *Romanian Journal of European Affairs*, Vol. 7, No. 4, 2007; Davies, G., "Services, Citizenship and the Country of Origin Principle", Mitchell Working Paper Series, no. 2, 2007.

contractual obligations', from its scope. The principle of mutual recognition is embodied in art. 16. The article prohibits Member States from making access to or the exercise of a service activity in their territory subject to compliance with any requirements which do not respect the principles enumerated in that article.[71] Art. 17 (15) provides that the prohibition does not apply to 'provisions regarding contractual and non-contractual obligations, including the form of contracts, determined pursuant to the rules of private international law'.

Whereas it might be debatable whether rules of private law are caught by the country of origin principle, the Services Directive indicates quite clearly that rules regarding contractual and non-contractual obligations are normally not caught by the principle of mutual recognition. The fierce opposition in the streets of Brussels towards the adoption of the country of origin principle indicates that one must be reluctant in giving an expansive scope to the case-law of the ECJ. The country of origin principle does not appear to have much relevance in the sphere of PIL.[72] As will be argued below, good reasons exist for differentiating between public and private law rules.

6.3 *Separating 'Public' from 'Private'*

Mutual recognition concerns public law rules; or, since the divide between public and private in Union law is fading more and more,[73] rules concerning administrative authorisations, prudential supervision

[71] The enumeration resembles in very broad lines the case-law of the ECJ, although the list of accepted mandatory requirements is defined more narrowly. See: Kalypso, N., and S. Schmidt, "Mutual recognition 'on trial': the long road to services liberalization", *Journal of European Public Policy*, Vol. 14, No. 5, 2007, pp. 717–734; Hatzopoulos, V., "Que reste-t-il de la directive sur les services?", *Cahiers de droit Européen*, 2007, pp. 299–358.

[72] In the same sense: Wilderspin and Lewis, *supra* note 61, pp. 23 ; De Baere, G., "'Is this a Conflict Rule which I see Before Me?' Looking for a Hidden Conflict Rule in the Principle of Origin as Implemented in Primary European Union law and in the 'Directive on Electronic Commerce'", *Maastricht Journal of Comparative Law*, Vol. 11, No. 3, 2004, pp. 287–319.

[73] Kennedy, D., "The Stages of Decline of the Public/Private Distinction", *University of Pennsylvania Law Review*, 1982, pp. 1349–1357; Loughlin, M., *The idea of public law*, Oxford University Press, Oxford, 2004; Wyatt, D., "Horizontal Effect of Fundamental Freedoms and the Right to Equality after Viking and Mangold, and the Implications for Union Competence", Oxford Legal Studies Research Paper No. 20/2008.

or product quality.[74] It has already been observed that Union law is in principle not interested in the origin or national classification of a rule. Rather the ECJ establishes the restrictive effects of a rule on the internal market. So, why would Union law care about the public/private distinction, especially since there is on the continent no common consensus about what is public and what is private and since, moreover, the distinction as such does not have much relevance in common law?[75] The meaning of the public/private divide should be interpreted in the light of the original objective of the Union: the creation of an internal market by the elimination of artificially created obstacles to trade. Union law thus, with the exception of competition laws, principally did not address horizontal relations but were addressed to Member States. It is beyond doubt that the Union lacked, and still lacks, a general competence in private law. Mutual recognition was developed in this framework. Starting with *Defrenne II*,[76] where the ECJ held that the non-discrimination principle embodied in art. 141 EC also applied in a contract between two private parties, the influence of Union law in private law was increasingly acknowledged. It has already been observed that the ECJ gradually began to apply the fundamental freedoms to private relationships. Regulations can also be directly applied between two individuals.[77]

Indeed the public/private distinction is of itself of little value, but its underlying rationale helps to explain why rules concerning administrative authorisations, prudential supervision or product quality should be approached differently from rules exclusively interfering with private relations. In general one has to be reluctant in the application of the fundamental freedoms to private law. The application of fundamental freedoms in the private sphere does not confer a privilege against the state upon a foreign service provider allowing for more consumer choice in host Member State, but changes the rights and obligations between the parties. Moreover in the area where harmonised conflict of laws rules are applicable, the traditional renvoi

---

[74] Muir Watt, H., "The Conflict of Laws as a Regulatory Tool", F. Cafaggi (ed.), *The Institutional Framework of European Private Law Volume II*, Oxford University Press, Oxford, 2006, pp. 107–148 (110).

[75] Heidemann, M., "Private Law in Europe: The Public/Private Dichotomy Revisited", *European Business Law Review*, Vol. 20, 2009, pp. 119–139.

[76] Case 43/75 *Defrenne II* [1975] ECR 455.

[77] Case 93/71 *Leonesio v Italian Ministry of Agriculture* [1972] ECR 293; case 39/72 *Commission v Italy* [1973] ECR 101.

argument arises. If Union law contained a rule leading to the applicability of the laws of the country of origin, the law of the host Member State would often still be applicable since the laws of the home Member State would lead in consumer contracts to the application of the laws of the host Member State. A Dutch service provider that targets the Belgian market could then not complain about the application of Belgian consumer protection law, since it would be the laws of the home Member State that lead to the application of Belgian law.

6.3.1 *Is Mutual Recognition Appropriate in Contract Law?*

In contract law, an even stronger argument can be made against the application of the fundamental freedoms. Public laws are by definition mandatory and their application can therefore not be evaded by private parties. Rules in contract law, even when they are mandatory, can be avoided by parties to an international contract. In *Ahlstom Atlantique* the ECJ held that rules whose application can be avoided by the parties by a simple choice of law are not able to constitute a restriction on the internal market.[78] Artificially created obstacles to trade created by 'public laws' cannot be effectively struck down by private parties, which creates the need for an instrument such as mutual recognition, but this does not apply to large parts of private law, where private autonomy is able to avoid the application of restrictive laws.[79] Moreover, there is no restrictive effect of a combined application of multiple laws since parties can identify a single applicable law. Mutual recognition can therefore not fulfil the same role with respect to private laws as it does to public laws.

6.3.2 *Mutual Recognition versus Vested Rights*

But has the Court not resorted in private law to mutual recognition? The private law restrictions that the Court has accepted on the fundamental freedoms and even European Citizenship underlie a different rationale. What was at stake was not the application of national private law in the strict sense, but rather non-recognition of the choice made between the legal systems of the Member States. The obligation

---

[78] Case C-339/89 *Ahlstom Atlantique* [1991] ECR 107, par. 29.

[79] Basedow, J., "Der kollisionsrechtliche Gehalt der Produktfreiheiten im europäischen Binnenmarkt: *favor offerentis*", *RabelsZ*, Vol. 59, 1995, pp. 1–55 (12); but critical: Fallon/Meeusen *supra* note 57, pp. 55–57.

to recognise fulfils a different function than mutual recognition. This hypothesis will be tested in the area of company law and in surname law before it will be explained why it is not suitable for even a reformulated principle of mutual recognition to be applied to contract law.

6.4 *Company Law*

Art. 54 in conjunction with art. 49 TFEU confers the freedom of establishment upon companies or firms that are formed in accordance with the law of a Member State and have their registered office, central administration or principal place of business within the Union. Two connecting factors are predominantly used by the Member States.[80] The incorporation theory declares the *lex societas* (law applicable to the company) to be the law of the place where company is registered, whereas the real seat doctrine declares as *lex societas* the law of the place applicable where the company has its main centre of business. Article 54 does not provide for a clear-cut right of transfer,[81] although the precise scope of the provision has been subject of controversy. In particular the question whether the ECJ favoured one of the connecting factors has been subject of debate.

In *Daily Mail* a company wished to move its headquarters from the United Kingdom to the Netherlands, but this was opposed by the UK authorities.[82] The Court, with a view to the widely differing connecting factors between the Member States, held that Union law as it stood did not confer a right upon Daily Mail, incorporated under the legislation of England and having its registered office there to transfer its central management and control to the Netherlands.

In *Centros* the Court held the refusal to register a branch of companies duly formed under the law of another Member State to be a restriction on the freedom of establishment.[83] The host Member State (Denmark) could not impose upon a company which had been duly formed in England its own substantive company law. Although Denmark was allowed to impose safeguards to avoid evasion of its

---

[80] See: Rammeloo, S., "Corporations in Private International Law: A European Perspective", Oxford University Press, Oxford, 2001.

[81] A proposal for the 14th Company Law Directive on the transfer of undertakings is in the pipeline. See: Draft Report with recommendations to the Commission on cross-borders transfers of company seats (2008/2196(INI)).

[82] Case 81/87 *Daily Mail v. UK* [1988] ECR 5483.

[83] Case C-212/97 *Centros* [1999] ECR I-1459, para. 20 and 21.

laws, the refusal did not pass the suitability test. The registration of the branch of a company that carried out business in the UK would have equally deprived Danish creditors of their protection.[84]

In *Überseering*, a company was denied legal standing as a plaintiff in a legal proceeding because after a transfer of ownership it had moved its actual centre of business from the Netherlands to Germany.[85] The shift of actual centre of business without any change in legal personality was possible under Dutch PIL, but not under German. The Court held that a company duly set up under the legislation of one Member State can 'transfer its registered office or its actual centre of administration to another Member State without losing its legal personality under the law of the Member State of incorporation, and, in certain circumstances, the rules relating to that transfer, are determined by the national law in accordance with which the company was incorporated'.[86]

In *Inspire Art* the Netherlands sought to impose additional registration requirements upon pseudo foreign companies, including a minimum capital requirement.[87] The additional requirements failed the proportionality test: potential creditors were already sufficiently warned by the fact that Inspire Art held itself out as a company governed by the law of England and not by the law of the Netherlands.[88] The Court favoured self-help: potential creditors in the Netherlands should apparently know that the minimum capital requirements in England are significantly more lenient than in the Netherlands and could therefore take appropriate securities to ascertain the fulfilment of Inspire Art's obligations.

In its judgments the ECJ did not seem to attach much importance to the distinction between primary and secondary establishment, nor to the intention of the undertaking to evade stricter standards in the host Member State. The essence of the internal market is that individuals can take advantages from differences between national legislations. The cases led academic commentators to predict regulatory competition, or a race to the bottom whereby Member States would try to attract as many companies as possible by offering the most lenient

---

[84] *Centros supra* note 82, par. 35.
[85] Case C-208/00 *Überseering* [2002] ECR I-9919.
[86] Case C-216-06 *Cartesio* [2008] ECR I-9641 par. 107.
[87] Case C-167/01 *Inspire Art* [2003] ECR I-10155.
[88] *Inspire Art, supra* note 87, par. 135.

standards.[89] It is true that after the judgments Member States started revising their company and private international laws. For example, in the Netherlands the European developments were specifically named as reason for the proposal to make the limited liability company (BV) more internationally competitive by abolishing the minimum capital requirement and introducing in general more flexibility.[90]

6.4.1 *Real Seat Doctrine under Pressure?*

The decisions in *Centros*, *Überseering*, and *Inspire Art* made many question whether *Daily Mail* was still standing. Did the ECJ, despite its vow to respect the plurality of connecting factors, not give a lethal blow to the real seat doctrine or at least gave preference to the incorporation theory?[91] The Austrian *Oberste Gerichtshof* (Supreme Court, OGH) answered that question apparently in the affirmative. The OGH held, without making a reference to the ECJ, the application of the real seat doctrine to companies established in other Member States to be

---

[89] On the debate: Siems, M., "Convergence, competition, Centros and Conflicts of Law: European Company Law in the 21st Century", *European Law Review*, Vol. 27, 2002, pp. 47–59; Spindler, G., and O. Berner, "Inspire Art - Der europäische Wettbewerb um das Gesellschaftsrecht ist endgültig eröffnet", *Recht der internationalen Wirtschaft*, Vol. 49, 2003, pp. 949–957; Kirchner, C., R. Painter and W. Kaal, "Regulatory Competition in EU Corporate Law After Inspire Art: Unbundling Delaware's Product for Europe", University of Illinois Law & Economics Research Paper no. LE04-001, 2004; Kieninger, E., "The Legal Framework of Regulatory Competition Based on Company Mobility: EU and US Compared", *German Law Journal*, Vol. 6, No. 4, 2005, pp. 741–770; McCahery, J., "Harmonisation in European Company Law: The Political Economy of Economic Integration", D. Curtin *et al* (eds.), *European Integration and Law*, Intersentia, Antwerpen, 2006, pp. 155–194.

[90] Memorie van Toelichting, Wijziging van Boek 2 van het Burgerlijk Wetboek in verband met de aanpassing van de regeling voor besloten vennootschappen met beperkte aansprakelijkheid (Wet vereenvoudiging en flexibilisering bv-recht), Tweede Kamer der Staten Generaal 2006-2007, 31 058, no. 3. At the time of writing, the bill was still pending in the Tweede Kamer (House of Commons).

[91] Halhuber, H., "Das ende der Sitztheorie als Kompetenztheorie- Das Urteil des Europäischen Gerichtshofs in der Rechtssache C- 208-00 (Überseering)", *Zeitschrift für Europäisches Privatrecht*, Vol. 8, No. 2, 2003, pp. 418–438; Rammeloo, S., "Vrij verkeer van rechtspersonen in Europa na HvJ EG *Überseering*. Ipr-zetelleeercontroverse beslecht?", *Nederlands Internationaal Privaatrecht*, 2003, pp. 134–144; Rammeloo, S., "Vrij verkeer van rechtspersonen in Europa na HvJ EG *Inspire Art*: zetelleercontroverse beslecht!", *Nederlands Internationaal Privaatrecht*, 2004, pp. 283–29; Rammeloo, S., "Freedom of Establishment for Legal Persons in Europe Accomplished", *Maastricht Journal of European and Comparative Law*, Vol. 11, No. 4, 2004, pp. 398–413. For an overview: Muir-Watt, H., "Case Note to *Inspire Art*", *Revue Critique de Droit International Privé*, Vol. 93, No. 1, 2004, pp. 151–184.

incompatible with the freedom of establishment.[92] There seemed to be a broad consensus that the rationale of the ECJ with regard to host Member State also affected the position of the Member State of origin. The distinction made by the Court between restrictions imposed by the host Member State and the Member State of origin was found to be unconvincing.[93] It even led an AG to conclude that the distinction was artificial and found no support in the wording of the judgments.[94] Although the Court reaffirmed in *Überseering* and *Inspire Art* its distinction between the relation of the company with the Member State of incorporation and the Member State of registration, it could not count on academic approval. To quote a leading textbook on EU law:

> Although the ECJ distinguished the *Daily Mail* case on its facts (where the restriction on the company's right to retain legal personality in the event of a transfer of registered office or centre of administration was imposed by the Member State of incorporation), the reality is that the reasoning in *Überseering* clearly moves away from the underlying broad rationale in *Daily Mail.*[95]

6.4.2 *Cartesio*

However, the ECJ felt apparently unconvinced by the criticism.[96] In *Cartesio* a company wished to transfer its real seat from Hungary to Italy whilst retaining its incorporation in Hungary and thus without changing the *lex societas*.[97] Hungary provided in such cases for the loss of Hungarian legal personality and required the prior winding up and

---

[92] OGH, Beschluss v. July 15, 1999 – 6 Ob 123/99 b, 'Der Begriff "Ansässigkeit" setze eine enge wirtschftliche Verbindung mit der Gemeinschaft voraus, es müsse somit Hauptverwaltung oder Hauptniederlassung in einem Mitgliedstaat, nicht notwendig aber im Gründungsstaat, begründet sein.' see: Heidinger, M., "Austria: Company Law – Branch Office", *Journal of International Banking Law*, Vol. 15, No. 2, 2000, pp. 8. More correct is the decision of the German BGH, Bundesgerichtshof 13 March 2003 (BGHZ 154/185): 'Diese Anknüpfungsregel (Sitztheorie) werde durch die im EG-Vertrag geregelte Niederlassungsfreiheit nicht verdrängt.'

[93] Ringe, W., "No freedom of migration for European Companies?" *European Business Law Review*, Vol. 16, 2005, pp. 621–642.

[94] AG Colomer in *Uberseering, supra* note 85, par. 37

[95] Craig, P., and G. de Burca, *EU Law: Text, Cases and Materials*, Oxford University Press, Oxford, Fourth Edition, 2007, pp. 810.

[96] AG Maduro joined AG Colomer in his critique. Maduro found the distinction between laws that restrict the freedom of establishment in the Member State of origin and the host Member State unconvincing. AG Maduro in *Cartesio supra* note 86, par. 28.

[97] *Cartesio, supra* note 86.

liquidation of the company.[98] The power to define the connecting factor would, for countries adhering to the incorporation theory, be jeopardised if other Member States could freely refuse to give effect to incorporation in that Member State. Leaving Member States the power to define the connecting factor requires balancing the powers of for example the United Kingdom and Germany. In order to leave the United Kingdom with the power to define its connecting factor, Germany has to exercise some restraint. Individuals can however never invoke more rights than they would have under UK law. The Court pointed out that while in *Überseering* Dutch law (incorporation theory) provided for a right for the company to transfer its actual centre of business abroad, Hungarian law did not.

> Consequently, in accordance with Article 48 EC, in the absence of a uniform Union law definition of the companies which may enjoy the right of establishment on the basis of a single connecting factor determining the national law applicable to a company, the question whether Article 43 EC applies to a company which seeks to rely on the fundamental freedom enshrined in that article – like the question whether a natural person is a national of a Member State, hence entitled to enjoy that freedom – is a preliminary matter which, as Union law now stands, can only be resolved by the applicable national law. In consequence, the question whether the company is faced with a restriction on the freedom of establishment, within the meaning of Article 43 EC, can arise only if it has been established, in the light of the conditions laid down in Article 48 EC, that the company actually has a right to that freedom.[99]

So the power of a Member State to define the connecting factor which determines whether a company is regarded as incorporated under its laws includes the power to refuse a company governed by its law to retain that status if it desires to re-establish in another Member State by moving its real seat. Did the ECJ then fully confirm *Daily Mail*? Not really, in an *obiter dictum* the Court continued that the power to define the connecting factor did not place the rules on transfer of undertakings outside the scope of Union law. Those rules came under

[98] There is confusion as to whether Hungary adheres to the real seat or incorporation doctrine. See: Korom, V., and P. Metzinger, "Freedom of Establishment for Companies: The European Court of Justice Confirms and Refines its Daily Mail Decision in the Cartesio Case C-210/06", *European Company and Financial Law Review*, Vol. 6, No. 1, 2009, pp. 125–161 (141-144). For the present purposes it is sufficient that Hungary did not foresee in the transfer of real seat without changing legal personality.

[99] *Cartesio*, par. 109.

the scrutiny of the freedom of establishment to the extent that the law of the Member State of origin allows for a transfer. Contrary to *Daily Mail* the Court held that the winding-up or liquidation of the company prior to a transfer to another Member State would violate the freedom of establishment if it could not be justified by an overriding public interest.[100]

Much can be said about the judgment.[101] The impossibility under the law of the Member State of incorporation to re-establish an undertaking in another Member States can be easily circumvented by performing a so-called 'vertical merger in reverse'.[102] If Hungarian law had not foreseen the possibility of re-incorporating in Italy, Cartesio could simply have established an empty shell in Italy and subsequently merged the two legal entities, then having the Hungarian company transfer all of it assets and be completely absorbed by the Italian company. The ECJ held in *Sevic Systems* that the commercial registrar of the Member State of the first undertaking (empty shell) is obliged to register a cross-border merger by dissolution without liquidation of one company and transfer of the whole of its assets to another company if such registration is possible when both companies are established within the Member State involved.[103] Cartesio would of course then have to accept that the *lex societas* of the new legal entity would fall to be determined by Italian law, and would presumably be Italian.

Cartesio could not invoke a right against Hungary since Hungary already recognised all privileges resulting from incorporation under Hungarian law.[104] Has the ECJ by refining, but in the main confirming *Daily Mail* implicitly overturned *Centros*? Is regulatory competition

[100] *Cartesio*, par. 112–113.

[101] Behrens, P., "Cartesio bestätigt, aber korrigiert Daily Mail", *Europäische Zeitschrift für Wirtschaftsrecht*, Vol. 20, No. 3, 2009, pp. 81–83; Pießkalla, M., "EuGH: Verhinderbare Gesellschaftssitzverlegung in einen anderen Mitgliedstaat als den Gründungsmitgliedstaat – Cartesio", *Europäische Zeitschrift für Wirtschaftsrecht*, Vol. 20, No. 3, 2009, pp. 75–83; Gerner-Beuerle, C., and M. Schillig, "The Mysteries of Freedom of Establishment after Cartesio", available at SSRN: http://ssrn.com/abstract=1340964 as of 15 March 2011; Korom/ Metzinger *supra* note 98.

[102] Klinke, U., "European Company Law and the ECJ: The Court's judgments in the years 2001–2004", *European Company and Financial Law Review*, 2005, pp. 275–304.

[103] It is assumed that the registration of a vertical merger without liquidation of one of the parties is possible under Italian law.

[104] There might conceivably be situations where a right against the home Member State can be invoked. For example when a tax scheme allows for the offsetting of losses incurred by subsidiaries for the benefit of the parent company, this right would also apply to subsidiaries set up and operating in other Member States. The home Member State of the parent is then bound to recognise the capacity of the subsidiary awarded by

now dead? The wide interpretation of *Centros* and *Überseering* as the end of the real seat doctrine can certainly no longer be maintained, but that interpretation was incorrect anyway. What the Court did in those cases was oblige the host Member State to recognise a company duly set up under the laws of another Member State. *Cartesio* fits in this approach. Cartesio could not invoke any additional right against Hungary, since Hungary already recognised all rights resulting from incorporation under Hungarian law.

6.5 *Surname Law*

The approach of the Court can also be seen in surname law. Comparing company and family law might seem a bit unusual, but one must realise that, for the purposes of the freedom of establishment, the Treaty draws a parallel between legal and natural persons. Family law is, just like company law, an area where the Union has no direct competence and where between Member States discrepancies in substantive law and connecting factors exist.

In *Konstantinidis* the transliteration of the name of a self-employed masseur into the Roman alphabet on his marriage certificate diverged from the transliteration in his Greek passport.[105] The ECJ held that the national rules on transliteration are incompatible with Union law if it causes a Greek national such a degree of inconvenience that it infringes his right of establishment. This would be case if the divergence in transliteration modifies the pronunciation and would create the risk that potential clients may confuse him with other persons. In other words: Konstantinidis had the right to use the name duly acquired under Greek law also in Germany.

In *Garcia Avello*, two children were born in Belgium out of a marriage between a Belgian and a Spanish national.[106] The question arose whether a change of surname under Spanish law had to be recognised in Belgium. Although the children were Belgian nationals having lived their whole live in Belgium, the ECJ used European Citizenship to

---

the home Member State of the subsidiary. Case C-446/03 *Marks & Spencer plc v HM's Inspector of Taxes* [2005] ECR I-10837.

[105] Case C-168/91 *Konstantinidis v Stadt Altensteig* [1993] ECR 1-1191.

[106] Case C-148/02 *Garcia Avello* ECR [2003], I-11613.

bring the situation into the scope of Union law.[107] The children were also Spanish nationals living in Belgium and could therefore not be discriminated against on the ground of nationality. Non-discrimination requires that equal situations should be treated equally and unequal situations unequal. Dual citizens are in a different situation compared to Belgians who only possess one nationality, since dual citizens can bear different surnames under different laws. Treating a request for the change of surname of a dual citizen equal to that of a 'single citizen' would therefore amount to unequal treatment.[108] Art. 12 in conjunction with art. 17 EC (now: resp. art. 18 and 20 TFEU) therefore prevented a Member State from refusing a change of surname if the requested surname would be in accordance with the law of a Member State whose nationality the applicant also possessed.

In *Grunkin-Paul*, a child was born out of a marriage between two German nationals living in Denmark.[109] Both the parents and the child possessed German nationality. 'Grunkin-Paul', an accumulation of the surname of both parents, was mentioned as surname on the Danish birth certificate of the child. Such an accumulation was possible under Danish law, but not under German law. Under Danish PIL, the law applicable to the determination of a surname is the law of the place of habitual residence, while German PIL uses nationality as the connecting factor. When the marriage broke down, the father moved to Germany and sought to register the child in Germany. Registration of the surname was refused since under German PIL the surname had to be determined according to German law, which required the parents to choose between the surname of the father and mother. A discrimination such as in *Garcia Avello* could not occur since the child only possessed German nationality and was treated equally compared to all other German nationals. The Court concluded however that a difference in surname could give rise to such an inconvenience (different surnames on diplomas, proof of identity) as to create a disadvantage merely because the child exercised its freedom to move and to reside in another Member State. The refusal therefore constituted a restriction

---

[107] Ballarino, T., and B. Ubertazzi, "On Avello and Other Judgments, A New Point of Departure in the Conflict of Laws?", *Yearbook of Private International Law*, Vol. 6, 2004, pp. 85–128. (106-111)

[108] Critical : Lagarde, P., Note to Garcia Avello, in: *Revue Critique de Droit International Privé*, Vol. 93, No. 1, 2004, pp. 184–202.

[109] Case C-353/06 *Grunkin Paul* [2008] ECR I-7639.

on European Citizenship that could not be justified by any overriding public interest.

Whereas the restriction in *Garcia Avello* originated in the joint reading of the general principle of non-discrimination on the grounds of nationality and European Citizenship, the Court based its judgment in *Grunkin Paul* on citizenship alone. The Court thus moved away from the discrimination test it established in *Garcia Avello* towards a prohibition of restriction approach and tested whether the difference in surname could create such a degree of inconvenience that it would become more difficult for the individual concerned to exercise his rights as a citizen of the Union to move and reside freely throughout the territory of the Member States. This shift by the Court fits into the gradually increasing attention given by the Union to the free movement of citizens other than from economic transactions.[110]

6.5.1 *The Recognition of Rights Acquired under the Laws of another Member State*

The obligation to recognise allows Member States to maintain their connecting factor and perhaps more importantly, does not require any change of the substantive law. National cultural identities can be preserved. Since the obligation to recognise only impacts the existing legal norms in a very limited way and operates independently from the connecting factors of the host Member State, it is possible to significantly simplify current legal problems.[111] The duty to recognise does not replace the normal conflict of laws system, but is aimed at the avoidance of 'limping relationships'; relationships that are lawful in one Member State but not in others.[112] Such situations are incompatible with the idea of a common European justice area. Legal fiction should be brought back in line with factual reality. The duty to recognise does require that purely domestic situations are treated differently from

[110] Fallon, M., "Les conflits de lois et de juridictions dans un espace économique intégré. L'expérience de la Communauté européenne", *Recueil des Cours*, Vol. 253, 1995, pp. 13–281 ; Meeusen, J., "Instrumentalisation of Private International Law in the European Union: Towards a European Conflicts Revolution?", *European Journal of Migration and Law*, Vol. 9, 2007, pp. 287–305.

[111] Coester-Waltjen, D., "Das Anerkunningsprinzip im Dornröschenschlaf?", H. Mansel *et al* (eds.), *Festschrift für Erik Jayme Band I*, Sellier, München, 2004, pp. 121–129 (123).

[112] Baratta, R., "Problematic elements of an implicit rule providing for mutual recognition of personal and family status in the EC", *IPRax*, Vol. 37, 2007, pp. 4–11 (5).

situations involving a link with another Member State. A different treatment of international situations is not anything substantially new for European PIL, but it narrows the question down. As AG Sharpston observed in her opinion in *Grunkin Paul*:

> I would stress therefore that my approach would not require any major change to Germany's substantive or choice of law rules in the field of names, but would simply require them to allow greater scope for recognising a prior choice of name validly made in accordance with the laws of another Member State. To that extent, it involves no more than an application of the principle of mutual recognition which underpins so much of Union law, not only in the economic sphere but also in civil matters.[113]

AG Jacobs, on the other hand, incorporated a fundamental rights perspective into his opinion in *Konstantinidis*.[114] European citizens could by relying on their status as such invoke a core of rights (*civis europeus sum*), in particular the observance of fundamental rights.[115] Such a political rights approach pushes back the role of PIL. From the outset it should be observed that citizenship and fundamental rights are two different things. Although both are claimed by individuals against the state, the latter are universal while the aim of the former is to make a distinction between the have and the have-nots. By reason of belonging to a certain political Union, the citizen can claim certain rights that cannot be exercised by individuals not belonging to that political Union.[116] Nevertheless, AG Jacobs held in *Konstantinidis* that the transliteration could infringe Konstantinidis' fundamental rights, in particular his right to private life as laid down in art. 8 of the European Convention on Human Rights. The obligation to bear different surnames under the law of different Member States would be incompatible with private life, and therefore the status and rights of a European Citizen, since a name forms an intrinsic part of a person's

[113] AG Sharpston, *Grunkin Paul, supra* note 109, par. 91.

[114] A fundamental rights perspective for the unilateral recognition of family relationships was also defended by Muir Watt. The recognition of the personal status is in her opinion is not dependent upon the possession of European Citizenship and may therefore have a more universal application. Muir Watt, H., Family Law: European Federalism and the "New Unilateralism", *Tulane Law Review*, Vol. 82, 2008, pp. 1983–1999.

[115] AG Jacobs, *Konstantinidis, supra* note 105, 46.

[116] Chalmers *et al*, D., *European Union Law*, Cambridge University Press, Cambridge, 2006, pp. 561–603.

identity.[117] Obviously, one cannot be required to maintain two different identities. A similar line can be discovered in his opinions in *Standesamt Niebüll*[118] and *Garcia Avello.*[119] The fundamental rights perspective does not come back in the decisions of the Court, which adopted a classical internal market rationale. One must be careful with such an approach since it could enormously expand the scrutiny of the ECJ over national measures.

Despite the hopeful words of AG Jacobs' '*civis europeus sum*'[120] European Citizenship is not in itself an autonomous generator of rights.[121] Legal scholars must be careful not to again take an over expansive interpretation of ECJ case-law, as they did in company law. In a Union law context, European Citizenship might be used to broaden the interpretation of pre-existing rights. European Citizenship becomes instrumental for bringing a situation within the scope of Union law, triggering the obligation to recognise duly acquired rights. European Citizenship then does not create any new rights, but instead ensures

---

117 The ECHR seems to interpret art. 8 differently: European Court of Human Rights, *Kuharec v Latvia* (2004) and European Court of Human Rights, *Mentzen v Latvia* (2004).

118 Case C-94/04 *Standesamt Niebüll* (Grunkin Paul I) [2006] ECR I-3561. The case was held inadmissible on procedural grounds but the same facts reappeared in 'Grunkin Paul'.

119 Meeusen, *supra* note 110, 295-297.

120 Further discussion and references: Binder, D., "The European Court of Justice and the Protection of Fundamental Rights in the European Union: New Developments and Future Possibilities in Expanding Fundamental Rights Review to Member State Action", Jean Monnet Working Paper 95/9504, 1995; see also: Cherednychenko, O., *Fundamental Rights, Contract Law and the Protection of the Weaker Party*, Molengraaff Instituut voor Privaatrecht, Utrecht, 2007, pp. 217–218.

121 European Citizenship has had a large impact on in social security matters and residency rights whereby the Court held that European Citizens lawfully resident on the territory of another Member State could not be discriminated against on the grounds of nationality. The rights are however limited to those conferred by the Treaties, although the introduction of European Citizenship has expanded the interpretation of those rights. See: Dougan, M., and E. Spaventa, "Educating Rudy and the (non-) English Patient: A double-bill on residency rights under Article 18 EC", *European Law Review*, Vol. 28, 2003, pp. 699–712.; Reich, N., "Union Citizenship—Metaphor or Source of Rights?", *European Law Journal*, Vol. 7, No. 1, 2001, pp. 4–23; Reich, N., and S. Harbacevica, "Citizenship and Family on Trial: a Fairly Optimistic Overview of Recent Court Practice with Regard to Free Movement of Persons", *Common Market Law Review*, Vol. 40, 2003, pp. 615–638; Wollenschläger, F., "Grundfreiheiten ohne Markt Die Herausbildung der Unionsbürgerschaft im unionsrechtlichen Freizügigkeitsregime", Mohr Siebeck, Tübingen, 2006. According to Marzo, the effect of European Citizenship goes further than the enlargement of pre-existing rights: Marzo, C., La *dimension sociale de la citoyenneté européenne*, EUI Thesis, 2009.

that rights obtained under Union law shall be sustained in Member States, but as well as rights duly created in other Member States. It is true that the Court has gradually moved away from establishing an economic link. One should be careful not to misinterpret this shift as replacing the red line of creating an internal market that runs through ECJ case-law with a political rights approach centred on the individual. European Citizenship is brought more in line with the economic freedoms where the convergence of the fundamental freedoms has led to an increasing importance of the prohibition of restriction approach. The case-law on European Citizenship should instead be seen as widening the red line so as to include, next to the creation of the internal market, the creation of a common justice area. The expansion of the Court's *Leitmotiv* also reappeared in the attribution of competences in the Lisbon Treaty; art. 81 TFEU would do away with the internal market criterion.[122]

The surname cases demonstrate that it is difficult to apply mutual recognition to private law cases. In *Garcia Avello* it does not seem possible to establish a country of origin. Could it not be argued that the Spanish embassy was bound to refuse the registration of the surname 'Garcia Weber' since a different surname had already been attributed to the child in Belgium? The case is less problematic from the point of view of theory based on the recognition of rights duly acquired in another Member State. In both Member States a right to a surname had been duly acquired under the same connecting factor (nationality), it is within the private autonomy of an individual to choose whether he desires to enforce a right or not.

Grunkin Paul also demonstrates the difficulty of perceiving the duty to recognise as a new form of mutual recognition combined with a country of origin approach. The parents exercised a fundamental freedom and, furthermore, the child although born on the territory of Denmark, only acquired German nationality; should Germany then not be classified as the country of origin? Rather, the Court resorted to a party autonomy orientated approach: a Member State is bound to respect a choice of law made by the parties. If the situation had been the reverse; namely that German surname law would have been more

---

[122] De Groot, G., and J. Kuipers, "The New Provisions on Private International Law in the Treaty of Lisbon", *Maastricht Journal of European and Comparative Law*, Vol. 15, 1, 2008, pp. 109–114 (111-112). Of course, the EU remains restricted by its general objectives.

liberal than Danish surname law, Denmark would have to respect German law had the parties wished to invoke their right under German substantive law for the determination of the surname on the Danish birth certificate.

6.6 *Vested Rights*

A company duly set up under the law of one Member State shall be recognised in other Member States. A name duly acquired in one Member States shall be recognised in other Member States. The language of the Court might sound familiar to the older generation common lawyers. It is the revival of a PIL doctrine declared dead many years ago. It was the Frisian scholar Ulrik Huber (1636–1694) who developed the idea that comity (fellowship of nations)[123] and the general pressure of international commerce required that acts duly performed in one jurisdiction shall be sustained in other jurisdictions. This idea became very influential in common law jurisdictions, in the form of the vested rights doctrine.[124] There has, however, never been a universal conception of this doctrine.[125] In England the theory was most notably promulgated by Dicey who presumed that in English courts the applicable law was always English, but that English law would enforce rights duly acquired under foreign law unless this would violate English public policy.[126] In the United States, Beale favoured the universal recognition of rights created by the appropriate law.[127] Unlike Dicey, Beale formulated a rule to determine the law that created those rights: the law of the place where the last legal act necessary for the completion of the right took place.[128] The vested rights theory was also

---

[123] Yntema, H., "The Comity Doctrine", E. von Caemmerer, A. Nikisch and K. Zweigert, (eds.), *Vom Deutschen zum Europäischen Recht, Festschrift für Hans Dölle*, Mohr Siebeck, Tübingen, 1963, pp. 65–72.

[124] North, P., and J. Fawcett, *Cheshire and North Private International Law*, Butterworths, London, Eleventh edition, 1987, pp. 21; Strikwerda, L., "Fries recht in Amerika. Over Ulrik Huber, Jospeh Story en internationale contracten", *Groninger Opmerkingen en Medelingen IV*, 1987, pp. 55.

[125] Maury, J., "Règles générales des conflits de lois", *Recueil des Cours*, Vol. 57, 1936, pp. 329.

[126] Dicey, A., "On Private International Law as a Branch of the Law of England", *Law Quarterly Review*, Vol. 6, 1890, pp. 1–21 and 113–137 (114-118).

[127] Beale, J., "Dicey's Conflict of Laws", *Harvard Law Review*, Vol. 10, 1896, pp. 168.

[128] Michaels, R., "EU Law as Private International Law? The Country-of-Origin Principle and Vested Rights Theory", *Journal of Private International Law*, Vol. 2, No. 2, 2006, pp. 195–242 (215).

influential in French academia.[129] For Pillet the enforcement of a vested right was not a conflict of laws; at stake was not the question of which jurisdiction was entitled to create it, but under which conditions a right had to be recognised in a jurisdiction different from which created it.[130] Pillet created, in addition to the acquired rights doctrine, a complete system for designating the applicable law.[131]

6.6.1 *Vested Rights versus Mutual Recognition*

The vested right doctrine has some striking similarities with the principle of mutual recognition.[132] It has already been observed that in essence the principle of mutual recognition is nothing more than the inability of the host Member State to apply its legislation to a situation when that situation is already governed by the laws of the home Member State.[133] Neither the principle of mutual recognition nor the vested rights doctrine determines on itself the applicable law.[134] The fact that Germany cannot apply its beer purity laws to French imports does not mean French law is applicable, but rather that Germany cannot apply its legislation to French beer when that legislation is more restrictive than French legislation. Vested rights can seem circular. The question that duly acquired rights have to be respected does not answer the question according to which law the rights have to be established. An additional concept that can determine the competent legal order(s)

---

[129] Muir Watt, H., "Quelques remarques sur la théorie anglo-américaine des droits acquis", *Revue Critique de droit international privé*, 1986, pp. 425–455.

[130] Pillet, A., *Traité pratique de droit international privé I*, Sirey, Paris, 1923.

[131] Michaels, *supra* note 128, pp. 216.

[132] Jayme, E., and C. Kohler, "Europäisches Kollisionsrecht 2001: Anerkennungsprinzip statt IPR?", *IPRax*, Vol. 21, No. 6, 2001, pp. 501–514; Israël, J., "Europees internationaal privaatrecht", *Nederlands Internationaal Privaatrecht*, Vol. 19, No. 2, 2001, pp. 135–149; Fallon/ Meeusen, *supra* note 57; Bogdan, M., Concise introduction to EU Private International Law, Europa Law Publishing, Groningen, 2006, 26-30. For the general influence of Union law upon PIL: Roth, W., "Der Einfluß des Europäischen Gemeinschaftsrechts auf das Internationale Privatrecht", *RabelsZ*, Vol. 55, 1991, pp. 623–673 ; Radicati di Brozolo, L., "L'influence sur les conflits de lois des principes de droit communautaire en matière de liberté de circulation", *Revue Critique de Droit International Privé*, Vol. 82, 1993, pp. 401–423.

[133] Commission Communication on Mutual Recognition, OJ C256/2 [2008]. Weiler, *supra* note 41; Steffenson, R., "The EU's Exportation of Mutual Recognition: A Case of Transatlantic Policy Transfer?", EUI Working Paper 2002/73.

[134] Israël, J., en K. Saarloos, "Europees Internationaal Privaat- en procesrecht", A. Hartkamp, C. Sieburg, L. Keus (eds.), *Serie Onderneming en Recht deel 42-II*, Deventer, Kluwer, 2007, pp. 629–698 (651).

is therefore necessary. Similarly, it is not within the scope of the principle of mutual recognition or vested rights to completely replace the otherwise applicable law. Regulatory gaps may therefore occur.[135] Finally, from a political legitimacy perspective it can be argued that neither doctrine attributes necessarily regulatory competence to the Member State with the largest regulatory interest. Was the regulatory interest of Germany to control the sale of spirits on its territory not larger than the regulatory interest of France to promote exports?[136] Did Denmark not have a larger regulatory interest in the registration of the Danish branch of an English company that factually carried out no business in the United Kingdom?

For Michaels, mutual recognition demonstrates a paradigm shift in PIL. The country of origin principle 'is a choice-of-law principle albeit not one according to classical conflict of laws but a new form of vested rights principle.'[137] Although it is beyond doubt that the vested rights doctrine is a PIL principle, one can doubt whether vested rights are really a new form of mutual recognition. Mutual recognition concerns rules of administrative authorisations, prudential supervision or product quality. On the other hand, vested rights are strongly centred around the individual. As observed in the literature, with regard to the recognition of acquired rights:

> L'individu acquiert une dimension autonome au plan transnational. Il résulte de cette consécration de l'autonomie que chaque situation ou rapport juridique n'est pas forcément rattaché à un seul ordre juridique mais rayonne et peut être appréhendé par plusieurs. Il en résulte également que l'hypothèse de l'autonomie participe à un besoin de réglementation d'un rapport par la collaboration des ordres juridiques concernés, sans porter, autant que possible, atteinte à la cohérence du rapport privé.[138]

Mutual recognition is about the avoidance of a double burden: a manufacturer should not be asked to comply with the rules of both the Member State of origin and the host Member State. These 'public' laws are perceived imposing duties, rather than creating rights. This is

[135] Michaels, *supra* note 128, 230.

[136] Case 120/78 *REWE-Zentral v Bundesmonopolverwaltung für Branntwein (Cassis de Dijon)* [1979] ECR 649.

[137] Michaels, R., "The New European Choice-of-Law Revolution", *Tulane Law Review*, Vol. 82, No. 5, 2008, pp. 1607–1644 (1628).

[138] Pamboukis, C., "La renaissance-métamorphose de la méthode de reconnaissance", *Revue Critique de Droit International Privé*, Vol. 97, No. 3, 2008, pp. 513–560 (527).

fundamentally different from 'private law' rules. Private law enables individuals to perform legal acts, to enter into legal relations, and subsequently to enforce the obtained rights. Private law thus ensures that individuals can create rights and obligations between each other. Legal subjects may benefit from the potential application of various sets of private law since this broadens the array of potential private law rights. On a European level, the impediment to free movement does not originate in the diversity of private law rights, but in the non-recognition of rights acquired under the private law system of a Member State by another Member State.

Vested rights are therefore more than the inability to apply the legislation of the host Member State to a situation already governed by the laws of the Member State of origin. Vested rights do not only require the host Member State to refrain from imposing its conditions to creation of the right, but also the duty to accommodate the foreign rights into its own legal system. For example if Überseering had gone bankrupt, it would not have been sufficient for the German authorities to establish that limited liability existed and subsequently to have treated the company as a GmbH (German private limited company).[139] Not only the creation but also the extent and conditions of the limited liability under Dutch law have to be incorporated into German law, even if the law applicable to the insolvency proceedings is German.[140]

6.6.2 *The Rebirth of Vested Rights*

Although the vested rights doctrine was declared dead many years ago, it may, within the European Union at least, be able to overcome the critique that led to its original decline. As von Savigny noted, it can only be ascertained if a right is duly acquired when one has identified the law applicable to the creation of that right.[141] Pillet developed a

---

[139] It is admitted that this does not follow explicitly from the case but in this respect an analogy can be drawn with the recognition of civil judgments. The ECJ held that the effects of the judgment had to be established according to the law of the jurisdiction where the decision was rendered and not by the jurisdiction recognising the decision. Case 145/86 *Hoffmann v Krieg* [1988] ECR 645, par. 22

[140] Art. 3 (1) of Regulation 1346/2000 confers jurisdiction in insolvency proceedings upon the courts of the Member State where the main centre of the debtors interest are situated, which is presumed to be the place of registration. A creditor would thus have to proof that although Überseering had its registered office in the Netherlands, the main centre of interest was situated in Germany. Art. 4 (1) declares the *lex fori* to be applicable to the insolvency proceedings.

[141] Von Savigny, F., *System des Heutige Römische Recht VIII Band*, 1849, pp. 132.

separate PIL system to determine the competent legal order. In the Union, the development of a new system to establish the law applicable to the creation of a right would not be necessary. It is true that the recognition of an existing right should separated from the applicable law, but the PIL systems of the Member States that determine the applicable law can be maintained. Subsequently, it may occur that different Member States declare themselves, or are declared, competent. It is then up to Union law to verify whether the connecting factor used by the Member State is legitimate. If several Member States use different legitimate connecting factors, it is for private autonomy to decide the law applicable to the creation of the right. By the introduction of party autonomy, the rigidity that brought the vested rights of Beale and Pillet down is thereby avoided. It should be recalled that the main criticism against the First Restatement in the US, where a vested rights doctrine was laid down, was not directed against vested rights as such but rather at the rigid way of determining the applicable law. Where the obligation for recognition was initially sought in the *comitas* doctrine of Huber and later in principles of international law, within the common European justice area it is beyond doubt that the duty to recognise directly originates in Union law.

6.6.3 *Vested Rights: A Better Insight to ECJ Case-Law?*

The vested rights theory can effectively distinguish between *Daily Mail* and *Cartesio* on the one hand, and *Centros* and *Überseering* on the other. The Court never distinguished between the right to exit and the right to enter. As soon as there exists a possibility under national law of the Member State of origin to re-establish in another Member State, Union law safeguards that right of establishment in the sense that a restriction of that right on either side has to be justified by an overriding provision of public interest.[142] What matters is whether the company can invoke a duly acquired right against the host Member State, that being the recognition of its privileges under a foreign law (for example limited liability). Whether a right is duly acquired depends on principle on the competent legal order. Art. 54 TFEU determines what the competent legal order is: either the jurisdiction where the company has its registered office, central administration or principal place of business. If the company desires to rely on its right, it may also very

[142] *Cartesio, supra* note 86, par. 113

well prefer to be incorporated under German law if it moves its real seat from the Netherlands to Germany, and the host Member State is then bound to respect it. *Cartesio* then perfectly fits in the pre-existing case law: there was no right that Cartesio could invoke against Hungary since Hungary already recognised all privileges resulting from incorporation under Hungarian law.

6.6.4 *Vested Rights Beyond Company and Surname law?*

The vested rights doctrine seems therefore to have returned in the case-law of the ECJ in two areas of private law. To what extent can it be incorporated into other areas of private law? Especially as concerns questions of personal status[143] the vested right doctrine may be able to make a more general contribution.[144] Rights in surname and company law are however unilaterally created by registration; private autonomy thus means the liberty of a legal or natural person to choose the applicable PIL. Although their rationale is different, the recognition of rights under surname and company law could be formulated as privileges invoked against the state. Could the vested rights doctrine also be applied against more horizontally acquired rights, where private autonomy of two or more individuals is at stake, as for example in contract or torts?[145] Especially with regard to security rights in (in)movables the vested rights doctrine may be useful. Should, for example, a lawfully established German retention of title clause (*Eigentumsvorbehalt*) on a delivery of computers be recognised in the context of the insolvency proceedings of the Latvian buyer in Latvia? Roth answers that question in the affirmative. He falls back on *Keck*, but concludes that a policy of

---

[143] Exploring the possibility for mutual recognition in mutual parentage, in particular implemented via positive harmonisation: Saarloos, K., *European private international law on legal parentage?*, Océ, Maastricht, 2010, pp. 261–331. In favour of extending the *Garcia Avello* and *Grunkin Paul* line to other personal status: Henrich, D., "Anerkennung statt IPR: Eine Grundsatzfrage", *IPRax*, Vol. 25, No. 5, 2005, pp. 422–424 (423). Against: Funken, K., *Das Anerkennungsprinzip im internationalen Privatrecht*, Mohr Siebeck, Tübingen, 2009, pp. 179. Funken argues that the case-law on surname law is justified since a person has to prove his identity in different Member States. The potential confusion of identity would be different than the inconveniences suffered as a consequence of liming relationships.

[144] Lagarde, P., "Développement futurs du droit international privé dans une Europe en voie d'unification: quelques conjectures", *RabelsZ*, Vol. 68, 2004, pp. 225–243; Coester-Waltjen, *supra* note 970; Lagarde, P., La Reconnaissance mode d'emploi, T. Azzi *et al* (eds.), *Vers de nouveaux équilibres entre ordres juridiques, Liber amicorum Hélène Gaudemet-Tallon*, Dalloz, Paris, 2008, pp. 481–501 (488-490).

[145] Coester-Waltjen, *supra* note 111, pp. 397–398.

non-recognition is neither a selling arrangement nor a product requirement but in fact a distant category. Non-recognition of securities works as a remote barrier to market access since the seller might abstain from exporting goods if he knows the security right might be lost when the goods cross a border.[146]

Pamboukis stresses that rights obtained through registration by a public authority is an *acte quasi public*. The state by exercising its authority confirms the existence of a right. The semi public nature justifies an analogy with the principle of mutual recognition of judgments.[147] With regard to horizontally acquired rights what Pamboukis finds troublesome is that without state interference it is difficult to establish whether a right has been truly created. Normal conflict of laws rules are not apt to deal with existing rights, leading to legal uncertainty and unforeseeability for the individual. Despite the difficulty of establishing whether a right has been truly created, Pamboukis accepts that effect should also be given to real and existing private relationships under a foreign law.[148]

From the outset, there is nothing that would prevent a party from relying in another Member State on a duly acquired right. Limited liability could be invoked against all creditors, thus including private parties. If duly acquired rights can be relied upon in horizontal situations, why could they also not be created in a horizontal situation? It does however not mean that vested rights are appropriate in all horizontal circumstances. Contract law might be one of those fields. The difficulty of ascertaining the establishment and content of a right created abroad without registration might prevent an effective application of the vested rights doctrine. Instead of answering the question whether it would appropriate to apply vested rights to contractual obligations, it will be

[146] Roth, W., "Secured Credit and the Internal Market: The Fundamental Freedoms and the EU's Mandate for Legislation", *European Company and Financial Law Review*, 2008, pp. 36–67 (50). The situation has to be distinguished from *Krantz* where the question was not whether the retention of title clause was recognised as such but whether Dutch tax legislation could take precedence over it.

[147] A similar analogy is drawn by: Mayer, P., "Les méthodes de la reconnaissance en droit international privé", *Le droit international privé : esprit et méthodes ; Mélanges en l'honneur de Paul Lagarde*, Dalloz, Paris, 2005, pp. 547–573.

[148] Pamboukis, *supra* note 138. Pamboukis proposes the approach of 'reconnaissance' for quasi public actes and 'relevance' for rights created without state intervention (545). On the recognition of public rights: Pamboukis, C., *L'Acte Public Étranger en Droit International Privé*, LGDJ, Paris, 1993. On the recognition of factual situations : Picone, P., "La méthode de la référence à l'ordre juridique compétent en droit international privé", *Recueil des Cours*, Vol. 197, 1986, pp. 229–419 (274-302).

demonstrated that vested rights do not have much explanatory power in European contract law. The case-law on the vested rights in the area of company and surname law allows us to deduce three conditions for the application of the vested rights doctrine. The situation should fall into the scope of Union law, the PIL rules of Member States must lead to the application of different substantive rules and finally, differences must exist between the potentially applicable legal systems.

6.6.5 *The Duty to Recognise Originates in Union Law*

Union law can only generate the duty to recognise a right duly acquired right when the situation falls into its scope of application.[149] The first important limitation is thereby already given. The vested rights doctrine cannot apply to rights duly acquired in a non-Member State. Germany is thus not obliged to recognise legal personality of a company incorporated under the laws of Switzerland, but with its main centre of business in Germany.[150] To bring the situation into the scope of Union law, European Citizenship is, with regard to personal status, of particular importance.[151] The test that a difference in surname could create such a degree of inconvenience that it causes a disadvantage to the right to freely reside in the territory of another Member State as adopted in *Grunkin Paul* can also be applied to other personal status areas such as the recognition of adoption, lack of legal capacity, marriage or divorce.

6.6.6 *Legitimate Divergence of National Connecting Factors*

The second condition for the application of the vested rights doctrine is that Member States can legitimately apply different connecting factors.[152] Union law places a check upon the content of the conflict of laws rule. The connecting factor determines the competent legal order(s). An excessive connecting factor, and thus an excessive claim

---

[149] Lagarde, *supra* note 144. 'Le droit communautaire n'impose pas de façon générale et inconditionnelle la reconnaissance de telles situations. Il n'en impose la reconnaissance que dans les cas où la non-reconnaissance serait une entrave non justifiée par l'intérêt général aux grandes libertés du traité.' (483)

[150] Bundesgerichtshof 27 October 2008, II ZR 158/06.

[151] More reluctant: Mansel, H., "Anerkennung als Grundprinzip des Europäischen Rechtraums", *RablesZ*, Vol. 70, 2006, pp. 651–731.

[152] Roth, W., "Methoden der Rechtsfindung und Rechtsanwendung im Europäischen Kollisionsrecht", *IPRax*, Vol. 26, No. 4, 2006, pp. 338–347 (344).

for regulatory competence, could potentially be struck down by the ECJ. A possible excessive connecting factor could be automatic application of the *lex fori*. The Court has accepted both habitual residence and nationality as legitimate connecting factors in the area of surname law. That would *mutatis mutandis* also apply to all other areas personal status. The different connecting factors lead to two or more potentially applicable legal systems. From a Union perspective all national private law systems are equal and Union law cannot come up with a rule to determine the competent legal order (should nationality prevail over habitual residence, or *vice versa*). Union law can only observe that two or more Member States can legitimately create the right, but the decision under which law the right has to be duly created must be left to private autonomy. It is after all for an individual to decide whether he desires to rely on a right or not.

Private autonomy becomes then an instrument for settling competing claims for regulatory authority. The Union does not have an interest in the application of the legal system of a particular Member State. In a common justice area characterised by legal diversity Member States should be left with sufficient leeway to decide when it is suitable to apply their own legislation. What matters for the Union is that the competing claims do not result in a barrier to trade or free movement. Instead of the allocation of regulatory authority on a horizontal level, party autonomy is equipped with a quasi-federal function.[153]

Party autonomy in the applicable PIL constitutes a paradigm shift in PIL. Courts always resorted to their own PIL to determine the competent legal order. Also, in the vested rights conception of Beale and Pillet it was the PIL of the forum that determined which legal order was competent to create the right concerned. However, *Grunkin Paul* clearly goes further. Private parties can avoid the application of national PIL. The German court could not establish the competent legal order itself but had to accept that under Union law Denmark could declare itself to be a competent legal order and the parties had chosen for the application of Danish PIL. By answering the question whether a right existed from the perspective of the PIL rules of the forum, private autonomy is in essence excluded and the conflict of laws norms are elevated to a

---

[153] Joerges has therefore favoured a constitutional foundation of private autonomy. Joerges, C., "The Challenges of Europeanization in the Realm of Private Law: A Plea for a New Legal Discipline", *Duke Journal of Comparative & International Law*, Vol. 14, 2004, pp. 149–196.

mandatory level. Since the barrier cannot be evaded by the private parties themselves, Union law has to step in.

The mandatory nature of the conflict of laws norms does not in principle affect a cross border trader when Member States use the same connecting factor. After all the applicable legal system is in principle the same, regardless under which PIL system that applicable legal system is determined. It could also occur that although Member States use different connecting factors they both refer to the same applicable legal system. If Spain had used domicile as connecting factor for the determination of a surname instead of nationality, both Spanish and Belgium PIL would have referred in *Garcia Avello* to Belgian law as the applicable law. The children would then not have acquired under Spanish law any right and could hence not have invoked it before the Belgian courts. It is in principal for the Member State concerned to determine whether an appropriate link with its legal system exists in order to trigger the application of its laws.[154]

Vested rights thus do not give an unlimited possibility of choices. In order for a right to be duly established, it is necessary that the law establishes that the right is designated as applicable by one of the PIL systems of the Member States. In *Grunkin Paul*, therefore, the parents could therefore not have relied on the Spanish tradition of establishing surnames. Usually this will require a link with the applicable legal system, but *Centros* and *Inspire Art* demonstrate that the link can be rather loose or even artificially created. Whereas with regard to the freedom of establishment the possible connecting factors are laid down in the Treaty (art. 54), this is not the case with surname law. The Court relied on state practice and international conventions to conclude that both the use of nationality as well as habitual residence as connecting factor was reasonable. In case of the threat of abuse, connecting factors should be harmonised to prevent abuse at the detriment of the weaker party.

6.6.7 *Legitimate Divergence between Potentially Applicable National Laws*

Obviously the legal norm applicable should differ on a substantive level from the otherwise potentially applicable law. If private law were

[154] In favour of a choice of law in such cases seem: De Groot, G., and S. Rutten, "Op weg naar een Europees IPR op het gebied van het personen- en familierecht", *Nederlands Internationaal Privaatrecht*, 2004, pp. 273–282 (275-276).

harmonised by the European legislator it would not matter whether one applied the law of Belgium or Ireland to a contract. Under both legal systems the outcome of the proceedings would be identical. Thus not only the importance of vested rights would be marginalised, but also that of PIL as a whole.[155]

6.6.8 *No Vested Rights Doctrine in Contract Law*

Vested rights do therefore not seem appropriate in contract law. The doctrine becomes unattractive because of the factual difficulties of proving that a situation lawful according to the laws of another Member State existed. Whereas practical difficulties might be overcome, the doctrine does not have much explanatory power in contracts. The harmonised conflict of laws rules have ensured that the question of applicable law is answered identically regardless of before which court the question is put. It will not for an Italian court be necessary to establish whether an Italian buyer duly acquired any rights under Greek law that could be enforced in an Italian court since the whole legal relationship has to be answered according to Greek law anyway. The doctrine of vested rights only has explanatory power when the right is invoked in a situation governed by a law different from the law that created the right. Moreover, Member States do not impose their national conflict of laws rules as mandatory, but instead harmonised Union rules. Within the Union a double burden to comply with the sets of mandatory conflict of laws rules, and the often mandatory application of national private law, does therefore not arise.

6.7 *The Free Movement and Private Autonomy*

Vested rights do however nicely illustrate the fact that private law rules should be treated different from rules concerning administrative authorisations, prudential supervision or product quality. The distinction between the categories is not always clear. The prohibition on cold calling in *Alpine Investments* affected the relation between two private parties since it prohibited a way of concluding a contract (formal validity). The requirement was however linked to a licence. Without the promise of an undertaking not to engage in cold calling it was

[155] Kegel, G., "The Crisis of Conflict of Laws", *Recueil des Cours*, Vol. 95, 1964, pp. 91–268.

impossible to obtain a licence and hence impossible to operate on the Dutch financial market. It therefore became a rule concerning an administrative authorisation. The requirement could not be avoided by choosing Belgian instead of Dutch private law. Rules may thus be caught by the free movement provisions, regardless their national classification. What matters is the effect of a provision, do parties have the possibility to evade the application of laws themselves or should they be assisted by Union law?

6.7.1 *The Possibility of Choosing the Applicable Law*

Rules that may be avoided by the parties themselves cannot have the effect of hindering the trade between Member States. It has been argued that the restrictive effects of a rule can in principle not depend upon the authority on the basis of which a rule is applied. It does thus not matter whether a rule is applied on the basis of the consent of the parties or is imposed by a state. What is decisive is whether a national rule prohibits or requires certain conduct and therefore potentially hinders the smooth functioning of the internal market.[156] Even if that submission were to be followed, *Alsthom Atlantique* however exactly suggests that where private autonomy is allowed, the rule is not capable of hindering the smooth functioning of the internal market.

6.7.2 *The Scope of Alsthom Atlantique*

In *Alsthom Atlantique*, the measure at stake was allegedly liable to hinder exports.[157] As such the French producer could therefore not invoke the law of his own Member State as an alternative. It is however difficult to distinguish on the basis of exports or imports or whether the restrictive rule originates in the legal system of the host or home Member State. The existence of transaction costs related to getting familiar with the legal system of the host Member State is not an argument as such since in an international contract those transaction costs have to be borne by one of the contracting parties in any case. Also Tassikas

[156] Franzen, M., *Privatrechtsangleichung durch die europäische Gemeinschaft*, W. de Gruyter, Berlin, 1999, pp. 144; Langner, O., "Das Kaufrecht auf dem Prüfstand der Warenverkehrsfreiheit des EG-Vertrages", *RabelsZ*, Vol. 65, 2001, pp. 222–244 (228-230).

[157] Gkoutisinis, A., "Free movement of Services in the EC Treaty and the Law of Contractual Obligations Relating to Banking and Financial Services", *Common Market Law Review*, Vol. 41, 2004, pp. 119–175 (126).

attempts to nuance the scope of *Alsthom Atlantique*. The distinction between mandatory and overriding mandatory provisions is in his opinion not of much help since a satisfying boundary between the two concepts has never been drawn.[158] Although that holds ground, it does not prevent the transposition of the distinction into the Union legal order. What matters in Union law is not the classification of a rule, but rather its potential effects. Union law steps in if a forum classifies a provision as overriding mandatory. Hence, the application of the fundamental freedoms takes place *ex post*, not *ex ante*. Tassikas goes even one step further; rules masquerading as non-mandatory can in some circumstances not factually be deviated from. They can therefore equally harm citizens' free movement rights and should therefore be subject to judicial scrutiny. The factual binding force of a non-mandatory rule however follows from the fact that one party enjoys a much stronger bargaining position and can insist upon the application of a specific rule.[159] It will undoubtedly be the stronger party that will engage in cross border trade. It would be rather odd to strengthen the position of that stronger party with the possibility of challenging a non-mandatory rule when after all it turns out that the law selected by him is more restrictive to trade.

Von Wilmowsky is critical as to whether the existence of private autonomy is sufficient for a provision to stay out of the reach of the free movement provisions.[160] In his opinion private autonomy may reduce the burden of traders, but not completely remove them. Supposedly there is not always a more liberal legal order at the disposal of parties, a choice of law involves information costs,[161] and finally the private parties that have the possibility to make a choice of law are not always identical to the parties that might suffer from the restrictive effects. These arguments carry only limited weight in respect of contractual obligations. With regard to contractual obligations, the parties can designate any law to govern their contract. Moreover, in contractual

[158] Tassikas, A., *Dispositives Recht und Rechtswahlfreiheit als Ausnahmebereiche der EG-Grundfreiheiten. Ein Beitrag zur Privatautonomie, Vertragsgestaltung und Rechtsfindung im Vertragsverkehr des Binnenmarktes*, Mohr Siebeck, Tübingen, 2004.

[159] See: Hesselink, M., "Non-Mandatory Rules in European Contract Law", *European Review of Contract Law*, Vol. 1, 2005, pp. 44–86 (73).

[160] Von Wilmowsky, P., "EG-Freiheiten und Vertragsrecht", *Juristenzeitung*, Vol. 12, 1996, pp. 590–596 (595); Von Wilmowsky, P., "EG-Vertrag und kollisionsrechtliche Rechtswahlfreiheit", *RabelsZ*, Vol 62, 1998, pp 1-37

[161] Basedow, J., "A Common Contract Law for the Common Market", *Common Market Law Review*, Vol. 33, 1996, pp. 1169–1195 (1174-1178).

obligations the choice of law will have to be made by the parties that suffer from the potential restrictive effects of the law. In fact, under the double burden rationale it is the frequent trader that suffers the most severe consequences of diverging laws. He is also often in a factually stronger bargaining position and can therefore push for a choice of law, or even make all contracts subject to the same law. The frequent trader party might prefer a law that he is familiar with, which will usually be the law of his home Member State. The frequent trader will thus only suffer information costs if he desires to make the contract subject to a law he is unfamiliar with. Information costs only appear in the need to identify the applicable law. Once a selection of a particular national law is made, the applicable law does not constitute a barrier to trade.[162]

The Union is based on individual responsibility, and consequently, it should be left to the individuals concerned to decide how best to safeguard their interests which they deem worthy of protection.[163] It should once again be recalled that even mandatory rules can be avoided by choosing a different legal system. A German mandatory provision will not apply if parties opt for the application of French law. The burden for a producer established in one Member State of complying with different national contract laws when it desires to engage in export could be prevented by the producer itself by ensuring the applicability of its own contract law. The double burden rationale presupposes that a foreign trader has to comply with the restrictive rules in two legal systems. That argument does not in principle apply to contract law. A French undertaking supplying beer in Germany can make its contract subject to either French or German law. Save for overriding mandatory provisions, neither France nor Germany will seek to impose its contract law. It does not seem that Union law should step in when the application of a rule is mandatory, but its application can be avoided by private parties.[164] If the parties fail to reach an agreement during their negotiations why would Union *ex post* disrupt legal relations and favour one party of the other? If a choice of law exists, what *CMC Motorradcenter* and

---

[162] Collins, H., The European Civil Code: The Way Forward, Cambridge University Press, Cambridge, 2008, 66.

[163] AG Trstnjak in: Case C-331/05 *Internationaler Hilfsfonds v Commission* [2007] ECR I-05475, par. 93. Note that the case did not concern contract law, but the question whether legal costs incurred in proceedings before the Ombudsman against the Commission were recoverable.

[164] Similar: Grundmann, S., "The Structure of European Contract Law", *European Review of Private Law*, Vol. 9, No. 4, 2001, pp. 505–528.

Alsthom Atlantique suggest is that the influence upon the trade between Member States is too remote and uncertain to warrant the conclusion that intra-Union trade might be hampered.

Unlike administrative authorisations, prudential supervision or rules on product quality, contract law does not work on the basis of territoriality. A rule is imposed upon a producer that either produces or markets its products on the territory of a Member State. The rule will only be applied if it meets the relevant criteria, but if it meets its application is mandatory. Contract law does in principle not have any territorial boundaries. It can regulate situations that are not exclusive to its territory or to situations that might even have no link with the relevant jurisdiction at all. On the other hand, contract law will not impose itself but only be applied in default of a choice of law by the parties.

6.8 *Specific Rules of Contract Law and the Fundamental Freedoms*

Where private autonomy is able to place contract law in general outside the scope of the fundamental freedoms, there are rules in contract law or affecting contract law that will be subject to the scrutiny of the fundamental freedoms. The first category of rules affecting contract law that are caught by the free movement provisions are thus rules concerning administrative authorisations, prudential supervision or product quality. These provisions often operate on the basis of the territoriality and cannot be evaded by the private parties. They directly impact upon private relations, but do not become part of the horizontal relationship as such. These rules will often be of a public law nature, but may be classified as rules of contract. The national classification of a rule is irrelevant for the purposes of Union law. In that sense, rules that are perceived on a national level to be private are caught by the principle of mutual recognition. An example is *Alpine Investments*, but also technical regulations such as in *Unilever* that impact upon the validity of performance.

The second category rules are not related to administrative authorisations, prudential supervision or product quality but can equally not be evaded by the private parties by a choice of law. Overriding mandatory provisions are applicable regardless of the applicable law. Their application cannot be prevented by a mere choice of law. Private autonomy is thus excluded. Since private individuals cannot evade the potential restrictive effects, Union law has to step in.[165] Although it remains open to each Member State to determine *which* legal rules are crucial for the safeguard of its political, social or economical order the application of overriding mandatory provisions can thus not completely be left to the national legal systems involved.

6.8.1 *How to Distinguish between Rules of Administrative Authorisations and Overriding Mandatory Provisions?*

The distinction between overriding mandatory provisions and rules concerning administrative authorisations, prudential supervision or product quality is hard to draw. Overriding mandatory provisions also underlie a clear public policy aim, such as the protection of the national labour market or protection of the subcontractor. Overriding mandatory provisions however become part of the applicable law, while the latter category affects the validity or modality of a contractual obligation without becoming part of the applicable law as such. Because the rule is part of a horizontal relationship a choice of law would normally be possible, but the overriding mandatory nature of the provision prevents opting out. Overriding mandatory provisions will therefore be applied whenever the contract enters their scope of application. In that sense, they function as territorial rules. Rules concerning administrative supervision do not depend at all upon being part of the applicable law as long as their interest pursued is realised. They often operate in the negative. The principle of mutual recognition can adequately address such impediments in trade because it imposes upon Member States the negative duty not to apply economic regulation.[166] The prohibition on cold calling in the licence in *Alpine Investments* or the Greek requirement that baby milk could only be sold in pharmacies did not depend upon the applicable law. The fact a contract will be made subject to a foreign law does not alter the nature of the prohibition on cold

[165] The control over the application of overriding mandatory provisions takes away from their character of rules of direct application. See: Poillot Peruzzetto, S., "Ordre Public et loi de police dans l'ordre communautaire", *Travaux du Comité Français de Droit International Privé 2002-2004*, pp. 65–106 (72).

[166] De Baere, G., "Houdt het communautair herkomstlandbeginsel een verborgen conflictregel in?", *Revue belge de droit international*, Vol. 36, No. 1, 2003, pp. 131–201; De Baere, G., "'Is this a Conflict Rule which I see Before Me?' Looking for a Hidden Conflict Rule in the Principle of Origin as Implemented in Primary European Union law and in the 'Directive on Electronic Commerce'", *Maastricht Journal of Comparative Law*, Vol. 11, No. 3, 2004, pp. 287–319 (302).

calling or the prohibition to sell baby milk outside pharmacies. On the other hand, the realisation of the purpose of a minimum wage requirement would not be served if a labour contract stipulating a wage below the minimum were declared void. Rather, the prevention of unfair competition and avoidance of social dumping requires actual application of the minimum wage requirement. It thus directly steps into the contractual obligation. The same would apply to a rule awarding jurisdiction relating to consumer contracts to a special tribunal in order to safeguard the rights of the consumer. That goal can only be realised when the actual provision is applied. The same was apparent in the examples discussed in the area of company and surname law. Mutual recognition performs less well when what at stake is the application of a specific rule, since the behaviour required by a Member State consists out of more than refraining from applying a national law.

The Television without Frontiers Directive (89/552 EEC, TVWF), for example, does not affect PIL since it concerns rules on administrative authorisation, prudential supervision or product quality.[167] Art. 2 imposes the obligation upon Member States to apply their legislation to broadcasters established on their territory and prevents other Member States from applying their legislation to the same broadcaster. The same principle of home country control combined with an obligation for the home Member State to enforce its laws also underpinning the Data Protection Directive. The obligations for the home Member State are one of supervision on issues such as on the promotion, distribution and production of television programmes, control against the unlawful broadcasting of cinematographic work and rules on television advertising and sponsorship. The core features have been preserved in the Audiovisual Mediaservices Directive (2007/65), updating the TVWF and taking into account the changed multimedia landscape. A provision stipulating that advertising for alcoholic beverages can only be made after nine o'clock obviously impacts upon the contractual relationship between a broadcaster and an advertiser since it limits their contractual possibilities. They cannot lawfully contract for commercials to be broadcasted at eight. That would not change even if parties were to make their private contract subject to the laws of another Member State. On the other hand, though the TVWF limits the

[167] Varney, M., "European Controls on Member State Promotion and Regulation of Public Service Broadcasting and Broadcasting Standards", *European Public Law*, Vol. 10, No. 3, 2004, pp. 503–530.

contractual possibilities it does however not say anything about the law applicable to the rights and obligations between broadcaster and sponsor or between broadcaster and viewer.

Although this category of rules therefore affects the relationship between private parties, they are not part of the contractual obligations in a strict sense. If looked from this wider perspective, primary law does contain a hidden conflict of laws rule.[168] The hidden conflict of laws rule does however not originate from a desire of Union law to comprehensively regulate a legal relationship, but rather from the fact that the traditional line between public and private is being drawn differently. The divide is being drawn on the basis of the effect of a rule, instead of its dogmatic classification. Legal areas that used to belong to private law, and hence, to private international law, now appear to be caught by the principle of mutual recognition. An example is given by the *GB-INNO-BM* case. At stake was a Luxembourgian decree stipulating that a special purchase offer may not mention the duration of the offer, nor the previous price.[169] Similar legislation did not exist in Belgium. Infringement procedures were brought by a non-profit making association against a Belgian supermarket after it had distributed leaflets in both Belgium and Luxembourg. The information requirements of a professional towards a consumer traditionally belonged to the realm of private law. The Luxembourgish measure did not find any grace with the ECJ. It held that the objective of preventing unfair competition and consumer protection could also be attained by less restrictive means. Whether classified as private or not, the regulation does not affect the rights and obligations in a specific consumer contract but rather regulates the general behaviour of the professional. The ECJ did not go into the classification of the rule as private but rather emphasised the potentially restrictive effects of the regulation.

6.8.2 *Free Movement and Protective Connecting Factors*

The use of protective connecting factors in consumer and labour contracts also excludes party autonomy to an extent. In certain circumstances a choice of law may not deprive the consumer or employee of the protection that is afforded to him by the law of respectively the place of habitual residence or the place where the labour contract is

[168] Bernard, *supra* note 60.

[169] Case C-362/88 *GB-INNO-BM v Confédération du commerce luxembourgeois* [1990] ECR I-0667.

habitually performed. Party autonomy is not fully excluded, since parties can still choose the law applicable to their contract even if that law has no factual connections with the contract whatsoever. However, the restrictive effects cannot be evaded. The only possibility for the non-application of the restrictive - from the point of view of traders - labour and consumer standards would be if the chosen law affords an equivalent or higher degree of protection. The burden of a trader of having to comply with the legal systems of 27 Member States could only be avoided if he complies with the highest national standard. That idea is be hardly compatible with the internal market. Mandatory consumer and labour laws are therefore eligible to be caught by the free movement provisions. It has already been demonstrated that, especially with regard to consumer law, the level of protection is to a large extent harmonised by Union law. National laws that go beyond the minimum protection offered by the harmonised standards are however subject to scrutiny under the free movement provisions.[170]

6.9 *Justification of a Restriction*

The dogmatic distinction between rules affecting the contract and rules that are part of the contract (as applicable law) might help us to better understand the interplay between PIL and Union law, however from the point of view of Union law the distinction is less relevant. In *Arblade* the Court held that the national classification of a rule as public order legislation did not place the rule outside the scope of Union law.[171] The Court does not seem to draw a distinction as to whether a provision is a rule concerning administrative authorisations, prudential supervision or product quality or an overriding mandatory provision. From a Union point of view there is also no reason why it should. Once again, what matters is the effect of a rule, not its classification. Both categories exclude private autonomy, albeit in different ways, which may lead to the creation of a dual burden.

Overriding mandatory provisions are applied regardless the applicable law. This means that they apply to all traders regardless whether they are established in the relevant jurisdiction or in another Member

[170] Case C-20/03 *Burmanjer* [2005] ECR I-4133; Case C-441/04 *A-Punkt Schmuckhandels* [2006] ECR I-2093, see: Dougan, M., "Minimum Harmonization and the Internal Market", *Common Market Law Review*, Vol. 37, 2000, pp. 863–885.

[171] Joined Cases C-369/96 and C-376/96 *Arblade* [1999] ECR I-8453, par. 31.

State. Overriding mandatory provisions are therefore indistinctly applicable measures.[172] Do they constitute selling arrangements within the meaning of the *Keck* doctrine or is the restriction not sufficient to impede market access?

Mazzoleni demonstrates that overriding mandatory provisions may have the effect of preventing market access in the field of services. A French company posted workers in Belgium and did not comply with the minimum wage requirement. From a Belgian perspective, the minimum wage requirement is regarded to be an overriding mandatory provision.[173] The Court held that the application of the free movement of services would be seriously undermined if it were made subject to all conditions of establishment. Therefore 'the application of the host Member State's national rules to service providers is liable to prohibit, impede or render less attractive the provision of services to the extent that it involves expenses and additional administrative and economic burdens'.[174]

6.9.1 *Legitimate Aim*

Overriding mandatory provisions do not therefore benefit *a priori* from the *Keck* exception and are capable of prohibiting market access.[175] The fact that a provision is caught by one the free movement provisions does not necessarily mean it is incompatible with it. Art. 9 (1) Rome I provides that overriding mandatory provisions 'are provisions the respect for which is regarded as crucial by a country for safeguarding its public interests, such as its political, social or *economic* organisation'. Many overriding mandatory provisions originated as economic

[172] AG Colomer in *Arblade, supra* note 171, par. 95; Gaudemet-Tallon, H., "Le droit international privé des contrats dans un ensemble regional", T. Einhorn *et al* (eds), *Intercontinental cooperation through private international law ; Essays in the honour of Peter Nygh*, T.M.C. Asser Press, The Hague, 2004, pp. 119–137.

[173] Cour de Cassation 4 December 1989, Arresten Cour de Cassation 1989-1990, 963; Arbeidshof Gent, 21 December 1988, Tijdschrift voor Sociaal Recht 1989, 239; Arbeidshof Brussel, 14 March 1983, Arbeidsrecht nr. 14023, 359. See: Meeusen, J., *Nationalisme en Internationalisme in het Internationaal Privaatrecht: Analyse van het Belgische Conflictenrecht*, Intersentia, Antwerpen, 1997.

[174] Case C-165/98 *Mazzoleni and ISA* [2001] ECR I-2189, par. 24. But see as well: Joined cases 62/81 and 63/81 *Seco and Desquenne & Giral* [1982] ECR 223; Case C-133/89 *Rush Portuguesa* [1990] ECR I-1417.

[175] Pataut, E., "Lois de police et ordre juridique communautaire", A. Fuchs *et al* (eds.), *Les conflits de lois et le système juridique communautaire*, Dalloz, Paris, 2004, pp. 117–143.

corrections to market liberalism and the conflict of laws based thereupon.[176] The ECJ has consistently held, however, that mere economic considerations cannot justify a barrier to the free movement provisions.[177] Does the Rome I alter that case-law if the provision concerned can be qualified as an overriding mandatory provision? Is there perhaps from a Union perspective a difference between economic considerations and rules safeguarding the economic organisation of a State? Both interpretations seem unlikely. As regards the latter, an analogy could perhaps be drawn with the doctrine of fiscal coherency.[178] Member States could then be allowed to invoke economic justifications if those considerations go to the heart of the economic organisation of the Member State involved. This reasoning is equally unconvincing, however. The fiscal argument correlates with the large autonomy of Member States in fiscal matters and cannot be extended to the economic organisation because Member States do not, in the latter field, enjoy such a large level of autonomy. As regards the former, the ECJ case-law concerns the interpretation of primary law. A regulation cannot limit the application of the freedom to provide services or the free movement of goods.

The most likely interpretation relates to the universal scope of application of Rome I. The Regulation could thus lead to the application of the laws of a third country. Union law does not impose restrictions on the application of purely economic legislation if it does not affect the free movement provisions. For example the application of a Swedish exchange control to a contract governed by Indian law between an Indian seller and a Swedish buyer will not impede the free movement of goods between the Member States. Overriding mandatory provisions that underlie exclusively economic considerations can only be applied when they do not affect the free movement provisions.

The impossibility of justifying the application of overriding mandatory provisions on mere economic grounds might, however, be less problematic than at first sight. Overriding mandatory provisions will

[176] Basedow, J., "Conflicts of Economic Regulation", *American Journal of Comparative Law*, Vol. 42, 1994, pp. 423–447.

[177] Case C-120/95 *Decker* [1998] ECR I-1831, par. 39. See: Craig, P. and G. De Burca, *EU Law: Text, Cases and Materials*, Oxford University Press, Oxford, Fourth Edition, 2007, pp. 705–720.

[178] Case C-204/90 *Bachmann* [1992] ECR I-249, para. 21–28; Case C-300/90 *Commission v Belgium* [1992] ECR I-305, para. 14–21 and case C-478/98 *Commission v Belgium* [2000] ECR I-07587, para. 31-35.

often not exclusively have an economic consideration as their underlying rationale but equally a social or a political one. There is a significant grey area in what constitutes for the purposes of PIL an economic regulation.[179] To return to the minimum wage requirement, one of the considerations in applying this requirement to posted workers in addition to national workers is to prevent national workers from being priced out of the market. The guarantee of equal terms of competition not only fulfils an economic aim, but the social and political structure of the host Member State may significantly be disrupted if posted workers take over jobs of national workers and cause large scale unemployment. Moreover, the host Member State may have a legitimate interest in the avoidance of social dumping of the posted worker. The example demonstrates that the difference between economic and non-economic policies might sometimes be hard to draw.[180] However it is beyond doubt that measures which try to counter the operation of the fundamental freedoms, or national protectionism, can never constitute a justified restriction upon the fundamental freedoms.

If it is established that an overriding mandatory provision pursues a legitimate aim, it should be established whether the protected interest falls within the sphere of responsibility of the jurisdiction from which the overriding mandatory provision originates. The ECJ held in *Alpine Investments* that the protection of the Belgian consumer was not a matter for the Dutch government.[181] Similarly, on an ordinary application of the free movement of goods it was found that the protection of live calves against being reared in systems in the importing Member State which are prohibited in the exporting Member State was outside the sphere of responsibility of the exporting Member State.[182] What is deemed to be the appropriate standard for the protection of calves has in principle to be determined by the Member State involved itself. The compatibility of the doctrine with mutual recognition is debatable. If it is accepted that under mutual recognition a Member State will be prevented from imposing consumer protection measures even if the home Member State provides for significantly laxer standards but not if the home Member State does not address consumer protection at all does

---

[179] Basedow, *supra* note 176, pp. 424–428.
[180] Israël/Saarloos, *supra* note 134, pp. 639.
[181] *Alpine Investments, supra* note 28, par. 43.
[182] Case C-1/96 *Compassion in World Farming* [1998] ECR I-1251. In particular AG Léger, par. 93.

this not imply that home Member State is supposed to take care of the consumers in the host Member State?

Despite this apparent doctrinal inconsistency the approach of the Court makes sense. Overriding mandatory provisions operate by exception in order to guarantee a particular national interest. If the protection of that national interest falls away there is in principle also no reason to maintain the exception.[183] The *Sonderanknüpfung*[184] and *bijzondere aanknoping*[185] of overriding mandatory provisions have exactly the same effect. An overriding mandatory provision is not automatically excluded if it does not belong to the *lex causae*, but equally an overriding mandatory provision is not automatically applied when it forms part of the *lex causae*. The overriding mandatory provision therefore has to justify its own application and can only do so when the interest it seeks to protect is at stake. In the UK, art. 27 (1) of the Unfair Contract Terms Act (1977) produces a similar effect when it stipulates that when a contract governed by the law of any part United Kingdom only by choice of the parties, and in the absence of a choice of law the law of some country outside the United Kingdom would have been applicable, certain consumer protection provisions do not apply.

In reaction to the Commission Proposal for a Rome I Regulation the Max Planck Institute suggested to introduce an art. 8 (4): 'The internationally mandatory rules of the law governing the contract under this Regulation apply to the contract if they so demand'.[186] The paragraph was justified with the argument that in some Member States (e.g. Germany) PIL rules could only refer to private law. Overriding mandatory provisions were understood to refer to public law. In other Member States (e.g. the United Kingdom) overriding mandatory provisions were applied as part of the governing law. Member States cannot however invoke their traditional public/private distinctions when interpreting a Union instrument. The idea of the limitation of national overriding mandatory provisions by the forum is however very useful.

---

[183] However some standards are deemed to be so universal that they should be applied by the forum even if the situation has no factual connections with the forum whatsoever. See: Mills, A., "The Dimensions of Public Policy in Private International Law", *Journal of Private International Law*, Vol. 4, No. 2, 2008, pp. 201–236.

[184] Par. 3.2.1

[185] Par. 3.3.1

[186] Max Planck Institute for Foreign Private and Private International Law, Comments on the European Commission's Proposal for a Regulation of the European Parliament and the Council on the law applicable to contractual obligations (Rome I), *RabelsZ*, vol. 71, 2007, pp. 225–344 (313).

Self-limitation should be seen a proximity requirement. In French legal doctrine *proximité*[187] means that the conflict of laws norm should designate the law that has the closest connection, or at least a close connection to the case at hand to legitimise the assumption of authority.[188] The limitation of public policy underlies a similar idea.[189] Application of the provision should only be required if there exist sufficiently strong links with the jurisdiction in which the overriding mandatory provision originates. Some close connection with the forum should exist for the application of local public policy to be appropriate since the forum state should be sufficiently interested in the dispute before it can assume partial regulatory authority.[190] Overriding mandatory provisions form an exception to the free movement provisions. There is no reason to limit a fundamental freedom when the interest that the exception aims to protect falls away.

6.9.2 *Suitability*

Once it has been established that the measure pursues a legitimate aim it has to be assessed whether the measure is suitable to attain the objective. The measure at stake must be able to attain its objective. Hence, a Belgian requirement that products should mention a notification number attributed by the Inspection Service for Foodstuffs could not be justified on the grounds of consumer protection since the number did not provide any information to the consumers about the

---

[187] German legal doctrine describes *proximité* as *Inlandsbeziehung*, but this not relevant with regard to overriding mandatory provisions since the *Sonderanknüpfung* presupposes a connection with the forum. A similar presupposition is not present in France.

[188] Lagarde, P., "Le principe de proximité dans le droit international privé contemporain", *Recueil des Cours*, vol. 196, 1986, 9-238 (26-27) ; Ballarino, T., and P. Romano, "Le principe de proximité chez Paul Lagarde", *Mélanges en l'honneur de Paul Lagarde ; Le droit international privé : esprit et méthodes*, Dalloz, Paris, 2005, pp. 37–54 ; Kessedjian, C., "Le principe de proximité vingt ans après", *Mélanges en l'honneur de Paul Lagarde" ; Le droit international privé : esprit et méthodes*, Dalloz, Paris, 2005, pp. 507–521.

[189] Courbe, P., "L'ordre public de proximité", *Mélanges en l'honneur de Paul Lagarde ; Le droit international privé : esprit et méthodes*, Dalloz, Paris, 2005, pp. 227–239 ; Fallon, M., "Le principe de proximité dans le droit de l'Union Européenne", *Mélanges en l'honneur de Paul Lagarde ; Le droit international privé : esprit et méthodes*, Dalloz, Paris, 2005, pp. 241–262 (255-256).

[190] Mills, *supra* note 183, pp. 211.

nutrients of the product or the checks carried out by the authorities.[191] In *Centros,* the refusal to registrar the Danish branch of a company duly set up under English law that factually carried out no business in the United Kingdom could not be justified on the grounds of creditor protection. The registration of a branch of a company that carried out business in the UK would have equally deprived Danish creditors of their protection. The suitability test does not seem to pose any particular problems with overriding mandatory provisions.

6.9.3 *Necessity*

It has already been observed that proportionality implies mutual recognition. That becomes apparent at the necessity stage of the proportionality test. It would go beyond what is necessary if a Member State were to apply its legislation to a situation already covered by the legislation of another Member State. Mutual recognition is however less effective with regard to overriding mandatory provisions. To the extent that mutual recognition can be applied to private laws, it must be observed that the principle applies to the level of standards imposed by the home Member State. It does not require Member States to accept rules 'enacted under a different regulatory philosophy and not functionally equivalent to their own."[192] Overriding mandatory provisions aim to protect a particular national interest. Their observation is after all crucial for the functioning of the social, political or economic organisation of that particular State. The Netherlands will, for example, in its contract or property law not have considered the Cypriot interest in the preservation of its cultural heritage. Similarly the protection of the labour market and the avoidance of social dumping in Sweden will not be embedded in the Latvian labour legislation. Overriding mandatory provisions relate to the specific characteristics of each jurisdiction. Legislation of another Member State will most often not have taken that particular interest into consideration. That interest is therefore free from regulation by the home Member State and the host Member State

[191] Case C-217/99 *Commission v Belgium* [2000] ECR I-10251, par. 26. In similar vein: Joined Cases C-158/04 and C-159/04 *Alfa Vita Vassilopoulos* [2006] ECR I-8135, par. 25.

[192] Bernard, N., "Flexibility in the European Single Market", C. Barnard and J. Scott (eds.), *The Law of the Single European Market: Unpacking the Premises*, Hart Publishing, Oxford, 2002, pp. 101–124 (104).

is therefore not prevented by the principle of mutual recognition from applying its own legislation.

Although mutual recognition might be less effective with regard to overriding mandatory provisions, the general proportionality principle still fulfils a significant role. In *Inspire Art* the Netherlands sought to impose additional requirements to companies incorporated under a foreign law (without changing the *lex societas*) but factually carrying out all of their activities in the Netherlands. The Court held that the imposition of for example a minimum capital requirement went beyond what was necessary since potential creditors were already sufficiently warned by the fact that *Inspire Art* held itself out as a company governed by English law. Potential creditors could thus demand adequate securities if they feared that the English minimum capital requirements were too lax.

Proportionality not only places a check upon the content of the legislation but also upon the quality. It would go beyond what was necessary if a foreign producer or service provider were required to meet excessive legal costs in order to get acquainted with the local legal system. In *Arblade* the minimum wage requirement could only pass the proportionality test if that requirement was sufficiently precise and accessible that it did not render it impossible or excessively difficult in practice for the foreign service provider to determine the obligations with which he was bound to comply.[193] Overriding mandatory provisions are thus also in the proportionality test not awarded a privileged position.

The application of overriding mandatory provisions is thus subject to the same process of justification as any other measure infringing one of the fundamental freedoms.[194] The test is however not identical. The specific characteristics of overriding mandatory provisions require a different analysis. Whereas the requirement of a legitimate aim must be read as imposing a requirement of proximity upon the application of the overriding mandatory provision, the *raison d'être* of overriding mandatory provisions makes the principle of mutual recognition less effective. Overriding mandatory provisions protect a particular national interest that is not protected by any other jurisdiction. However, it is stating the obvious that overriding mandatory provisions cannot escape the scrutiny of the tests of suitability and necessity.

---

[193] *Arblade, supra* note 28, par. 43.

[194] Similar: Piroddi, P., "The French Plumber, Subcontracting and the Internal Market", *Yearbook of Private International Law*, Vol. 10, 2008, pp. 593–616.

6.10 *The E-Commerce Directive*

A particular instrument in the discussion on the relation between the Union law and private international law on the internal market is the E-Commerce Directive.[195] Whether or not the Directive affects PIL has been the subject of large controversy.[196] Although art. 1 (4) explicitly provides that the Directive does not lay down any additional rules on PIL,[197] some authors have however claimed that the Directive also precludes the application of private laws. The core of the E-Commerce Directive is art. 3, which lays down an internal market clause. According to the second subparagraph 'Member States may not, for reasons falling within the coordinated field, restrict the freedom to provide information society services from another Member State'. According to the proponents of the country of origin principle, the duty to ensure the free movement of information society services would contain a hidden conflict of laws rule insofar as the harmonised field covers private law. Since the host Member State may not restrict the freedom to provide services in the coordinated field, the Directive favours the application of the private law of the home Member State. However, the precise scope of the coordinated field remains open to debate. Art. 2 (i)

---

[195] Van Haersolte- van Hof, J., "Richtlijn elektronische handel – internationaal privaatrechtelijke aspecten", *Nederlands Tijdschift voor Europees Recht*, vol. 6, 2000, pp. 325–327; Lodder, A., "Directive 2000/31/EC", A. Lodder and H. Kaspersen (eds), *eDirectives: Guide to European Union Law on E-commerce*, Kluwer Law International, The Hague, 2002, pp. 67–93.

[196] On this discussion : Cachard, O., *La régulation internationale du marché électronique*, LGDJ, Paris, 2001, pp. 155 ; Spindler, G., "Internet, Kapitalmarkt und Kollisionsrecht unter besonderer Berücksichtigung der E-Commerce Richtlinien", *Zeitschrift für das gesamte Handelsrecht und Wirtschaftsrecht*, Vol. 165, 2001, pp. 324–361; Fallon, M., and J. Meeusen, "Le commerce électronique, la directive 2000/31/CE et le droit international privé", *Revue Critique de Droit International Privé*, Vol. 91, No. 3, 2002, pp. 435–489 ; Vogel, H., "E-Commerce : Directives of the European Union and Implementation in German Law", *E-Commerce : Law & Jurisdiction*, Kluwer, Deventer, 2002, pp. 29–78 (49-50) ; Saxby, S., "UK Implements E-Commerce Directive", *Computer Law & Security Report*, Vol. 18, No. 5, 2002, pp. 306; Walk, F., *Das Herkunftsprinzip der E-Commerce-Richtlinie: Art. 3 der Richtlinie 2000/31 EG und seine Umsetzung in deutsches Recht*, Herbert Ultz München, 2002; Grundmann, S., "Das Internationale Privatrecht der E-Commerce-Richtlinie – was ist kategorial anders im Kollisionsrecht des Binnenmarkts und warum?", *Rabelsz*, Vol. 67, No. 2, 2003, pp. 246–297; Brière, C., "Le droit international privé européen des contrats et la coordination des sources", *Journal du Droit International*, Vol. 136, No. 3, 2009, pp. 791–807.

[197] The complexities of PIL with regard to electronic commerce are described in: Gillies, L., *Electronic Commerce and International Private Law: A Study of Electronic Consumer Contracts*, Ashgate, Aldershot, 2008.

provides that the harmonised field includes 'requirements regarding the quality or content of the service including those applicable to advertising and contracts'. The European Parliament and Commission did indeed argue in the process of drafting the Directive that private law rules would also be covered by the internal market clause. In the process of implementation, however, Member States appear to have taken different views on the matter.[198]

6.10.1 *Should Article 1 (4) be Ignored?*

The Annex to the E- Commerce Directive provides that the internal market clause does not apply to the right to freely choose the law applicable to a contract. Moreover, according to the Annex, the internal market clause also does not apply to contractual obligations arising out of consumer contracts. Member States may thus impose general consumer protection rules in addition to the protection in the directive conferred upon receiver of services provided that the information society service provider targets its activities towards the territory of that Member State. The wording of the Annex is rather confusing. The provisions of art. 3 of the Directive 'do not apply' instead of 'do not affect' or 'are without prejudice to' art. 3 and 6 Rome I. A contrario reasoning would suggest that if it had not been for the Annex, the internal market clause would have prevented the application of art. 3 and 6 Rome I. By confirming the pertinence of a choice of law and the protective connecting factor for consumers, it is implied that the internal market clause would normally affect the conflict of laws.

Departing from the presumption that private law is also covered by the harmonised field, Mankowski observes that the 22nd recital, which provides that 'information society services should in principle be subject to the law of the Member State in which the service provider is established', conflicts with art. 1 (4). Since in reality the Directive does lay down a conflict of laws rule, the declaration contained in art. 1 (4)

[198] Hellner, M., "The Country of Origin Principle in the E-Commerce Directive: A Conflict with Conflict of Laws?", A. Fuchs *et al* (eds.), *Les conflits de lois et le système juridique communautaire*, Dalloz, Paris, 2004, pp. 205–224. On 211, with further references: The Nordic countries for example are of the opinion that the E-Commerce Directive does not cover private law rules, other Member States such as France have not touched upon the issue; Jayme, E., and C. Kohler, *Europäisches Kollisionsrecht 2002: Zu Wiederkehr des Internationalen Privatrechts*, *IPRax*, Vol. 22, No. 6, 2002, pp. 461–471 (463).

should be ignored.[199] In any case, art. 1 (4) would not allow for PIL limitations of the country of origin principle. In such an interpretation, the freedom to provide services is perceived to be an absolute freedom. The analysis developed in this chapter has however demonstrated that not all private law rules are caught by the fundamental freedoms, and above all, the fundamental freedoms allow for derogations.

It is therefore rather doubtful whether the 22nd recital could in reality be attributed such a wide meaning. The recital starts with the observation that, in order to ensure an effective protection of public interest objectives, information society services should be supervised at the source of the activity. As will be argued below, the distinction between rules of administrative authorisations, prudential supervision and product quality on the one hand and conflict of laws on the other should also be applied to E-Commerce. When referring to the applicable law, the 22nd recital refers to supervisory rules rather than to the law applicable to the contract. The Directive therefore seeks the allocation of regulatory authority between the Member States without determining the law applicable to the horizontal relation between the private parties. An uncareful drafting of the wording of the Annex would not change that principle.[200] The internal market clause does, with regard to private law, not go beyond the fundamental freedoms. Art. 3 (4) of the Directive recognises that Member States are not prevented from applying to foreign information society service providers national provisions necessary for the safeguard of public policy, protection of health, public security or the protection of consumers. Even proponents of a country of origin principle have acknowledged that the ECJ will interpret these grounds and their scope in a manner similar to the derogations to the free movement provisions.[201]

A restriction to the freedom to provide services and the non-application of the law of the home Member State of the information society service provider are not identical. The fact that the freedom to provide

---

[199] Mankowski, P., "Herkunftslandprinzip und deutsches Umsetzungsgesetz zur e-commerce-Richtlinie", *IPRax*, Vol. 22, No. 4, 2002, pp. 257–266; Spindler, G., "Herkunftslandprinzip und Kollisionsrecht -Binnenmarktintegration ohne Harmonisierung?", *RabelsZ*, Vol. 66, 2002, pp. 633–709 (651).

[200] Placing a question mark at the legal value of the Annex: Lopez-Tarruella, A., "A European Union Regulatory Framework for Electronic Commerce", *Common Market Law Review*, Vol. 38, No. 6, 2006, pp. 1337–1384 (1346).

[201] Hörnle, J., "Country of Origin Regulation in Cross-Border Media: One Step Beyond the Freedom to Provide Services?", *International Comparative Law Quarterly*, Vol. 54, 2005, pp. 89–126 (104).

information society services should not be restricted does not result in the automatic application of the law of the Member State of origin. Since art. 3 (2) of the E-Commerce Directive does not lead automatically to the comprehensive application of the law of the Member State of origin, it cannot be read as a proper country or origin principle. The provision differs in this respect from, for example, the Bolkestein proposal. Art. 16 (1) Bolkestein proposal explicitly stipulated that Member States should ensure that service providers were only subject to the laws of the Member State of origin.[202] Such a formulation would not leave any scope to the conflict of laws. However, the country of origin principle in the Services Directive as such became the subject of fierce criticism and was ultimately deleted.

The discussion on the country of origin principle in the Bolkenstein proposal coincided from a temporal point of view with the transformation of the Rome Convention into the Rome I Regulation. Art. 22 of the Rome I Proposal contained a subparagraph (c) which provided that Rome I would not prejudice the application of instruments of secondary law which 'lay down rules to promote the smooth operation of the internal market, where such rules cannot apply at the same time as the law designated by the rules of private international law'. A similar provision was laid down in the draft Rome II Regulation.[203] Although the provisions do not mention the E-Commerce Directive explicitly, it was clear that the provisions were meant to make the make internal market clause, read as a country of origin principle, prevail over Rome I and Rome II. The provisions met with strong resistance and were ultimately dropped in the final instrument and instead a more neutral reference to the E-Commerce Directive was inserted in the preamble to Rome I.[204]

---

[202] Proposal for a Directive of the European Parliament and of the Council on services in the internal market, COM (2004) 002, final.

[203] Proposal for a Rome II Regulation, COM (2004) 28 2, final.

[204] The 40th recital of the preamble to Rome I: '(..) This Regulation should not prejudice the application of other instruments laying down provisions designed to contribute to the proper functioning of the internal market in so far as they cannot be applied in conjunction with the law designated by the rules of this Regulation. The application of provisions of the applicable law designated by the rules of this Regulation should not restrict the free movement of goods and services as regulated by Community instruments, such as Directive 2000/31/EC of the European Parliament and of the Council of 8 June 2000 on certain legal aspects of information society services, in particular electronic commerce, in the Internal Market (Directive on electronic commerce).' Unfortunately the preamble 'still leaves room for the assumption that the E-Commerce Directive does have some kind of interference with private international law',

The adoption of proposed provisions would have made it difficult to apply the conflict of laws rules alongside sectoral instruments adopting a country of origin approach. The deletion of subparagraph (c) thus has broader implications for the relationship between the country of origin principle and Rome I. Wilderspin has phrased with regard to Rome II that 'it might be premature to conclude that this result marks the demise of the country of origin's claim to be a conflict of laws rule but it is certainly true to say that it marks a triumphant resurgence of a more traditional Savignyian conflict of laws approach (…)'.[205]

6.10.2 *The Harmonised Field as Overriding Mandatory Provisions*

The view that the E-Commerce Directive lays down a conflict of laws rule fails to convince completely. A second point of view that has been advanced by scholars concerning the relationship between the 'country of origin principle' in the Directive and PIL is that though the E-Commerce Directive does not lay down an additional choice of law, the coordinated field should be seen as a set of overriding mandatory provisions.[206] The substantive rules would override the law designated by the conflict of laws rules. In a strict sense, art. 3 of the Directive would therefore not lay down any additional PIL rules. Also this view fails to convince. It is doubtful whether the information requirements could really be classified as crucial for the safeguard of a country's political, social or economical order. Once again it must be repeated that the concept of overriding mandatory provisions is traditionally interpreted narrowly in the Member States. The classification of the coordinated field as overriding mandatory provisions would in any event bring little additional benefits.

6.10.3 *eDate Advertising*

The scope of interference of the E-Commerce Directive in the conflict of laws process, if any, therefore remains open to debate. Fortunately, the ECJ has been invited in *eDate Advertising* to rule upon the

see: Kramer, X., "The Rome II Regulation on the Law Applicable to Non-Contractual Obligations: The European private international law tradition continued", *Nederlands Internationaal Privaatrecht*, Vol. 26, 2008, pp. 414–424 (417).

205 Wilderspin, M., "The Rome II Regulation; Some Policy Observations", *Nederlands Internationaal Privaatrecht*, Vol. 26, 2008, pp. 408–413 (410).

206 Fallon/Meeusen *supra* note 196, pp. 486–488 ; Hellner, *supra* note 198, pp. 217–223.

relationship between the E-Commerce Directive and PIL.[207] If the Court were to follow the line of reasoning developed in this chapter, it would find that the Directive does not lay down any additional conflict of laws rule, although it may regulate areas traditionally belonging to the area of private law. However, what matters in European law is not the national classification of a rule, but rather its effects. The E-Commerce Directive provides for a duty of supervision over information society service providers established in the territory of the Member States, and gives minimum requirements and rules concerning the formal validity of the contract. The Directive constitutes a specific interpretation of the freedom to provide services and should therefore follow the lines of art. 56 TFEU as much as possible.[208] The freedom to provide services does not settle the question of applicable law, but can make corrections to it insofar as the applicable law would constitute a barrier to trade that could not be justified by an overriding public interest.

6.10.4 *The Directive may Affect Private law, but not Conflict of Laws*

What the Directive aims for is that if a society service provider can lawfully exercise his profession or lawfully make promotional sales in its own Member State, he should in principle also be allowed to do so in other Member States. The host Member State cannot impose additional restrictions. To that extent, the Directive contains nothing more than the application of the principle of mutual recognition to administrative authorisations, prudential supervision or rules concerning product quality to E-Commerce. Rules relating to administrative authorisations, prudential supervision or product quality should, however, be treated different from rules exclusively interfering with private relations.[209] The *Alpine Investment* distinction previously drawn in the Data Protection Directive should also be applied to the E-Commerce Directive.[210] The fact that due to the physical establishment of an undertaking the Netherlands was in the best position to regulate, did not

---

[207] Case C-509/09 *eDate Advertising* (pending case).

[208] Fezer, K., and S. Koos, "Das gemeinschaftsrechtliche Herkunftslandprinzip und die e-commerce-Richtlinie", *IPRax*, Vol. 20, No. 5, 2000, pp. 349–354; Fallon, M., and J. Meeusen, "Private International Law in the European Union and the Exception of Mutual Recognition", *Yearbook of Private International Law*, Vol. 4, 2002, pp. 37–66.

[209] See par. 6.3

[210] See par. 4.1.1.

settle the law applicable to a contract concluded between the Dutch undertaking and a consumer approached in Belgium. The harmonised field of the E-Commerce Directive would also cover private laws insofar as these provisions are in essence rules of supervision. However, the fact that private law is not caught by the supervision at source principle underpinning the directive does not mean that the application of the private rule cannot contravene the fundamental freedoms.[211] General contract law will in principle be excluded, but provisions that cannot be derogated from by agreement may nevertheless constitute a restriction upon the functioning of the internal market.

Also the fact that the internal market clause does not interfere in the conflict of laws process, does not mean that the directive does not affect private law. An example would be the information requirements imposed by the Directive (art. 5, 6 and 10). The requirement that a promotional offer should be clearly identifiable as such, and the conditions which are to be met to qualify for them should be easily accessible and be presented clearly and unambiguously would traditionally fall into the domain of private law. What is at stake here, is however not private law as such, but the public enforcement of these provisions. The home Member State has the duty to ensure that the information society services provided by a service provider established on its territory shall comply with the national provisions applicable in the Member State in question which fall within the coordinated field (art. 3 (1)). Because of the home supervision, the host Member State may not impose any further checks. From this angle, art. 3 (2) will have relevance for private law. Contrary to contract law, the public enforcement of mandatory norms also functions on the basis of territorial criteria. Without harmonisation, the risk would occur that a service provider would be confronted with public enforcement in both the Member State in which it is established and in the Member State where it provides the service.

Art. 3 distributes the duty of enforcement. In line with *Alpine Investments*, the Member State in which the service provider is established is best placed to enforce legislation, but the Directive does not define the law applicable to horizontal relationship between the service provider and the recipient. Even with regard to the rules of

---

[211] Compare the 23rd recital of the preamble to the E-Commerce Directive: '(…) provisions of the applicable law designated by rules of private international law must not restrict the freedom to provide information society services as established in this Directive.'

administrative authorisations, prudential supervision and product quality, the Directive does not automatically lead to the application of the laws of the Member State of origin. If the Directive somehow contained a hidden conflict of laws rule in favour of the 'home' of the information society service provider, that conflict of laws rule would automatically lead to the applicability of the information requirements as defined by the law of the Member State of origin. In *Gysbrechts* the ECJ however held that the public enforcement of a rule Belgian on consumer protection to a service provider established in Belgium in relation to a contract concluded with a French consumer could constitute a restriction of art. 35 TFEU.[212] The public enforcement of the *lex fori* to service providers established in its territory may be incompatible with the free movement of goods. Therefore the national provisions applicable in the Member State of origin to a cross border provision of services may diverge as compared to a purely national provision of services. If the Directive would require the automatic enforcement of the laws of the Member State of origin, it would thus under circumstances violate the free movement of goods or services. The E-Commerce Directive thus regulates primarily who may enforce, instead of what should be enforced.

Hence the Directive, although it may affect rules that were traditionally perceived as private law, does not lay down any additional rules on PIL. The Directive might cover rules that are traditionally considered to be part of private law in some Member States, but are essentially meant to supervise the information society service provider. However, even the observance of these information requirements is the subject of public enforcement. The Directive primarily allocates the duty of supervision between the Member States without determining the law applicable to the horizontal relationship between the service provider and the recipient. Evidently, the private law declared applicable by the PIL rules of the forum affecting E-Commerce remain subject to the rule that they may not restrict the freedom to provide services.[213]

[212] *Gysbrechts*, *supra* note 29.

[213] Even here it is doubtful whether private laws can constitute a restriction on the free movement provisions. The ECJ held in *Motorradcenter* that the effects of an obligation to provide information prior to contract on the free movement of goods were too indirect and uncertain to warrant the conclusion that it may hinder trade between Member States. Case C-93/92 *CMC Motorradcenter* [1993] ECR I-5009

6.11 *Conclusions*

Mutual recognition and conflict of laws fulfil a mutually complentary function. Mutual recognition is about rules concerning administrative authorisations, prudential supervision or product quality. The application of these laws, generally and traditionally perceived to be public laws, is by definition mandatory and cannot be evaded by private parties. Because application is territorial, a risk occurs that a service provider has to comply with the legislation of two Member States, creating a double regulatory burden. Union law therefore must step in. Despite that conflict of laws norms may operate on the basis of territorial criteria, private law is not necessarily territorial. The conflict of laws norms lead to the designation of a single applicable law. Moreover, private parties have in contract law the possibility of a choice of law. In contract law only minimal checks are placed upon private autonomy. Parties can even evade mandatory private laws by evading the application of the legal system involved altogether. Union law is based upon individual responsibility; it should in principle be left to the private parties themselves how to best protect their rights. Union law thus fulfils a different role. *CMC Motorradcenter* and *Alhstom Atlantique* seem to suggest that if parties possess the possibility to choose the applicable law, the effects of application of that law will be too remote and uncertain to constitute a restriction upon the fundamental freedoms.

Mutual recognition is in areas outside administrative authorisations, prudential supervision and product quality less appropriate. The case-law in the field of company and surname law demonstrates that not the application of the conflict of laws norm in itself, but rather the non-recognition of the operation of the conflict of laws mechanism of other Member States is able to restrict the fundamental freedoms or European Citizenship. The national conflict of laws rules would otherwise be elevated to the level of mandatory laws and exclude private autonomy. Logically, differences in rights for the individual can only occur when the conflict of laws systems lead to the application of different, diverging national laws. The violation of the fundamental freedoms is not a dual burden in the strict sense, but the non-recognition of rights duly acquired under the laws of another Member State. Private autonomy is used to decide about the observance of national legislations competing over application. In that sense, Union law empowers the individual to evade mandatory choice of law rules, but only to the extent that an alternative is being offered by another Member State.

Vested rights might be able to provide much explanatory power in company, surname and property law, but less in contracts. There exists a practical difficulty in proving that a vested right has been duly acquired if that right has never been registered by the state or in any official registrar. The conflict of laws norms in contractual obligations have been harmonised by Rome I. The application of the conflict of laws norms will thus always lead to the designation of the same applicable law. The only mechanism for designating the applicable law not harmonised by Rome I is overriding mandatory provisions.

The examples of company and surname law demonstrate that mutual recognition can have only limited effect in private law. Mutual recognition is a privilege that is invoked against the state and not against another individual. Mutual recognition leads to an obligation for the host Member States not to apply its law, whereas the non-application does not suffice in private law. What is required is the application of a specific law. The public/private distinction should not be taken too strictly. The effects of the fundamental freedoms on private law can to a certain extent be explained by the fact that the dividing line is drawn differently. Union law is not concerned with the national classification of a rule, but rather with its effects. Rules on administrative authorisation, prudential supervision and product quality will thus be caught by the principle of mutual recognition regardless of whether such a rule is qualified as public or private in a Member State.

Overriding mandatory provisions represent in this distinction a particular category. On the basis of the interests they seek to interpret, they require more than the non-application of foreign law, instead ascertaining their own application. Contrary to general contract law or the conflict of laws norms dealing with contractual obligations overriding mandatory provisions do not allow for private autonomy. They apply regardless of the applicable law and thus regardless of the choice made by the private parties. The exclusion of private autonomy makes it difficult for parties to evade the application of the overriding mandatory provisions. Union law should thus step in. There is no principal reason why overriding mandatory provisions should a priori be excluded from the scope of the fundamental freedoms. Overriding mandatory provisions do also not a priori benefit from the *Keck* exception in the area of goods, nor are they incapable of preventing market access in the area of services. Although the particular characteristics of overriding mandatory provisions should be taken into account, they are in principle subject to the same process of justification as any other national rule infringing one of the fundamental freedoms.

BIBLIOGRAPHY

Allison, J., "Variation of View on English Legal Distinctions between Public and Private", *Cambridge Law Journal*, Vol. 66, No. 3, 2007, pp. 698–711

Amstuz, M., "In-between Worlds: *Marleasing* and the Emergence of Interlegality in Legal Reasoning", *European Law Journal*, Vol. 11, No. 6, 2005, pp. 766–784

Anagnostaras, G., "The Unfair Commercial Practices Directive in Context: From Legal Disparity to Legal Complexity", *Common Market Law Review*, Vol. 47, 2010, pp. 147–171

Ancel, B., and Y. Lequette, *Grand arrêts de la jurisprudence française de droit international privé*, 4e édition, 2001

Ancel, M., *La prestation caractéristique du contrat*, Economica, Paris, 2002

Ancel, B., "Destinées de l'article 3 du Code civil", *Mélanges en l'honneur de Paul Lagarde ; Le droit international privé : esprit et méthodes*, Dalloz, Paris, 2005, pp. 1–18

Badiali, G., "Le droit international privé des Communautés européennes", *Recueil des Cours*, Vol. 191, 1985, pp. 9–182

Baere (de), G., "Houdt het Communautair herkomstlandbeginsel een verborgen conflictregel in?", *Revue Belge de Droit International*, Vol. 36, 2003, pp. 131–201

De Baere, G., "'Is this a Conflict Rule which I see Before Me?' Looking for a Hidden Conflict Rule in the Principle of Origin as Implemented in Primary European Union law and in the 'Directive on Electronic Commerce", *Maastricht Journal of Comparative Law*, Vol. 11, No. 3, 2004, pp. 287–319

Bagheri, M., International Contracts and National Economic Regulation, Kluwer Law International, The Hague, 2000

Ballarino, T., and B. Ubertazzi, "On Avello and Other Judgments, A New Point of Departure in the Conflict of Laws?", *Yearbook of Private International Law*, Vol. 6, 2004, pp. 85–128

Ballarino, T., and P. Romano, "Le principe de proximité chez Paul Lagarde", *Mélanges en l'honneur de Paul Lagarde ; Le droit international privé : esprit et méthodes*, Dalloz, Paris, 2005, pp. 37–54

Bar (von), C., and P. Mankowski, *Internationales Privatrecht, Band I: Allgemeine Lehren*, Beck'sche Verlagsbuchhandlung, München 2. Auflage, 2003

Bar (von), C., "Coverage and Structure of the Academic Common Frame of Reference", *European Review of Contract Law*, Vol. 3, 2007, pp. 350–361

Barnard, C., "Social Dumping and the Race to the Bottom", *European Law Review*, Vol. 25, 2000, pp. 57–78

Barnard, C., EC Employment Law, Oxford University Press, Oxford, 3rd edition, 2006

Barnard, C., "Trailing a new approach to free movement of goods?", *Cambridge Law Journal*, Vol. 68, 2009, pp. 288–290

Barrière Brousse, I., "Le Traité de Lisbonne et le droit international privé", *Journal du Droit International*, Vol. 137, No. 1, 2010, pp. 3–34

Basedow, J., "Wirtschaftskollisionsrecht", *RabelsZ*, Vol. 52, 1988, pp. 8–40

Basedow, J., "Conflicts of Economic Regulation", *American Journal of Comparative Law*, Vol. 42, 1994, pp. 423–447

Basedow, J., "Der kollisionsrecheteliche Gehalt der Produktfreiheiten im europäischen Binnenmarkt: favor offerentis", *RabelsZ*, Vol. 95, 1995, pp. 1–55

Basedow, J., "A Common Contract Law for the Common Market", *Common Market Law Review*, Vol. 33, 1996, pp. 1169–1195

Basedow, J., "The Efffects of Globalization on Private International Law", in: J. Basedow and T. Kono (eds.), Legal Aspects of Globalization, Kluwer Law International, The Hague, 1999, pp. 1–10

Basedow, J., "Anforderungen an eine Europäische Zivilrechtsdogmatik", R. Zimmermann, R. Knütel and J.P. Meincke (eds), *Rechtsgeschichte und Privatrechtsdogmatik*, C.F. Müller, Heidelberg, 1999, pp. 81–82

Basedow, J., "The Communitarisation of the Conflict of laws under the Treaty of Amsterdam", *Common Market Law Review*, Vol. 37, No. 3, 2000, pp. 687–708

Basedow, J., "The Gradual Emergence of European Private Law", T. Einhorn and K. Siehr (eds.), *Intercontinental Cooperation through Private International Law: Essays in Memory of Peter E Nygh*, TMC Asser Press, The Hague, 2004, pp. 1–18

Basedow, J., "Dienstleistungsrichtlinie, Herkunftslandprinzip und Internationales Privatrecht", *Europäisches Zeitschrift für Wirtschaftsrecht*, Vol. 15, 2004, pp. 423–424

Basedow, J., "Recherches sur la formation de l'ordre public européen dans la jurisprudence", B. Ancel, *Le droit international privé : esprit et méthodes ; Mélanges en l'honneur de Paul Lagarde*, Dalloz, Paris, 2005, pp. 291–319

Basedow, J., "European Private International Law of Obligations and Internal Market Legislation – A matter of Coordination", J. Erauw *et al* (eds.), *Liber Memorialis Petar Šarčević: Universalism, Tradition and the Individual*, Sellier, München, 2006, pp. 13–24

Basedow, J., "Freedom of Contract in the European Union", *European Review of Private Law*, vol. 16, 2008, pp. 901–923

Basedow, J., "Der Grundsatz der Nichtdiskriminierung im europäischen Privatrecht", *Zeitschrift für Europäisches Privatrecht*, 2008, pp. 230–251

Batiffol, H., *Traite élémentaire de droit international privé*, Librairie générale de droit et de jurisprudence, Paris, 1949

Batifol, H., and P.Lagarde, *Traité de Droit International Privé*, Paris, Tome I, 8e édition, 1993

Beale, H., "The Draft Directive on Consumer Rights and UK Consumer law: Where now", G. Howells and R. Schulze (eds.), *Modernising and harmonising consumer contract law*, Sellier, München, 2009, pp. 289–302

Beale, H., "European Contract Law: The Common Frame of Reference and Beyond", C. Twigg-Flesner, *The Cambridge Companion to European Union Private Law*, Cambridge University Press, Cambridge, 2010, pp. 116–130

Behrens, P., "Cartesio bestätigt, aber korrigiert Daily Mail", *Europäische Zeitschrift für Wirtschaftsrecht*, Vol. 20, No. 3, 2009, pp. 81–83

Bell, M., *Anti-Discrimination Law and the European Union*, Oxford University Press, New York, 2002

Benöhr, I., *Consumer Law between Market Integration and Human Rights Protection*, EUI Thesis (2009)

Bercusson, B., *European Labour Law*, Butterworths, London 1996; Teyssié, B., *Droit européen du travail*, Litec, Paris, 2e edition, 2003

Betti, I., "The Italian torpedo is dead: long live the Italian torpedo, *Journal of Intellectual Property Law & Practice*, Vol. 3, No. 1, 2008, 6–7

Berg (van den), R., "Subsidiarity as an Economic Demarcation Principle and the Emergence of European Private Law", *Maastricht Journal of International and Comparative Law*, Vol. 5, 1998, pp. 129–152

Bergh, R. (van den), "Uneasy Case for Harmonising Consumer Law", K. Heine and W. Kerber, *Zentralität und dezentralität von Regulierung in Europa*, Lucius Lucius, Stuttgart, 2007, pp. 183–206

Berg (van den), P., *The Politics of European Codification. A History of the Unification of Law in France, Prussia, the Austrian Monarchy and the Netherlands*, European Law Publishing, Groningen, 2007

Bermann, G., (ed.), *Party autonomy: constitutional and international law limits in comparative perspective, XVIth Quadrennial Congress of Comparative Law*, Juris Publishing, New York, 2005

Bernard, P., "Cassis de Dijon und Kollisionsrecht - am Beispiel des unlauteren Wettbewerbs", *Europäisches Zeitschrift für Wirtschaftsrecht*, Vol. 14, 1992, pp. 437–438

Bernard, N., "Flexibility in the European Single Market", C. Barnard and J. Scott (eds.), *The Law of the Single European Market: Unpacking the Premises*, Hart Publishing, Oxford, 2002, pp. 101–124

Bertoli, P., "The Court of Justice and Private International Law", *Yearbook of Private International Law*, Vol. 8, 2006, pp. 375–412

Bertoli, P., "Party Autonomy and Choice-Of-Law Methods in the "Rome II" Regulation on the Law Applicable to Non-Contractual Obligations", *Il Diritto dell'Unione europea*, Vol. 14, 2009, pp. 229–264

Bertrams, R., and S. Kruisinga, *Overeenkomsten in het internationaal privaatrecht en het Weens Koopverdrag*, Kluwer, Deventer, 2007

Bervoets, Th., "Een rechtstheoretisch onderzoek naar het beginsel van rechtskeuze", *Partij-invloed in het international privaatrecht; Vier opstellen ter gelegenheid van het 25-jarig bestaan van het Centrum voor Buitenlands Recht en Internationaal Privaatrecht aan de Universiteit van Amsterdam*, Deventer, Kluwer, 1974, pp. 31–45

Besson, S., "L'Égalité de Traitement entre Particuliers en Droit Communautaire", F. Werro (ed.), *L'Européanisation du Droit Privé*, Editions Universitaires Fribourg, Fribourg, 1998, pp. 51–96

Betlem, G., "The Doctrine of Consistent Interpretation; Managing Legal Uncertainty", J. Prinssen and A. Schrauwen (eds.), *Direct Effect: Rethinking a Classic of EC Legal Doctrine*, European Law Publishers, Groningen, 2001, pp. 79–105

Betlem, G., Beyond *Francovich*: Completing the Unified Member State and EU Liability Regime, D. Obradovic and N. Lavranos (eds.), *Interface between EU Law and National Law*, European Law Publishers, Groningen, 2007, pp. 297–309

Binder, D., "The European Court of Justice and the Protection of Fundamental Rights in the European Union: New Developments and Future Possibilities in Expanding Fundamental Rights Review to Member State Action", Jean Monnet Working Paper 95/9504, 1995

Boele-Woelki, K., "Unification and Harmonization of Private International Law in Europe", J. Basedow *et al* (eds.) *Private Law in the International Arena: Liber Amicorum Kurt Siehr*, T.M.C. Asser Press, The Hague, 2000, pp. 61–78

Boele-Woelki, K., and R. Van Ooik, "The Communitarization of Private International Law", *Yearbook of Private International Law*, Vol. 4, 2002, pp. 1–36

Boer (de), Th., "Forty years on : the evolution of postwar private international law in Europe", *Symposium in celebration of the 40th anniversary of the Centre of Foreign Law and Private International Law*, Kluwer, Deventer, 1990

Boer (de), Th., "Party Autonomy and its Limitations in the Rome II Regulation", *Yearbook of Private International Law*, Vol. 9, 2007, pp. 19–29

Bogaert (van den), S., "Horizontality: The Courts Attacks?" C. Barnard (ed.), *The Law of Single European Market*, Hart Publishing, Oxford, 2002, pp. 123–152

Bogdan, M., *Concise Introduction to EU Private International Law*, Europa Law Publishing, Groningen, 2006, pp. 6–14

Bogdan, M., "Foreign Public Law and Article 7 (1) of the Rome Convention: Some Reflections from Sweden", T. Azzi *et al* (eds.), *Vers de nouveaux équilibres entre ordres juridiques, Liber amicorum Hélène Gaudemet-Tallon*, Dalloz, Paris, 2008, pp. 671–682

Bonomi, A., "Mandatory Rules in Private International Law: The quest for uniformity of decisions in a global environment", *Yearbook of Private International Law*, Vol. 1, 1999, pp. 215–247

Bonomi, A., "Note – Article 7(1) of the European Contracts Convention: Codifying the Practice of Applying Foreign Mandatory Rules", *Harvard Law Review*, Vol. 114, 2001, pp. 2462–2477

Bonomi, A., "Conversion of the Rome Convention on Contracts into an EC Instrument: Some Remarks on the Green Paper of the EC Commission", *Yearbook of Private International Law*, Vol. 5, 2003, pp. 53–98

Borrás, A., "Les clauses de déconnexion et le droit international privé communautaire", H. Mansel *et al* (eds.), *Festschrift für Erik Jayme*, Sellier, München, 2004, pp. 57–72

Borrás, A., "Le droit international privé communautaire : réalités, problèmes et perspectives d'avenir", *Recueil des Cours*, Vol. 317, 2005, pp. 323–526

Braams, B., "Equal Opportunities between Men and Women and Gender Mainstreaming under the European Employment Strategy (EES) and the Open Method of Coordination (OMC) – A New Policy Approach to Combat Gender Discrimination?", *European Integration online Papers*, Vol. 11, 2007

Brand, R., "Union Competence for Matters of Judicial Cooperation at the Hague Conference on Private International Law: A View from the United States", *Journal of Law and Commerce*, Vol. 21, 2002, pp. 191–208

Brand, R., "The Lugano Case in the European Court of Justice: Evolving European Union Competence in Private International Law", *ILSA Journal of International & Comparative Law*, Vol. 11, 2005, pp. 297–303

Brand, R., "Balancing Sovereignty and Party Autonomy in Private International Law",Erauw J., *et al* (eds.), *Liber Memorialis Petar Šarčević, Universalism, Tradition and the Individual*, Sellier, München, 2006, pp. 35–52

Brand, R., "The European Magnet and the U.S. Centrifuge: Ten Selected Private International Law Developments of 2008", University of Pittsburgh Working Paper No. 2009–01

Brière, C., "Le Droit International Privé Européen des Contrats et la Coordination des Sources", *Journal du Droit International*, Vol. 136, No. 3, 2009, pp. 792–807

Briggs, P., *The Conflict of Laws*, Oxford University Press, Oxford, 2002

Briggs, P., *Agreements on Jurisdiction and Choice of Law*, Oxford University Press, Oxford, 2008, pp. 396–399.

Brilmayer, L., "The Role of Substantive and Choice of Law Policies in the Formation and Application of Choice of Law Rules", *Recueil des Cours*, Vol. 252, 1995, pp. 9–122

Brüning, S., *Die Beachtlichkeit des fremden ordre public*, Duncker & Humblot, Berlin, 1996

Bucher, A., "L'Ordre Public et le But Social des Lois en Droit International Privé", *Recueil des Cours*, Vol. 239, 1993, pp. 9–116

Búrca (de), G., "The Principle of Proportionality and its Application in EC Law", *Yearbook of European Law*, Vol. 13, 1993, pp. 105–150

Bureau, D., and H. Muir Watt, *Droit international privé*, Presses Universitaires de France, Paris, 2007

Buxbaum, R., and K. Hopt, *Legal Harmonization and the Business Enterprise*, Walter de Gruyter, Berlin, 1988

Bygrave, L., "Determining Applicable Law pursuant to European Data Protection Legislation", *Computer Law & Security Report*, Vol. 16, 2000, pp. 252–257

Cachard, O., *La régulation internationale du marché électronique*, LGDJ, Paris, 2001

Cafaggi, F., and H. Muir-Watt, "The Making of European Private Law: Regulation and Governance Design", European Governance Paper N-07–02, 2007

Carbonara, E., and F. Parisi, "Choice of Law and Legal Evolution: Rethinking the Market for Legal Rules", University of Minnesota Law School Legal Studies Research Paper Series no. 07–38, 2007

Chalmers, D., *et al*, *European Union Law*, Cambridge University Press, Cambridge, 2006

Cherednychenko, O., *Fundamental Rights, Contract Law and the Protection of the Weaker Party, A Comparative Analysis of the Constitutionalisation of Contract Law, with Emphasis on Risky Financial Transaction*, Sellier, München, 2007

Chong, A., "The Public Policy and Mandatory Rules of Third Countries in International Contracts" *Journal of Private International Law*, Vol. 2, No. 1, 2006, pp. 27–70

Claringbould, M., "Artikel 5 Rome I en vervoerovereenkomsten", *Nederlands Internationaal Privaatrecht*, Vol. 27, No. 4, 2009, pp. 426–436

Coester-Waltjen, D., "Das Anerkunningsprinzip im Dornröschenschlaf? ", H. Mansel *et al* (eds.), *Festschrift für Erik Jayme Band I*, Sellier, München, 2004, pp. 121–129

Collins, H., *Regulating Contracts*, Oxford University Press, Oxford, 1999

Collins, H., "Why Europe Needs a Civil Code: European Identity and the Social Model", M. Andenas *et al* (eds.), *Private Law Beyond the National Systems: Liber Amicorum Guido Alpa*, British Institute for International and Comparative Law London, 2007, pp. 259–269

Collins, H., *The European civil code : the way forward*, Cambridge University Press, Cambridge, 2008

Collins, L., *et al* (eds.), *Dicey, Albert Morris and Collins on the Conflicts of Laws*, Sweet Maxwell, London, fourteenth edition, Volume II, 2006

Corkin, J., "European Law as <Conflicts Law>: The Implications for Individual Autonomy", A. Furrer (ed.), *Europäisches Privatrecht im wissenschaftlichen Diskurs*, Stämpfli Verlag, Bern, 2006, pp. 391–415

Courbe, P., "L'ordre public de proximité", *Mélanges en l'honneur de Paul Lagarde ; Le droit international privé : esprit et méthodes*, Dalloz, Paris, 2005, pp. 227–239

Cox, R., L. Merett and M. Smith, *Private International Law of Reinsurance and Insurance*, Informa, London 2006

Cremona, M., EU External Action in the JHA Domain: A Legal Perspective, EUI Working Papers Law, No. 24, 2008

Crettez, B., and R. Deloche, "On the unification of legal rules in the European Union", *European Journal of Law and Economics*, Vol. 21, 2006, pp. 203–214

Crettez, B., B. Deffains and R. Deloche, "On the optimal complexity of law and legal rules harmonization", *European Journal of Law and Economics*, Vol. 27, 2009, pp. 129–142

Cutler, C., Private Power and Global Authority: Transnational Merchant Law in the Global Political Economy, Cambridge University Press, Cambridge, 2003, pp. 48–49

Czernich, D., and H. Heiss (eds.), *EVÜ: Das Europäische Schuldvertragsübereinkommen*, Wien: Verlag Orac, 1999, pp. 155.

Dagan, H., "The Limited Autonomy of Private Law" *American Journal of Comparative Law*, Vol. 56, 2008, pp. 809–834

Danwitz (von), T., "Der Grundsatz der Verhältnismäßigkeit im Gemeinschaftsrecht", *Europäisches Wirtschafts & Steuerrecht*, Vol. 14, No. 9, 2003, pp. 393–402

Davies, G., "Services, Citizenship and the Country of Origin Principle", Mitchell Working Paper Series, no. 2, 2007

Deelen, J., *Rechtskeuze in het Nederlands internationaal contractenrecht*, W.L.G. Lemaire, Amsterdam 1965

Deelen, J., *De blinddoek van von Savigny*, Scheltema & Holkema, Amsterdam, 1966

De Lima Pinheiro, L., "Competition between Legal Systems in the European Union and Private International Law", *IPRax*, Vol. 28, 2008, pp. 206–213

Dickinson, A., "Cross-Border Torts in EC Courts – A Response to the proposed 'Rome II' Regulation", *European Business Law Review*, Vol. 13, 2002, pp. 369–388

Dickinson, A., "European Private International Law: Embracing New Horizons or Mourning the Past", *Journal of Private International Law*, Vol. 1, No. 2, 2005, pp. 197–236

Dickinson, A., "The law applicable to contracts – uncertainty on the horizon?" *Butterworths Journal of International Banking and Financial Law*, 2006, pp. 171–173

Dickinson, A., "Third-Country Mandatory Rules in the Law Applicable to Contractual Obligations, so long, farewell, auf wiedersehem, adieu?" *Journal of Private International Law*, Vol. 3, No. 1, 2007, pp. 53–88

Diederiks-Verschoor, I., and M. Butler, An introduction to air law, Kluwer, Deventer, 8th edition, 2006

Dougan, M., "The "Disguised" Vertical Effect of Directives", *Cambridge Law Journal*, Vol. 59, No. 3, 2000, pp. 586–612

Dougan, M., "Minimum Harmonization and the Internal Market", *Common Market Law Review*, Vol. 37, 2000, pp. 863–885

Dougan, M., and E. Spaventa, "Educating Rudy and the (non-) English Patient: A double-bill on residency rights under Article 18 EC", *European Law Review*, Vol. 28, 2003, pp. 699–712

Downes, N., "More about Timeshare: A Revised Directive of a Regulation? Incidents of Other Instruments of Consumer Protection", *European Review of Private Law*, Vol. 16, 2008, pp. 607–625

Duintjer Tebbens, H., "Les règles de conflit contenues dans les instruments de droit dérivé", A. Fuchs *et al* (eds.), *Les conflits de lois et le système juridique communautaire*, Dalloz, Paris, 2004, pp. 101–115

Ebers, M., "From *Océano* to *Asturcom*", *European Review of Private Law*, Vol. 18, 2010, pp. 823–846

Eeckhout (van den), V., "Promoting Human Rights within the Union: The Role of European Private International Law", *European Law Journal*, Vol. 14, No. 1, 2008, pp. 105–127

Eeckhout (van den), V., "Het beroep op het bezit van een nationaliteit in geval van dubbele nationaliteit", *Nederlands Tijdschrift voor Europees Recht*, Vol. 15, 2009, 307–316

Eidenmüller, H., *et al*, "Der Gemeinsame Referenzrahmen für das Europäische Privatrecht – Wertungsfragen und Kodifikationsprobleme –", *Juristenzeitung*, Vol. 63, 2008, pp. 529–550

Eidenmüller, H., "Party Autonomy, Distributive Justice and the Conclusion of Contracts in the DCFR", *European Review of Contract Law*, Vol. 5, No. 2, 2009, pp. 109–131

Enchelmaier, S., "The Awkward Selling of a Good Idea, or a Traditionalist Interpretation of *Keck*", *Yearbook of European Law*, Vol. 22, 2003, pp. 249–322

Fallon, M., "Les conflits de lois et de juridictions dans un espace économique intégré", *Receuil des Cours*, Vol. 253, 1995, pp. 9–281

Fallon, M., and S. Francq, "Towards Internationally Mandatory Directives for Consumer Contracts?", J. Basedow *et al* (eds.) *Private Law in the International Arena: Liber Amicorum Kurt Siehr*, T.M.C. Asser Press, The Hague, 2000, pp. 155–178

Fallon, M., and J. Meeusen, "Private International Law in the European Union and the Exception of Mutual Recognition", *Yearbook of Private International Law*, Vol. 4, 2002, pp. 37–66

Fallon, M., and J. Meeusen, "Le commerce électronique, la directive 2000/31/CE et le droit international privé", *Revue Critique de Droit International Privé*, Vol. 91, No. 3, 2002, pp. 435–489

Fallon, M., "Libertés communautaires et règles de conflit de lois", A. Fuchs *et al* (eds.), Les conflits de lois et le système juridique communautaire, Dalloz, Paris, 2004, pp. 31–80

Fallon, M., "Le principe de proximité dans le droit de l'Union Européenne", *Mélanges en l'honneur de Paul Lagarde ; Le droit international privé : esprit et méthodes*, Dalloz, Paris, 2005, pp. 241–262

Fallon, M., "L'applicabilité du règlement ‹Bruxelles I› aux situations externes après l'avis 1/03", T. Azzi *et al* (eds.), *Vers de nouveaux équilibres entre ordres juridiques, Liber amicorum Hélène Gaudemet-Tallon*, Dalloz, Paris, 2008, pp. 241–264

Farrand, B., "The Case that Never Was: An Analysis of the Apple iTunes Case Presented by the Commission and Potential Future Issues", *European Intellectual Property Law Review*, Vol. 31, 2009, pp. 508–513

Fawcett, J., "Evasion of Law and Mandatory Rules in Private International Law", *Cambridge Law Journal*, Vol. 44, 1990, pp. 44–62

Fawcett, J., "The Impact of Art. 6 (1) of the ECHR on Private International Law", *International and Comparative Law Quarterly*, Vol. 56, 2007, pp. 1–48

Fentiman, R., *Foreign Law in English Courts: Pleading, Proof and Choice of Law*, Oxford University Press, Oxford, 1998

Fetsch, J., *Eingriffsnormen und EG-Vertrag*, Mohr Siebeck, Tübingen, 2002

Fezer, K., and S. Koos, "Das gemeinschaftsrechtliche Herkunftslandprinzip und die e-commerce-Richtlinie", *IPRax*, Vol. 20, No. 5, 2000, pp. 349–354

Flessner, A., Interessenjurisprudenz im IPR, Mohr Siebeck, Tübingen, 1990

Forder, C., "The Bredius Museum Case: Public Interest and Private International Law", *International Journal of Cultural Property*, vol. 2, 1993, pp. 117–126

Fourtoy, F., *L'impact du droit communautaire secondaire sur le droit international privé français*, EUI Thesis, 2003

Francescakis, Ph., "Quelque précisions sur les 'lois d'application immédiate' et leur rapports avec les règles de conflits de lois", *Répertoire Dalloz de droit international privé, V° Conflit de lois*, 1966, n° 137

Francq, S., *L'applicabilité du droit Communautaire dérivé au regard des méthodes du droit international privé*, Bruylant, Brussels, 2005

Franq, S., "The Scope of Secondary Union Law in the Light of the Methods of Private International Law – or the Other Way Around?", *Yearbook of Private International Law*, Vol. 8, 2006, pp. 333–374

Franzen, M., *Privatrechtsangleichung durch die europäische Gemeinschaft*, W. de Gruyter, Berlin, 1999

Franzosi, M., "Worldwide Patent Litigation and the Italian Torpedo", *European Intellectual Property Law Review*, Vol. 19, No. 7, 1997, pp. 382-385

Funken, K., *Das Anerkennungsprinzip im internationalen Privatrecht*, Mohr Siebeck, Tübingen, 2009

Garcimartin Alfarez, F., "The Rome I Regulation: Exceptions to the Rule on Consumers Contracts and Financial Instruments", *Journal of Private International Law*, Vol. 5, No. 1, 2009, pp. 85–103

Gaudemet-Tallon, H., "Le droit international privé des contrats dans un ensemble régional: l'exemple du droit communautaire", T. Einhorn and K. Siehr (eds.), *Intercontinental Cooperation through Private International Law: Essays in Memory of Peter E Nygh*, TMC Asser Press, The Hague, 2004, pp. 119–137

Gerven (van), W., "The ECJ Case-Law as a Means of Unification of Private Law?", A. Hartkamp (ed.), *Towards a European Civil Code*, Ars Aequi Libri, Nijmegen, 2005, pp. 101–124

Gillies, L., "Choice-of-law Rules for Electronic Consumer Contracts: Replacement of the Rome Convention by the Rome I Regulation", *Journal of Private International Law*, Vol. 3, No. 1, 2007, pp. 89–112

Gillies, L., *Electronic Commerce and International Private Law: A Study of Electronic Consumer Contracts*, Ashgate, Aldershot, 2008

Gkoutisinis, A., "Free movement of Services in the EC Treaty and the Law of Contractual Obligations Relating to Banking and Financial Services", *Common Market Law Review*, Vol. 41, 2004, pp. 119–175

Gómez, F., and J. Ganuza. "Optimal Harmonized Standards to Promote Cross-Border Trade", Universitat Pompeu Fabra Working Paper, 2008

Gomez, F., "The Harmonization of Contract Law through European Rules: a Law and Economics Perspective", *European Review of Contract Law*, Vol. 4, 2008, pp. 89–118

Gomez, F., The Economics of Harmonized Law-Making in Private Law: Mechanisms, Modes and Standards, R. Brownsword *et al* (eds.), *Foundations of European Private Law*, Hart Publishing: Portland, 2010

González Campos, J., "La Cour de Justice de Communautés Européennes et le non-Droit international privé", H. Mansel *et al* (eds.), *Festschrift für Erik Jayme Band I*, Sellier, München, 2004, pp. 261–275

Groot (de), G., and S. Rutten, "Op weg naar een Europees IPR op het gebied van het personen- en familierecht", *Nederlands Internationaal Privaatrecht*, 2004, pp. 273–282

Groot (de), G., and J. Kuipers, "The New Provisions on Private International Law in the Treaty of Lisbon", *Maastricht Journal of European and Comparative Law*, Vol. 15, No. 1, 2008, pp. 109–114

Gruber, U., "Insurance Contracts", F. Ferrari and S. Leible, *Rome I Regulation: The Law Applicable to Contractual Obligations in Europe*, Sellier, Münich, 2009, pp. 109–128

Grundmann, S., *Europäisches Schuldvertragsrecht*, 1999

Grundmann, S., "Binnenmarktkollisionsrecht - vom klassischen IPR zur Integrationsordnung", *RabelsZ*, Vol. 64, 2000, pp. 457–477

Grundmann, S., "The Structure of European Contract Law", *European Review of Private Law*, Vol. 9, No. 4, 2001, pp. 505–528

Grundmann, S., "Information, Party Autonomy and Economic Agents", *Common Market Law Review*, Vol. 39, 2002, pp. 269–293

Grundmann, S., and W. Kerber, "European System of Contract Laws. A Map for Combining the Advantages of Centralised and Decentralised Rule-making", S. Grundmann and J. Stuyck (eds.), *An Academic Greenpaper on European Contract Law*, Kluwer Law International, The Hague, 2002, pp. 295–342

Grundmann, S., "Das Internationale Privatrecht der E-Commerce-Richtlinie – was ist kategorial anders im Kollisionsrecht des Binnenmarkts und warum? ", *Rabelsz*, Vol. 67, No. 2, 2003, pp. 246–297

Grundmann, S., "Internal Market Conflict of Laws…", A. Fuchs *et al* (eds.), *Les conflits de lois et le système juridique communautaire*, Dalloz, Paris, 2004, pp. 5–29

Grundmann, S., "Grand European Code Napoléon or Concise Uniform Contract Law? : Defining the Scope of a Common Frame of Reference", A. Somma (ed.), *The politics of the draft common frame of reference*, Kluwer, Alphen a/d Rijn, 2009, pp. 19–37

Guedj, T., "The Theory of the Lois de Police, A Functional Trend In Continental Private International Law – A Comparative Analysis With Modern American Theories", *American Journal of Comparative Law*, Vol. 39, 1991, pp. 661–697

Gunst, D., *Die charakteristische Leistung: Zur funktionellen Anknüpfung im Internationalen Vertragsrecht Deutschlands der Schweiz und der Europäischen Gemeinschaft*, Hartung Gorre, Konstanz, 1994

Gutzwiller, M., *Der Einfluss Savignys auf die Entwicklung des Internationalprivatrechts*, Fribourg, 1923

Haersolte- van Hof (van), J., "Richtlijn elektronische handel – internationaal privaatrechtelijke aspecten", *Nederlands Tijdschift voor Europees Recht*, vol. 6, 2000, pp. 325–327

Halhuber, H., "Das ende der Sitztheorie als Kompetenztheorie- Das Urteil des Europäischen Gerichtshofs in der Rechtssache C- 208–00 (Überseering)", *Zeitschrift für Europäisches Privatrecht*, Vol. 8, No. 2, 2003, pp. 418–438

Hammje, P., "L'ordre public de rattachement", *Travaux du Comité de Droit International Privé 2006–2008*, pp. 153–186

Hansen, L., "Applicable Employment Law after Rome I - The Draft Rome I Regulation and Its Importance for Employment Contracts", *European Business Law Review*, Vol. 19, 2008, pp. 767–774

Harris, J., "Understanding the English response to the Europeanisation of Private International Law", *Journal of Private International Law*, Vol. 4, No. 3, 2008, pp. 347–395

Harris, J., "Mandatory Rules and Public Policy under the Rome I Regulation", F. Ferrari and S. Leible, *Rome I Regulation: The Law Applicable to Contractual Obligations in Europe*, Sellier, Münich, 2009, pp. 269–342

Hartkamp, A., "The Effect of the EC Treaty in Private Law: On Direct and Indirect Effects of Primary Community Law", *European Review of Private Law*, Vol. 18, 2010, pp. 527–548

Hartley, T., "Pleading and Proof of Foreign Law: The Major European Legal Systems Compared", *International & Comparative Law Quarterly*, Vol. 45, 1996, pp. 271–292

Hartley, T., "Mandatory Rules in International Contracts", *Recueil des Cours*, Vol. 266, 1997, pp. 337- 431

Hartley, T., "The European Union and the Systematic Dismantling of the Common Law of Conflict of Laws", *International Comparative Law Quarterly*, Vol. 54, 2005, pp. 813–828

Hartley, T., "The Modern Approach to Private International Law: International Litigation and Transactions from a Common-Law Perspective: General Course on Private International Law", *Recueil des Cours*, Vol. 319, No. 9, 2006, pp. 9–324

Hatzopoulos, V., "Legal Aspects in Establishing the Internal Market for services", College of Europe, Research Papers in Law, no. 6. 2007

Hatzopoulos, V., "Que reste-t-il de la directive sur les services?", *Cahiers de droit Européen*, 2007, pp. 299–358

Hayek, F., "Der Wettbewerb als Entdeckungsverfahren", Kieler Vorträge N.S. 56, Kiel, 1968; O'Hara, E., and L. Ribstein, *The Law Market*, Oxford University Press, Oxford, 2009, pp. 32–33

Heidemann, M., "Private Law in Europe: The Public/Private Dichotomy Revisited", *European Business Law Review*, Vol. 20, 2009, pp. 119–139

Heidinger, M., "Austria: Company Law – Branch Office", *Journal of International Banking Law*, Vol. 15, No. 2, 2000, pp. 8

Heinze, C., "Insurance contracts under the Rome I Regulation", *Nederlands Internationaal Privaatrecht*, Vol. 27, 2009, pp. 445- 453

Heiss, H., and N. Downes, "Non-optional elements in a Optional European Contract Law. Reflections from a Private International Perspective", *European Review of Private Law*, Vol. 13, 2005, pp. 693–712

Heiss, H., "Insurance Contracts in Rome I: Another Recent Failure of the European Legislature", *Yearbook of Private International Law*, Vol. 10, 2008, pp. 261–283

Heiss, H., "Party Autonomy", F. Ferrari and S. Leible, *Rome I Regulation: The Law Applicable to Contractual Obligations in Europe*, Sellier, Münich, 2009, pp. 1–16

Hellner, M., "The Country of Origin Principle in the E-Commerce Directive: A Conflict with Conflict of Laws?", A. Fuchs *et al* (eds.), *Les conflits de lois et le système juridique communautaire*, Dalloz, Paris, 2004, pp. 205–224

Henrich, D., "Anerkennung statt IPR: Eine Grundsatzfrage", *IPRax*, Vol. 25, No. 5, 2005, pp. 422- 424

Herings, J., and J. Kanning, "Unifying Commercial Laws of nation-states, Coordination of Legal Systems and Economics Growth", METEOR Working Paper no. 027, 2002

Hertel, C., "Preventive Consumer Protection in an Optional Instrument - A Practitioner's View", *ERA Forum*, Vol. 4, No. 2, 2003, pp. 70–84

Hess, B., "Les compétences externes de la Communauté européenne dans le cadre de l'article 65 CE", A. Fuchs *et al* (eds.), *Les conflits de lois et le système juridique communautaire*, Dalloz, Paris, 2004, pp. 81–100

Hesselink, M., *et al*, "Social Justice in European Contract Law: a Manifesto", *European Law Journal*, Vol. 10, No. 6, 2004, pp. 656–674

Hesselink, M., "Non-Mandatory Rules in European Contract Law", *European Review of Contract Law*, Vol. 1, 2005, pp. 44–86

Hesselink, M., "European Contract Law: A Matter of Consumer Protection, Citizenship, or Justice?" *European Review of Contract Law*, Vol. 15, No. 3, 2007, pp. 323–348

Hesselink, M., J. Rutgers and T. De Booys, "The Legal Basis for an Optional Instrument on European Contract Law", Centre for the Study of European Contract Law Working Paper no. 2007/04

Hesselink, M., "The Common Frame of Reference as a Source of European Private Law", *Tulane Law Review*, Vol. 83, 2009, pp. 919

Heuzé, V., *La réglementation française des contrats internationaux*, GLN Joly Éditions, Paris, 1990

Heuzé, V., "De la compétence de la loi du pays d'origine en matière contractuelle ou l'anti-droit Européen", B. Ancel, *Le droit international privé : esprit et méthodes ; Mélanges en l'honneur de Paul Lagarde*, Dalloz, Paris, 2005, pp. 393–415

Hoek (van), A., *Internationale mobiliteit van werknemers: Een onderzoek naar de interactie tussen arbeidsrecht, EG-recht en IPR aan de hand van de detacheringsrichtlijn*, SDU Uitgevers: Den Haag, 2000

Hoek (van), A., "De Bilaterisering van de Voorrangsleer in Europa", Th. de Boer (ed.), *Voorkeur voor de lex fori; Symposium ter gelegenheid van het afscheid van Prof. Th. de Boer*, Kluwer, Deventer, 2004, pp. 5–36

Hoffmann (von), B., "Inländische Sachnormen mit zwingendem internationalem Anwendungsbereich", *IPRax*, vol. 9, 1989, pp. 261–272

Hoffmann, J., and V. Primaczenko, "Die kollisionsrechtliche Absicherung des Verbraucherschutzes in Europa: Zu Anerkennung ungeschriebenen Richtlinienkollisionrecht", *IPRax*, Vol. 27, No. 3, 2007, pp 173–179

Hood, K., *Conflict of Laws within the UK*, Oxford University Press, Oxford, 2007

Hondius, E., "CISG and a European Civil Code: Some Reflexions", *RabelsZ*, Vol. 71, 2007, pp. 99–114

Hondius, E., "The Proposal for a European Directive on Consumer Rights: A Step Forward", *European Review of Private Law*, vol. 18, 2010, pp. 103–127

Hörnle, J., "Country of Origin Regulation in Cross-Border Media: One Step Beyond the Freedom to Provide Services?", *International Comparative Law Quarterly*, Vol. 54, 2005, pp. 89–126

Hös, N., "The Principle of Proportionality in the *Viking* and *Laval* cases: An Appropriate Standard of Judicial Review", EUI Working Paper Law, no. 6, 2009

Houwerzijl, M., *De Detacheringsrichtlijn: Over de inhoud, achtergrond en implementatie van Richtlijn 96/71/EG*, Kluwer, Deventer, 2005

Howells, G., and T. Wilhelmsson, *EC Consumer Law*, Ashgate, Darmouth, 1997

Howells, G., and R. Schulze (eds.), *Modernising and Harmonising Consumer Contract Law*, Sellier, München, 2009

Huber, P., "European Private International Law, Uniform Law and the Optional Instrument", *ERA Forum*, Vol. 4, No. 2, 2003, pp. 85–98

Inman, R., and D. Rubinfeld, "Federalism", B. Bouckaert and G. de Geest (eds.), *Encyclopedia of Law and Economics, Volume V: The Economics of Crime and Litigation*, Edward Elgar Cheltenham, 2000, pp. 661–691

Israël, J., "Conflicts of Law and the EC after Amsterdam: A Change for the Worse?", *Maastricht Journal of European and Comparative Law*, Vol. 7, No. 1, 2000, pp. 81–99

Israël, J., "Europees Internationaal Privaatrecht", *Nederlands Internationaal Privaatrecht*", Vol. 18, 2001, pp. 135–149

Israël, J., *European Cross-Border Insolvency Regulation*, Intersentia, Antwerpen, 2005

Israël, J., and K. Saarloos, "Europees Internationaal Privaat- en procesrecht", A. Hartkamp, C. Sieburg, L. Keus (eds.) *Serie Onderneming en Recht deel 42-II*, Deventer, Kluwer, 2007, pp. 629–698

Jacquet, J., *Principe d'autonomie et contrats internationaux*, Economica, Paris, 1983

Jacquet, J., *Le Contrat International*, Dalloz, Paris, 1992

Jacquet, J., "La Fonction Supranationale de la Règle de Conflit de Lois", *Recueil des Cours*, Vol. 292, 2001, pp. 155–248

Jakubowski, A., "Return of Illicitly Trafficked Cultural Objects Pursuant to Private International Law: Current Developments", A. Vrdoljak and F. Francioni, *The Illicit Traffic of Cultural Objects in the Mediterranean*, EUI Working Paper Law, 2/2009, pp. 137–148

Jans, J., "Proportionality Revisited", *Legal Issues of Economic Integration*, Vol. 27, No. 3, 2000, pp. 239–265

Jans, J., "The Effect in National Legal Systems of the Prohibition of Discrimination on Grounds of Age as a General Principle of Union Law", *Legal Issues of Economic Integration*, Vol. 3, No. 1, 2007, pp. 53–66

Jansen, N. and R. Michaels, "Private Law Beyond the State? Europeanization, Globalization and Privatization", *American Journal of Comparative Law*, Vol. 54, 2006, pp. 843–890

Jansen, N. and R. Michaels, "Private Law and the State Comparative Perceptions and Historical Observations", *RabelsZ*, Vol. 71, 2007, 345–397

Jansen, N., and R. Michaels, "Beyond the State – Rethinking Private Law", *American Journal of Comparative Law*, Vol. 56, 2008, pp. 527–540

Jansen, N., and R. Zimmermann, "Restating the Acquis? A critical examination of the 'Principles of the existing European Contract Law", *Modern Law Review*, Vol. 71, No, 4, 2008, pp. 505–534

Jansen, N., and R. Zimmermann, ""A European Civil Code in all but name" Discussing the nature and purposes of the Draft Common Frame of Reference", *Cambridge Law Journal*, Vol. 69, 2010, pp. 98–112

Jarass, H., "Elemente einer Dogmatik der Grundfreitheiten", *Europarecht*, 1995, pp. 202–226

Jarass, H., "A Unified Approach to the Fundamental Freedoms", M. Andenas and W. Roth, *Services and Free Movement in EU Law*, Oxford University Press, Oxford, 2002, pp. 141–162

Jayme, E., *Pasquale Stanislao Mancini, Internationales Privatrecht zwischen Risorgimento und praktischer Jurisprudenz*, Gremer, Ebelsbach, 1980

Jayme, E., and C. Kohler, "Das Internationale Privat- und Verfahrensrecht der EG 1993 – Spannungen zwischen Staatsverträgen und Richtlinien", *IPRax*, Vol. 13, No. 6, 1993, pp. 357–371

Jayme, E., and C. Kohler, "L'interaction des règles de conflit contenues dans le droit dérivé de la Communauté européenne et des conventions de Bruxelles et de Rome", *Revue Critique de Droit International Privé*, Vol. 84, No. 1, 1995, pp. 1–36

Jayme, E., and C. Kohler, "Europäisches Kollisionsrecht 2001: Anerkennungsprinzip statt IPR?", *IPRax*, Vol. 21, No. 6, 2001, pp. 501–514

Jayme, E., and C. Kohler, *Europäisches Kollisionsrecht 2002: Zu Wiederkehr des Internationalen Privatrechts, IPRax*, Vol. 22, No. 6, 2002, pp. 461–471

Jayme, E., "Globalization in Art Law: Clash of Interests and International Tendencies", *Vanderbilt Journal of Transnational Law*, Vol. 38, 2005, pp. 927–945

Jessurun d'Oliveria, H., "The EU and a Metamorphosis of Private International Law", J. Fawcett (ed.), *Reform and Development of Private International Law: Essays in honours of Sir Peter North*, Oxford University Press, Oxford, 2002, pp. 111–136

Joerges, C., "Die klassische Konzeption des Internationalen Privatrechts und das Recht des unlauteren Wettbewerbs", *RabelsZ*, Vol. 36, 1972, pp. 421–491

Joerges, C., "The Europeanization of Private Law as a Rationalisation Process and as a Contest of Disciplines – an Analysis of the Directive on Unfair Terms in Consumer Contracts", *European Review of Private Law*, Vol. 3, 1995, pp. 175–191

Joerges, C., "The Challenges of Europeanization in the Realm of Private Law: A Plea for a New Legal Discipline", *Duke Journal of Comparative and International Law*, Vol. 14, 2004, pp. 149–193

Joerges, C., "Working through "Bitter Experiences" towards Constitutionalisation. A Critique of the Disregard for History in European Constitutional Theory", EUI Working Paper Law No. 2005/14

Joerges, C., "Rethinking European Law's Supremacy", EUI Working Paper Law, No. 2005/12

Johns, F., "Performing Party Autonomy", *Law and Contemporary Problems*, Vol. 71, No. 3, 2008, pp. 243–271

Johnston, A., and H. Unberath, "Law at, to or from the Centre? The European Court of Justice and the Harmonization of Private Law in the European Union", F. Cafaggi (ed.), *The Institutional Framework of European Private Law*, Oxford, University Press Oxford, 2006, pp. 149–190

Joustra, C., "Europese Richtlijnen en internationaal privaatrecht", *Weekblad voor het Privaatrecht Notariaat en Registratie*, 1999, pp. 664–670

Joustra, C., "Het voorstel voor een Rome I Verordening: een nieuwe kans voor het ipr voor verzekeringsovereenkomsten?" *Nederlands Tijdschrift voor het Handelsrecht*, vol. 4, 2006, pp. 130–137

Junker, A., "Die einheitliche europäische Auslegung nach dem EG-Schulvertragsübereinkommen", *RabelsZ*, Vol. 55, 1991, pp. 674–696

Junker, A., "Empfiehlt es sich, Art. 7 EVÜ zu revidieren oder aufgrund der bisherigen Erfahrungen zu präzisieren?", *IPRax*, Vol. 20, 2000, pp. 65–73

Kadner Graziano, T., "Das auf außervertragliche Schuldverhältnisse anzuwendende Recht nach Inkrafttreten der Rom II-Verordnung", *RabelsZ*, Vol. 73, 2009, pp. 1–77

Kalypso, N., and S. Schmidt, "Mutual recognition 'on trial': the long road to services liberalization", *Journal of European Public Policy*, Vol. 14, No. 5, 2007, pp. 717–734

Kaplow, L., and S. Shavell, "Why the Legal System Is Less Efficient Than the Income Tax in Redistributing Income", *Journal of Legal Studies*, Vol. 23, 1994, pp. 667–681

Kaplow, L., and. S. Shavell, "Should Legal Rules Favor the Poor? Clarifying the Role of Legal Rules and the Income Tax in Redistributing Income", *Journal of Legal Studies*, Vol. 29, 2000, pp. 821–836

Kaplow, L., and S. Shavell, "Fairness versus Social Welfare: Notes on the Pareto Principle, Preferences and Distributive Justice", Harvard Discussion Paper no. 411, 2003

Karydis, G. "Ordre public dans l'ordre juridique communautaire", *Revue Trimestrielle de Droit Européen*, Vol. 38, 2002, pp. 1–26

Kassis, A., *Le nouveau droit européen des contrats internationaux*, LGDJ, Paris, 1993

Kaye, P., *The New International Law of Contract of the European Community*, Aldershot, Brookfield, 1993

Kegel, G., "The Crisis of Conflict of Laws", *Recueil des Cours*, Vol. 95, 1964, pp. 91–268

Kegel, G., "Zum Territorialitätsprinzip im internationalen öffentlichen Recht", A. Heldrich, D. Henrich and H. Sonnenberger (eds.), *Konflikt und Ordnung; Festschrift für Murad Ferid zum 70. Geburtsdag*, C.H. Beck'sche Verlagsbuchhandlung, München, 1978, pp. 233–278

Kegel, G., "Story and von Savigny", *American Journal of Comparative Law*, Vol. 37, No. 1, 1989, pp. 39–66

Kegel, G., and H. Schurig, *Internationales Privatrecht*, Verlag C.H. Beck, München:, 9. Auflage, 2004

Kennedy, D., "The Stages of Decline of the Public/Private Distinction", *University of Pennsylvania Law Review*, 1982, pp. 1349–1357

Kerber, W., "Interjurisdictional Competition within the European Union", *Fordham International Law Journal*, Vol. 23, 2000, pp. 217–249

Kerber, W., and S. Grundmann, "An optional European contract law code: Advantages and disadvantages", *European Journal of Law and Economics*, Vol. 21, No. 3, 2006, pp. 215–236

Kerber, W., and R. van den Bergh, "Mutual Recognition Revisited: Misunderstandings, Inconsistencies, and a Suggested Reinterpretation", *Kyklos*, Vol. 61, 2008, pp. 447–465

Kerber, W., "European system of private laws: an economic perspective", F. Cafaggi and H. Muir Watt (eds.), *Making European Private Law: Governance Design*, Edward Elgar, Cheltenham, 2008, pp. 64–97

Kessedjian, C., Le droit international privé et l'intégration juridique européene, T. Einhorn and K. Siehr (eds.), *Intercontinental Cooperation through Private International Law: Essays in Memory of Peter E Nygh*, TMC Asser Press, The Hague, 2004, pp. 187–196

Kessedjian, C., "Le principe de proximité vingt ans après", *Mélanges en l'honneur de Paul Lagarde" ; Le droit international privé : esprit et méthodes*, Dalloz, Paris, 2005, pp. 507–521

Keyes, M., "Statutes, Choice of Law, and the Role of Forum Choice", *Journal of Private International Law*, Vol. 4, No. 1, 2008, pp. 1–33

Kieninger, E., "The Legal Framework of Regulatory Competition Based on Company Mobility: EU and US Compared", *German Law Journal*, Vol. 6, No. 4, 2005, pp. 741–770

Kinsch, P., "Droits de l'Homme, Droits Fondamentaux et Droit International Privé", *Recueil des Cours*, Vol. 318, 2005, pp. 19–331

Kirchner, C., R. Painter and W. Kaal, "Regulatory Competition in EU Corporate Law After Inspire Art: Unbundling Delaware's Product for Europe", University of Illinois Law & Economics Research Paper no. LE04-001, 2004

Kitch, E., "Business Organization law: State or federal?", Buxbaum *et al* (eds.), *European Business Law: Legal and Economic Analysis on Integration and Harmonization*, 1991, pp. 35–50

Klauer, I., *Die Europäisierung des Privatrechts*, Nomos Verlagsgesellschaft, Baden-Baden, 1997

Klauer, S., *Das europäische Kollisionsrecht der Verbraucherverträge zwischen Römer-EVÜ und EG-Richtlinien*, Mohr Siebeck, Tübingen, 2002

Klinke, U., "European Company Law and the ECJ: The Court's judgments in the years 2001–2004", *European Company and Financial Law Review*, 2005, pp. 275–304

Kohler, C., "Travaux de Comité français de droit international privé (1993–94)", 75–76

Kohler, C., "Interrogations sur les sources de droit international privé européen après le traité d'Amsterdam", *Revue Critique de Droit International Privé*, Vol. 88, No. 1, 1999, pp. 3–30

Kohler, C., "Verständigungsschwierigkeiten zwischen europäischem Gemeinschaftsrecht und internationales Privatrecht", H. Mansel *et al* (eds.), *Festschrift für Erik Jayme Band I*, Sellier, München, 2004, pp. 445–459

Korom, V., and P. Metzinger, "Freedom of Establishment for Companies: The European Court of Justice Confirms and Refines its Daily Mail Decision in the Cartesio Case C-210/06", *European Company and Financial Law Review*, Vol. 6, No. 1, 2009, pp. 125–161

Korte (de), J., "De *ligging van het risico* in het conflictenrecht voor directe schadeverzekeringsovereenkomsten", *Aansprakelijkheid, Verzekering & Schade*, Vol. 5, No. 3, 2007, pp. 115–119

Kostoris Padoa Schioppa, F., *The Principle of Mutual Recognition in the European Integration Process*, Palgrave Macmillan, New York, 2005

Kuckein, M., *Die 'Berüksichtigung' von Eingriffsnormen im deutschen und englischen internationalen Vertragsrecht*, Mohr Siebeck, Tübingen, 2008

Kühne, G., "Die Parteiautonomie zwischen kollisionsrechtlichter und materiellrechtlichter Gerechtigkeit", H. Krüger and H. Mansel, *Liber Amicorum Gerhard Kegel*, C.H. Beck Verlag, München, 2002, pp. 65–82

Kuijper, P., "The Opinion on the Lugano Convention and Implied External Relations Powers", B. Martenczuk and S. van Thiel, *Justice, Liberty and Security: New Challenges for EU External Relations*, Brussels University Press, Brussels, 2008, pp. 187–210

Kuipers, J. and S. Migliorini, Qu'est-ce que sont les lois de police ? Une controverse franco-allemande, in: *European Review of Private Law*, vol. 18, No. 2, 2011, pp. 187–207

Kuipers, J., "The Exclusive External Competence of the Union under art. 81 TFEU: Lugano re-opened?", M. Cremona, J. Monar and S. Poli (eds.), *The External Dimension of the Area of Freedom Security and Justice*

Kramer, L., "Return to Renvoi", *New York University Law Review*, Vol. 66, No. 4, 1991, pp. 979–1044

Kramer, X., "Enforcement Under the Brussels Convention: Procedural Public Policy and the Influence of Article 6 ECHR", *International Lis*, 2003, pp. 16–20

Kramer, X., "The Rome II Regulation on the Law Applicable to Non-Contractual Obligations: The European private international law tradition continued", *Nederlands Internationaal Privaatrecht*, Vol. 26, 2008, pp. 414–424

Kramer, X., "The New European Conflict of Law Rules on Insurance Contracts in Rome I: A Complex Compromise", *The Icfai University Journal of Insurance Law*, Vol. 6, 2008, pp. 23- 42

Kraus, J., "Legal Design and the Evolution of Commercial Norms", *Journal of Legal Studies*, Vol. 26, No. 2, 1997, pp. 377–411

Kropholler, J., *Internationales Privatrecht*, Mohr Siebeck, Tübingen, 5. Auflage, 2004

Kyriacou, A., "Decision rules, membership and political centralization in the European Union", *European Journal of Law and Economics*, Vol. 27, 2009, pp. 143–158

Lagarde, P., "Le principe de proximité dans le droit international privé contemporain", *Recueil des Cours*, vol. 196, 1986, 9–238

Lagarde, P. "Développement futurs du droit international privé dans une Europe en voie d'unification: quelques conjectures", *RabelsZ*, Vol. 68, 2004, pp. 225–24

Lagarde, P., La Reconnaissance mode d'emploi, T. Azzi *et al* (eds.), *Vers de nouveaux équilibres entre ordres juridiques, Liber amicorum Hélène Gaudemet-Tallon*, Dalloz, Paris, 2008, pp. 481–501

Lando, O., "The EEC Convention on the Law Applicable to Contractual Obligations", *Common Market Law Review*, Vol. 24, 1987, pp. 172–180

Lando, O., *et al* (eds.), *Principles of European Contract Law*, Kluwer Law International, The Hague, 2003

Lando, O., "Liberal, Social and 'Ethical' Justice in European Contract Law", *Common Market Law Review*, Vol. 43, 2006, pp. 817–833

Lando, O., "Culture and Contract Laws", *European Review of Contract Law*, Vol. 3, No. 1, 2007, pp. 1–20

Lando, O., and P. Nielsen, "The Rome I Regulation", *Common Market Law Review*, Vol. 45, 2008, pp. 1687–1725

Lando, O., "Have the PECL been a success or a failure?" *European Review of Private Law*, Vol. 17, 2009, pp. 367–375

Lang, T., "Community Constitutional Law: Article 5 EEC Treaty", *Common Market Law Review*, Vol. 27, 1990, pp. 645–682

Langner, O., "Das Kaufrecht auf dem Prüfstand der Warenverkehrsfreiheit des EG-Vertrages", *RabelsZ*, Vol. 65, 2001, pp. 222–244

Lecuyer, S., *Appréciation critique du droit international privé conventionnel*, L.G.D.J., Paris, 2007

Leebron, D., "Lying Down with Procrustes: An Analysis of Harmonization Claims", J. Bhagwati and. R. Hudec, *Fair Trade and Harmonization*, Vol. 1, 1996, pp. 41–117

Legrand, P., "A Diabolical Idea", A. Hartkamp (ed.), *Towards a European Civil Code*, Kluwer Law International, Nijmegen, 3rd edition, 2004, pp. 245–272

Leible, S., "Parteiautonomie im IPR – Allgemeines Anknüpfungsprinzip oder Verlegenheitslösung?", H. Mansel *et al* (eds.), *Festschrift für Erik Jayme*, Band I, Sellier, München, 2004, pp. 485–503

Lein, E., "The New Rome I / Rome II / Brussels I Synergy", *Yearbook of Private International Law*, Vol. 10, 2008, pp. 177–198

Legrand, P., "European Legal Systems are not Converging", *International and Comparative Law Quarterly*, Vol. 45, 1996, pp. 52–81

Lévay-Fazekas, J., "Connection between the CFR and the Proposal for a Directive on Consumer Rights", R. Schulze, *Common frame of reference and existing EC contract law*, Sellier, Münich, 2009, pp. 309–313

Liebscher, C., "Arbitral & Judicial Decision: European public policy after Eco Swiss", *American Review of International Arbitration*, Vol. 10. 1999, pp. 81–94

Lodder, A., "Directive 2000/31/EC", A. Lodder and H. Kaspersen (eds), *eDirectives: Guide to European Union Law on E-commerce*, Kluwer Law International, The Hague, 2002, pp. 67–93

Loon (van), H., and A. Schulz, "The European Union and the Hague Conference on Private International Law", B. Martenczuk and S. van Thiel, *Justice, Liberty and Security: New Challenges for EU External Relations*, Brussels University Press, Brussels, 2008, pp. 257–299

Lopez-Tarruella, A., "A European Union Regulatory Framework for Electronic Commerce", *Common Market Law Review*, Vol. 38, No. 6, 2006, pp. 1337–1384

Loquin E., "Les règles matérielles internationals", *Recueil des Cours*, Vol. 322, 2006, pp. 21–241

Loughlin, M., *The idea of public law*, Oxford University Press, Oxford, 2004

Loussouarn, Y., "Cours général de droit international privé", *Recueil des Cours*, Vol. 139, 1973, pp. 271–385

Low, G., "How and Why We Are (Not) Bothered By the Costs of Legal Diversity - A Behavioural Approach to the Harmonization of European Contract Law", Tilburg Institute of Comparative and Transnational Law Working Paper No. 2009/8

Low, G., "The (Ir)Relevance of Harmonization and Legal Diversity to European Contract Law: A Perspective from Psychology", *European Review of Private Law*, Vol. 18, 2010, pp. 285–305

Lurger, B., "The Future of European Contract Law between Freedom of Contract, Social Justice, and Market Rationality", *European Review of Contract Law*, Vol. 1, No. 4, 2005, pp. 442–468

Madsen-Mygdal, N., "The Bretton Woods Agreement Article VIII, Sec. 2 (b)", *Nordic Journal of International Law*, Vol. 25, No. 1, 1955, pp. 63–78

Maduro, M., "Harmony and Dissonance in Free Movement", Andenas, M. and W. Roth, *Services and Free Movement in EU Law*, Oxford University Press, Oxford, 2002, pp. 41–68

Magagni, M., *La Prestazione Caratteristica nella Convenzione di Roma del 19 Giugno 1980*, Giuffrè, Milano, 1989

Magnus, U., "Article 4 Rome I Regulation: The Law Applicable in the Absence of a Choice", F. Ferrari and S. Leible, *Rome I Regulation: The Law Applicable to Contractual Obligations in Europe*, Sellier, Münich, 2009, pp. 27–50

Mak, C., *Fundamental Rights in European Contract Law: A Comparison of the Impact of Fundamental Rights on Contractual Relationships in Germany, the Netherlands, Italy and England*, Wolters Kluwer, Alphen a/d Rijn, 2008

Mak, V., "Review of the Consumer Acquis: Towards Maximum Harmonization", *European Review of Private Law*, Vol. 17, No. 1, 2009, pp. 55–73

Mak, V., "Harmonisation through 'Directive-Related' Case Law", *Zeitschrift fúr Europäisches Privatrecht*, Vol. 18, 2010, pp. 129–146

Mankowski, P., "Wichtige Klärungen im Internationalen Arbeitsrecht", *IPRax*, 1994, pp. 88–98

Mankowski, P., "Keine Sonderanknüpfung deutschen Verbraucherschutzrechts über Art. 34 EGBGB", *Deutsche Zeitschrift für Wirtschaftsrecht*, 1996, pp. 273–280

Mankowski, P., "Herkunftslandprinzip und deutsches Umsetzungsgesetz zur e-commerce-Richtlinie", *IPRax*, Vol. 22, No. 4, 2002, pp. 257–266

Mankowski, P., "Stillschweigende Rechtswahl und wählbares Recht", S. Leible (ed.), *Das Grünbuch zum Internationalen Vertragsrecht*, Sellier, München, 2004, pp. 63–108

Mankowski, P., "Wieder ein Herkunftslandprinzip für Dienstleistungen im Binnenmarkt", *IPRax*, Vol. 24, No. 5, 2004, pp. 385–395

Mankowski, P., "Der Vorschlag für die Rom I-Verordnung", *IPRax*, Vol. 26, No. 2, 2006, pp. 101–113

Mankowski, P., "Employment Contracts under Article 8 of the Rome I Regulation", F. Ferrari and S. Leible, *Rome I Regulation: The Law Applicable to Contractual Obligations in Europe*, Sellier, Münich, 2009, pp. 171–216

Mann, F., "Eingriffsgesetze und Internationales Privatrecht", Klaus Müller (ed.), *Festschrift für Eduard Wahl zum siebzigsten Geburtstag*, Universität Heidelberg, Heidelberg, 1973, pp. 139–160

Mann, F., "Contracts: Effects of Mandatory Rules", K. Lipstein (ed.), *Harmonisation of Private International Law by the E.E.C.*, Chameleon Press Limited, London, 1978

Mann, F., *Foreign Affairs in English Courts*, Clarendon Press, Oxford, 1986

Mann, F., "The Proper Law in the Conflict of Laws", *International & Comparative Law Quarterly*, Vol. 36, 1987, pp. 437–453

Mansel, H., "Anerkennung als Grundprinzip des Europäischen Rechtraums", *RablesZ*, Vol. 70, 2006, pp. 651–731

Mansel, H., K. Thorn and R. Wagner, "Europäisches Kollisionsrecht 2009 : Hoffnungen durch den Vertrag von Lissabon", *IPRax*, Vol. 30, No. 1, 2010, pp. 1–27

Marchadier, F., *Les objectifs généraux du droit international privé à l'épreuve de la convention européenne des droits de l'homme*, Bruylant, Bruxelles, 2007, pp. 601–609

Marenco, G., "Pour une interprétation traditionnelle de la notion de mesure d'effet équivalent à une restriction quantitative", *Cahier droit européen*, Vol. 20, 1984, pp. 291–326

Martinek, M., "The Seven Pillars of Wisdom in Private International Law: The German and the Swiss Experience with the Codification of Conflicts Law Rules", *Chinese Yearbook of Private International Law and Comparative Law*, 2001, pp. 15–54

Martiny, D., "Die Zukunft des europäischen ordre public im Internationalen Privat-Zivelverfahrensrecht", M. Coester, D. Martiny and K. Prinz von Sachsen Gessaphe (eds.), *Privatrecht in Europe, Festschrift für Hans Jürgen Sonnenberger*, Verlag C.H. Beck, München, 2004, pp. 523–548

Martiny, D., "Europäisches Internationales Vertragsrecht in Erwartung der Rom-I Verordnung", *Zeitschrift für Europäisches Privatrecht*, Vol.16, 2008, pp. 79–10

Marzal Yetano, T., "The Constitutionalisation of Party Autonomy in European Family Law", *Journal of Private International Law*, Vol. 6, No. 1, 2010, pp. 155–193

Marzo, C., La *dimension sociale de la citoyenneté européenne*, EUI Thesis, 2009

Mäsch, G., *Rechtswahlfreiheit und Verbraucherschutz ; Eine Untersuchung zu den Art. 29 I, 27 III und 34 EGBGBI*, Duncker & Humblot, Berlin 1993, pp. 114–125

Mattei, U., "Hard Code Now!", *Global Jurist Frontiers*, Vol. 2, No. 1, 2002, article 1

Mayer, P. and V. Heuzé, Droit International Privé, 9e édition, Paris, Montchrestien, 2007

Mayer, P., "Les méthodes de la reconnaissance en droit international privé", *Le droit international privé : esprit et méthodes ; Mélanges en l'honneur de Paul Lagarde*, Dalloz, Paris, 2005, pp. 547–573

Mayer, P., "Le Phénomène de la Coordination des Ordres Juridiques Étatiques en Droit Privé" *Recueil des Cours*, Vol. 327, 2007, 23–377

McCahery, J., "Harmonisation in European Company Law: The Political Economy of Economic Integration", D. Curtin *et al* (eds.), *European Integration and Law*, Intersentia, Antwerpen, 2006, pp. 155–194

McClean, D., and K. Beevers, *The Conflict of Laws*, Sweet & Maxwell, London, Sixth edition, 2006, pp. 359–361.

McKendrick, E., "The State We Are In, in: The Harmonisation of European Contract Law; Implications for European Private Laws, Business and Legal Practice", S. Vogenauer and S. Weatherill (eds.), Hart Publishing, Portland, 2006, 5–29

Meeusen, J., *Nationalisme en Internationalisme in het Internationaal Privaatrecht: Analyse van het Belgische Conflictenrecht*, Intersentia, Antwerpen, 1997

Meeusen, J., "Instrumentalisation of Private International Law in the European Union: Towards a European Conflicts Revolution? " *European Journal of Migration and Law*, Vol. 9, 2007, pp. 287–305

Meeusen, J., "Who is afraid of European Private International Law", G. Venturini and S. Bariatti (eds), *Liber Fausto Pocar: New Instruments of Private International Law*, Giuffrè, Milano, 2009, pp. 685–700

Meeusen, J., "Grunkin and Paul judgment" *Zeitschrift für Europäisches Privatrecht*, Vol. 18, No. 1, 2010, pp. 186–201

Meidanis, H., "Public Policy and *ordre public* in the private international law of the EC/EU: Traditional positions of the Member States and modern trends", *European Law Review*, Vol. 30, 2005, pp. 95–110

Meijers, E., "L'Histoire des principes fondamentaux du droit international privé à partir du moyen âge spécialement dans l'Europe occidentale", *Recueil des Cours,* Vol. 3, 1934, pp. 543–686

Meijers, E., "The Benelux Convention on Private International Law", *American Journal of Comparative Law*, Vol. II, No. 1, 1953, pp. 1–11

Merett, L., "Choice of Law in Insurance Contracts under the Rome I Regulation" *Journal of Private International Law*, Vol. 5, 2009, pp. 49–67

Merkin, R., "The Rome I Regulation and Reinsurance", *Journal of Private International Law*, Vol. 5, 2009, pp. 69 – 84

Michaels, R., and H. Kamann, "Grundlagen eines allgemeinen gemeinschaftlichten Richtlinienkollisionsrechts – "Amerikanisierung" des Gemeinschafts-IPR?", *Europäisches Wirtschafts- & Steuerrecht*, Vol. 12, No. 6, 2001, pp. 301–311

Michaels, R., "The Re-*State*-ment of Non-State Law: The State, Choice of Law and the Challenges from Global Legal Pluralism", *Wayne Law Review*, Vol. 51, 2005, pp. 1209–1259

Micheals, R., "Globalizing Savigny? The State in Savigny's Private International Law and the Challenge of Europeanization and Globalization", Duke Law School Working Paper Series 15, 2005

Michaels, R., "Two Economists, Three Opinions? Economic Models for Private International Law – Cross-Border Torts as Example", J. Basedow and T. Tono (eds.) *An Economic Analysis of Private International Law,* Mohr Siebeck, Tübingen, 2006, pp. 143–186

Michaels, R., "EU Law as Private International Law? The Country-of-Origin Principle and Vested Rights Theory", *Journal of Private International Law*, Vol. 2, No. 2, 2006, pp. 195–242

Michaels, R., "The New European Choice-of-Law Revolution", *Tulane Law Review*, Vol. 82, No. 5, 2008, pp. 1607–1644

Micklitz, H., "Review of Academic Approaches to the European Contract Law Codification Project", M. Andenas *et al* (eds.), *Liber Amicorum Guido Alpa: Private Law beyond the National Systems*, British Institute of International and Comparative Law, London, 2007, pp. 699–726

Micklitz, H., "Failures or Ideological Preconceptions? : Thoughts on two Grand Projects: the European Constitution and the European Civil Code", S. Sankari (ed.), *The Many Constitutions of Europe*, Ashgate, Farnham, 2010, pp. 109–140

Mills, A., *The Confluence of Public and Private International Law: Justice, Pluralism and Subsidiarity in the International Constitutional Ordering of Private Law*, Cambridge University Press, Cambridge, 2009

Mohamed Mahmoud, M., "Loi d'autonomie et méthodes de protection de la partie faible et droit international privé", *Recueil des Cours*, Vol. 315, 2005, pp. 141–264

Monéger, F., *Droit International Privé*, Litec, Paris, 2001

Moreau, M., *Structure du rattachement et conflits de lois en matière de responsabilité civile délictuelle*, Thèse Université de droit, d'économie et de sciences sociales de Paris, 1985

Moreau, M., "Le détachement des travailleurs effectuant une prestation de services dans l'Union européenne", *Journal de droit international*, Vol. 123, No. 3, 1996, pp. 889–908

Moreau, M., H. Muir Watt and P. Rodière (eds.), *Justice et mondialisation en droit du travail : Du rôle du juge aux conflits alternatifs*, Dalloz, Paris, 2010

Morse, C., "The EEC Convention on the Law applicable to Contractual Obligations", *Yearbook of European Law*, Vol. 2, 1982, pp. 107- 171

Morse, C., "Consumer Contracts, Employments Contracts and the Rome Convention", *International Comparative Law Quarterly*, Vol. 41, 1992, pp. 1–21

Mosconi, F., "Exceptions to the Operation of Choice of Law Rules", *Recueil des Cours*, Vol. 217, 1989, pp. 13–214

Muir Watt, H., "Quelques remarques sur la théorie anglo-américaine des droits acquis", *Revue Critique de droit international privé*, 1986, pp. 425–455

Muir-Watt, H., "Evidence of an Emergent European Legal Culture : Public Policy Requirements of Procedural Fairness under the Brussels and Lugano Conventions", *Texas International Law Journal*, Vol. 36, 2001, pp. 539–554

Muir Watt, H., "Choice of Law in Integrated and Interconnected Markets: A Matter of Political Economy": *Electronic Journal of Comparative Law*, Vol 7, No. 3, 2003

Muir Watt, H., "Choice of Law in Integrated and Interconnected Markets: A Matter of Political Economy", *Columbia Journal of European Law*, Vol. 9, 2003, pp. 383–409

Muir Watt, H., "The Challenge of Market Integration for European Conflicts Theory", A. Hartkamp and. E. Hondius, *Towards a European Civil Code*, Kluwer Law International, Deventer, 2004, pp. 191–204

Muir Watt, H., "Aspects économiques du droit international privé", *Recueil des Cours*, Vol. 307, 2004, pp. 25–384

Muir Watt, H., "European Integration, legal diversity and the Conflict of Laws", *Edinburgh Law Review*, Vol. 9, 2005, pp. 6–31

Muir Watt, H., "The Conflict of Laws as a Regulatory Tool", F. Cafaggi (ed.), *The Institutional Framework of European Private Law Volume II*, Oxford University Press, Oxford, 2006, pp. 107–148

Muir Watt, H., Family Law: European Federalism and the "New Unilateralism", *Tulane Law Review*, Vol. 82, 2008, pp. 1983–1999

Müller-Graff, P., "EC Directives as a Means of Private Law Unification", A. Hartkamp and E. Hondius, *Towards a European Civil Code*, Kluwer Law International, Deventer, 2004, pp. 77–100

Nadaud, S., *Codifier le droit civil européen*, Larcier, Brussels, 2008

Niboyet, M., and G. de Geouffre de La Pradelle, *Droit International Privé*, Librairie Générale de Droit et de Jurisprudence, Paris, 2007

Nick, C., Ausweitung der Parteiautonomie und objektive Anknüpfung im Erbkollisionsrecht, *European Journal of Legal Studies*, Vol. 2, No. 1, 2008, pp. 286–324

Nielsen, R., *European Labour Law*, DJØF Publishing, Copenhagen, 2000, pp. 43–46

Nielsen, P., "Brussels I and Denmark", *IPRax*, Vol. 27, No. 6, 2007, pp. 506–509

Nielsen, P., "The Law Applicable and Contracts of Carriage", F. Ferrari and S. Leible, *Rome I Regulation: The Law Applicable to Contractual Obligations in Europe*, Sellier, Münich, 2009, pp. 99–108

Nojack, J., *Exclusivnormen im IPR: Interessenanalyse, dogmatische Einordnung und Anwendungsprobleme*, Mohr Siebeck, Tübingen, 2005

North, P., "Is European Harmonisation of Private International Law a Myth or Reality", T. de Boer (ed.) *Forty Years on: the Evolution of Postwar Private International Law in Europe*, Kluwer, Deventer, 1990, pp. 29–48

North, P., *Essays in Private International Law*, Clarendon Press, Oxford, 1993

Nuener, J., "Protection Against Discrimination in European Contract Law", *European Review of Contract Law*, Vol. 2, No. 1, 2006, pp. 35–50

Nygh, P., *Autonomy in International Contracts*, Clarendon Press, Oxford, 1999

Ogus, Anthony, "Competition between National Legal Systems: A contribution of Economic Analysis to Comparative Law", *International and Comparative Law Quarterly*, Vol. 48, 1999, pp. 405–418

O'Hara, E. and L. Ribstein, "From Politics to Efficiency in Choice of Law", George Mason Law and Economics Working Paper No. 00–04, 1999

O'Leary, S., and J. Fernández-Martin, "Judicially-Created Exceptions to the Free Provision of Services", M. Andenas and W. Roth, *Services and Free Movement in EU Law*, Oxford University Press, Oxford, 2002, pp. 163–195

Ooik (van), R., "The European Court of Justice and the Division of Competence in the European Union", D. Obradovic and N. Lavranos (eds.), *Interface between EU Law and National Law*, European Law Publishers, Groningen, 2007, pp. 11–40

Øren, J., "International Jurisdiction over Consumer Contracts in e-Europe", *International Comparative Law Quarterly*, Vol. 52, 2003, pp. 665–696

Overbeck (von), A., "The Fate of Two Remarkable Provisions on the Swiss Statute on Private International Law", *Yearbook of Private International Law*, Vol. 1, 1999, pp. 119–133

Pamboukis, C., *L'Acte Public Étranger en Droit International Privé*, LGDJ, Paris, 1993

Pamboukis, C., "La renaissance-métamorphose de la méthode de reconnaissance", *Revue Critique de Droit International Privé*, Vol. 97, No. 3, 2008, pp. 513–560

Pataut, E., "Lois de police et ordre juridique communautaire", A. Fuchs *et al* (eds.), *Les conflits de lois et le système juridique communautaire*, Dalloz, Paris, 2004, pp. 117–143

Pelkmans, J., "Deepening Services Market Integration: A critical assessment", *Romanian Journal of European Affairs*, Vol. 7, No. 4, 2007

Perner, S., "Das Internationale Versicherungsvertragsrecht nach Rom I", *IPRax*, Vol. 29, 2009, pp. 218–222

Picheval, C., *L'ordre public européen droit communautaire et droit européen des droit de l'homme*, CERIC, Aix-Marseille, 2001

Picone, P., "La méthode de la référence à l'ordre juridique compétent en droit international privé", *Recueil des Cours*, Vol. 197, 1986, pp. 229–419

Pießkalla, M., "EuGH: Verhinderbare Gesellschaftssitzverlegung in einen anderen Mitgliedstaat als den Gründungsmitgliedstaat – Cartesio", *Europäische Zeitschrift für Wirtschaftsrecht*, Vol. 20, No. 3, 2009, pp. 75–83

Piroddi, P., "The French Plumber, Subcontracting and the Internal Market", *Yearbook of Private International Law*, Vol. 10, 2008, pp. 593–616

Pizzolante, G., "I contratti con i consumatori e la nuova disciplina comunitaria in material di legge applicablile obbiligazioni contrattuali", *Cuadernos de Derecho Transnacional*, Vol. 1, 2009, pp. 221–236

Plas (van der), C., *De taak van de rechter en het IPR: een verkenning van de grenzen van de taak van de Nederlandse rechter bij de toepassing van vreemd privaat- en publiekrecht*, Kluwer, Deventer, 2005

Plas (van der), C., "Verbintenissen uit overeenkomst: van EVO-Verdrag naar Rome I Verordening", *Nederlands Tijdschrift voor Europees Recht*, Vol. 14, 2008, pp. 318–329

Plender, R., *The European Contracts Convention: The Rome Convention on the Law Applicable to Contractual Obligations*, Sweet & Maxwell, London, 2001

Plender, R., and Wilderspin, M., "The European Private International Law of Obligations", Sweet & Maxwell, London, Third Edition, 2009

Poillot, E., *Droit Européen de la Consommation et Uniformisation du Droit des Contrats*, LGDJ, Paris, 2006

Poillot Peruzzetto, S.,"Ordre Public et loi de police dans l'ordre communautaire", *Travaux du Comité Français de Droit International Privé 2002–2004*, pp. 65–106

Polak, M., *Arbeidsverhoudingen in het Nederlands internationaal privaatrecht*, Kluwer, Deventer, 1988

Pommier, J., *Principe d'autonomie et loi du contrat en droit international privé conventionnel*, Economica, Paris, 1980, pp. 30–36

Poncibò, C., "The Challenges of EC Consumer Law", EUI Working Paper MWP No. 2007/24

Porte (de la), C., "Is the Open Method of Coordination Appropriate for Organising Activities at European Level in Sensitive Policy Areas?" *European Law Journal*, Vol. 8, 2002, pp. 38–58

Puljak, M., *Le droit international privé à l'épreuve du principe communautaire de non-discrimination en raison de la nationalité*, Presses Universitaires d'Aix-Marseille, Aix en Marseille, 2003

Radicati di Brozolo, L., "L'influence sur les conflits de lois des principes de droit communautaire en matière de liberté de circulation", *Revue Critique de Droit International Privé*, Vol. 82, No. 3, 1993, pp. 401–423

Radicati di Brozolo, L., "Mondialisation, juridiction, arbitrage : vers des règles d'application semi-nécessaires ?", *Revue Critique de Droit International Privé*, 2003, pp. 1–36

Radtke, R., "Schuldstatut und Eingriffsrecht", *Zeitschrift für Vergleichende Rechtswissenschaft*, Vol. 84, 1985, pp. 326–357

Ragno, F., "The Law Applicable to Consumer Contracts under the Rome I Regulation", F. Ferrari and S. Leible, *Rome I Regulation: The Law Applicable to Contractual Obligations in Europe*, Sellier, Münich, 2009, pp. 129–170

Rammeloo, S., Das Neue EG-Vertragskollisionrecht, Carl Heymanns Verlag KG, Köln, 1992

Rammeloo, S., "Die Auslegung von Art.4 Abs. 2 und Abs. 5 EVÜ: Eine niederländische Perspektive", *Iprax*, Vol. 14, 1994, pp. 234–245

Rammeloo, S., "Corporations in Private International Law: A European Perspective", Oxford University Press, Oxford, 2001

Rammeloo, S., "Freedom of Establishment for Legal Persons in Europe Accomplished", *Maastricht Journal of European and Comparative Law*, Vol. 11, No. 4, 2004, pp. 398–413

Rammeloo, S., "*Via Romana*. Van EVO naar Rome I - Nieuw Europees IPR inzake het recht dat van toepassing is op verbintenissen uit overeenkomst", *Nederlands Internationaal Privaatrecht*, Vol. 3, 2006, pp. 239–253

Rauscher, T., "Gran Canaria — Isle of Man — Was kommt danach", *Europäische Zeitschrift für Wirtschaftsrecht*, vol.7 (1996), 650–3

Reding, V., "Warum Europa ein Optionales Europäisches Vertragsrecht benötigt", *Zeitschrift für Europäisches Privatrecht*, Vol. 19, 2011, pp. 1–6

Reich, N., "Competition Between Legal Orders: A New Paradigm of EC Law", *Common Market Law Review*, Vol. 29, 1992, pp. 861–896

Reich, N., *Europäisches Verbraucherschutzrecht: Binnenmarkt und Verbraucherinteresse*, Nomos Verlagsgesellschaft, Baden-Baden, 1993

Reich, N. and G. Woodroffe (eds.), *European Consumer Policy after Maastricht*, Kluwer, Deventer, 1994

Reich, N., "EuGH: Handelsvertreterrichtlinie unabdingbar gegenüber Drittlandprinzipial", *Europäische Zeitschrift für Wirtschaftsrecht*, Vol. 12, 2001, pp. 50–52

Reich, N., "Union Citizenship—Metaphor or Source of Rights?", *European Law Journal*, Vol. 7, No. 1, 2001, pp. 4–23

Reich, N., and H. Micklitz, *Europäisches Verbraucherrecht*, Nomos Verlagsgesellschaft, Baden-Baden, 4. Auflage, 2003

Reich, N., and S. Harbacevica, "Citizenship and Family on Trial: a Fairly Optimistic Overview of Recent Court Practice with Regard to Free Movement of Persons", *Common Market Law Review*, Vol. 40, 2003, pp. 615–638

Reich, N., "Der Common Frame of Reference und Sonderprivatrechte im 'Europäischen Vertragsrecht' ", *Zeitschrift für Europäisches Privatrecht*, Vol. 15, 2007, pp. 161–179

Reich, N., and H. Micklitz,"Crónica de una muerte anunciada: The Commission Proposal for a 'Directive on Consumer Rights", *Common Market Law Review*, Vol. 46, No. 2, 2009, pp. 471–519

Reich, N., "The Public/Private Divide in European Law", H. Micklitz and F. Cafaggi, *European Private Law after the Common Frame of Reference*, Edward Elgar, Cheltenham, 2010, pp. 56–89

Reithmann, C., und D. Martiny, *Internationales Vertragsrecht: das Internationale Privatrecht*

der Schuldvertrage, Verlag Dr Otto Schmidt KG, Köln, 1988

Remien, O., "Private International Law, the European Union and its Emerging Area of Freedom, Security and Justice," *Common Market Law Review*, 2001, pp. 53–86

Remy, B., *Exception d'ordre public et mécanisme des lois de police en droit international privé*, Dalloz, Paris, 2008, pp. 176–208

Rich, W., and W. Burress, "Economic Analysis and Distributive Justice", *Research in Law and Economics*, Vol. 18, 1997, pp. 15–64

Rigaux, F., and M. Fallon, *Droit International Privé*, Larcier, Bruxelles, 3e édition, 2005

Ringe, W., "No freedom of migration for European Companies?" *European Business Law Review*, Vol. 16, 2005, pp. 621–642

Rodière, P., *La convention collective de travail en droit international*, Litec, Paris, 1987

Rooij (van), R., and M. Polak, *Private International Law in the Netherlands*, Kluwer, Deventer, 1987, pp. 121

Rösler, H., "Schutz des Schwächeren im Europäischen Vertragsrecht", *Rabelsz*, Vol. 73, 2009, pp. 889–911

Ross, G., "Assessing the Delors Era and Social Policy", S. Leibfried and P. Pierson (eds), *European Social Policy: Between Fragmentation and Integration*, Brookings Institution, Washington DC, 1995, pp. 357–388

Roth, W., "Der Einfluß des Europäischen Gemeinschaftsrechts auf das Internationale Privatrecht", *RabelsZ*, Vol. 55, 1991, pp. 623–673

Roth, W., "Die Freiheiten des EG-Vertrages und das nationale Privatrecht", *Zeitschrift für Europäisches Privatrecht*, Vol. 2, No. 1, 1994, pp. 5–33

Roth, W., "ECJ Case Law on Freedom to Provide Services : Keck", M. Andenas and W. Roth, *Services and Free Movement in EU Law*, Oxford University Press, Oxford, 2002, pp. 1–24

Roth, W., "Zur Wälbarkeit nichtstaatlichen Rechts", H. Mansel *et al* (eds.), *Festschrift für Erik Jayme*, Band I, Sellier, München, 2004, pp. 757–772

Roth, W., "Methoden der Rechtsfindung und Rechtsanwendung im Europäischen Kollisionsrecht", *IPRax*, Vol. 26, No. 4, 2006, pp. 338–347

Roth, W., "Secured Credit and the Internal Market: The Fundamental Freedoms and the EU's Mandate for Legislation", *European Company and Financial Law Review*, 2008, pp. 36–67

Rott, P., and R. Terryn, "The Proposal for a Directive on Consumer Rights : No Single Set of Rules", *Zeitschrift für europäisches Privatrecht*, Vol. 17, 2009, pp. 456–488

Röttinger, M., "Towards a European Code Napoléon/ABGB/BGB? Recent EC Activities for a European Contract Law", *European Law Journal*, Vol. 12, 2006, pp. 807–827

Rühl, G., "Extending *Ingmar* to Jurisdiction and Arbitration Clauses: The End of Party Autonomy in Contracts with Commercial Agents?", *European Review of Private Law*, Vol. 15, No. 6, 2007, pp. 891–903

Rühl, G., "Party Autonomy in the Private International Law of Contracts: Transatlantic Convergence and Economic Efficiency", CLPE Research Paper 4/2007, Vol. 03 No. 1, 2007, pp. 32–34

Rühl, G., "Die Kosten der Rechtswahlfreiheit: Zur Anwendung ausländischen Rechts durch Deutsche Gerichte", *Rabelsz*, Vol. 71, 2007, pp. 559–596

Rutgers, J., "An Optional Instrument and Social Dumping", Centre for the Study of European Contract Law Working Paper Series no. 2006/03

Rutgers, J., and R. Sefton-Green, "Revising the Consumer *Acquis*: (Half) Opening the Doors of the Trojan Horse", *European Review of Private Law*, Vol. 16, No. 3, 2008, pp. 427–442

Sack, A., "Conflict of Laws in the History of English Law", *Law: A Century of Progress 1835–1935*, New York Vol. III, 1937, pp. 342–454

Sanchirico, C., "Taxes Versus Legal Rules as Instruments for Equity, A More Equitable View", *Journal of Legal Studies*, Vol. 29, 2000, pp. 797–820

Sargeant, M., "The Employment Equality (Age) Regulations 2006: A Legitimisation of Age Discrimination in Employment", *Industrial Law Journal*, Vol. 35, No. 3, 2006, pp. 209–227

Savigny (von), F., *System des heutige Römische Recht,* VIII System

Schäfer, B., and Z. Bankowski, "Mistaken Identities: The Integrative Force of Private Law", M. van Hoecke and François Ost (eds.), *The Harmonisation of European Private Law*, Hart Publishing, Oxford, 2000, pp. 21–45

Schäfer, H., "Direktiven als Ersatz für Humankapital: Empfehlen sich für Entwicklungs- und Transformationsländer präzisere Rechtsnormen als für hochentwickelte Staaten? " *RabelsZ*, Vol. 67, 2003, pp. 550–580

Scharpf, F., "The European Social Model: Coping with the Challenges of Diversity", *Journal of Common Market Studies*, Vol. 40, No. 4, 2002, pp. 645–670

Schebesta, H., "Does the national Court know Union Law? A note on ex-officio application after Asturcom" *European Review of Private Law*, Vol. 18, 2010, pp. 847–880

Schillig, M., "The Contribution of Law and Economics as a Method for Legal Reasoning in European Private Law", *European Review of Private Law*, Vol. 17, 2009, pp. 853–893

Schilling, K., *Binnenmarktskollisionsrecht*, De Gruyter, Berlin, 2006

Schmidtchen, D., "Vereinheitlichung des Vertragsrechts in Europa – eine Lösung auf der Suche nach dem Problem?", T. Eger and H. Schäfer, *Ökonomische Analyse der europäischen Zivilrechtsentwicklung*, Mohr Siebeck, Tübingen, 2007, pp. 1–45

Schnyder, A., "Parteiautonomie im Internationalen Namensrecht", J. Basedow *et al* (eds.) *Private Law in the International Arena: Liber Amicorum Kurt Siehr*, T.M.C. Asser Press, The Hague (2000), pp. 667–672

Schulte-Nölke, H., "The way forward in European consumer contract law: optional instrument instead of further deconstruction of national private laws", C. Twigg-Flesner, *The Cambridge Companion to European Union Private Law*, Cambridge University Press, Cambridge, 2010, pp. 131–146

Schultsz, J., "Dutch Antecedents and Parallels to Article 7 of the EEC Contracts Convention of 1980", *RabelsZ*, Vol. 47, 1983, pp. 267–283

Schulz, A., "The Accession of the European Union to the Hague Conference on Private International Law", *International and Comparative Law Quarterly,* Vol. 56, 2006, pp. 939–950

Schurig, K., *Kollisionsnorm und Sachrecht: zu Struktur, Standort und Methode des internationalen Privatrechts*, Duncker & Humblot, Berlin, 1981, pp. 89–106

Schurr, F., "The relevance of the European consumer protection law for the development of the European Contract Law", *Victoria University of Wellington Law Review*, vol. 38, 2007, pp. 131–144

Schutter (de), O., and S. Franq, "La proposition de directive relative aux services dans le marché intérieur: reconnaissance mutuelle et conflits de lois dans l'Europe élargie", *Cahiers de droit Européen*, 2005, pp. 603–660

Schwarz, S., "Das international Handelsvertreterrecht im Lichte von "Ingmar" – Droht das Ende der Parteiautonomie im Gemeinschaftsprivatrecht?", *Zeitschrift für Vergleichende Rechtswissenschaft*, Vol. 101, 2002, pp. 45–74

Seatzu, F., *Insurance in Private International Law: A European Perspective*, Hart Publishing, Oxford, 2003

Siehr, K., *Internationales Privatrecht*, C.F. Müller Verlag, Heidelberg, 2001

Siems, M., "Convergence, competition, Centros and Conflicts of Law: European Company Law in the 21st Century", *European Law Review*, Vol. 27, 2002, pp. 47–59

Sinai, A., "Inclusion of Mandatory Rules in an Optical EC Contract Law Instrument", *European Business Law Review*, Vol. 15, 2004, pp. 41–72

Slater, D., "The Scope of the EC harmonising powers: The ECJ Tobacco Case", *German Law Journal*, Vol. 4, 2003, pp. 137–148

Smith, G., *Internet Law and Regulation*, Sweet & Maxwell, London, 2007

Smits, Jan, *The Making of European Private Law: Toward a Ius Commune Europaeum as a Mixed Legel System*, Intersentia, Antwerpen, 2002

Smits, Jan, "How to predict the differences in uniformity between different areas of a future European private law? An evolutionary approach", A. Marciano and J. Josselin, (eds.), *The Economics of Harmonizing European Law*, Edgar Elgar, Cheltenham, 2002, pp. 50–70

Smits, Jan, "The Principles of European Contract Law and the Harmonisation of Private Law in Europe", Antoni Vacquer (ed.), *La Tercera Parte de Los Principios de Derecho Contractual Europeo*, Tirant, Valencia, 2005, pp. 567–590

Smits, Jan, "Private Law and Fundamental Rights: a skeptical view", Maastricht Working Papers Faculty of Law, no. 8, 2006

Smits, Jan, Editorial: "The Draft-Common Frame of Reference for a European Private Law; Fit for its purpose?" *Maastricht Journal of International and Comparative Law*, Vol. 15, 2008, pp. 145–148

Smits, Jan, "Full Harmonization of Consumer Law? A Critique on the Draft Directive on Consumer Rights", *European Review of Private Law*, Vol. 18, 2008, pp. 5–14

Smorto, G., "Efficiency and Justice in European Contract Law", *European Review of Private Law*, Vol. 16, No. 6, 2008, pp. 925–948

Snell, J., *Goods and Services in EC Law*, Oxford University Press, Oxford, 2002

Snell, J., and M. Andenas, "Exploring the Outer Limits: Restrictions on the Free Movement of Goods and Services", M. Andenas and W. Roth, *Services and Free Movement in EU Law*, Oxford University Press, Oxford, 2002, pp. 69–139

Snell, J., "The Notion of Market Access: A Concept or a Slogan", *Common Market Law Review*, Vol. 47, 2010, pp. 437–472

Solomon, D., "The Private International Law of Contracts in Europe: Advances and Retreats", *Tulane Law Review*, Vol. 82, 2008, 1709–1740

Sonnenberger, H., "Eingriffsrecht – Das trojanische Pferd im IPR oder notwendige Ergänzung?", *IPRax*, vol. 23, 2003, pp. 104–116

Spaventa, E., "Leaving Keck behind? The free movement of goods after the rulings in Commission v Italy and Mickelsson and Roos", *European Law Review*, Vol. 34, 2009, pp. 914–932

Spickhoff, A., *Der ordre public im internationalen Privatrecht ; Entwicklung – Struktur – Konkretisierung*, Alfred Metzner Verlag, Neuwied, 1989

Spindler, G., "Internet, Kapitalmarkt und Kollisionsrecht unter besonderer Berücksichtigung der E-Commerce Richtlinien", *Zeitschrift für das gesamte Handelsrecht und Wirtschaftsrecht*, Vol. 165, 2001, pp. 324–361

Spindler, G., "Herkunftslandprinzip und Kollisionsrecht –Binnenmarktintegration ohne Harmonisierung? ", *RabelsZ*, Vol. 66, 2002, pp. 633–709

Spindler, G., and O. Berner, "Inspire Art - Der europäische Wettbewerb um das Gesellschaftsrecht ist endgültig eröffnet", *Recht der internationalen Wirtschaft*, Vol. 49, 2003, pp. 949–957

Stalla-Bourdillon, S., "Re-allocating horizontal and vertical regulatory powers in the electronic marketplace: what to do with private international law", F. Cafaggi and H. Muir Watt (eds.), *The Regulatory Function of European Private Law*, Edward Elgar, Chelthenham, 2009, pp. 290–342

Staudinger, A., "Die ungeschriebenen kollisionsrechtlichen Regelungsgebote der Handelsvertreter-, Haustürwiderrufs- und Produkthaftungsrichtlinie", *Neue Juristische Wochenschrift*, Vol. 54, 2001, pp. 1974–1978

Staudinger, A., "Internationales Versicherungsvertragsrecht – (k)ein Thema für Rom I?", F. Ferrari and S. Leible (eds.), *Ein neues Internationales Vertragsrecht für Europa, Jena: Jenaer Wissenschaftliche Verlagsgesellschaft*, 2007, pp. 226–243

Staudenmayer, D., "Un instrument optionnel en droit européen des contrats", *Revue trimestrielle de droit* civil, 2003, pp. 629–644

Steele, J., "Damages in Tort and Under the Human Rights Act: Remedial or Functional Separation", *Cambridge Law Journal*, Vol. 67 No. 3, 2008, pp. 606–634

Steinmann, T., P. Kenel and I. Billotte, *Le contract d'agence commercial en Europe*, Schulthess, Zürich, 2005

Stone, P., *European private international law*, Edward Edgar, Cheltenham, 2006

Straalen, (van) P., *Behoud van rechten van werknemers bij overgang van onderneming*, Kluwer, Deventer, 1999

Strikwerda, L., *Semipubliekrecht in het conflictenrecht : verkenningen op een kruispunt van methoden*, Tjeen Willink, Alphen a/d Rijn, 1978

Strikwerda, L., *De overeenkomst in het IPR*, Kluwer, Deventer, 2004

Strikwerda, L., Inleiding tot het Nederlandse Internationaal Privaatrecht, Kluwer, Deventer, 2005

Struycken, A., "Les conséquences de l'intégration européenne sur le développement du droit international privé," *Recueil des Cours*, Vol. 232, 1992, pp. 257–383

Struycken, A., "La Contribution de l'Académie au développement de la science et de la pratique du droit international privé", *Recueil des Cours*, Vol. 271, 1998, pp. 15–56

Struycken, A., "L'ordre public de la Communauté Européenne", T. Azzi *et al* (eds.), *Vers de nouveaux équilibres entre ordres juridiques, Liber amicorum Hélène Gaudemet-Tallon*, Dalloz, Paris, 2008, pp. 617–632

Stuyck, J., "The Consumer Law Compendium, A New Era for European Consumer Law?" *European Business Law Review*, Vol. 20, 2009, pp. 377–382

Stuyck, J., Case Note to *Pannon* and *Asturcom*, *Common Market Law Review*, Vol. 47, 2010, pp. 879–898

Sun, J., and J. Pelkmans, "Regulatory Competition in the Single Market", *Journal of Common Market Studies*, Vol. 33, 1995, pp. 67–89

Svantesson, B., *Private International Law and the Internet*, Kluwer Law International, Deventer, 2007

Symeonides, S., *American Private International Law*, Kluwer Law International, Deventer, 2008, pp. 208–209

Syrpis, P., "Should the EU be attempting to harmonise national systems of labour law?", *European Business Law Review*, Vol. 21, 2010, pp. 143–163

Szydło, M., Export Restrictions within the Structure of the Free Movement of Goods. Reconsideration of an old paradigm, *Common Market Law Review*, Vol. 47, 2010, pp. 753–789

Szyszczak, E., "Experimental Governance: The Open Method of Coordination", *European Law Journal*, Vol. 12 No. 4, 1996, pp. 486–502

Tang, Z., "The Interrelationship of European Jurisdiction and Choice of Law in Contract", *Journal of Private International Law*, Vol. 4, No. 1, 2008, pp. 35–82

Tassikas, A., *Dispositives Recht und Rechtswahlfreiheit als Ausnahmebereiche der EG-Grundfreiheiten. Ein Beitrag zur Privatautonomie, Vertragsgestaltung und Rechtsfindung im Vertragsverkehr des Binnenmarktes*, Mohr Siebeck, Tübingen, 2004

Taupitz, J., "Kaffeefahrten deutscher Urlauber auf Gran Canaria: Deutscher Verbraucherschutz im Urlaubsgepäck?", *Betriebsberater*, 1990, pp. 642–652

Tenreiro, M., and J. Karsten, "Unfair Terms in Consumer Contracts: Uncertainties, contradictions and novelties of a Directive", H. Schulte-Nölke (ed.), *Europäische Rechtsangleichung und nationale Privatrechte*, Nomos Verlagsgesellschaft, Baden-Baden, 1999, pp. 223–276

Tiebout, C., "A Pure Theory of Local Expenditures", *Journal of Political Economy*, Vol. 64, 1956, pp. 416–424

Tison, M., *De interne markt voor bank- en beleggingsdiensten*, Intersentia, Antwerpen, 1999

Tobler, C., "Endlich "Keck" im Freien Dienstleistungsverkehr", *Jus & News*, 2005, pp. 159–171

Traest, M., *De Europese Gemeenschap en de Haagse Conferentie voor het Internationaal Privaatrecht*, Maklu, Antwerpen, 2003

Tridimas, T., "Proportionality in Union law: searching for the appropriate standard of scrutiny", E. Ellis (ed.), *The Principle of proportionality in the laws of Europe*, Hart Publishing, Oxford, 1999, pp. 65–84

Tridimas, T., *The General Principles of EU Law*, Oxford University Press, Oxford, 2nd edition, 2006, pp. 214–215

Twigg-Flesner, C., "No Sense of purpose or direction? The modernisation of European Consumer Law", *European Review of Contract Law*, 2007, pp. 198–213

Unberath, H., and A. Johnston, "The Double-Headed Approach of the ECJ concerning Consumer Protection", *Common Market Law Review*, Vol. 44, 2007, pp. 1237–1284

Vareilles-Sommières (de), P., "La Compétence internationale de l'espace judicaire européen", T. Azzi *et al* (eds.), *Vers de nouveaux équilibres entre ordres juridiques, Liber amicorum Hélène Gaudemet-Tallon*, Dalloz, Paris, 2008, pp. 397–417

Varney, M., "European Controls on Member State Promotion and Regulation of Public Service Broadcasting and Broadcasting Standards", *European Public Law*, Vol. 10, No. 3, 2004, pp. 503–530

Vékás, L., "Der Weg zur Vergemeinschaftung des Internationalen Privat- und Verfahrensrechts – eine Skizze", J. Erauw *et al* (eds.), *Liber Memorialis Petar Šarčević, Universalism, Tradition and the Individual*, Sellier, München, 2006, pp. 171–187

Verhagen, H., "Het spanningsveld tussen de vrijheid van rechtskeuze en het communautaire harmonisatie-proces", *Nederlands Internationaal Privaatrecht*, Vol. 19, No. 1, 2001, pp. 27–33

Verhagen, H., "The tension between party autonomy and European Union law: some observations on Ingmar", *International Law and Comparative Law Quarterly*, Vol. 51, 2002, pp. 135–154

Vignal, T., *Droit international privé*, Dalloz, Paris, 2005

Vogel, H., "E-Commerce : Directives of the European Union and Implementation in German Law", *E-Commerce : Law & Jurisdiction*, Kluwer, Deventer, 2002, pp. 29–78

Vogenauer, S. and S. Weatherill, "The EC's Competence to Pursue Harmonisation", S. Vogenauer and S. Weatherill (eds.), *The Harmonisation of European Contract Law; Implications for European Private Laws, Business and Legal Practice*, Hart Publishing, Portland, 2006, pp. 105- 148

Vonk, O., *Dual Nationality in the European Union*, EUI Thesis (2010)

Vos (de), M., *European Union Employment and Labour Law : Law and Cases*, Knops Publishing, Herentals, 2007

Vrellis, S., "Conflit ou Coordination de Valeurs en Droit International Privé : Al la recherche de justice", *Recueil des Cours*, Vol. 328, 2007, pp. 189–485

Wagner, G., "The Economics of Harmonization: the Case of Contract Law", *Common Market Law Review*, Vol. 39, 2002, pp. 995–1023

Wagner, G., "The Virtues of Diversity in European Private Law", *The Need for a European Contract Law: Empirical and Legal Perspectives*, European Law Publishing, Groningen, 2005, pp. 3–24

Wagner (von), R., Das Haager Übereinkommen vom 30. 6. 2005 über Gerichtsstandsvereinbarungen, *RabelsZ*, Vol. 73, No. 1, 2009, pp. 100–149

Wagner (von), R., "Die Haager Konferenz für Internationales Privatrecht zehn Jahre nach der Vergemeinschaftung der Gesetzgebungskompetenz in der justiziellen Zusammenarbeit in Zivilsachen", *RabelsZ*, Vol. 73, 2009, pp. 215–240

Wai, R., "Transnational Liftoff and Juridicial Touchdown: The Regulatory Function of Private International Law in an Era of Globalization", *Columbia Journal of Transnational Law*, Vol. 40, 2002, pp. 209–274

Waldron, J., "Locating Distribution", *Journal of Legal Studies*, Vol. 32, 2003, pp. 277–302

Walk, F., *Das Herkunftsprinzip der E-Commerce-Richtlinie: Art. 3 der Richtlinie 2000/31 EG und seine Umsetzung in deutsches Recht*, Herbert Ultz München, 2002

Weatherill, S., "After *Keck*: Some thoughts on How to Clarify the Clarifcation", *Common Market Law Review*, Vol. 33, 1996, pp. 885–906

Weatherhill, S., *EU Consumer Law and Policy*,: Elgar European Law, Cheltenham, 2005

Weatherhill, S., "Constitutional Issues – How Much is Best Left Unsaid?", *The Harmonisation of European Contract Law*, 2006, pp. 89–104

Weatherill, S., "Maximum or Minimum Harmonisation: What Kind of 'Europe' do we want?", K. Boele-Woelki and W. Grosheide (eds.), *The Future of European Contract Law*, Wolters Kluwers, Alpen a/d Rijn, 2007, pp. 133–146

Weatherhill, S., "An Ever Tighter Grip: The European Court's Pro-Consumer Interpretation of the EC's Directives Affecting Contract Law", M. Andenas *et al* (eds.) *Liber Amicorum Guido Alpa*, British Institute of International and Comparative Law, London, 2007, pp. 1037–1069

Weatherhill, S., "Current developments", *International and Comparative Law Quarterly*, Vol. 58, 2009, pp. 985–992

Weiler, J., "The Transformation of Europe", *Yale Law Journal*, Vol. 100, No. 8, 1991, pp. 2403–2483

Wengler, W., "Die anknüpfung des zwingenden Schuldrechts im IPR", *ZVergRWiss*, 1941, pp. 168–212

Wenneras, P., and K. Boe Moen, "Selling Arrangments, keeping Keck', *European Law Review*, Vol. 35, 2010, pp. 387–400

Werlauff, E., "A 'Copenhagen Effect'?", *European Company Law*, Vol. 4, No. 4, 2009, pp. 160–168

Wiese, V., *Der Einfluss des EG-rechts auf das internationale Sachenrecht der Kulturgüter*, Mohr Siebeck, Tübingen, 2004

Wilderspin, M., and X. Lewis, "Les relations entre le droit communautaire et les règles de conflits de lois des Etats membres", *Revue Critique de Droit International Privé*, 2002, pp. 1–37

Wilderspin, M., "The Rome I Regulation: Communitarisation and modernisation of the Rome Convention", *ERA Forum*, Vol. 9, 2008, pp. 259–274

Wilderspin, M., "The Rome II Regulation; Some Policy Observations", *Nederlands Internationaal Privaatrecht*, Vol. 26, 2008, pp. 408–413

Williams, P., "The EEC Convention on the Law Applicable to Contractual Obligations", *International and Comparative Law Quarterly*, Vol. 35. 1986, pp. 1–31

Wilmowsky (von), P., "EG-Freiheiten und Vertragsrecht", *Juristenzeitung*, Vol. 12, 1996, pp. 590–596

Wilmowsky (von), P., "EG-Vertrag und kollisionsrechtliche Rechtswahlfreiheit", *RabelsZ*, Vol. 62, 1998, pp. 1–37

Winchop, M., and Keyes, M., "Statutes Domains in Private International Law: An Economic Theory of the Limits of Mandatory Rules", 1998. Available at SSRN

Winter (de), L., "Enige Beschouwingen over de Wet van de Karakteristieke Prestatie", *Met eerbiedigende werking, opstellen aangeobden aan prof. Hijmans van den Bergh*, Kluwer, Deventer, 1971

Wollenschläger, F., "Grundfreiheiten ohne Markt Die Herausbildung der Unionsbürgerschaft im unionsrechtlichen Freizügigkeitsregime", Mohr Siebeck, Tübingen, 2006

Woodward, J., "Contractual Choice of Law: Legislative Choice in an Era of Party Autonomy", *Southern Methodist University Law Review*, Vol. 54. No. 2, 2001, pp. 697–786

Woolcock, S., "Competition Among Rules in the Single European Market", W. Bratton *et al* (eds), *International Regulatory Competition and Coordination: Perspectives on Economic Regulation in Europe and the United States,*Clarendon Press, Oxford, 1996, pp. 289–321

Wördemann, N., *International zwingende Normen im internationalen Privatrecht des europäischen Versicherungsvertrages: Eine kollisionsrechtliche Untersuchung zur Bedeutung und Tragweite des Art. 7 ABS. 2 zweite Ri Schadenv sowie des Art. 4 ABS. 4 zweite Ri LEBV*, Verlag Versicherungswirtschaft, Karlsruhe, 1997

Wyatt, D., "Horizontal Effect of Fundamental Freedoms and the Right to Equality after Viking and Mangold, and the Implications for Union Competence", Oxford Legal Studies Research Paper No. 20/2008

Yntema, H., "The Historic Basis of Private International Law", *American Journal of Comparative Law*, Vol. 2, 1953, pp. 297–317

Yntema, H., " The Comity Doctrine", E. von Caemmerer, A. Nikisch and K. Zweigert, (eds.), *Vom Deutschen zum Europäischen Recht, Festschrift für Hans Dölle*, Mohr Siebeck, Tübingen, 1963, pp. 65–72

Zhang, M., "Party Autonomy :An International Perspective of Contractual Choice of Law", *Emory International Law Review*, Vol. 20, 2006, pp. 511–562

Zimmer, D., "Auslandisches Wirtschaftsrecht vor deutschen Zivilgerichten: Zur Unterscheidungg zwischen einer normativen Berücksichtigung fremder zwingender Normen und einer bloßen Beachtung ihrer tatsachlichen Folgen", *IPRax,* 1993, pp. 65–69

Zweigert, K., Nichterfüllung auf Grund ausländische Leistungsverbote", *RabelsZ*, Vol. 14 (1942), pp. 283

INDEX

www.ingramcontent.com/pod-product-compliance
Lightning Source LLC
LaVergne TN
LVHW020650300926
849161LV00004B/887